ANGLO-NORMAN STUDIES XII

PROCEEDINGS OF THE BATTLE CONFERENCE

1989

ANGLO-NORMAN STUDIES

XII

PROCEEDINGS OF THE BATTLE CONFERENCE

1989

Edited by Marjorie Chibnall

THE BOYDELL PRESS

First published 1990 by The Boydell Press, Woodbridge

The Boydell Press is an imprint of Boydell & Brewer Ltd
PO Box 9, Woodbridge, Suffolk IP12 3DF
and of Boydell & Brewer Inc.
PO Box 41026, Rochester, NY 14604, USA

ISBN 0 85115 257 0   ꞌ19011 66172ꞌ

ISSN 0954-9927
Anglo-Norman Studies
(Formerly ISSN 0261-9857: Proceedings of the Battle Conference
on Anglo-Norman Studies)

British Library Cataloguing in Publication Data

Battle Conference, (*12th ; 1989*)
   Proceedings of the Battle Conference 1989. - (Anglo -
   Norman studies, ISSN 0954-9927; 12).
   1. Western Europe. Normans, history
   I. Title   II. Chibnall, Marjorie   III. Series
   940.0441
   ISBN 0-85115-257 – 0

Library of Congress Catalog Card Number: 89–646512

The cover illustration is from BL MS Cotton Domitian AII f.21
and is reproduced by kind permission of
the Trustees of the British Library

This publication is printed on acid-free paper

Printed in Great Britain by St Edmundsbury Press, Bury St Edmunds, Suffolk

CONTENTS

ILLUSTRATIONS

EDITOR'S PREFACE

The twelfth volume of the Proceedings of the Battle Conference in Anglo-Norman Studies is dedicated in memory of Professor R. Allen Brown, founder, for eleven years Director, and at all times inspiration of the Conference. The twelfth Conference opened in the Library of the Abbey with tributes to him from Councillor Barry Gray, Chairman of East Sussex Education Committee, Mr Allen Denny, Chairman of the Battle and District Historical Society, Dr Maylis Baylé of Paris, Professor C. Warren Hollister of Santa Barbara, California, and myself. A setting of the *Firmetur*, originally composed for the coronation of William the Conqueror, was played in a recording made at Allen Brown's Memorial Service by the choir of King's College London. The Memorial Address delivered at that service by Professor Christopher Holdsworth is printed in this volume.

The strength of support for the Conference, shown in the very large attendance by scholars from many countries and the lively interchange of ideas both in the conference room at Pyke House and in the 'Chequers', is perhaps the tribute that would have pleased Allen Brown best of all. Thirteen papers were read, and are published in this year's *Proceedings*. Mr Ian Peirce showed some of the medieval arms and armour from his unique collection, and escorted members round both the Abbey House, in process of alteration and restoration, and the battlefield. The Outing this year was to Romsey Abbey by way of East Meon and Corhampton, and we are greatly indebted to all who contributed to its success: to the Vicars of Romsey and East Meon and the Rector of Corhampton both for access and for their personal welcome at the churches, to Dr Richard Gem and Dr Jeffrey West for their invaluable guiding, and to Mr Francis J. Green, the Field Director of the Test Valley Archaeological Trust, for an illustrated exposition of the recent excavations at Romsey. For the comfort and refreshment, both of the Outing and of the entire conference, we once again owe a very great deal to the skill and indefatigable energies of Mr Peter Birch and the staff at Pyke House. More than ever this year the smooth running of the Conference is due to them and to Mrs Gillian Murton, whose enthusiasm, experience and practical guidance were invaluable to a new and very raw Director. Once again we thank the East Sussex County Council for their sponsorship and support, and the Headmaster and Deputy Head of the Abbey School, who made available both the Library and the Abbey Hall for the opening memorial tributes and the Reception given by the East Sussex County Council.

Photographs in Dr Tudor-Craig's paper are reproduced by courtesy of the British Library Board, the Trustees of the Bodleian Library, the Syndics of Cambridge University Library, the President and Fellows of St John's College Oxford, the Master and Fellows of Trinity College Cambridge and the Trustees of the British Museum.

Clare Hall, Cambridge

Marjorie Chibnall

ABBREVIATIONS

Antiqs Journ.	*The Antiquaries Journal* (Society of Antiquaries of London)
Arch. Journ.	*Archaeological Journal* (Royal Archaelogical Institute)
ASC	*Anglo-Saxon Chronicle*, ed. D. Whitelock *et al.*, London 1969
Battle Chronicle	*The Chronicle of Battle Abbey*, ed. Eleanor Searle, Oxford Medieval Texts, 1980
BIHR	*Bulletin of the Institute of Historical Research*
BL	British Library
BN	Bibliothèque Nationale
Cal. Docs France	*Calendar of Documents preserved in France* ... i, 918–1206, ed. J. H. Round, HMSO, 1899
Carmen	*The Carmen de Hastingae Proelio of Guy bishop of Amiens*, ed. Catherine Morton and Hope Munz, Oxford Medieval Texts, 1972
De gestis pontificum	William of Malmesbury, *De gestis pontificum Anglorum*, ed. N. E. S. A. Hamilton, RS 1870
De gestis regum	William of Malmesbury, *De gestis regum Anglorum*, ed. W. Stubbs, RS 1887
Domesday Book	*Domesday Book, seu liber censualis* ..., ed. A. Farley, 2 vols, 'Record Commission', 1783
Dudo	*De moribus et actis primorum Normanniae Ducum auctore Dudone Sancti Quintini Decano*, ed. J. Lair, Société des Antiquaires de Normandie, 1865
Eadmer	*Historia novorum in Anglia*, ed. M. Rule, RS 1884
EHD	*English Historical Documents* i, ed. D. Whitelock, London 1955; ii, ed. D. C. Douglas, London 1953
EHR	*English Historical Review*
Fauroux	*Recueil des actes des ducs de Normandie (911–1066)*, ed. M. Fauroux, Mémoires de la Société des Antiquaires de Normandie xxxvi, 1961
GEC	*Complete Peerage of England, Scotland, Ireland, Great Britain and the United Kingdom*, 13 vols in 14, London 1910–59
Gesta Guillelmi	William of Poitiers, *Gesta Guillelmi* ..., ed. R. Foreville, Paris 1952
Historia Novella	William of Malmesbury, *Historia Novella*, ed. K. R. Potter, Nelson's Medieval Texts, London 1955
HMSO	Her Majesty's Stationery Office, London
Huntingdon	Henry of Huntingdon, *Historia Anglorum*, ed. T. Arnold, RS 1879
Journ. BAA	*Journal of the British Archaeological Association*
Jumièges	William of Jumièges, *Gesta Normannorum Ducum*, ed. J. Marx, Société de l'histoire de Normandie, 1914

Lanfranc's Letters	*The Letters of Lanfranc Archbishop of Canterbury*, ed. H. Clover and M. Gibson, Oxford Medieval Texts, 1979
Med. Arch.	*Medieval Archaeology*
MGH	*Monumenta Germaniae Historica*, Scriptores
Monasticon	William Dugdale, *Monasticon Anglicanum*, ed. J. Caley, H. Ellis and B. Bandinel, 6 vols in 8, London 1817–30
ns	New Series
Orderic	Ordericus Vitalis, *Historia Ecclesiastica*, ed. M. Chibnall, Oxford Medieval Texts, 1969–80
PRO	Public Record Office
Procs BA	*Proceedings of the British Academy*
Regesta	*Regesta Regum Anglo-Normannorum*, i, ed. H. W. C. Davis, Oxford 1913; ii, ed. C. Johnson, H. A. Cronne, Oxford 1956; iii, H. A. Cronne, R. H. C. Davis, Oxford 1968
RS	Rolls Series, London
ser.	series
Trans.	Transactions
TRHS	*Transactions of the Royal Historical Society*
VCH	Victoria County History
Vita Eadwardi	*The Life of Edward the Confessor*, ed. F. Barlow, Nelson's Medieval Texts, London 1962
Wace	Wace, *Le Roman de Rou*, ed. A. J. Holden, 3 vols, Société des anciens textes français, Paris 1970–3
Worcester	Florence of Worcester, *Chronicon ex Chronicis*, ed. B. Thorpe, English Historical Society, London 1848–9

R. ALLEN BROWN

An Address given at the Service of Thanksgiving for the Life of Allen Brown, held on Tuesday, 14 March 1989 in the Chapel of King's College London

We are met here this evening to recall with thankfulness the life and work of Reginald Allen Brown. A few of us knew him as a central figure in family life, more of us as a colleague, still more as friend and teacher. This address is not, I sense, the occasion on which to say very much about Allen with his family, for in that area he kept himself, and those whom he loved, to himself: yet it is patent how much he was involved with that closest circle, how great was his delight in his children, more especially in the dedication of Giles and Philippa to just the kind of scholarship to which he had devoted himself, as well as in Abigail's prowess with a camera. Life at home, in the country and around the house he so much loved, was absolutely central to his being; there was the 'jardin enclos' from which his great energy and strength came, never more so than since the moment when he knew that he was fighting cancer. Remembering him, the hackneyed saying 'The Englishman's home is his castle' has peculiar resonance and appositeness, and there we may briefly envisage him, giving thanks to all those who shared that side of his life.

But today all of us can recall three other sides of his life to which I now turn; Allen as scholar, teacher and friend. If, sometimes, I draw here on my own experiences, I hope you will not feel excluded by them, but rather be encouraged as you listen, to complement them with your own.

Allen as scholar achieved a very great deal, directing his attention mainly towards the noble and royal world of the Anglo-Norman and Plantagenet periods. Chronicles, diplomas and writs, castles and palaces won his interest, people and high politics were his concern. It would be otiose to recall the titles of his books and articles, but they make a goodly and solid company, reaching, perhaps, their greatest originality and force when he was able to combine his mastery of written and physical sources together, as when writing about Dover Castle or the Tower of London.[1] He gloried in belonging to the category of 'old' historian, among which he had been placed by his former supervisor, John Prestwich, in a speech marking his own retirement from the Queen's College, Oxford. 'Certainly', Allen wrote later, 'as an historian I have always been as old as possible, and I become

---

[1] Cf. Vivien Brown's bibliography in *Studies in Medieval History presented to R. Allen Brown*, ed. Christopher Harper-Bill, Christopher Holdsworth and Janet L. Nelson, Woodbridge 1989, 353–57. Happily Allen was able to receive this book. In what follows I am indebted to the 'Personal Appreciation' by Christopher Harper-Bill which it contains, 1–5, as well as to Miss June Walker, secretary to the History Department.

unrepentantly older as time passes and fashions change.'[2] By old, of course, he meant not old in age, but in the use of tried and tested methods, whether for understanding a text or reading a building – not for him holograms or tables of percentages. He exaggerated his antiquity, we may be sure, after all he used the 'modern camera' and accurate plans often, but his mastery of the severely taxing business of editing a charter, or discerning in the subtle variations of technique and style the successive seasons in which a building was erected, was formidable. Charter lore and mason's craft he felt, as it were, in his hands. But he knew another mystery, in his seat, for he had experienced – first as a soldier during the Second World War – the understanding that develops between a horse and his rider, and how it can only come about over time when what each partner has to learn becomes habitual, and mutual trust is complete. He once confessed that 'there are not many horsey figures among academics, any more than the sheer love of war, – ''fresh and joyful war'' [as Bloch put it, the Bloch whom he had first read by candle-light] – and physical achievement does not find much sympathy in academe.'[3] There he was probably correct, and it is interesting to note that although he disagreed over many things with Reginald Darlington, their shared love of horses probably enabled Allen to write a very sympathetic obituary about him in the Proceedings of the British Academy.[4] Certainly Allen's horsemanship gave a peculiar strength to his ability to recreate both the larger and smaller sides of medieval warfare. He realised, for example, that just as one needed a string of ponies to play polo for an afternoon on Smith's Lawn, so knights going to Hastings would have ridden there on their second-best horse, whilst their 'great stallion warhorse' was gently trotted or led by an esquire.[5]

All these skills of body, eye and mind he used for a purpose to which he gave the most serious attention, the establishment of truth about the past, that past which lies all about us, if we have but eyes to see it. For him it was a land worth discovering, and the journey there had its own delights. He was a master, for instance, of the concise footnote, in which occasionally he would courteously deflate someone else, and of which he wrote that it should have an honourable place in scholarship since the footnote leads 'all those who wish to follow into the deep woods, green pastures and rewarding byways which lie on either side of the motorway of the text.'[6] I cannot forbear here to hazard that he would have created a nice note to explain how it came about that one of those who wrote his obituary recently came to misplace the start of the Battle Conference by a year.[7]

Mention of Battle leads me to the second aspect of Allen about which I want to speak; Allen as teacher. By this I mean not merely his work as lecturer or supervisor, but his role as communicator and stimulus. Just because he had himself been seized by the need to understand the past he was convinced that he needed to share his discovery with others. It is not always so – some scholars appear to

---

[2] 'The Status of the Norman Knight' in *War and Government in the Middle Ages*, ed. John Gillingham and J. C. Holt, Woodbridge 1984, 18.
[3] 'Norman Knight', 30 and 19.
[4] *Proceedings of the British Academy* lxvi, 1982, 427–37.
[5] 'Norman Knight', 28–9.
[6] *The Normans and the Norman Conquest*, 1969, ix.
[7] *The Daily Telegraph* nodded, but so did I. When revising this text for publication I found that I had displaced the origins to 1968.

commune best alone, and the ability to communicate is not always given to each person who wishes to write or speak. Yet Allen found such gifts and used them to the full. His writing is clear and fluent, without sacrificing the highest standard of faithfulness to the complex, and often refractory evidence. His lecturing had that same energy too, often enhanced with the wearing of a gown (which he sported long after most of us had renounced it), or with a carefully planted handkerchief, or (do I recall aright?) a discreet button hole, whilst his sword could make a formidable aid for slides. I was never his pupil so I can only imagine what it might have been like from attending to those who were, who speak of his skill in combining deflation with encouragement. The number of you here today who received his guidance whether as undergraduates or later on, is sufficient testimony to the lasting effects which his teaching had.

One side of his teaching, his Special Subject on the Norman Conquest, did impinge upon me since Allen was instrumental in persuading the Board of Examiners to appoint me as second marker for a number of years. Then, each June, I recognised in scripts that those very qualities of accuracy, engagement and imagination had been awakened in his pupils. I saw, too, how these things had been stimulated by the trips he organised to Normandy, a considerable undertaking for the winter vacation, and yet one which had extraordinary results in the level of scholarship and *enjoyment* attained. This note should, I believe, have occurred before, and now needs underlining, since Allen so evidently relished his work as teacher and scholar. It points us also to the fact that he surely would have wished us today to enjoy our memories of him, rather than to mourn.

Most of Allen's teaching life occurred here at King's College where he became an Assistant Lecturer thirty years ago in 1959. His potential was recognised by C. H. Williams who was farsighted enough to risk the appointment of Allen at 35, and whose trust was well placed. I have the impression that over the years Allen was allowed admirable freedom to develop his teaching and writing as he liked, and was not burdened with a great deal of administration. These days it is cheering to recall all this, and to mark that he never seemed to want to cut a figure on university committees.

But now one must remember with peculiar thanks how he and Gillian Murton, of East Sussex County Council Education Department, brought into being the first Battle Conference in 1978. Here was a wider arena for his skills; in some sense the conferences with their combination of papers and visits were a development from his Norman odysseys. At Battle, too, Allen was very much in the leading role, he invited scholars, set in motion the plans to visit a place of outstanding interest like Canterbury or Winchester, and normally presided over each paper. Then his ability to listen with eyes gently closed could be observed, but when a paper ended he at once showed how wakeful his spirit had been, even though at his feet his dog slept on. At Battle he elicited an extraordinary range of papers, catholic indeed, and attracted scholars from across both the narrower and broader seas which separate Sussex from the Duchy, or from America. To be 'at Battle' was to be brought into touch with the growing points of scholarship, and to receive there new ideas, and to see the possibility of following new roads towards the country of the past, an appreciation which all travellers there need from time to time (perhaps not all of these roads proved to be motorways, some of them more like tracks, but all of them leading towards new pastures and woods). One saw, too, his courtesy, nay patience, when someone displaying a building to visitors from the conference lingered rather too long over an architectural feature dear to their hearts, and, more jovially, experienced his pleasure in conversation spiced with the ease of mild conviviality in the Chequers, placed neatly cheek-by-jowl with the conference house. In Battle, finally, scholars with whom he might have crossed swords in print, were made welcome, the hearth was wide enough to welcome enthusiasts with views often very different from his own.

Such qualities derived, of course, from that third side of Allen to which I referred at the start, Allen as friend. He was warm-hearted, generous and eager to share his delight in living with others, and to be warmed by them in turn. He would, I believe, have said Amen to Ailred of Rievaulx's dictum that 'the best medicine in life is a friend'.[8] To me he was magnaminous and encouraging to a humbling degree, especially when I remember that University College took me in to the History Department in 1956 when they could have had him, preferring, I suppose, the slightly younger man. Typically, Allen never, I think, referred to this, and when much later we were both candidates for a chair in another London College (which neither of us got), this brought about no strain in our relationship. Long before that he opened to me one of the most important doors in my life when he invited me to share in, and later to take over, the task of editing the charters of a Midland Cistercian abbey, Rufford, which I might never have had the opportunity to do otherwise. I shall never forget that first time he took me to Chancery Lane, where in a room normally denied to mere readers, a black deed box was opened and he spread out a few of the charters within, stopping from time to time to draw attention to a famous name or a luscious seal. A few years later I was able to repay a small part of my debt to him by reading the draft of his book *The Normans and the Norman Conquest*. Here tonight there must be many others who have received similar crucial acts of friendship from him, suggestions which have coloured their lives. And it is because he was that kind of person that we loved him, and sense him from time to time even now. 'Wherefore friends, says Tullius' (I quote Ailred again, perhaps because I was at Rievaulx last Saturday) 'though absent are present . . . and – what seems stranger still – though dead are alive.'[9]

And so we give thanks for Allen's life, for him as husband, father, brother, scholar, teacher and friend, for the *largesse* of spirit which he always showed, never more so than in the last year and a half of his life. At Caen, only a few months into his illness, he rejoiced in the company of his friends in a transplanted Battle Conference, and displayed the old energy and delight to an astounding degree. In succeeding months he managed in a marvellous way to continue active in writing and teaching, as well as to commit himself to a further stage in his membership of Christ's church. I never spoke to Allen of 'religion', but from those who saw him in that last eighteen months I have heard not merely of his courage, but also of his confidence, as though things were somehow or other, thanks be to God, being made one. And so perhaps, not inappropriately, I may make as our valediction, words which Bernard of Clairvaux wrote for the Knights of the Temple, as he pointed them towards Christ's burial place. They seem apt for Allen both because they contain a fundamental message of hope and because they do so

---

[8] *De Spirituali Amicitia*, II.13 (*Aelredi Rievallensis Opera*, ed. A. Hoste, C. H. Talbot, Turnhout 1971, 304). I quote the translation by Mary Eugenia Laker, *Aelred of Rievaulx: Spiritual Friendship* (Cistercian Fathers Series, 5, Kalamazoo 1977), 72.

[9] *De Spirit. Amic.*, II.13 (305); translation, 72–3. Ailred here quotes Cicero, *De Amicitia*, 23.

in imagery drawn from that feudal world which he so much enjoyed and about which he has revealed so much to us;

'How sweet it must be for pilgrims after the fatigue of their long journey and their many perils on land and sea, to find rest there at last,' Bernard wrote, 'there where their own Lord has rested. I should think that in their joy, they no longer feel their weariness, nor regret their expenses, but claim the reward of their labour and the prize of their course.'[10]

Laus Deo.

Christopher Holdsworth

---

[10] *De Laude Novae Militiae*, XI.29 (*S. Bernardi Opera*, ed. J. Leclercq and H. M. Rochais, Rome 1963, III, 236). I quote the translation by Conrad Greenia, *Bernard of Clairvaux: Treatises III* (Cist. Fathers 19, Kalamazoo 1977), 162–3.

THE BAYEUX TAPESTRY:
WHY EUSTACE, ODO AND WILLIAM?

Shirley Ann Brown

In the early 1730s an embroidery representing the story of the dynastic struggle between Harold Godwinson and William of Normandy for the kingship of England was brought to the attention of the French Royal Academy, primarily through the efforts of Antoine Lancelot and Dom Bernard de Montfaucon. In the subsequent 260 years, this object, now known as the Bayeux Tapestry in spite of its being an embroidery of wool on linen, has spawned innumerable writings, ranging from scholarly studies to popular rhapsodies.[1] It has been regarded from every conceivable viewpoint and has yielded much information about eleventh-century England and Normandy, their way of life and their manner of looking at things.

Everyone who is familiar with this most famous work of art to survive from the Middle Ages[2] knows that the subject represented on the Bayeux Tapestry is the Norman Conquest of England with the Battle of Hastings as its climax. The first half of the Tapestry's narrative is concerned with elucidating the justification, from an apparently Norman viewpoint, of Duke William of Normandy's decision to invade a foreign sovereign state and to take over its seat of power.[3] The middle section is filled with details of the preparation and provisioning of the invasion fleet and the activities of the Duke's forces from the time they land on English soil until the first shock of battle. The actual encounter between the two armies[4] is taken up in what remains, less than one-quarter of the total length of the embroidery.[5]

* I would like to thank David Bates for his generosity in reading the draft of this paper and for help with some of the historical material concerning Odo of Bayeux and his vassals.

[1] See S. A. Brown, *The Bayeux Tapestry: History and Bibliography*, Woodbridge 1988.

[2] For a history of the Bayeux Tapestry and its survival, see S. A. Brown, 'Bayeux Tapestry', 1–22.

[3] The Norman claim that King Edward had sent Harold to Normandy to renew the pledge of succession to William is obviously the basis for the first part of the embroidery's narrative, in spite of certain ambiguities in the inscriptions. Edward's designation and Harold's oath of support, clearly shown as the climax of his stay in Normandy, formed the foundation of William's claim, and were seen as over-ruling Edward's deathbed designation of Harold as his successor, which is also clearly represented. The secret inclusion in the Tapestry's narrative of an underlying Anglo-Saxon sympathy or even protest is highly possible, given the probability of its English manufacture, but this does not outweigh the apparent Norman element. See Richard D. Wissolik, 'The Monk Eadmer as historian of the Norman succession: Körner and Freeman examined', *The American Benedictine Review* xxx, 1979, 32–43; and his 'The Saxon Statement: Code in the Bayeux Tapestry', *Annuale Mediaevale* xix, 1979, 69–97; also, David J. Bernstein, *The Mystery of the Bayeux Tapestry*, Chicago and London 1986.

[4] I will call the opposing factions French and English, in deference to the Tapestry's own inscriptions, in which the combined forces fighting under William at Hastings are described as French; the term 'Norman' is used in the embroidery only as part of William's ducal title, but will be used in this paper where the context is clearly meant to refer to Norman matters as opposed to those Anglo-Saxon or French.

[5] The hanging currently measures between 48 and 51cm in height by about 69.55 metres in length,

Plate 1 BT: The 'rout' of the French forces

The Bayeux Tapestry has rewarded its viewers with untold enjoyment on the one hand, and with seemingly unsolvable puzzles of interpretation on the other. This paper is concerned with one of those seeming puzzles, one which is deeply imbedded in the depiction of the Battle of Hastings, and which seems not to have been asked before, at least not in print. This paper asks the question: Why Eustace? Why was the Count of Boulogne heroically portrayed in a crucial scene on the Bayeux Tapestry, and why was he shown specifically in close association with Duke William and Odo, Bishop of Bayeux? (Pl. 1). To answer these questions it is necessary to study the relationship between this version of events in the Bayeux Tapestry and those found in the poetical and so-called 'historical' sources, and to ask whether or not we have been reading the illustrations in the embroidery correctly. Should we consider another way of dividing the scenes that depict the battle sequence?

The depiction of William, Odo and Eustace in battle together is crucial to the understanding of the Bayeux Tapestry, and because one should not take too much for granted when looking at a heavily restored section of the embroidery, this segment must be scrutinized to see if there is any doubt about the genuineness of its current appearance and the subsequent identification of the standard-bearing figure as Eustace of Boulogne. (Pl. 2)

It is to be noticed immediately that the inscription, which lies at the upper edge of the linen and which identifies the figure with the banner, is incomplete, with a major portion missing in the middle. The remaining letters are heavily restored, the initial E in a blackish wool and the rest in a green wool. Looking at early reproductions and descriptions is one way to determine the validity of the restorations.

The first two descriptions of this section of the embroidery date from 1730. Bernard de Montfaucon, who introduced the hanging to the antiquarian world in

being composed of eight unequal lengths of material carefully stitched together. The right end is ragged and torn and it is impossible to calculate how much is currently missing.

Plate 2 BT: Eustace of Boulogne and Duke William

his *Monumens de la Monarchie françoise* did not mention the presence of any inscription between HIC EST WILLELMUS DUX and HIC FRANCI PUGNANT,[6] and in his explanatory narrative, he did not identify the standard-bearer.[7] Neither did Antoine Lancelot, in a paper read to the Académie royale in May 1730, indicate any identification of this figure by the inscription, nor did he posit an identification beyond calling him the standard-bearer; he then quoted a section of Wace's *Roman de Rou* which identifies the French standard-bearer as Tostain of Caux.[8]

In the engravings which accompany these writings, it is evidenced that a semi-circular piece was already missing from the upper border above this figure. There is no inscription, partial or otherwise, in the plates for Lancelot. (Pl. 3) But in the plates produced for de Montfaucon from the drawings of Antoine Benoît who was sent to Bayeux to make an accurate drawing of the hanging, the IUS is shown as

[6] Bernard de Montfaucon, *Les Monumens de la Monarchie françoise*, vol. 2, Paris 1730, 28–29.

[7] At this point in his exposition of the Bayeux Tapestry's narrative, de Montfaucon interjects the story, based on William of Poitiers and later writers, that Eustace of Boulogne lost his courage and resolve when he saw the retreat of part of the French force, turned back himself, counselling William to flee for his life. De Montfaucon adds that as he was doing this, Eustace was struck by an arrow and fell dead on the spot! De Montfaucon does not identify any of the figures in the Tapestry as Eustace, although if he had done so, he probably would have chosen either the knight actually fleeing, or one of the fallen figures in the lower border.

[8] Antoine Lancelot, 'Suite de l'explication d'un monument de *Guillaume le Conquérant*', *Mémoires de littérature tirés des registres de l'Académie royale des Inscriptions et Belles-Lettres depuis l'année MDCCXXVI jusques et compris l'année MDCCXXX* viii, 1732, 667.

Plate 3 BT: The 'rout' as shown in Lancelot's engraving of 1730

clearly readable.[9] (Pl. 4) This indicates that at least some remnants of the thread remained or that the needle-holes could be discerned.

The next set of complete drawings of the Bayeux Tapestry still available was delivered to the Society of Antiquaries in London by the artist Charles Stothard in 1819, with an accompanying essay. (Pl. 5) His description of the part of the embroidery in question warrants attention:

> In that part of the battle between William and Harold, where the former is pulling off his helmet, to shew himself to his soldiers, under the words HIC EST DUX WILELMI, there is on his left hand a figure with outstretched arms, bearing a standard; above which a part of the Tapestry has been torn away, and only the last two letters U S of an inscription apparently remaining. On carefully examining the torn and ragged edges, which had been doubled under and sewed down, I discovered three other letters, the first of the inscription an E, and T I, preceding U S, a space remaining in the middle but for *four* letters, the number being confirmed by the alternations of green and buff in the colours of the letters remaining. I therefore conjecture that the letters as they now stand may be read *Eustatius*, and that the person bearing the standard beneath is intended for Eustace, Earl of Boulogne, who I believe was a principal commander in the army of William.[10]

The colour alternations have disappeared, presumably with the subsequent restorations of the letters, but there is no reason to doubt Stothard's description of

---

[9] There is no indication that de Montfaucon had ever gone to Bayeux to look at the Bayeux Tapestry or that he had even bothered to look closely at the drawings he commissioned. One more inconsistency in this scene between what he wrote and the evidence of the engravings supports this contention. De Montfaucon suggests that HIC ODO EPS BACULUM TENENS CONFOR... which was clearly legible, should be completed with -TAT FRANCOS 'or something similar'. Benoît clearly drew -TAT PUEROS on the evidence of the needleholes. Benoît's version is corroborated in the Lancelot engravings in which -TAT PUEROS also appeared, although in a different spot, Lancelot having stated that this part of the inscription had been confirmed for him in a letter from the Bishop of Bayeux. Today the inscription follows the Benoît placement.

[10] Charles A. Stothard, 'Some Observations on the Bayeux Tapestry', *Archaeologia* xix, 1821, 185.

Plate 4 BT: The 'rout' as shown in de Montfaucon's engraving of 1730

what he found. While it is unfortunate that the inscription is fragmentary at this point, I think we can be certain that the restored letters we see today are based on good authority and that the figure bearing the standard was meant to be recognized as Eustace II, Count of Boulogne.[11]

The critical viewer is faced with the question of why Eustace was represented at this point in the embroidery and in such distinguished company. To attempt an answer to this problem, I suggest it is once more necessary to take a fresh look at the Tapestry's version of the Battle of Hastings and at its possible links with other renditions of these momentous events.

The Battle of Hastings, as shown in the Bayeux Tapestry, is composed of a series of episodes, each clearly following one another, leading to the death of Harold and the English flight. The visual designer and the narrator, who may or may not have been the same person, obviously strove to be vivid and endeavoured to make clear what must have been essentially a confused picture.[12] The viewer is shown a carefully organized battle in which several stages are depicted: the French cavalry attacking the English infantry; the deaths of Leofwine and Gyrth Godwinson; a tumultuous scene of tumbling horses and riders giving way before the lightly-armed English levy which occupies a hillock; the French rout being reversed by the combined efforts of Odo of Bayeux, Duke William and Eustace of Boulogne; the

---

[11] If one looks closely at the figure now identified as Eustace, one immediately notices that he sports flowing mustachios. These have grown since the 1730 drawings in which this figure is clean-shaven, as are all the other French knights. Either Benoît missed them, they had been added during the eighteenth century, or Stothard invented them. They seem to have become a permanent attribute of the figure. That these mustachios are seen as an anomaly on a French knight led one writer to wonder if Stothard might have been aware of Eustace's nickname, *Aux grenons*. See Charles Dawson, *The 'Restorations' of the Bayeux Tapestry*, London 1907, 9, who characteristically gives no source for his information about Eustace's nickname. This anomaly of French mustachios does not necessarily affect the identification of the figure as Eustace, but it does make one aware of the difficulties of relying upon small visual details, such as haircuts and mustachios, to prove points about the Bayeux Tapestry.

[12] R. C. Smail, *Crusading Warfare (1097–1193)*, Cambridge 1956, 166–167 used this argument when warning historians against using art and poetry as a source of realistic accounts of battles. Obviously there would have been no-one who could have related the sequence of encounters in a battle of the size, complexity and duration of the Battle of Hastings; there would be as many differing versions as there were survivors.

Plate 5 BT: Eustace as shown in Stothard's facsimile of 1819

renewed French offensive leading to the death of Harold and the English flight, where the Tapestry is so heavily restored as to be useless for artistic consideration.

It must be remembered that the Bayeux Tapestry's version of the Battle of Hastings is an assemblage of carefully chosen events of the day, consciously arranged in a sequence determined by the story-teller, or 'librettist' as I like to call this still-anonymous person, in response to the conditions of the commission. Although his version of what happened on Saturday, 14 October 1066, is a story determined in part by extraneous influences, the embroidery has long been regarded by some scholars as one of the most accurate and reliable sources of information about how this battle was fought. Some writers have reconstructed the day according to William of Poitiers, the Bayeux Tapestry, and until a few years ago, the *Carmen de Hastingae Proelio*.[13] The principle of 'artistic license' is not deemed, by some of these scholars, to have had much, if any, effect upon the

---

[13] The list is almost endless, but most recently see, N. P. Brooks, 'The authority and interpretation of the Bayeux Tapestry', *ante* i, 1978, 1–34 and 191–199 for a careful, even-handed view; and R. A. Brown, 'The Battle of Hastings', *ante* iii, 1980, 1–21 and 197–201 for a reconstruction according to William of Poitiers and the Bayeux Tapestry. For the reconstruction according to the *Carmen*, see *Carmen*, especially Appendices B, C and D.

formation of the Bayeux Tapestry's story.[14] But a careful look at the version of the Battle of Hastings as presented in the famous embroidery will show that 'artistic license' did indeed come into play in its narrative and that what we call 'historical accuracy' was not its principal objective.

With its similarities to such other roughly contemporary versions of the story of Harold and William as found in the *Gesta Guillelmi* of William of Poitiers and the *Carmen de Hastingae Proelio*,[15] the borrowing of Edward's deathbed scene from the *Vita Aedwardi*, the parallels with the *Chanson de Roland*,[16] the inclusion of a number of *fabliaux*,[17] and if we are to agree with the latest suggestion, references to Old Testament iconography,[18] it should have become uncomfortable, if not impossible, for scholars to continue to regard the Bayeux Tapestry as primarily an historical chronicle. Although it is felt by some scholars that he was independently depicting events that were common knowledge, it seems to me rather that the Bayeux Tapestry's 'librettist' made so many allusions to so many episodes found in such a wide range of contemporary literary works, that unless it can be postulated that there was one all-encompassing source for all versions, it would appear that he was consciously gleaning information to form his own story, shaped by his own purposes, and those initially laid down by his patron(s).

All the stages of the Battle of Hastings as shown in the Bayeux Tapestry are variously described, or at least mentioned by William of Poitiers and the poet of the *Carmen de Hastingae Proelio*. The probability that the embroidery's 'librettist' knew the *Gesta Guillelmi* has often been argued. But for some scholars the *Carmen*, with its poetic description of the Battle of Hastings, has fallen from grace. Since its discovery in 1826, two opposing camps have gathered around the poem: those who support its attribution to Guy, Bishop of Amiens, and thus a dating of between 1067 and 1074/75;[19] and those who would deny Guy's authorship and place it in the twelfth century.[20] Some who accepted the early dating also regarded the *Carmen* as a valuable historical source to be mined for information used in reconstructing the Norman Campaign. This reached its apogee in the latest edition of the poem in which the editors, regarding it as being, 'at once fuller than the *Gesta Normannorum Ducum*, more honest and reliable than the *Gesta Guillelmi*, and more explicit than the Bayeux Tapestry', set out to rewrite the currently accepted reconstruction of that famous battle, according to the poetic description.[21]

[14] The same attitude pervades the attempts to late-date and discredit the *Carmen*. See R. H. C. Davis, 'The Carmen de Hastingae Proelio', *EHR* ccclxvii, 1978, 241–261.

[15] Morton and Muntz's comparative tables of parallel texts in *Carmen*, Appendix A, are valuable, but their unrelenting use of the poem as an absolutely reliable historical document cannot be accepted.

[16] See C. R. Dodwell, 'The Bayeux Tapestry and French Secular Epic', *Burlington Magazine* cviii, 1966, 549–560; and S. A. Brown, 'The Bayeux Tapestry and the Song of Roland', *Olifant* vi, 1979, 339–350.

[17] Hélène Chefneux, 'Les Fables dans la Tapisserie de Bayeux', *Romania* lx, 1934, 1–35; 153–194; also, though fairly unreliable, L. Herrmann, *Les fables antiques de la broderie de Bayeux*, Brussels 1964.

[18] D. Bernstein, 'The Blinding of Harold and the Meaning of the Bayeux Tapestry', *ante* v, 1982, 40–64; and developed further in *Mystery*.

[19] Pertz, Petrie, Hardie, Körner, Barlow, Morton and Muntz, Engels, Foreville, Jaschke, van Houts.

[20] White, Davis, R. A. Brown.

[21] *Carmen*, 73–120.

Morton and Muntz's remarkable effort was soundly rejected on several grounds by R. H. C. Davis, who concluded his arguments by writing that the *Carmen de Hastingae Proelio* was actually a twelfth-century literary exercise produced in the French court circle, and, in his oft-quoted words, 'as a source for the history of the Norman Conquest it is simply ridiculous'.[22] The discussion became animated with L. J. Engels' rebuttal of the Davis arguments,[23] and Raymonde Foreville's reiteration of her continuing support for the early dating and attribution [24] on the one hand, and R. A. Brown's rejection of the *Carmen* as an historical source [25] on the other.

Much of the difficulty arises from the desire to see the *Carmen* as a reliable historical source and the subsequent realization that its version of events differs from that of parallel accounts found in William of Poitiers and the Bayeux Tapestry. But the historical and literary evidence do not necessarily point in different directions and it is perfectly possible to accept the early dating for the poem and its attribution to Guy of Amiens, without regarding it as a primary source of historical information. Elisabeth van Houts' very recent study of the poem in the light of other Latin poetry written for the early Anglo-Norman and French courts, and her conclusion that the early dating is reliable, has reopened the discussion.[26]

In my opinion, not all of Professor Davis' suggestions of anachronisms in the poem are conclusive and his discussion of the manuscript does not necessarily require a late date for the poem's composition. His argument that WIDO was an unusual form for Guy in the eleventh century disregards the fact that another Guy, from Ponthieu, the Bishop of Amiens' nephew, was distinctly labelled as WIDO four times in the Bayeux Tapestry. But Davis' suggestion that the *Carmen*'s poet 'is more intent on how he sings than on what he sings about' should be kept in mind by parties on both sides of the argument.[27] The poem should be seen as an artistic creation whose tone, shape, and even story, are determined, at least partially, by the circumstances surrounding its creation. This latter viewpoint had been put forth by Frank Barlow, who suggested that the *Carmen* was never meant to be taken as a completely accurate description of events, but as a literary work.[28]

I suggest that it is profitable to look carefully at the parallels between the narratives in the Bayeux Tapestry, in William of Poitiers' *Gesta Guillelmi* and in the *Carmen de Hastingae Proelio*, narratives which are closer than has been noticed before. But even if there are inevitable similarities among different versions of the same events, it is immediately recognizable that the sequential arrangement of the Bayeux Tapestry's version is unique. One oft-quoted example is that in the embroidery the Breton Campaign occurs before Harold receives arms from Duke William, the reverse of the sequence as relayed by William of Poitiers. In the Tapestry this allows the bestowal of arms to lead directly to the oath scene, and

---

[22] Davis, 'Carmen', 261.

[23] L. J. Engels, 'Once more: The Carmen de Hastingae Proelio', *ante* ii, 1979, 3–20 and 165–167.

[24] R. Foreville, in 'The Carmen de Hastingae Proelio: a discussion', *ante* ii, 1979, 18–19.

[25] R. A. Brown, 'The Battle of Hastings'.

[26] Elisabeth van Houts, 'Latin Poetry and the Anglo-Norman Court 1066–1135: The *Carmen de Hastingae Proelio*', *Journal of Medieval History* xv, 1989, 39–62.

[27] Davis, 'Carmen', 242.

[28] Frank Barlow, 'The Carmen de Hastingae Proelio', *Studies in International History*, ed. by K. Bourne and D. C. Watt, London 1967, 35–67.

thus to augment the importance of the oath and Harold's links to William. It can be seen here that the embroidery's 'librettist' was a consummate storyteller and clearly arranged his tale to produce a desired effect.

Every battle has a beginning, but the argument as to who surprised whom at Telham Hill is allowed no importance in the Tapestry's version, for before the onset of battle, we are shown scouts from each side bringing news of the opposing force. The Tapestry's depiction of the initial encounter between the French archers and cavalry and the English infantry with its 'shield-wall' has much in common with other descriptions, even to the exaggeration of how closely closely-bunched, fully-armed warriors could stand.[29] The next episode in the Bayeux Tapestry's battle sequence is the death of Harold's brothers Leofwine and Gyrth. It was common knowledge that they had fallen in the fighting, but most sources simply allude to their demise, along with that of Harold.[30] Of the literary versions, only the *Carmen* describes the death of Gyrth, and in heroic and epic terms: Gyrth having wounded Duke William's horse and forcing him to fight on foot, is killed in hand-to-hand combat by the enraged Norman. Leofwine goes unmentioned in the poem.[31] It is worth remarking that the only casualties singled out for specific identification in the Bayeux Tapestry are the three Godwinsons and that the deaths of Leofwine and Gyrth were considered important enough by the Tapestry's 'librettist' to warrant a depiction separate from the killing of Harold. I have argued elsewhere that the 'librettist' may have seized the opportunity to indicate the destruction of the family unit as one of the punishments for treason.[32]

Gyrth's heroic, saga-like death occurs after the Norman rout in the *Carmen*'s account, and conversely, before the rout in the Bayeux Tapestry. Although this may represent different traditions, I suggest that once more we witness the narrator striving to create the most effective sequence. The placing of Leofwine and Gyrth's deaths together and at this point in the embroidery's version allows the remainder of the narrative to be read as a continuous sequence leading to the flight of the vanquished English.

It is of paramount importance to read the following scenes not as a series of separate events, but as one action leading directly into another.[33] One of my contentions is that it is in this carefully orchestrated battle sequence that the Bayeux

---

[29] *Gesta Guillelmi*, ii, 16; *Carmen*, vv. 356–372; 406–422.

[30] *Anglo-Saxon Chronicle D*, 1066; *Gesta Guillelmi* ii, 23.

[31] *Carmen*, vv. 471–480.

[32] S. A. Brown, 'The Bayeux Tapestry and the Song of Roland', 343.

[33] Since the numbers were written onto the top margin of the backing cloth to divide the narrative into scenes for quick identification, and the creation of photographic reproductions, we have become accustomed to looking at, and consequently studying, the Bayeux Tapestry in a piecemeal fashion. One of the unavoidable problems with the book format, no matter how wonderful the quality of the photographs, is that it arbitrarily cuts the images and thus the narrative into bits and pieces. Anyone who has seen the original will immediately realize what a different impact the visual narrative produces, and how differently we read it, when it can be seen without a break, as it was originally meant to be viewed. The current method of exhibition, in which space and fire safety were necessarily deemed of primary importance, unfortunately folds the Tapestry in the wrong direction and does not allow the viewer to stand far enough back from the images. The embroidery should ideally be wrapped around the walls of a room which affords continuous viewing, from both close and distant standingpoints. In order to follow my arguments suggesting that we must look at longer sections of the Bayeux Tapestry than can be shown in book illustrations, I suggest the use of the continuous fold-out reproduction that is available.

Tapestry narrative exhibits certain features which are curiously reminiscent of, or at least analogous to, the *Carmen de Hastingae Proelio*'s poetic version, and is where the story-teller may be giving us clues to his underlying purpose.

The Bayeux Tapestry's dramatic scene of the total disarray of the French, falling in a tumbling mass of horses and knights before the group of lightly-armed English who occupy the hill has attracted attention before. It may very well reflect knowledge of the so-called *Malfosse* incident found much later in the sequence in William of Poitier's account, but put into a different context by the Tapestry's narrator.[34] It may also be interpreted in the context of the *Carmen*'s lengthy description of a feigned flight which turns into a real rout as the French give way before the English shire levies.[35]

This wonderfully chaotic scene was included in the Bayeux Tapestry's narrative to provide the reason for the rout of the French which results directly from it. These two episodes should be seen as one continuous action, for they even overlap in design. The rout is understatedly indicated by the lone knight riding in a direction opposite the general movement, with his lance over his shoulder and his shield covering his back. (Pl. 7) Although this would have been a common precautionary method, the parallel in the *Carmen* is interestingly close: 'The Normans fled, their shields covering their backs'.[36] In the matter of the French retreat, the *Carmen* and William of Poitiers relate basically the same story: one section of the French forces, believing William to have been slain, fled from the English; Duke William rushed to check their flight; haranguing them for their cowardice, he lifted his helmet to bare his head so that his men could see he was still alive; inflamed anew, they followed him into battle.[37]

In agreement with this generally-known story, the Bayeux Tapestry clearly depicts the Duke's legendary action; but the 'librettist' added new and unique elements to the tale. (Pl. 1) The Bayeux Tapestry narrator assigns a very important role to Bishop Odo of Bayeux in reversing the rout, and in this, it is unique. The story-teller also adds another hero into this melée – Eustace of Boulogne – the second hero of the *Carmen de Hastingae Proelio*! But the inclusion of the Count of Boulogne in this particular episode is also peculiar to the Bayeux Tapestry, for neither the *Carmen* nor William of Poitiers mentions him as active during this crisis. Eustace may be something of a hero in the *Carmen*, but it is only later in the action that he is described as fighting alongside the Duke.[38] The telescoping of events in the Tapestry must be deliberate, so that the three men – Odo, William, and Eustace – can be shown together.

In the embroidery, the grouping of William and Eustace leads without any visual break into the renewed attack on the English position. This is precisely analogous to the passage in the *Carmen*: 'the count and the duke, joining forces, renewed the battle together wherever the clashing arms glittered most brightly'.[39] The poem

---

[34] *Gesta Guillelmi* ii, 24; T. Davies Pryce, 'Earthworks of the moated mound type', *Journ. BAA* lxii, 1906, 231–268, especially 257–260; R. A. Brown, 'The Battle of Hastings', 18–21 gives a good overview of the various versions of the 'malfosse' incident and the complications introduced by different sources.

[35] *Carmen*, vv. 424–444.

[36] *Carmen*, v. 444.

[37] *Gesta Guillelmi*, ii, 18; *Carmen*, vv. 445–470.

[38] *Carmen*, vv. 525–526.

[39] *Carmen*, vv. 525–526.

describes how this led to the deaths of scores of Englishmen – the Bayeux Tapestry shows the French attacking 'those who were with Harold', presumably the remnants of the household guard. Harold's death follows immediately in both versions. Thus, in the Tapestry, the sequential arrangement of the chosen highlights of the Battle of Hastings was carefully orchestrated so that the ultimate French victory is seen as a direct result of an action stemming from the alliance of Odo of Bayeux, Duke William, and Eustace of Boulogne.

Only the Bayeux Tapestry and the *Carmen de Hastingae Proelio* furnish detailed accounts of the king's demise. (Pl. 6) The scene of Harold's death presents one of the thorniest and most sensitive of the interpretational problems created by the Bayeux Tapestry. There are basically three readings of the scene: (1) only the arrow-in-the-eye figure is Harold; (2) only the falling figure about to lose the leg is Harold; (3) both figures are Harold and represent two stages of the slaying. The inscription is bald: HIC HAROLD REX INTERFECTUS EST – and by its placement, it does nothing to alleviate the perhaps deliberate ambiguity of the scene. The *Carmen* contains the only other contemporary description of Harold's final moments, and as improbable as its account may seem to some scholars, it gives us clues, not necessarily to what actually happened, but to what is depicted on the Bayeux Tapestry.

The *Carmen* states that the French had all but won the day and that plundering of the dead already had begun, when Duke William spotted Harold stubbornly resisting. The Duke called three men to his aid – Eustace of Boulogne, Hugh of Ponthieu, and Giffard – and together they killed Harold.[40] The King of England was literally hacked to pieces: William pierced his breast clean through his shield, drenching the earth with blood; Eustace decapitated him; Hugh pierced his belly with his lance; and Giffard cut off his leg at the thigh.[41] So much for William of Poitiers' statement that William would have fought Harold single-handed had he been given the opportunity![42]

The Bayeux Tapestry's depiction of Harold's death is surprisingly similar. But we must look at the scene in the embroidery in a manner different from the usual – it is important to see the episode as encompassing the whole section from the horseman beneath the beginning of the inscription HIC HAROLD REX INTERFECTUS EST to the last pair of knights moving to the left, just before the English flight. (Pl. 6) The previous action with Odo, William, and Eustace leads to this culmination of the fighting and Harold dies accompanied by his faithful housecarls, who valiantly attempt to fend off the attack from both directions. As in the *Carmen*, the plundering of the dead begins in the Bayeux Tapestry's lower border at the point where the first knight attacks the English holdouts. Also akin to the poem, four mounted knights participate in this final assault, although in the embroidery it is impossible to identify individual attackers. Harold is undoubtedly the figure being cut down by a sword blow beneath the inscription INTERFECTUS EST, coinciding with the *Carmen*'s account of the mutilation of the leg. But there is no denying that the scene in the Tapestry is made ambiguous, at least for modern commentators, with the insertion of the arrow-in-the-eye figure. This may very well represent one of Harold's last defenders. On the other hand, it may represent

[40] Morton and Muntz seem to have been correct in their identification of the four men in the *Carmen*.
[41] *Carmen*, vv. 530–550.
[42] *Gesta Guillelmi* ii, 22.

the king suffering a wound to the face before being hacked down, a story now reflected only in later written sources.[43]

The similarities found between the Tapestry and the *Carmen*'s description of the Battle of Hastings are not invalidated by the ambiguities in the visual images. But there are also important differences between the two versions which must be taken into consideration. Although the story of Duke William baring his face during battle is found in the majority of accounts of the Battle of Hastings and has the ring of authenticity to it, only the Bayeux Tapestry shows Odo of Bayeux and Eustace of Boulogne as his companions in this derring-do. The critical viewer is faced with the puzzle of why the scene is so constructed. In the Bayeux Tapestry, Eustace is portrayed as a close comrade-in-arms of William, helping to turn back the fleeing knights. He holds the banner high as he rides slightly ahead of the Duke, pointing him out to his troops to rally their courage. At the same time, he is shown leading the renewed fighting which results in King Harold's death and the French victory.

In the *Carmen* the Count of Boulogne has nothing to do with this episode; the killing of Gyrth Godwinson and the double unhorsing of William intervene between the head-baring incident and the introduction of Eustace. By giving a very special place to Eustace as a companion to the Conqueror, the Bayeux Tapestry narrative here exhibits the tenor, if not the sequence, of the *Carmen*, for both the embroidery and the poem draw attention to the heroism of the Count of Boulogne. In the poem, Eustace is singled out for special praise for his action in rescuing the Duke who had been unhorsed and half-stunned during the most intense part of the fighting. Eustace and his knights sweep to the rescue and the Count gives his own war-horse to William.[44] When Harold is seen fighting on the hill, it is Eustace whom the Duke calls first to help him break the king's resistance.[45] When the English flee the battle at the day's end, and while William rests, Eustace ceaselessly pursues the English and is engaged all night in countless skirmishes.[46]

It is noteworthy that the portrayal of Eustace of Boulogne in both the *Carmen* and the Tapestry is at complete variance with William of Poitiers' picture of the man. Although at one point in the *Gesta Guillelmi* Eustace is described as one of William's companions,[47] he is also described as the worst of cowards, one who turns in flight after the French setback at the ditch, taking his troops with him, fleeing after the main battle had already been fought and won! To compound this cowardice, William of Poitiers' Eustace urges the Duke to retreat, and is seriously wounded in the back, requiring aid from his men.[48] The author of the Bayeux Tapestry's narrative may very well have been familiar with the image of the cowardly Eustace found in the *Gesta*. Instead, he deliberately chose to immortalize a Eustace as heroic as the man reflected in the *Carmen*, even labelling the Count of Boulogne so that his identity could not be mistaken! The curious dichotomy of contemporary opinion about the performance of Eustace of Boulogne and the choice made as to the manner of his portrayal in the Bayeux Tapestry may provide clues as to the function of the embroidery's story.

[43] See N. P. Brooks for a full account of the arrow-in-the-eye controversy; also, D. Bernstein for an alternate view and interpretation.
[44] *Carmen*, vv. 505–522.
[45] *Carmen*, vv. 533–535.
[46] *Carmen*, vv. 561–566.
[47] *Gesta Guillelmi* ii, 22.
[48] *Gesta Guillelmi* ii, 24.

Plate 6 BT: The death of Harold

Plate 7 BT: Bishop Odo of Bayeux rallying the French

Just as the Bayeux Tapestry is alone in placing Eustace at the head-baring incident, so it alone attests the participation of Odo of Bayeux. The Duke's half-brother is shown at the rout scene, wearing a most unusual hauberk, a helmet, without a protective shield, brandishing a club. (Pl. 7) That his presence and action are to be considered seriously by the viewer is indicated by the inscription – HIC ODO EPISCOPUS BACULUM TENENS CONFOR(TAT PUEROS)[49] – which leaves no doubt about the identification of the figure. The bishop's appearance in this scene with William and Eustace has to be looked at from two angles – why is he shown at this particular point in the Bayeux Tapestry's story, and what degree of 'historical truth' is being depicted. Odo of Bayeux is now generally considered to be the most likely patron of the Bayeux Tapestry, and the manner in which he is represented in the embroidery is of paramount importance.[50]

Willliam of Poitiers wrote that two bishops, Odo of Bayeux and Geoffrey of Coutances, accompanied the invading force to England as spiritual advisors. Geoffrey does not appear in the Bayeux Tapestry while Odo appears definitely four times and in three of these he is labelled as EPISCOPUS, so that there is an obvious, repeated reference to his religious status. But paradoxically, Odo's role

---

[49] The last part of the inscription -TAT PUEROS, is restoration, and although there are questions about the choice of words, they are not relevent to this discussion.
[50] My preliminary study of Odo as possible patron of the Bayeux Tapestry, using much of the information supplied by David Bates in 'The Character and Career of Odo, Bishop of Bayeux (1049/50–1097)', *Speculum* i, 1975, 1–20, appeared in my unpublished doctoral disseration, *The Bayeux Tapestry: Its Purpose and Dating* Ithaca, New York, 1977. The arguments for Odo's patronage have been summarized most recently in Bernstein, 'The Mystery of the Bayeux Tapestry', 28–36.

Plate 8 BT: Bishop Odo of Bayeux blessing the meal at Hastings

as a Man of God seems to be downplayed visually, for the only instance of his being shown performing a priestly function is when he says grace at the meal before the fighting begins. (Pl. 8) I used to think that this was done so as to place a greater emphasis on Odo's military prowess, and that the obvious visual resemblance between the Hastings meal and a Last Supper was the result of an adaptation of a convenient design model. But on further reflection, I now think it more probable that the coincidence between the two designs was more deliberate, so that in fact attention is drawn to Odo's double status after Hastings – ecclesiastical and secular – Bishop of Bayeux and Earl of Kent.

Although we can be almost certain that Odo was present at Telham Hill, we cannot be certain of the amount of fighting in which he participated, if any. He is not mentioned specifically as taking part in the Battle of Hastings as described in the *Carmen de Hastingae Proelio*. Odo is never described in contemporary sources as a warrior bishop actually wielding a sword in battle although he is held responsible for ordering military actions and suppressing revolts in conquered England.[51] Odo's role in battle, as depicted in the Bayeux Tapestry, may very well have been fictionalized. (Pl. 7) The popular attribution of military prowess to Odo may well be a result of this image of him in the embroidery; it is only recently that an attempt has been made to unfictionalize his history.[52]

---

[51] For the best study of Odo see David R. Bates, 'The Character and Career of Odo of Bayeux', and *Normandy before 1066*, London and New York, 1982; also see *Gesta Guillelmi* ii, 37 and ii, 46.

[52] As an adjunct to the main argument of this paper, it is difficult to escape the conclusion that the image of the fighting Odo found in the Tapestry was created partially to evoke a parallel with that of the popular heroic figure of Turpin, the battling Archbishop of Reims in the Roland legend. The arguments for the dating of the *Chanson de Roland* are ongoing, but the majority of scholars agree that

Plate 9 BT: Bishop Odo of Bayeux and Duke William ordering ships to be built.

But the question remains. Why deliberately show Odo of Bayeux wielding what is probably a baton of command similar to William's [as shown earlier in the Tapestry, and not a fighting cudgel] in the same scene as Duke William and the Count of Boulogne? To answer this we must look at the lives of the two men, for obviously some relationship among Eustace, William, and Odo is being alluded to.

Although the Bayeux Tapestry may exaggerate Odo's actual participation in the fighting at Hastings, his portrayal as an important counsellor to William is probably accurate, albeit somewhat overstated. He is shown twice in this capacity. Shortly after Harold's coronation, Odo is seen in council with William. (Pl. 9) The tonsured Odo appears to be taking the initiative by directing the Duke to have ships built for the invasion of England, although the inscription states that William, as Duke, gave the order.[53] Once in England, Odo appears in a war council with William and his other brother, Robert of Mortain, both of whom seem to be turning to the bishop for advice. (Pl. 10) The council issues the order to erect fortifications at Hastings.

---

it assumed its present form c.1100. There is evidence for the growth of the Roland, and thus the Turpin, legend all through the eleventh century. The Bayeux Tapestry's 'librettist' could have been aware of the saga, either in an earlier written version, or, more likely, in an oral version. In the poem, after a lull in the battle, the French lose heart at the sight of being surrounded by the Saracen reinforcements arriving with King Marsile. They despairingly turn to their leaders for encouragement and it is Archbishop Turpin who begs them not to flee. He promises them Paradise that day. Rejoicing, the Franks once more shout their battle cry, 'Monjoie' and the slaughter resumes. The parallel circumstances are apparent. For further discussion of this point, see S. A. Brown, 'The Bayeux Tapestry and the Song of Roland'.

[53] That Odo contributed a great number of ships to the invasion force is attested by the historical sources, although they disagree on the number. The Ship List of William the Conqueror lists 100 ships

Plate 10 BT: Bishop Odo of Bayeux, Duke William, and Robert of Mortain

From an early age, Odo had followed the career path of many of the younger sons of the powerful Norman families. He was prepared for an administrative career in which he could help advance the causes of his older brother William and had been appointed to the strategic see of Bayeux while still below the canonical age of thirty.[54] He played an important contributory role in the invasion of England and was created Earl of Kent very soon after the Battle of Hastings. He became the wealthiest tenant-in-chief under the new king of England, being allowed to display his ability as a secular lord rather than as a guiding light of the English Church. That latter position went to Lanfranc.

Odo's later career was a dramatic series of political ups-and-downs. He was deprived of his English lands and power by William in 1082, ostensibly for aspiring to the papacy,[55] but it is more probable that he had interfered in the rancourous disputes between William and his eldest son, Robert Curthose.[56] Whatever the

---

as his contribution. See Elisabeth van Houts, 'The Ship List of William the Conqueror', *ante* x, 1987, 168 and Appendix I.

[54] While we know little of his activities before 1066, Odo's signature appears on ducal charters, on lists of participants at ecclesiastical councils, and it is probable that his appointment to the bishopric of Bayeux in 1049/50 was part of Duke William's strategy to reassert his authority in the region after the rebellious fighting at Val-ès-Dunes in 1047. See Bates, 'The Career and Character of Odo of Bayeux', 5.

[55] Orderic Vitalis, VII, iii.189–192 (Chibnall, vol. 4, 39–45). On Odo's trial and imprisonment, see also Chibnall, vol. 4, xxvii–xxx.

[56] Bates, 'The Character and Career of Odo of Bayeux', 15–17. Although one must argue backwards from his later behaviour, it is possible that Odo had sided with Robert in his desire to have some real authority in Normandy while his father was still alive. Odo supported Robert's claims to both Normandy and the English crown as long as he lived, as did Robert of Mortain. Robert Curthose rebelled twice. The first instance was in late 1077 or early 1078, culminating in William's siege of Gerberoy shortly after Christmas 1078–79; reconciliation followed by May 1080. Robert apparently left England

reason, Odo was kept in confinement in Rouen, but there was no move to deprive him of his Norman bishopric. When Odo had claimed ecclesiastical immunity against charges of treason, apparently he was informed he was being tried not as a churchman, but as Earl of Kent.[57] William was adamant and unrelenting in his refusal to pardon his younger half-brother. Released upon the death of William in 1087, not due to a real change of heart on William's part, but as a result of the pleading of Robert of Mortain and others, Odo attended the funeral and then returned to England where he regained his possessions in Kent. But the bishop was an unstinting supporter of the regal claims of Robert Curthose, and shortly thereafter, in the Spring of 1088, Odo, along with Robert of Mortain and Eustace of Boulogne, played a prominent role in an unsuccessful rebellion against King William Rufus. As a result he was deprived of his English revenues and honours and left England permanently, returning to his See in Bayeux and the protection of his nephew Robert. He set off on the First Crusade with Robert in 1096 and while wintering in Palermo, he died and was buried with great honour in the Cathedral.

As mentioned, the other companion of the Conqueror shown in the Bayeux Tapestry was Eustace of Boulogne, who also was no stranger to English matters. Like Harold Godwinson, he had been a brother-in-law of King Edward, for his first wife, who had died in 1049, was Godgifu, daughter of King Ethelred and Emma of Normandy, thus Edward's full sister. Eustace had been involved in a serious incident with the citizens of Dover in 1051 during one of his English visits. That he was an important participant in the Norman Invasion of England can be surmised from the size of his land settlement after 1066.[58] But shortly after the Battle of Hastings, he and William were already quarreling, and while William was in Normandy between March and December of 1067, the dissatisfied Count of Boulogne allied himself with subversive elements in Kent and landed an invasion force at Dover, a strategic site for which Odo of Bayeux was responsible. This attempt at power was quickly squashed and as a result, Eustace lost his English lands. It was several years before William and he were reconciled. Their

sometime between 1081 and 1084, after quarelling once more with his father, and was still in exile when William died. On his deathbed, William had to be convinced by his barons, including Robert of Mortain, not to disinherit Robert completely. The dying king also had to be convinced to release Odo from prison. William's anger with those who supported or helped his rebellious son is seen in his threat to seize and blind Samson le Breton, who had served as messenger between Queen Matilde and Robert when she secretly sent her son money against her husband's orders. The man fled to Normandy where he entered the safety of the monastery at Saint-Evroul where he lived for twenty-six years. Ordericus. V, ii.383. (Chibnall, vol. 3, 105) For information about Robert Curthose, see Charles Wendell David, *Robert Curthose, Duke of Normandy*, Cambridge, Mass. 1920.

[57] Apparently Archbishop Lanfranc, with whom Odo had frequently clashed, was party to the accusations. At the trial of William of St Calais, Bishop of Durham, in November 1088, the final rebellion and expulsion of Odo of Bayeux against William Rufus was still a very recent and painful memory for the king. The Bishop of Durham was charged with treason for his actions in the same rebellion and demanded that he be tried as a bishop according to canon law and not as a feudal tenant. Lanfranc is said to have refused this demand and replied that the court of William the Conqueror several years earlier had passed judgement on Odo of Bayeux and that 'the king did not then summon to trial the bishop of Bayeux, but his earl and his brother'. The trial proceedings are included in *EHD* ii, 652–669.

[58] See C. Warren Hollister, 'The Greater Domesday Tenants-in-chief', *Domesday Studies. Novocentenary Conference . . . Winchester 1986*, ed. J. Holt, Woodbridge 1987, 219–248, especially Appendix A.

reconciliation came about sometime before 1075 or 1077, for William of Poitiers mentions this renewed friendship.[59] Eustace received his English lands back and succeeded in establishing his family in England.[60]

Some of the scholars who support an early dating for the *Carmen de Hastingae Proelio* and assign its creation to Guy, Bishop of Amiens, suggest that the poem is connected with the estrangement between Eustace of Boulogne and William the Conqueror. Frank Barlow suggested that Guy, a supporter of Eustace of Boulogne, wrote the poem sometime between 1068 and 1070, after he had visited London in Queen Matilde's entourage, sending it to Lanfranc who sailed to England in 1070, presumably for delivery to William. In his view, the poem was meant to remind the king of Eustace's contribution at Hastings and was aimed at healing the rift between the two men.[61] Morton and Muntz believed that it had to be written early in 1067, before Eustace's ill-fated attack on Dover Castle, but after the initial quarrel with William.[62] L. J. Engels felt that it may even have been written before Lent, 1067, to accompany King William's triumphant return to Normandy and to remind him of Eustace's contribution.[63] Elisabeth van Houts has retained the 1067 dating of the poem but suggests that it was a gift to obtain Abbot Lanfranc's cooperation in healing the rift between Bishop Guy and Pope Alexander II.[64] If the poem can be attributed with confidence to Guy of Amiens, it must have been completed before his death in 1074/75.

We have seen that there are some curious and remarkable similarities between the narrative shown in the Bayeux Tapestry and the *Carmen*. By keeping in mind the methodology underlying the argument of a possible link between the poem and Eustace of Boulogne's political fortunes and his fall from grace, and by calling to mind analogies in the Bayeux Tapestry's images, it becomes possible to postulate an explanation for the peculiar composition of the so-called 'rout-scene' in the embroidery. A reason might even be suggested as to why the 'librettist' deliberately teamed Odo and Eustace together in their support for Duke William. As stated earlier, obviously some relationship among Eustace, William, and Odo is being alluded to, and I would like to suggest that we have an instance of the use of political typology. Both Eustace and Odo had played important roles in the Hastings venture, and at certain points in their careers both (Eustace in 1067 and Odo in 1082) had suffered the disgrace of a falling out with the king, losing their extensive

---

[59] *Gesta Guillelmi* ii, 47. R. H. C. Davis feels that this reconciliation had occurred shortly before William of Poitiers entered it into his work. See Davis, 'William of Poitiers and his History of William the Conqueror', in R. H. C. Davis and J. M. Wallace-Hadrill (eds), *The Writing of History in the Middle Ages. Essays Presented to Richard William Southern* Oxford, 1981, 81–82. For information on Eustace and the comital family of Boulogne, see *Carmen*, xvi–xxxix and Geneaological Table IV.

[60] As attested in Domesday Book. He was one of two non-Normans who were among the eleven men upon whom William had bestowed about half the land held by lay tenure in England. See David Douglas, *William the Conqueror* London, 1964, 269.

[61] Frank Barlow, 'Carmen', 46. Barlow felt that although it would be preferable to see the poem predating Lanfranc's elevation to the Archbishopric of Canterbury in 1070, the only firm *terminus ante quem* is 1074 or 1075, when Guy of Amiens died. Whether or not the poem was a successful plea-gift and instrumental in affecting the reconciliation of the two men we will of course never know. It is even debatable that Guy of Amiens lived to know about Eustace's return to grace – the bishop died in 1074 or 1075, and William of Poitiers may have recorded their reconciliation as late as 1077.

[62] *Carmen*, xxii, xxviii.

[63] Engels, 'Once more: The Carmen', 5.

[64] van Houts, 'Carmen', 53–56.

English lands and revenues as punishment. Forced back across the Channel, each man would have had to launch pleas for his reinstatement. Both may have chosen to do so, at least as one avenue open to them, by reminding William of their contribution to his successful invasion of England. The heroism of Eustace became part of a poem about the Battle of Hastings, and Odo's multi-faceted, key role was highlighted in a visual account of the larger story of William and Harold's struggle for power. Since by 1077 the Count of Boulogne had been received back into William's good standing, he could be used by Odo and his apologist as a topical example in a plea for clemency and reconciliation.

It is commonly accepted that the Bayeux Tapestry was commissioned by Odo of Bayeux, produced in England, and was meant to decorate the nave of Bayeux Cathedral during its consecration in 1077.[65] But it has also been suggested that the embroidery was meant as a secular work and thus could be dated before 1083 while Odo was at the height of his power.[66] I would like to suggest, alternatively, that the Bayeux Tapestry was indeed a *pièce justificative*, to borrow Dodwell's term, but that it was commissioned by Odo in response to the troubles between himself and William which came to a head in 1082, as a gift to his brother, to remind the king that the debt he owed Odo was greater than the charges preferred against him.[67] In the Tapestry, Odo's contribution of a large number of ships to the invasion fleet is directly referred to; his role as war counsellor along with Robert of Mortain, is shown; his role as spiritual advisor is briefly alluded to; and his prowess in battle is depicted. This would also explain the Tapestry designer's repeated insistence on referring to Odo as EPISCOPUS in the inscriptions, a reference to his religious status which had been ignored at his trial in England, but which he retained during his incarceration in Normandy.

I would also like to suggest that Odo affected the production through three of his trusted Kentish vassals – Turold, Vital and Wadard. Their sponsorship would provide a reason for the inclusion in the Bayeux Tapestry of these three particular men.[68] Under these circumstances, it is possible that Odo initiated the work on the Tapestry late in 1081 or early in 1082 while he was still in England, undoubtedly trying to avoid being brought to trial, as a feudal tenant, in the king's court. He would then be in a position to issue instructions and oversee the production. But a commission as ambitious as the Bayeux Tapestry would have required at least a

---

[65] This suggestion was first made by Delauney in 1824, and acquired the power of fact when put forth by Sir Frank Stenton in 1957. R. H. C. Davis has suggested that although the Tapestry was meant for the cathedral, it would have to be later than William of Poitiers' *Gesta* which he dates c.1077. See Davis, 'William of Poitiers', 81–82.

[66] Dodwell, 'BT and French Secular Epic', 560.

[67] The idea of using other people – relatives or friends – to plead a case for restoration of power and the connected use of an artistic gift was a tradition of long standing. R. H. C. Davis has made the interesting suggestion that there might have been a connection between William of Poitiers and Odo of Bayeux and that with his fulsome praise of Odo in Book II, William might have been trying to defend Odo from the king's suspicion. After Odo's disgrace, William of Poitiers seems to have suffered an eclipse of fortune. See Davis, 'William of Poitiers', 90–93.

[68] These men have long been recognized as Odo's tenants and their presence in the Bayeux Tapestry has usually been taken merely as evidence for Odo's patronage. For a brief reference to their holdings, see H. E. J. Cowdrey, 'Towards an Interpretation of the Bayeux Tapestry' *ante* x, 1987, 50, fn. 2. For a more complete study of Odo's vassals see David Bates, *Odo, Bishop of Bayeux, 1049/50–1097* Exeter University Ph.D. Thesis, 1970. But the question as to why these three particular tenants, among all his vassals in England, were chosen for depiction must also be addressed.

couple of years to complete, by which time he was confined in Rouen. Trusted friends would then have had to assume the responsibility for the undertaking, if they had not already done so. It would have been possible, if more difficult, for Odo to initiate the undertaking from prison, using his three tenants as go-betweens.

If the Bayeux Tapestry was meant to be a *pièce justificative*, not only for the Conquest, but also for Odo's appeal for a pardon, this would explain the pointed inclusion of Eustace of Boulogne as a leader of the fighting at Telham Hill, rather than one of the Norman lords, as one might expect. If William could forgive a French vassal's breach of loyalty, surely he could accept his own brother's plea for a return to good grace.

Audacious? Yes. But Odo was an audacious person. Potentially angering to William who was implacably opposed to Odo's release? Yes, but once in prison Odo had very little to lose. Untrue to the events and obviously boosting Odo's public image? Perhaps. But the more years which intervened between the events of 1066 and the time of the Bayeux Tapestry's images, the fuzzier memories would become, and the more chance there would be of a proliferation of even contradictory versions of what had happened. All this would work to the advantage of both the patron and the person or persons who were charged with the task of creating the story and the design to be executed by the needle-workers.

But who was the Bayeux Tapestry's 'librettist', and what chance might he have had to become familiar with the *Carmen*, since the poem seems to have enjoyed very little circulation? Morton and Muntz speculated that the original may have been deposited in the monasteries of Liège, or at St-Bertin in St-Omer, or even at St-Riquier. In spite of its minimal circulation, it could thus easily have been available at one of the teaching centres in northern France to which young clerics were sent for training. If the poem accompanied Guy of Amiens to England in 1068, as Morton and Muntz conjectured, or if it was carried there by Lanfranc in 1070, as Barlow suggested, it may well have been known among the royal entourage [69] or have been deposited in one of the libraries at Canterbury. If the last suggestion were the case, there would then be a good likelihood of a direct use of the poem as a source for the embroidery's iconography, for visual evidence seems to establish a connection between the Bayeux Tapestry and St Augustine's in Canterbury. But although it is a tempting conclusion to make, the similarities between the works do not prove that the Bayeux Tapestry's anonymous story-teller used the poem as a direct model for his narrative. Certainly, he may have been making allusions to the poem, but on the other hand, he may have been familiar with the oral tradition it reflects.

There is evidence that Odo of Bayeux was a patron of the arts and used his great wealth to encourage learning in clerics more naturally inclined in that direction than he himself was.[70] According to Orderic, he sent promising young clerics to study, at his expense, in major centres such as Liège. It is one of these clerics, (he could have been Norman, English, or Anglo-Norman) who had been supported by Odo, who I am suggesting was responsible for the creation of the Bayeux Tapestry's version of the Conquest story. Making himself familiar with the oral tradition and

---

[69] *Carmen*, lix–lxiii.

[70] Ordericus, VIII, iii. 263–267 (Chibnall, vol. 4, 115–119). For a good discussion of Odo as a patron of the arts and learning, see Bates, 'The Character and Career of Odo of Bayeux', 11–15.

literature of contemporary northern France and England, he chose what he felt best suited his purpose, amalgamated his ideas, to produce the schema for the embroidery. He was given a golden opportunity both to praise his patron and to exhibit his own literary skills. If what we today call 'historical truth' was sacrificed to 'poetic license', that did not seem to be a cause of worry, for it served his purpose. Throughout his narrative, the exceedingly gifted story-teller responsible for the Bayeux Tapestry's tale combined propaganda and literary art, not the least in his choice of creating the telling combination of Eustace of Boulogne and Odo of Bayeux as companions-at-arms to William, Duke of Normandy and King of England.[71]

[71] Like the *Carmen de Hastingae Proelio* and the *Gesta Guillelmi* of William of Poitiers, the Bayeux Tapestry seems to have enjoyed very little circulation and was generally unknown in both England and Normandy. It appears to have gone 'underground' almost as soon as it was finished, or the work may even have been abandoned. Davis has suggested that in the case of the *Gesta* this was possibly due to the praise it heaped upon Odo and its author's possible connection with the disgraced bishop. In the case of the *Carmen* and the embroidery, we have images which praise Eustace of Boulogne and Odo of Bayeux respectively. It should be remembered that these two men were both deeply implicated, along with Robert of Mortain, in the attempt in 1088 to overthrow King William Rufus and place Robert Curthose on the English throne. In the matter of the sieges of Pevensey and Rochester it had come to direct confrontation. I suggest that once that revolt was suppressed and Odo had been permanently expelled from England, not only would the Bayeux Tapestry have no purpose to serve, but it would even have been considered as odious by William Rufus. As Normandy came once more within the grasp of the King of England under Rufus and Henry I, the embroidery would have found no venue for exhibition, even in Bayeux. It had to wait until the eighteenth century before it gained any recognition.

DONORS AND DAUGHTERS: SHAFTESBURY ABBEY'S BENEFACTORS, ENDOWMENTS AND NUNS c.1086–1130

Kathleen Cooke

Shaftesbury abbey, along with the other pre-Conquest nunneries, has often been described as a 'preserve of the upper class', drawing its recruits from among the daughters of the Anglo-Saxon aristocracy and continuing this trend in the Norman period.[1] Unquestionably Shaftesbury was a wealthy and prestigious house in the Anglo-Saxon period. Founded by Alfred the Great claiming his daughter as its first abbess, the abbey had received extensive benefactions from the Anglo-Saxon kings and endowments from the local nobility.[2] And as the centre of the cult of the martyred King Edward, the abbey increased its prestige in the later Anglo-Saxon period. The abbey's wealth remained undiminished after the Norman Conquest: by the time of the Domesday survey, Shaftesbury was the wealthiest nunnery in England.[3]

But a closer look at the family connections of Shaftesbury's nuns in the Anglo-Norman period may allow us to determine more precisely the composition of the abbey – its abbesses and nuns – in those crucial years after the Conquest. Specifically, a study of Shaftesbury's benefactors and endowments may permit us to determine to what degree and how soon after the Conquest the new Norman landowners and barons supported a religious institution with such close affiliations to the Anglo-Saxon royal family and aristocracy and to the Anglo-Saxon past.

British Library MS Harley 61, the early fifteenth-century Shaftesbury cartulary, contains copies of two important groups of documents which have a bearing on this question. The first is a copy of a list headed 'Has scriptas terras dederunt homines cum filiabus eorum ad ecclesiam Sancti Edwardi Shafton' which records thirteen donations of property made to the abbey as entry gifts of dowries accompanying new entrants.[4] Of the thirteen donations recorded, all but two specifically state that the donation was made by the father 'cum filia sua'.[5] Eight of the thirteen can

[1] David Knowles, *The Monastic Order in England: A History of Development from the Times of St Dunstan to the Fourth Lateran Council, 943–1216* 2nd edn, Cambridge 1963, 137.
[2] On Alfred's foundation see *Asser's Life of King Alfred*, ed. W. H. Stevenson, Oxford 1904, 85, § 98. For Shaftesbury's early history see *Monasticon*, ii, 471–88 and M. M. C. Caltrop's article in VCH *Dorset*, ii, 73–4 For benefactions see Marc A. Meyer, 'Patronage of the West Saxon Royal Nunneries in Late Anglo-Saxon England', *Revue Bénédictine* xci (no. 3–4), 1981, 332–58, esp. 341–2, 350.
[3] For Shaftesbury's estates see *Domesday Book* i, fols 17v, 67v, 75r, 78v, 82v, 83v, 91r; iv, 193v.
[4] MS BL Harley 61, fol. 54r. This is printed in *Monasticon* ii, 482–83.
[5] Eudo Brito's donation omits this phrase; Ernulf de Hesding's donation is recorded here as having been made 'cum quadam parente sua' but in the later confirmation charters as 'cum quadam cognata sua moniali'. Latham, *Revised Medieval Latin Word-List from the British and Irish Sources*, London 1965, 332.

be identified from Domesday Book as landholders in the south-west in 1086, and though the precise locations of the estates thus acquired are not always given in this list, other evidence from the cartulary does allow us to identify all but four of the unspecified places.[6] The donation is usually expressed in the following form: 'Hugh Calvus tenet ii hidas quas Drogo de Monte Acuto dedit cum filia sua, et valet xv s'. Six of the individual entries include the current tenant's name and the value of the land or holding, suggesting that the list was not originally drawn up solely as a memorandum of benefactors and their daughters, but rather as a record of the abbey's claims to services and rights over those lands.[7]

Although the list itself is not dated, its content and form suggest a composition sometime after 1089, the date of a confirmation charter issued by William II but before 1121, when Abbess Emma apparently sought and received confirmation of these donations and other lands acquired since the Conquest. Although the reason for its composition remains somewhat obscure, the list relates to donations made in the period c.1086–1121; it thus serves as an important (and, additionally, a rather unusual) record of entry gifts to a nunnery in the early Norman period.

Further evidence relating to Shaftesbury's entrants and endowments in this period is provided by a group of six royal charters preserved in the abbey's cartulary.[8] The documents purport to be charters issued by William II, Henry I (two versions), Stephen, Henry II and John confirming the abbey's claims to rights and services which had apparently been usurped or unfulfilled by some of the abbey's tenants or neighbours. With the exception of William II's charter, which is shorter and confirms only four of the donations, these charters fill in some *lacunae* in the above-mentioned list of donors and daughters and give us an additional five entry gifts to consider. Despite the doubts that have been raised as to the authenticity and reliability of both William II's charter and the two versions of Henry I's charter, their over-all accuracy is confirmed by the independent list of donors and daughters, by entries in Shaftesbury's early estate survey contained in the cartulary, and by entries in Domesday Book and other eleventh- and twelfth-century charters.[9]

We have, then, a total of eighteen entry gifts made to the abbey in the period c.1086 to c.1121 to consider. And though we may justifiably ask how representative and comprehensive a record this is, I think we can use this evidence – along with some additional materials – to at least open a discussion about the possible 'Normanization' of Shaftesbury abbey.

In particular, three aspects of this process may be examined: first, the identity, position, and possible motives of the donors whose daughters entered the nunnery;

---

[6] Only Serlo de Burci's, Ernulf de Hesding's and Eudo Brito's are specified as to location.

[7] Aiulf's donation of 4½ hides 'sicut ipse dicit' and Harding's donation 'valet lx s, sicut homines eiusdam ville dicunt' suggests an inquest.

[8] Fol. 23r (William II's charter, calendered in *Regesta* i, 80, no. 309); fols 23r–v, 30r–v (two versions of Henry I's charter, fol. 23 version printed in *Regesta* ii, 346–47, no. 1347); fol. 24 (Stephen's charter; printed in full *Regesta* iii, 301, no. 818); fol. 24v–25r (Henry II's charter); fols 26r–27r (John's charter, enrolled in *Rotuli Chartarum in Turri Londinensi Asservati. Vol. I. Pars. I. Ab Anno MCXCIX ad Annum MCCXVI*, ed. T. D. Hardy, Record commission 1831, 150 and printed in *Monasticon* ii, 483).

[9] I have argued elsewhere for the acceptance of these charters ('Shaftesbury Abbey in the Eleventh and Twelfth Centuries: The Nuns and Their Estates', unpublished Oxford M.Litt., 1982, 16–24); see also Ann Williams, 'The Knights of Shaftesbury Abbey' *ante* viii, 1985, 224 for a discussion of William II's charter.

secondly, the type and exact nature of these entry gifts or dowries; and finally the importance to the abbey of these benefactions and benefactors. Shaftesbury's evidence does, I believe, raise some new questions about the role and functions of religious institutions for women in Anglo-Saxon England.

Perhaps the most important conclusion to be drawn from an examination of these entry gifts is that very soon after the Conquest, Shaftesbury was supported by the new Norman landowners who held estates in the south-west, close to the abbey, and that those families who sent their daughters to the abbey were not members of the richest barons in post-Conquest England. We might begin by looking at the evidence regarding the indentity of these donors, specifically with a view towards determining the Norman element in the abbey in the years after the Conquest.

As can be seen from Table 1, ten of these donors can be identified fairly certainly from Domesday Book. Seven of these, Aiulf the Sheriff (no. 1), Serlo de Burci (no. 3), Harding Fitz Alnoth (no. 4), Roger de Berkeley (no. 5), Ernulf de Hesding (no. 6), Odo fitz Gamelin (no. 8) and Goscelin de Rivera (no. 9) were tenants-in-chief in the south-west in 1086. Two, Alvred *pincerna* (no. 2) and Drogo de Monte Acuto (no. 7) were important tenants of Robert, Count of Mortain; and the remaining donor, Richard de Sancto Claro (no. 10) can probably be indentified as the tenant of Ralph de Bella Fago, Domesday tenant-in-chief in Suffolk and Norfolk. This group of donors, then, represents a largely Norman element.[10] Insofar as we know, only Harding, son of Alnoth (or Eadnoth) the Staller, can be definitely identified as coming from Anglo-Saxon family.[11]

It is impossible to be wholly certain of the family backgrounds of those donors who do not appear in Domesday Book and for whom we have little or no evidence other than their name, occupation or place of residence, but it appears that of this group there was a fairly even balance between Anglo-Saxon and French families. Alvric 'de Hecche' (no. 11) and Leowin 'de Bristow' (no. 12) both made donations with their daughters, and although they cannot be identified any further than to say that they were from the south-west, their names indicate an Anglo-Saxon background.[12] The family of Aileva (Aethelgifu) (no. 18), nun of Shaftesbury, was also probably of Anglo-Saxon descent.[13] Two of the five remaining but so far unidentified donors were probably French: Eudo Brito (no. 13), probably a Breton, and Gundreda, who donated a church and its tithes in Wiltshire for her relative Albereda (Aubrey) de Bosco Rohardi.[14] Her relative, Albereda, may have also

[10] Ernulf de Hesding (Arnulf de Hesdin) was apparently from Hesdin in the Pas de Calais: L. C. Loyd, *The Origins of Some Anglo-Norman Families* ed. C. T. Clay and D. C. Douglas, Harleian Soc. ciii, 1951, 51. Serlo de Burci was probably from Vire in Calvados: H. M. Maxwell-Lyte, 'Burci, Falaise, and Martin' *Proceedings of the Somerset Archaeological and Natural History Society* lxv, 1919, 1.

[11] For Harding see R. R. Darlington in VCH *Wilts.* ii, 66, 71 and J. H. Round in VCH *Somerset* i, 417. Aiulf the sheriff presents an unusual case: his name may be from the Old Norse *Eyidlfr* (O. von Feilitzen, *Pre-Conquest Personal Names of Domesday Book*, Uppsala 1937, 191; but see Cecily Clark, 'Starting from *Youlthorpe* (East Riding of Yorkshire): An Onomastic Circular Tour', *English Place-Name Society Journal* xvi, 1983–84, 27–30 for the most recent and most comprehensive discussion of Aiulf's descent.

[12] von Feilitzen, 176–180, 317–10. Prof. John Moore has suggested that Leowin de Bristow was the son of an Anglo-Saxon resident of Bristol (personal communication.)

[13] von Feilitzen, 183. See also Williams, 'Knights of Shaftesbury', 228.

[14] 'Brito' was commonly used to indicate a Breton: von Feilitzen, 208. In 1110 a Ralf Brito held a messuage in Winchester, the only 'Brito' mentioned in that survey. *Winchester in the Early Middle Ages: An Edition and Discussion of the Winton Domesday*, ed. M. Biddle et al., Oxford 1976, 17, 39.

Table 1   Shaftesbury abbey's donors and daughters.   c. 1086–1121

Name of Donor	Location, Amount and Value (per annum) of Donation	Donor's Domesday Book Holdings (1086): Location and Value
1. Aiulf, Sheriff of Dorset and Somerset; Deputy Chamberlain	i. (For wife) Blandford St Mary, Dorset 1½ hides, 30s ii. (with daughter) Farnham, Dorset, ½ hide	£70 Dorset and Wilts (£1 enfeoffed)
2. Alvred *pincerna* to Robert, Count of Mortain	Shilvinghampton, Dorset 5 virgates, 15s	£65 Dorset and Somerset (of Robert Count of Mortain) (£32 in other countries)
3. Serlo de Burci	Kilmington, Somerset 1 hide, 40s	£36 Dorset and Somerset (£17 enfeoffed)
4. Harding, son of Eadnoth the Staller	? unspecified. 1 hide later exchanged for 3 hides, Caundle, Dorset	c. £40 Wilts and Somerset (£1 enfeoffed)
5. Roger de Berkeley	Foxley, Wilts 2 hides (or 1 hide + 3 virgates), 60s	£32 Gloucester (+ farm of Berkeley £170)
6. Ernulf de Hesding (for his relative)	Keevil, Wilts Church and tithes, 20s	£272 in 10 countries (£80 in Wilts) (£54 enfeoffed)
7. Drogo de Monte Acuto	Nyland, Dorset 2 hides, *valet* 15s (*Domesday Bk* = waste)	£34 (of Robert, Count of Mortain)
8. Odo fitz Gamelin (with 2 daughters)	i. Gt Torrington, Devon Church and tithes ii. Little Wear, Devon 10s	£52 Devon (+ 1 manor in Somerset)
9. Goscelin de Rivera	Fosbury, Wilts 2 hides, waste (*Domesday Bk* value = 30s)	£1 10s as t-in-chief £17 as tenant of Robert Fitz Gerald and Humphrey de Insula
10. Richard de Sancto Claro 'de Wertham'	Wortham, Suffolk Tithes and 30 acres	£5 13s as t-in-chief £14 as tenant of Ralph Bello Fago
11. Alvric 'de Hecche'	? unspecified = 2 hides (no value given)	
12. Leowin 'de Bristow'	? unspecified = 2 houses 1 mark	
13. Eudo Brito	Winchester = 2 houses 1 mark	
14. Duncan	*Bremlega* (Broomleigh?) 1 virgate	
15. Garmundus	Tarrant Hinton, Dorset 1 hide	
16. Gundreda (for her relative Albereda de Bosco Rohard)	Broughton Giffard, Wilts Church and tithes	
17. 'A certain merchant of London'	1 house, *valet nihil*	
18. ? with Aileva	Gussage, Dorset 2 hides	

been a relative of the brothers William and Roger de Bosco Rohardi, Domesday tenants of Robert de Tosny.[15] A 'Duncan' and a 'Garmundus' also appear as donors, and though these names do not occur in Domesday as pre-Conquest names and are thus probably not Anglo-Saxon, it is impossible to be certain of their family origins.[16] Occurring only on the abbey list of donors and daughters but not mentioned in any of the confirmation charters is a 'certain merchant of London' who gave one house to the abbey with his daughter. Although his family antecedents cannot be identified further, it is important to note that, along with Eudo Brito, probably from Winchester, and Leowin de Bristow, probably from Bristol, families from urban areas also chose to send their daughters to Shaftesbury.

The daughters of at least four of these donors entered Shaftesbury before 1089: Serlo de Burci's (his daughter had entered by 1086), Roger de Berkeley's, Aiulf the sheriff's, and Alvred *pincera*'s.[17] Thus, these new Norman landowners were beginning to send their daughters to the same abbey that for two hundred years had received the daughters of the Anglo-Saxon aristocracy. It is less easy to be sure exactly when other girls entered the nunnery, except that it was before 1121. It is therefore difficult to say with certainty what proportion of nuns were, at any one time in this period, from Anglo-Saxon or Norman families. But there is some further evidence which helps to chart the Normanization of the abbey in the years after the Conquest: the appointment of Abbess Eularia or Eulalia, presumably a Norman, by the crown in 1074.[18] Her successor, Cecily, the daughter of Robert fitz Hamon (an important baron in William II's and the early part of Henry I's reign) was appointed sometime after 1107; the fact that Abbess Cecily was also the sister-in-law of Robert of Caen, Earl of Gloucester, may help, too, to explain the strong Gloucestershire connections of the abbey we see in examining the pattern of benefactions.[19]

The earliest evidence of the proportion of Anglo-Saxon to Norman nuns comes from the mortuary rolls circulating in England c.1113.[20] The roll originated at the abbey of Caen and commemorates the memory of its abbess, Matilda, daughter of

---

Gundreda and Alb(e)reda are names derived from Old German: von Feilitzen, 113, 277 and T. Forssner, *Continental-Germanic Personal Names in England*, Uppsala 1916, 134.

[15] *Domesday Book*i, fol. 149. The family was from Bosc-le-Hard, Dieppe. See Loyd, 18–19 and G. H. Fowler, 'Early Records of Turvey and its Neighbourhood', *Publications of the Bedfordshire Historical Record Society* xl, 1927, 72–4. I can find no Albereda mentioned.

[16] von Feilitzen gives no entry for Duncan or Garmundus.

[17] These are the four donations specified in William II's charter of 1089 (MS BL Harley 61, fol. 23r). Serlo de Burci's daughter's entrance is noted in *Domesday Book* i, fol. 98r and iv, fol. 453r.

[18] Knowles, *Monastic Order*, 137–8. He notes the English tendencies in 'personnel and sentiment' of nunneries in the post-Conquest period. See also David Knowles, et al., eds, *Heads of Religious Houses in England and Wales 940–1216*, Cambridge 1972, 219.

[19] Knowles, et al., *Heads*, 219. According to Tewkesbury legend, Henry I appointed Cecily abbess of Shaftesbury and her sister, Hawise, abbess of Wilton, sometime after Robert's death in 1107; their sister Matilda married Robert of Caen, who became Earl of Gloucester. See *Monasticon* ii, 60–1. On Robert fitz Hamon see Orderic, iii, 228; iv, 129, 182, 220; vi, 57, 60–1, 78–9, 518; I. J. Sanders, *English Baronies*, Oxford 1960, 6; and GEC, v, 682–83. Another daughter of Robert's may also have been a nun at Malling: see *Regesta* ii, no. 791.

[20] Léopold Delisle, *Rouleaux des morts du ixe au xve siècle*, Société de l'Histoire de France 1866, 177 ff. The Shaftesbury entry is on p. 190. The mortuary roll of 1122–23 for Abbot Vitalis of Savigny also records the names of 3 nuns of Shaftesbury, including those names of Abbess Eulalia and Albereda, prioress. *Rouleau mortuaire du b. Vital. abbé de Savigni* ed. Leopold Delisle, Paris 1909, Plate xliv, no. 187.

William I; the nunneries of Winchester, Wherwell, Amesbury and Wilton each contributed verses or a list of those nuns for whom prayers should be offered, but the list from Shaftesbury is the most extensive. The names of sixteen nuns are entered; of these, ten appear to have been Norman and only six Anglo-Saxon.[21] From this evidence, then, it does appear that by c.1100, and certainly by the end of the first quarter of the twelfth century, Shaftesbury did have as its nuns a number – perhaps even a majority – of daughters from Norman families who had settled in the south-west and that these families, for a variety of reasons, supported the abbey, one with strong connections to Anglo-Saxon royal and aristocratic circles.

One of the most interesting features of the evidence about the families associating themselves with Shaftesbury is that though they were often important landowners in the south-west, they were not from the wealthiest group. Looking at the resources of these families, as shown by the value of their holdings in Domesday Book for 1086, we can see that none of the donors belonged to the class of the richest barons in the post-Conquest England.[22] Although in most cases their holdings in the south-west were substantial, and were also where the preponderance of their estates lay, only one of Shaftesbury's donors had resources above £200 per annum. With the exception of Ernulf de Hesding, whose total Domesday holdings were spread over ten countries and valued at c.£272 p.a. in 1086, the donors who sent their daughters to Shaftesbury and who were also tenants-in-chief, were members of the bottom rank of this group.[23] They belonged to the ninety to one hundred families in the country whose baronies were valued at less than £100 p.a.[24] What is, perhaps, even more startling is that most of these could be grouped at the lower end of even this category. Aiulf the Sheriff had total resources of £70 in Dorset and Wiltshire, and the Devon baron Odo fitz Gamelin, who sent two daughters to Shaftesbury, held estates valued at £52.[25] But the remaining donors in this group held estates of smaller value: Harding fitz Alnoth's estates in 1086 were valued at £40 p.a.; Roger de Berkeley, though he farmed the manor of Berkeley for £170 p.a., had in his own right as tenant-in-chief estates valued at only £32 p.a.; and Serlo de Burci's estates were valued at about £32 p.a.[26] Three of the abbey's benefactors did not hold any of their estates in chief: Drogo de Monte Acuto held estates valued at £35 p.a. of Robert, Count of Mortain, and Alvred, the count's *pincerna*, held estates from him worth £65 p.a. in Dorset and Somerset,

---

[21] Two of the names, Albereda and Aileva, are identical to those on the abbey's list of donors and daughters (MS BL Harley 61, fol. 54r). For women's names in the post-Conquest period see Cecily Clark, 'Women's Names in Post-Conquest England: Observations and Speculations', *Speculum* liii, 1978, 223–51, where she concludes we are likely to see insular rather than continental names persisting longer for females. E. A. Freeman, *The History of the Norman Conquest of England*, 6 vols, Oxford 1867–79, v, 558, concludes also that women's names remain 'more distinctively English' than men's.

[22] Using W. J. Corbett's classification in 'England, 1087–1154', *The Cambridge Medieval History, Vol. v: Contest of Empire and Papacy*, eds J. R. Tanner et al., Cambridge 1926, 510–11.

[23] These are my figures. Sidney Painter, *Studies in the History of the English Feudal Barony*, Baltimore 1943, 18, gives £268 as the total of Ernulf de Hesding's holdings.

[24] Corbett, 510–11.

[25] For Aiulf, see VCH *Dorset* iii, 66–7, 83, 100–101; VCH *Wilts* ii, 138, 157; for Odo fitz Gamelin see VCH *Somerset* i, 517; VCH *Devon* i, 491–95.

[26] For Harding, see VCH *Dorset* iii, 97; VCH *Wilts* ii, 128, 133–34, 163; VCH *Somerset* i, 466, 522–3, 532; For Roger be Berkeley, see VCH *Wilts* ii, 113, 154; *Domesday Book* i, fols 162r, 163r, 168r; for Serlo de Burci see VCH *Dorset* iii, 72, 99; VCH *Somerset* i, 436, 439, 463–64, 466, 516–17.

considerably more than some tenants-in-chief.[27] The donor with apparently the most limited resources was Richard de Sancto Claro, who held two manors in Wortham, Suffolk, valued at only £5 13s p.a. from Ralph de Bello Fago.[28] To be sure, this does not represent the full range of Norman families who could have sent their daughters to Shaftesbury or were otherwise benefactors to the abbey, but the figures do show that it was not primarily from the highest rank of the nobility that Shaftesbury drew its recruits. Instead, many of those girls who entered the nunnery in the generation or two after the Conquest seem to have been the daughters of the less substantial barons or of those men who had received their estates through service to the crown or to their lord.

We might note some other interesting features about this group of families who had daughters or relatives at Shaftesbury. One, Ernulf de Hesding, was certainly a substantial landholder and had been well-rewarded by William I, but it was more characteristic of these families to belong to the circle of prominent administrators and royal officials active in the south-west. Harding fitz Alnoth is one such example. He was the son of Edward the Confessor's staller and was one of the few English thegns recorded in Domesday Book as continuing to hold lands of William I. During William II's reign he served as itinerant justice in Devon and Cornwall and perhaps served as provost of Bristol as well.[29] Harding's son Robert, brother of the Shaftesbury nun, who apparently succeeded his father as provost of Bristol, was a close associate of the young Henry I and was the founder of St Augustine's abbey in Bristol.[30] Roger de Berkeley, another of Shaftesbury's benefactors, was appointed provost of the manor of Berkeley c.1068–1071 by Earl William fitz Osbern and was confirmed in this office by William I c.1080.[31]

The local official probably the most important from Shaftesbury's point of view was Aiulf, sheriff of both Dorset and Somerset at various times from 1084 to c.1123.[32] Also styled *camerarius* in the abbey's records and in royal charters, he may have served as deputy chamberlain to Robert Malet during Henry I's reign.[33] His 'donations' to Shaftesbury were, in fact, not solely pious benefactions. Both Farnham and Blandford St Mary were apparently Shaftesbury's, or claimed as being the abbey's, in 1066, but Aiulf also claimed these as his estates held in chief

---

[27] For Drogo de Monte Acuto see VCH *Dorset* iii, 84, 88; VCH *Somerset* i, 474, 476–78, 483–83, 526; for Alvred see VCH *Dorset* iii, 81, 86, 88; VCH *Somerset* i, 478, 480–83. Alvred also held estates in 7 other counties worth £32: L.F. Salzmann, 'Some Sussex Domesday Tenants: I. Alvred Pincerna and His Descendants', *Sussex Archaeological Collections* lvii, 1915, 162.

[28] VCH *Suffolk* i, 490; VCH *Norfolk* ii, 149–50. He may be the same Richard who held other estates from Ralph; if so, his total resources were closer to £20.

[29] J. H. Round in VCH *Somerset* i, 417; J. Smyth, *The Berkeley Manuscripts: The Lives of the Berkeleys ... from 1066 to 1618*, ed. J. Maclean, 2 vols, Bristol and Gloucestershire Archaelogical Society 1883, i, 19–20.

[30] *Berkeley Manuscripts* i, 20, 22; D. Knowles and R. N. Hadcock, *Medieval Religious Houses: England and Wales*, rev. edn, London 1971, 150.

[31] H. Barkly, 'The Earlier House of Berkeley', *Transactions of the Bristol and Gloucestershire Archaeological Society* viii, 1883–4, 195; GEC, ii, 123–4.

[32] W. A. Morris, *The Medieval English Sheriff to 1300*, Manchester 1927, 47–8, 52–3, 76, 81; Judith A. Green, *The Government of England under Henry I*, Cambridge 1986, 155 identifies him as sheriff of Wiltshire as well.

[33] T. F. Tout, *Chapters in the Administrative History of Medieval England*, 6 vols, Manchester 1920–33, i, 89; *Regesta* ii, xiv; J. H. Round, *The King's Serjeants and Officers of State*, London 1911, 123; Judith A. Green, 'The Sheriffs of William the Conqueror', *Anglo-Norman Studies* v, 1982, 135 points to Aiulf's possible association with Queen Matilda's household.

in 1086. When his daughter entered Shaftesbury (sometime before 1089), he restored Farnham to the abbey; he made a second 'donation' sometime after this date when he restored Blandford St Mary 'pro anima uxoris sue'.[34] He is, it seems, a good example of the Norman sheriff adept at enhancing his own position by seizing church lands and later, when it was to his advantage, restoring them (and himself) to the church.[35] Another important landholder and administrator in the area, though not a royal official, was Alvred, the count of Mortain's *pincerna*. With holdings from the count valued at c.£65 in 1086, he was in a more advantageous position than some of the other donors to Shaftesbury who held their estates in chief, and when the count's estates escheated to the crown in 1091, he, along with Drogo de Monte Acuto, whose daughter also entered Shaftesbury, became in fact a tenant in chief.[36] Although there is no evidence that Robert Count of Mortain himself had any relative at Shaftesbury or that he endowed the abbey, the fact that two of his tenants chose Shaftesbury for their daughters is a further example of the 'corporate solidarity within a feudal grouping' often shown in benefactions to religious houses in this period.[37]

As landholders and administrations in the area, these men – the new service nobility created in the wake of the Conquest – were brought into Shaftesbury's orbit. As a group, too, we find that although some (Ernulf de Hesding, Roger de Berkeley, Odo fitz Gamelin, and Alvred *pincerna*) did support other religious houses in the area they made comparatively small gifts to those houses as well, even though these gifts were often more substantial than the ones given to Shaftesbury.[38] And judging by Shaftesbury's cartulary, it seems that these families made no further endowments to the abbey other than the dowries provided when their daughters entered. Indeed, available evidence suggests that it was the next generation – the sons and married daughters – of these donors who became the stronger supporters of religious houses. Despite the fact that a member of this later generation may have had a sister or an aunt at Shaftesbury, it appears that they often preferred to found or support a new house and thus associate themselves with the newer orders, than to continue benefactions to a representative of the older, more established and richer Benedictine order.[39]

---

[34] *Domesday Book* i, fols 78v, 82v, 83v; MS BL Harley 61, fol. 54r.

[35] Morris, 50, and Green, 'Sheriffs', give other examples of sheriffs following Aiulf's example. C. Harper-Bill, 'The Piety of the Anglo-Norman Knightly Class' in R. A. Brown, ed, *Proceedings of the Battle Conference* ii, 1979, 63 discusses and gives examples of 'the predatory and pious instincts' of many Anglo-Norman knights and argues that 'consciousness of guilt in specific matters was a frequent motivation for grants' (69). Aiulf's act of restitution can, perhaps, be seen as such.

[36] VCH *Somerset* i, 410; Painter, *Feudal Barony*, 23.

[37] Richard Mortimer, 'The Beginnings of the Honour of Clare', *ante* iii, 1980, 140. See also Marjorie Chibnall, 'Ecclesiastical Patronage and the Growth of Feudal Estates at the Time of the Norman Conquest', *Annales de Normandie* viii, 1958, 115–16 for tenants following their lords in donations to religious houses.

[38] Ernulf de Hesding, Roger de Berkeley and Odo fitz Gamelin were all benefactors of St Peter's, Gloucester: *Regesta* i, nos 130; ii, nos 1565, 1657, 1940 and nos 136a, 379a, 436a as addenda to *Regesta* i.

[39] Thus, for example, the benefactions of Roger de Berkeley's descendants to Leonard Stanley and Kingswood: C. Swynnerton, 'The Priory of St Leonard Stanley, Co. Gloucester', *Archaeologia* vol. 71, second ser. xxi, 1921, 198, and those of Serlo de Burci's descendants to many houses in the south-west, including Stogursey in Somerset and St Dogmael's in Wales: *Stogursey Charters*, ed. T. D. Tremlett and N. Blakiston, Somerset Record Society lxi, 1945, xiii, 1–2; Maxwell-Lyte, 3, 7–8, 10.

What, then were the reasons for our group of donors sending a daughter to Shaftesbury? We need to consider two aspects of this question: first, the decision of marriage versus the cloister, and secondly, why Shaftesbury, in particular, was the chosen house. Given the fact that infant donations or child oblations were still the practice in the late eleventh and early twelfth centuries, it is probable that many of these daughters entered the nunnery before adolescence and that the decision to do so was made by the girl's parents.[40] And for these families, there may have been some very compelling economic reasons for this decision. As has been shown, this group of donors, although in some cases prominent landholders in the area, was a group of fairly moderate means. Sidney Painter has discussed in some detail the drain on baronial resources produced by enfeoffments and by other necessary feudal obligations in the early twelfth century and has pointed out in particular the importance of looking at a baron's disposable income or resources in estimating his true economic position.[41] This position could have an important effect on a baron's ability to provide for his offspring and on the choices that were made for his children, particularly for his daughters:

> only an extremely rich lord could afford to marry many of his children well. ... And every daughter to be married needed a marriage portion. Not even a career in the church was free. ... When a son or daughter was placed in a religious house, a gift of land was expected to accompany the child. While it was cheaper to place a girl in a nunnery, than to marry her well, it still cost something.[42]

This last assertion needs to be examined more fully, and Shaftesbury's evidence, as well as evidence from other nunneries can be helpful in this respect. Considering first, then, the disposable resources of Shaftesbury's benefactors, Domesday Book shows in general the relatively small size of their baronies as measured by the valuation of 1086. This is particularly true of Serlo de Burci, Drogo de Monte Acuto, Goscelin de Rivers and Richard de Sancto Claro, whose holdings were all valued at less than £40 per annum, the last two with annual incomes probably not exceeding £20. With the exception of Richard de Sancto Claro, each of these donors had at least one other child in addition to the daughter who entered Shaftesbury, and in view of their relatively small resources, entering a daughter in a religous house may have been a less expensive alternative to providing a marriage portion from an already small demesne.[43]

The case of Serlo de Burci illustrates this problem well. His holdings in chief in Dorset and Somerset were numerous (two Dorset manors valued at £13 p.a. and

---

[40] Knowles, *Monastic Order*, 417–22. See J. H. Lynch, *Simoniacal Entry into Religious Life from 1000 to 1260*, Columbus (Ohio) 1976, 36–50 for a discussion of the practice and its persistence into the twelfth century.

[41] Painter, *Feudal Barony, passim*; and S. Painter, 'The Family and the Feudal System in 12th Century England *Speculum* xxxv, 1960, 1–16. On the scale of subinfeudation and its effects see also S. Harvey, 'The Knight and the Knight's Fee in England' *Past and Present* xlix, 1970, 6–8, 13.

[42] Painter, 'Family and the Feudal System', 9. See also J. C. Holt, 'Politics and Property in Early Medieval England' *Past and Present* lvii, 1972, 12–14, for inheritance practices and provisions for sons; however, he does not refer to marriage portions for daughters.

[43] For Serlo, see below; for Drogo de Monte Acuto see GEC ix, 75; for Goscelin de Rivera's son Walter see *Regesta* ii, no. 958 and *The Pipe Roll of 31 Henry I, Michaelmas 1130*, reproduced in facsimile from the edition of 1833, ed. J. Hunter, HMSO 1929, 125.

twelve Somerset manors with a total value of £23 5s p.a. in 1086), but they were
individually quite small: only two manors were worth more than £5 p.a. In addition
to those manors held in chief, he also held one manor from the bishop of Wells
in Somerset and six manors from Glastonbury abbey in Somerset and Wiltshire
whose values are not given in 1086.[44] If we remember Painter's argument that
'from the baron's point of view one manor yielding £20 was far more useful than
ten worth £2 each', Serlo de Burci's holdings, viewed in this light, seem less
valuable than the total value per annum implies.[45] Furthermore, and this is
important when examining his disposable resources, of his total holdings in chief
(valued at £37 10s p.a.), Serlo had enfeoffed lands worth £17 10s or nearly one-
half. His disposable revenues, then, seem more on a par with Goscelin de Rivera's,
although it is true that he did have the income from other manors not held in chief.

 Serlo de Burci's case is interesting also because this is the only instance for
Shaftesbury where we can compare the size of a marriage portion to the size of an
entry gift to a religious house. His donation on behalf of the daughter who entered
Shaftesbury is noted in Domesday Book. The entry shows that the abbey held
Kilmington, valued at £2 p.a. from Serlo 'for his daughter who is there'.[46] Serlo's
other daughter, Geva, had by 1086 married William de Falaise. He, as is noted in
Domesday, had received from his father-in-law the Somerset manor of Woodspring
valued at £5 p.a. as Geva's marriage portion.[47] This is, of course, only one
example of the relative size of a marriage portion versus the size of a dowry for
a religious house, but such evidence for the eleventh century is very scarce.[48]
Geva's marriage portion was more than twice as valuable as the endowment given
to Shaftesbury for Serlo's other daughter, and this donation itself, like the other
entry gifts to the abbey, was small. The evidence is not conclusive, but shows, I
think, that for some barons in the same position as Serlo de Burci, choosing a
religious house for a daughter, particularly if there were two or more daughters,
was sensible and could be motivated in part by financial considerations.[49]

 These considerations may have operated as well for all donors and may explain
the size, nature and location of those estates alienated to religious houses as entry
gifts. Shaftesbury's evidence alone shows the relatively small value of these
donations: of the eighteen donations we have a record of in this period, none, where

---

[44] For Serlo's holdings from Glastonbury abbey, see N. E. Stacy 'The Estates of Glastonbury Abbey
c.1050–1200,' Unpublished Oxford D.Phil. 1971, 56.

[45] Painter, *Feudal Barony*, 22.

[46] VCH *Somerset* i, 516.

[47] VCH *Somerset* i, 508.

[48] There are few references to either marriage portions or dowries for those entering religious houses
in Domesday. H. Ellis, *A General Introduction to Domesday Book*, 2 vols, Record Commission 1833,
i, 337 lists 7; the amounts range from ½ hide to more than 3 hides. Under Wilton's lands we find
mention of a donation made by a 'Toret' of 2 hides with his two daughters who entered that nunnery:
Domesday Book i, 68r. Evidence for the values of marriage portions *vs* values of entry gifts is more
abundant in the later Middle Ages. In this period, too, the dowries provided an intending nun were less:
see J. P. Cooper, 'Patterns of Inheritance and Settlement by Great Landowners from the Fifteenth to
the Eighteenth Centuries', in J. Goody et al., eds. *Family and Inheritance, Rural Society in Western
Europe 1200–1800*, Cambridge 1976, 293, 302, 308–9. I hope to assemble more evidence for the 11th
and 12th centuries on this question.

[49] V. Chandler, 'Politics and Piety; Influences on Charitable Donations during the Anglo-Norman
period', *Revue Bénédictine* xc, 1980, 64, considers the 'quasi-religious' motivation of donations made
as entry gifts in this light as well.

a value is assigned, was worth more than £3 per annum, and most gifts were in the range of £2 and assessed at either one or two hides. Similar examples, though they are not extensive, of the relatively small value of entry gifts accompanying nuns in the late eleventh and in the twelfth century can be found for Romsey, Clerkenwell, Godstow and Malling.[50] On the whole, the estates or revenues accompanying entrants to Shaftesbury even from donors who had slightly greater resources than Serlo de Burci, Goscelin de Rivera or Drogo de Monte Acuto were small. Harding fitz Alnoth, for example, whose Domesday Book holdings were somewhat more than £40 per annum, gave to Shaftesbury with his daughter land assessed at only one hide. In Harding's case the comparative smallness of the entry gift is not surprising: he had three other daughters and five sons to provide for.[51] Two donors, Aiulf the Sheriff and Odo fitz Gamelin (who sent two daughters to Shaftesbury), each gave more than one estate to the abbey, but again, each was valued at under £3 p.a., and in Aiulf's case, as we have seen, the donation was actually more in the nature of a restitution for lands he had seized.[52]

Four donors gave to Shaftesbury as entry gifts or dowries churches and/or their tithes. Gifts of churches and tithes, as others have pointed out, were popular forms of donations to monasteries in the late eleventh and early twelfth centuries.[53] It may be that in some cases the donations of tithes were simply a transfer of income from one ecclesiastical recipient to another and thus cost the donor little or nothing.[54] If the latter condition applied, these gifts to Shaftesbury may have been, from the donor's point of view, a painless and inexpensive way of both providing for a daughter and becoming a known and commemorated benefactor to the church.

As can be seen, both the resources of the donors and the entry gifts to Shaftesbury tended to be modest and suggest, then, the compelling nature of the economic reasons for choosing a life of religion rather than marriage for their daughters. We might ask whether for these families a life of religion was an 'inferior' choice, if a respectable one – especially if an illustrious house were chosen.

Why, though, was it Shaftesbury that these families chose? If families such as these chose – for whatever reason – religion rather than marriage for their daughters, the alternatives were limited. At the time of the Conquest there were only nine nunneries in the whole of England; by c.1125 the number had risen to twenty-five, but compared to the number of monastic houses available to the sons of these families, the range of houses available to daughters was extremely narrow.[55] Shaftesbury was not, of course, the only nunnery in the south-west. Romsey, Wherwell, and Winchester, all in Hampshire, and Wilton in Wiltshire, were all long-established Wessex houses and were thus also placed in the role of

[50] *Records of Romsey Abbey*, ed. H. G. Liveing, Winchester 1906, 54 and *Regesta* ii, nos 630, 874, 883; *Cartulary of St Mary Clerkenwell*, ed W. O. Hassall, Camden Society, 3rd ser. lxxi, 1949, *passim*; *The English Register of Godstow Nunnery*, ed. A. Clark, 3 vols, EETS, original ser. 1905–11, nos 129, 130, 142, *passim*; and for Malling *Regesta* ii, no. 791.

[51] *Berkeley Manuscripts* i, 17, 20.

[52] MS BL Harley 61, fol. 54r.

[53] Giles Constable, *Monastic Tithes: From their Origins to the Twelfth Century*, Cambridge 1964, 99–136.

[54] Constable, 99. See also Chibnall, 'Ecclesiastical Patronage', 107–8 for the popularity of tithes and churches in benefactions.

[55] Knowles and Hadcock, 493, show that in the period 100–1154 the number rose from 26 to 47 houses for women.

competitors for entrants and endowments in this region. But Shaftesbury's location on the Somerset-Wiltshire border meant that it was easily accessible not only to Dorset and Wiltshire families but also to the families from Somerset, Devon and Gloucestershire. A look at the geographical distribution of the benefactors' estates shows that the abbey's central and favourable location should be considered an important factor in attracting entrants. All the identified benefactors, with the exception of 'a certain merchant of London' and Richard de Sancto Claro (and he may have had family connections to the south-west), had their holdings concentrated in the south-west, and it was here, for the most part, that their principal manors, residences or castles lay.[56] For example, although Ernulf de Hesding held estates in ten counties, the greatest single concentration of his holdings (twenty-four manors valued at c.£80 p.a.) lay in Wiltshire. His principal manor, and the location of the endowment he provided to Shaftesbury with his relative, was at Keevil, not far from Shaftesbury's largest manor, Bradford-on-Avon.

Some of the donors possessed estates centred in the eastern part of Somerset, not far from the abbey: Harding fitz Alnoth's Somerset manor of Meriet became the *caput* of his barony; Alvred *pincerna* and Drogo de Monte Acuto, the two tennants of the count of Mortain who sent their daughters to Shaftesbury, also had their principal holdings here at Chiselborough and Shepton Montacute. The only Devonshire landholder among the Shaftesbury donors was Odo fitz Gamelin, and although his estates were centred at Plymtree some distance from the abbey, he did hold one manor in Somerset. For the Somerset landowners as well as for Odo fitz Gamelin, the choice of Shaftesbury was probably very simple: there were no nunneries in either Devonshire or Somerset before 1138, and therefore the Dorset house of Shaftesbury was the most convenient one.

Many Norman families of the immediate post-Conquest era maintained ties with family monasteries or other religious houses in Normandy and may thus have considered such a house as, also, a logical choice for their son or daughter entering religion.[57] For a family of considerable wealth or one which still held estates in Normandy, it may have been relatively easy to finance such an undertaking, but the families who sent their daughters to Shaftesbury were not in this position. Among the known Shaftesbury donors, only three, Ernulf de Hesding, Roger de Berekeley and Alvred *pincerna* were donors to continental as well as to English houses, and it is important to remember that Ernulf de Hesding's resources far outdistanced those of other Shaftesbury benefactors.[58]

Geographical factors and the growing attachment to England explain in part why these particular landowners chose Shaftesbury for their daughters. It is also clear that Shaftesbury was able to attract recruits, with or without a true religious vocation, from the families of the lesser ranks of the Norman barons in the south-west. Both the small number of nunneries available in the area and the abbey's advantageous location worked in Shaftesbury's favour in this respect.

[56] See Sanders, 84, for the St Clair family in the south-west.
[57] D. Matthew, *The Norman Monasteries and their English Possessions*, Oxford 1962, 27–71 and Chibnall, Ecclesiastical Patronage', 103–18 discuss and illustrate this point. See also John Le Patourel, *The Norman Empire*, Oxford 1976, 37.
[58] For Ernulf de Hesding's donation see *Cal. Docs France*, nos 318, 1033; for Roger de Berkeley's donation to St Aumale in Normandy see Swynnerton, 198; for Alvred's donation to the Norman abbey of Grestain see Salzmann, 163.

It is evident that family circumstances and economic position should be considered important in a study of Shaftesbury's donors, recruits and endowments in the late eleventh century and the early twelfth. The number of children in the family, particularly the number of daughters, and the extent of baronial resources were significant factors in determining whether a daughter entered a nunnery. The value, location and extent of the family's holdings to a large degree governed the size, the particular parcel of land, and the nature of the resources which constituted her dowry to the abbey. There is, furthermore, some evidence to suggest that entry gifts to Shaftesbury and to nunneries in general were often of less value than what was provided and expected as a marriage portion, raising the question of whether entering a nunnery was a second choice – second to marriage – and thus less valued.

But the recruitment to Shaftesbury, or to any religious house, should not be seen solely in terms of family convenience or economic circumstances. Shaftesbury was an important religious institution. As a royal foundation tracing its origins back to King Alfred, it could and did claim a long tradition of royal support and interest from the Anglo-Saxon rulers and aristocracy. Royal endowments had been given in return for prayers, and King Ethlered had apparently encouraged the cult of Edward King and Martyr which was centred at the abbey. The *Passio Sancti Edwardi* was composed from an earlier Shaftesbury life of King Edward in the last quarter of the eleventh or the first few years of the twelfth century, a fact which lends support to the view that this cult was still actively flourishing after the Conquest.[59] Although more evidence needs to be brought to bear on the development and importance of this cult throughout the Norman and Angevin period, its existence should be seen as a factor in attracting recruits to the abbey. Shaftesbury, like any monastic house, did serve a spiritual function: the prayers of its members were valuable, and these prayers would also have commemorated the abbey's benefactors.[60] A study of the specific terms of donation as contained in private charters for this period from other nunneries (for we have no such documents save Ernulf de Hesding's for Shaftesbury) shows that spiritual benefits were expected and conferred on the donors who gave estates and endowments with their daughters.[61] There is, to be sure, a regrettable lack of information on the liturgical life at Shaftesbury in this period, and it has been argued that by the eleventh century the intercessory functions of a house of nuns were seen as being less valuable than those performed in a house of monks.[62] But these points should not obscure or minimize Shaftesbury's importance as a religious and spiritual institution and what that implied in terms of attracting endowments and recruits. Family considerations were undoubtedly important, economic concerns were also surely a factor; but from the donor's point of view, there were also the ultimately

---

[59] C. Fell, *Edward King and Martyr*, Leeds Texts and Monographs 1971, xx.

[60] See H. E. J. Cowdrey, *The Cluniacs and the Gregorian Reform*, Oxford 1970, 121–33 for a valuable discussion of lay piety and benefactions in the 11th century. A. Murray, *Reason and Society in the Middle Ages*, Oxford 1978, 317–82 also examines the motivations of the nobility, and Harper-Bill, 66, cautions against neglecting 'religious sentiments' as a motive for benefactions.

[61] Ernulf de Hesding's private charter is in MS BL Harley 61, fols 28v–29r. The text is corrupt, and Dugdale's transcription (*Monasticon* ii, 483) hardly illuminating; this document was probably issued by Ernulf II, not by Ernulf I, the original benefactor. See, for example, the terms in the charters in *Cartulary of St Mary Clerkenwell*, nos 34, 58, 105, 116, 125, 129, 133.

[62] See R. W. Southern, *Western Society and the Church in the Middle Ages*, Harmondsworth 1970, 310 for this view. The abbey did have at least one chaplain in this period.

more important spiritual rewards accruing to him and to his family as a benefactor of the church.

It is important also to examine these endowments and the families thereby associated with Shaftesbury from the abbey's point of view. Clearly Shaftesbury was, by the late eleventh century, brought into the feudal and manorial framework within which the donors operated, and this had important and sometimes troublesome consequences for the abbey. Two of the donors, Aiulf the Sheriff and Harding fitz Alnoth were also men against whom the abbey pursued land claims. In Aiulf's case, the land in Farnham, Dorset, which he donated at his daughter's entrance was essentially a restitution; in this instance, then, Aiulf's entry gift provided with his daughter merely secured for the abbey land it regarded as rightfully its own.

A somewhat similar situation, one which illustrates the dual role an important neighbour and tenant could assume *via à vis* a local religious house, can be found in the case of the abbey's relations with Harding fitz Alnoth. His donation of land assessed at only one hide (in an unspecified location) is recorded in the abbey's list of donors and their daughters, and here it is noted that the abbess, with the consent of the king, had exchanged this land for an estate assessed at three hides in Caundle, probably in an effort to consolidate its possessions.[63] This, then, seems to have been a straight forward and, to the abbey, an ultimately beneficial transaction. Although the estate given with Harding's daughter was not the subject of any later dispute, another property he claimed, the manor of Beechingstoke, was. And as both the list of donated lands and the charters of Henry I from c.1121 make clear, Abbess Emma had to go to considerable lengths to recover the disputed estate for the abbey.[64] It is not without interest that Harding fitz Alnoth had also intruded upon an estate belonging to Glastonbury abbey and refused to surrender it until Abbot Herelewin (1101–1120) took legal action against him.[65] Both Aiulf the Sheriff and Harding were locally powerful men. They were in a position to seize Shaftesbury's lands, and they did so. Yet these men also turned to the abbey when providing for their daughters. It may be that the rather elusive entries in our surviving documents conceal from us considerable bargaining and negotiations over entry gifts. It is possible, I think, to regard an abbey's reception of an important landholder's, or a troublesome neighbour's, offspring as being to some degree conditional upon the settlement of outstanding claims in land: it is, I think, a strong possibility that this was the case when both Aiulf the Sheriff and Harding fitz Alnoth chose Shaftesbury for their daughters. As J.H. Lynch has pointed out, such negotiations over entry gifts reflect well the *quid pro quo* element present in the 'pious benefactions' of the period.[66].

From the abbey's point of view such negotiations were probably wise, especially during the post-Conquest years when rights in land, that is, conditions of tenure, rights of inheritance and the ability to alienate estates were particularly questionable. That the abbey, too, experienced such difficulties in this period is

---

[63] MS BL Harley 61, fol. 54r: 'postea Abbatissa excambiavit cancellarium pro tribus hidis de Candel concessu regis'.
[64] MS BL Harley 61, fols 54r, 23r. see also Williams, 227.
[65] *Berkeley Manuscripts*, 17, with no reference given. this must refer to the manor of Cranmore, Somerset. VCH *Somerset* i, 466.
[66] Lynch, 3–24.

evident, for at least five of the estates given as entry gifts in the period prior to 1221/2 became the subject of legal action in Henry I's reign. The circumstances surrounding each case are not, by any means, clear, but the donations which Serlo de Burci, Roger de Berkeley, Alvred *pincerna* and Garmund made at their daughters' entrances and the estate accompanying Aileva were each mentioned in Henry I's charter of 1121/2 confirming these possessions to the abbey.[67] And for each of these estates the charter names an individual against whom ('contra') Abbess Emma proved her claim. There was, then, evidently some insecurity of tenure or of rights associated with the abbey's ownership of these estates (as well as of other lands which may or may not have been entry gifts), a condition which possibly arose from the terms of the original endowment.[68] And it may be, too, that the insecurity of tenure was associated with the creation of knights' fees on the abbey's estates, which seems to have been the case with Harding's claims over the manor of Beechingstoke.[69] A further possibilty is that these particular disputes arose as the result of the vacancy occurring between the death of Abbess Cecily and the accession of Abbess Emma.

Not all the entry gifts brought problems, but some certainly did. Whatever the precise nature of these disputes (and their threads are difficult to unravel) it is clear that Shaftesbury abbey, like other religious houses, and particularly those upon whom the *servitium debitum* was levied, was being drawn into the complex feudal and manorial arrangements of the local lords.[70] Its very popularity made this enevitable, and some of the abbey's problems in the late eleventh century and in the early twelfth century arose from its association with the local landholders, perhaps especially with those who chose to send their daughters to the house.

In assessing the impact of such entry gifts to Shaftesbury it is important to note also that these endowments did not significantly augment the abbey's resources. In 1086 Shaftesbury had estates with an assessed value of 360 hides and £356 per annum. Yet, as has been shown, the individual endowments given by the eighteen donors were quite small, and the income from these estates probably totalled no more than about £25 p.a. in 1121. Most of the estates donated were located close to or in areas where the abbey already by 1086 possessed lands and rights. The two most distant, Odo fitz Gamelin's donation of the church and tithes in great Torrington (together with the manor of Little Wear), Devon, and Richard de Sancto Claro's gift of the tithes in Suffolk, must have been difficult to oversee properly. Indeed, the abbey subsequently exchanged the advowson of the great Torrington church and apparently lost completely the income from the Suffolk land.[71]

---

[67] MS BL Harley 61, fols 23, 30.

[68] There may have been questions over the ability to alienate freely, or the donors may have retained a life interest in these estates which their heirs or successors attempted to continue. See F. Pollock and F. W. Maitland, *The History of English Law*, 2 vols, 2nd edn, Cambridge 1911, i, 332–34, 340–42, 346; S. E. Thorne, 'English Feudalism and Estates in Land', *Cambridge Law Journal* 1959, 125, 205–9.

[69] Shaftesbury's early estate survey (c.1221–1130) and a contemporary list of landholders shows lands held for knight service in some of the disputed estates: MS BL Harley 61, fols 39r, 45v, 53. See Williams, 214–37 for a complete discussion of the creation of knights' fees on Shaftesbury's estates.

[70] H. M. Chew, *The English Ecclesiastical Tenants-in-Chief and Knight Service*, London 1932, 148.

[71] MS BL Harley 61, fol. 27. The abbey did not have the tithes from Wortham at the Dissolution (*Valor Ecclesiasticus*, iii, 481), and I can find no further reference to these tithes in the abbey's records.

There were, then, both legal and administrative difficulties resulting from some of these entry gifts; nevertheless, entry gifts were an important element at Shaftesbury and at other nunneries in this period. There is no question but that the system of entrance dowries for nuns was the usual practice in the late eleventh century.[72] But it was a system which came under increasing attack by the church during the twelfth century, when canon lawyers began arguing that requiring a dowry as a condition of entrance was simoniacal as well as a violation of the Benedictine Rule.[73]

There is, unfortunately, no hard evidence from Shaftesbury which indicates whether or not the nunnery had, in fact, required a dowry as a prerequisite for admission, but the consistency of the values of such endowments suggests the nunnery may have 'strongly encouraged' such a benefaction and may have suggested an appropriate amount. Because Shaftesbury was, compared to the other nunneries in early twelfth-century England, an extremely well-endowed abbey, the endowments thus acquired were probably not an essential part of its resources. To the smaller, poorer houses of recent foundation, particularly those of the new orders in the North, such gifts were necessary for the nuns' support.[74] Shaftesbury was not in this category; however, these gifts would have allowed the abbey to support additional members without increasing the burden on previously existing resources. There is little direct evidence about the number of nuns at the abbey in the late eleventh and early twelfth century, but there may have been around one hundred nuns by 1218: in that year Pope Honorius prohibited the abbey from having more than that number, 'the monastery being unable to support more or to give alms to the poor'.[75] Given the few places available as an alternative and given the support shown in such house as Shaftesbury by the Normans, it is probable that the nunnery increased its numbers during the Anglo-Norman period. Certainly Shaftesbury, like other nunneries, suffered no lack of recruits. Judging by the rapid expansion of nunneries in the middle and later decades of the twelfth century, the demand had exceeded the supply.[76]

It is by no means clear what factor was uppermost in the mind of each family choosing to send a daughter to Shaftesbury. For some girls the decision to enter the house may have been the result of a true vocation, for others it may have been seen as preferable to an unattractive marriage. But in view of what we have learned of this group of Shaftesbury's donors and daughters, the decision may have been the result of the family's financial and economic circumstance: they couldn't afford a suitable marriage portion. We might, then, begin to study this aspect of family history in assessing the role and function of other nunneries in Anglo-Norman England.

[72] Eileen Power, *Medieval English Nunneries, c.1275 to 1535*, Cambridge 1922, 16, 21–3. See also J. E. Burton, *The Yorkshire Nunneries in the 12th and 13th Centuries*, Borthwick Papers no. 56, 1979, 21–3 and Lynch, 39, 153–5.

[73] *Councils and Synods with other Documents Relating to the English Church: I. A.D. 871–1204* ed. D. Whitelock et al., Oxford 1981, ii, 747, 987; Lynch, 83–105.

[74] Burton, 22; see also A. Clark, *The English Register of Godstow Nunnery* i, xxv, for their importance to that nunnery.

[75] *Calendar of Entries in the Papal Registers relating to Great Britian and Ireland: Papal Letters, i, 1198–1304*, ed. W. H. Bliss, HMSO 1893, 51.

[76] Knowles and Hadcock, 493; F. Barlow, *The English Church 1066–1154*, London 1979, 193–95.

What is clear in the case of Shaftesbury, however, is that very soon after the Conquest, the abbey began drawing its recruits from the ranks of the new Norman families in the south-west, and that these families, while important local landowners, were very often families of comparatively modest means. For a variety of reasons – economic, social and spiritual – local families supported the abbey, and Shaftesbury – an abbey so rich in its Anglo-Saxon associations – moved in a Norman direction and continued to flourish in the post-Conquest era.

THE BISHOPS OF WINCHESTER AND THE MONASTIC REVOLUTION

M.J.Franklin

Recent historians coined the term 'crisis of western monasticism' to express the alleged dissatisfaction with traditional Benedictine monasticism and consequent burgeoning of the new orders at the expense of the old in the early part of the twelfth century. It was argued that revolutionary new perceptions of both the purpose of the monastic life itself, and of the relationship between monks and society were behind the mushrooming numbers of principally Cistercian and Augustinian houses in the period concerned. Important revisions have been made to these ideas based principally on the realisation that the Benedictines more than held their own in the early part of the twelfth century and that the crisis of numbers only struck c.1180–1215, when the consumption-oriented Benedictine economy hit trouble as the supply of gifts from pious laymen began to dry up with the onset of more general economic difficulties.[1] Moreover, it is now realised that from a global standpoint the differences between the various orders were often much less than their contemporary protagonists would have us believe. The *Libellus de diversis ordinibus* is the only work of the twelfth century which calmly and systematically analyses the monastic order as a whole, with a view to showing that every class of monks or canons had its proper place and calling, and its circulation was very limited.[2] In the local context, however, differences must have been sharper and more discernible. Even though patrons might perceive little difference between Cistercian and Augustinian, the decision to support new monastic endeavour, as opposed to the older established houses or collegiate churches, must have been made consciously. This paper will first examine in detail the monastic patronage of two bishops of Winchester, William Giffard and Henry of Blois, who held office in the crucial period and have been customarily assessed as old-style prelates and politicans at heart, to see what signs of the new attitudes emerge, and then go on to compare them, insofar as this is possible, with their contemporaries.

Giffard gave crucial support to the fledgling Cistercian house of Waverley, the first house of that order in England. This monastery was founded on the large episcopal manor of Farnham by Giffard on 24 November 1128.[3] According to the version of the foundation charter recorded on the Patent Rolls in the early fourteenth century the bishop gave to the monks merely the land of Waverley, two

---

[1] See J. Van Engen, 'The "crisis of cenobitism" reconsidered: Benedictine monasticism 1050–1150', *Speculum* LXI (1986), 269–304 which revises in particular N. F. Cantor, 'The crisis of western monasticism, 1050–1130', *American Historical Review* LXVI (1960–1), 47–67.
[2] C. N. L. Brooke, 'Monk and canon: some patterns in the religious life of the 12th century', *Studies in Church History* XXII (1985), 118.
[3] VCH *Surrey* II, 77 citing *Annales Monastici*, ed. H. R. Luard, 5 vols, RS, 1864–9, II, 221.

further acres of land at Helestede, pannage for their pigs quit of all customary payments in the woods of the manor of Farnham and some firewood.[4] This was hardly endowment on a grand scale. In spite of St Bernard's censures, his successor Blois was nevertheless a benefactor of the Cistercians; he augmented his predecessor's grant of land to Waverley by the gift of a further virgate and also added another piece of land whose bounds were listed in his *actum* in the manner of a classic Anglo-Saxon charter.[5] He also augmented their rights of pasture and extended pannage to their other beasts as well as giving them various other valuable rights.[6]

In two places at least it would also appear that Bishop Giffard was responsible for the transformation of ancient minsters into Augustinian priories. In neither case do any original charters survive, but though the bishop's precise role, or more important the timing of it, is not entirely clear, he does appear to have played a significant part.

At Taunton, the focus of a considerable episcopal manor throughout the Middle Ages, in 904 Edward the Elder had granted Danewulf, bishop of Winchester certain privileges for the presumably secular *monasterium* of Taunton.[7] By 1086 there were two priests left in possession and Giffard seems to have transformed the church into a priory for five canons from Merton c.1120.[8] He was described in the fourteenth century as the founder of the house and the account which speaks of this taking place 'before the time of King Edmund Ironside' is probably the result of the garbling of these two phases of the priory's history.[9] A slightly later charter of *inspeximus* recites a confirmatory charter of Henry II dating from 1155x8 which makes patent the importance of William's donation and also that the bishops'

---

[4] '. . . eidem terram de Waverli solute et quiete in eternum possidendam cum omnibus eidem terre pertinentibus in pratis et in pascuis et ii acras prati apud Helestede; et pasnagium porcorum suorum ab omni consuetudine quietum in boscis de Ferneham, et ligna ad usum ardendi et ad alia necessaria . . .': PRO C66/149 memb. 36r (cal. *Cal. Pat. Rolls 1317–21*, 104 and printed *Monasticon* V, 241, ii).

[5] 'unam virgatam terre . . . in augmentum terre sue de Waverl' quam terram cum pertinentiis suis venerabilis pater Willelmus Giffard, predecessor noster, assensu regis Henrici et tocius fratrum Wynton' ecclesie conventus in elemosina dedit eis . . . volentes et concedentes pro nobis et successoribus nostris ut dictas terras claudant ubi voluerint infra bundas suas que se extendunt a quercu de Tileford que vocatur Kyngboc per viam regiam versus Farnham usque ad Wynterborn et inde per ripam que currit de Ferneham ad montem quam dicitur Ricardishulle et per transitum illius montis et pontem de Waneford usque ad pratum de Tileford quod dicitur Yluethammesmede et inde sursum directe ad predictum quercum . . .': PRO C66/149 memb. 36r (cal. *Cal. Pat. Rolls 1317–21*, 104 and printed *Monasticon* V, 241, iii).

[6] 'Ut etiam habeant in communi pastura de Farnham porcos suos et alia averia sua et omnibus locis ubi liberi tenentes et alii de hundredo habeant et habere solent et ubicumque sibi magis viderint expedire: brueriam, petram, sabulum et aliam terram pro voluntate sua capiant ad omnes usus sibi necessarios sine calumpnia . . .': *ibid.*

[7] BL MS Additional 15350 fos 65v–66r / *Anglo-Saxon charters. An annotated list and bibliography*, ed. P. H. Sawyer, Royal Historical Society, Guides and Handbooks VIII, London 1968, no. 373.

[8] D. Knowles and R. N. Hadcock, *Medieval religious houses: England and Wales*, 2nd edn, London 1971, 175. The link with Merton is based upon BL MS Royal 8.E.ix fo. 93v (printed M. L. Colker, 'The life of Guy of Merton by Rainald of Merton', *Mediaeval Studies* XXXI (1969), 257 and cited J. C. Dickinson, *The origins of the Austin canons and their introduction into England*, London 1950, 118 n. 8).

[9] The house is described as being 'de fundatione cuiusdam Willelmi Giffard quondam episcopi Wynton' ante tempus regis Edmundi Iryneside . . .' in an Inquisition of 1317: PRO C145/78/9 printed *Monasticon* VI, 166, i and calendared *Cal Inq Misc* II, no. 295.

interest in the priory on their western outpost did not diminish in the time of his successors.[10]

In the case of Southwark there are even surviving *acta*. They do not, on the whole, seem to confirm that Giffard was deservedly called founder by the canons of St Mary Overy. Two *acta* survive: both only by virtue of later royal charters of *inspeximus*, and neither of these seems to show the bishop granting anything of significance to the canons.[11] Domesday confirms the existence of a minster in Southwark before 1066[12] and this institution was traditionally refounded as a priory by William de Pont-de-l'Arche and William Dauncey in 1106,[13] Giffard becoming known as founder because of his generosity in the building of the nave of the priory church the following year.[14] Dickinson called this story into question,[15] because this makes Southwark earlier than either Holy Trinity, Aldgate or Merton, but arguing thus ignores the possibility that St Mary Overy could have been colonised from a French house.[16] Giffard's involvement with currents of reform in Normandy is known by virtue of his status as the founder of the priory of Hamble, of the order of Tiron, apparently in c.1109,[17] though no documents actually issued by him seem to survive. Many of the muniments of Hamble went to William of Wykeham's foundation of Winchester College at the demise of the priory in 1392. Though explicit mentions of one, and possibly two charters issued by Giffard in favour of Hamble survive among the muniments of Winchester College, the originals do not seem to have survived into the fourteenth century.[18] It is true that Giffard only came into full possession of his see in 1107,

---

[10] 'ex dono Willelmi episcopi fundatoris eiusdem ecclesie omnes ecclesias Tantonie cum capellis et omnibus pertinentibus suis et terram de Blakecliva et ecclesiam de Kyngestona cum capellis et pertinentiis suis, ecclesiam de Lydyard cum pertinentiis suis, ecclesiam de Legha cum pertinentiis suis, ecclesiam de Hilla cum pertinentiis suis; ex dono Henrici episcopi ecclesiam de Pypeminster cum pertinentiis suis et cum capellis ...': *Cal. Chr Rolls 1327-41*, 312; *Monasticon* VI, 166.

[11] One *actum* confirms the grant of St Margaret's church to the priory despite the judgement of a diocesan synod – PRO C53/131 memb. 3r (*Inspeximus* of 1344), recited in BL MS Additional Charter 44694 (*temp.* Henry VI) – while the second confirms the donation by Alured, *presbiter de Stokes* of his church on his taking the habit: BL MS Additional Charter 44694 (text also printed in an abbreviated form *Monasticon* VI, 172 and said to be 'Ex Coll Vincent' i.e. from the transcript of the lost priory cartulary in the College of Arms).

[12] *Domesday Book*, I, 32a.

[13] *Annales Monastici* III, 430; IV, 374 cf. Knowles and Hadcock, 174.

[14] VCH *Surrey* II, 107.

[15] Dickinson, 119-20.

[16] So Knowles and Hadcock, 174.

[17] VCH *Hants* II, 221.

[18] An original of an *actum* issued by Bishop Henry of Blois confirms 'Donationem quod predecessor bone memorie Willelmus Giffard regis H senioris assensu & conventus Winton' concessione fecit deo et monachis de santo Andrea de una hida terre que vocatur Hama sicut eorum carte testant ...' (Winchester College Muniments no. 10630 [Hamble no. 6] – this charter was unaccountably ommitted by Voss, from her *Henrich von Blois*, though she did cite muniments from the College). Bishop Richard, a generation later, seems to have granted to the monks a pension of three marks in the church of Bishopstoke, noting 'quam [sc. the church of Bishopstoke] asserebant ad se pertinere ex concessione predecessorum Willelmi et Henrici bone recordacionis episcoporum': Winchester College Muniments nos 4222 [Bishopstoke no. 1] (an *inspeximus* of Bishop Woodlock), 4227 [Bishopstoke no. 6] (*inspeximus* of Bishop William of Wykeham); printed *Registrum Henrici Woodlock diocesis Wintoniensis episcopi a.d. 1305-1316*, ed. A. W. Goodman, 2 vols, Canterbury and York Society 1940-1, 646-7. That Bishop Henry should refer to his predecessor in this way invites suspicion, but the charter, which bears his seal, in admittedly a poor impression, appears genuine enough. No trace

but the lack of anything approaching a foundation charter for Southwark is probably primarily due to the loss of the main priory cartulary.

That Giffard showed concern for the progress of the Augustinians in his diocese is confirmed by his involvement in the early years of Merton, possibly one of the most significant of the early houses of that order in the country,[19] and, of course, located within the diocese of Winchester. Giffard was not the founder, since that honour fell to Gilbert Norman, the sheriff of Surrey, but he did consecrate a wooden chapel there very early in the days of the priory.[20] Of so early a bishop we should not expect to have much of an idea of the range of his episcopal activities; however, given that by his death in 1129 there were perhaps sixteen monastic houses in total within the diocese, only six of which were actually founded during his episcopate, it would seem significant that records of Giffard's intervention in the affairs of seven, or possibly eight houses exist, four of which considered him very important in their foundation. The seven houses are Carisbrooke, Chertsey, Winchester cathedral priory, Hamble, Merton, Southwark and Waverley, the last four of which, as we have seen considered Giffard to have played a significant part in their foundation. The eighth house is Southwick, where it is possible that Giffard was also involved in some way with the foundation of the priory, in its first incarnation at Porchester. There is some difficulty with this, particularly since the conventional foundation date for this house is 1133,[21] based on the royal charter of confirmation which is dated 'Apud Burnham in transfretatione', that is in July of that year, some four years after the bishop's death. The real founder of Porchester was William de Pont-de-l'Arche, the sheriff of Wiltshire and Hampshire, not Henry I at all, as the royal charter makes clear.[22] Dickinson made the point about the promoters of the Augustinians being Henry I's curialists;[23] of greater significance here may well have been the working relationship between Giffard and the local sheriff. They almost certainly co-operated in the setting-up of Southwark, unless this results from a misreading of Southwick as Dickinson suggested,[24] and William de Pont-de-l'Arche witnessed the reconciliation between the bishop and his monks.[25] There are two *acta* of Blois which purport to record gifts of Giffard to the canons of Porchester/Southwick;[26] they are of some suspicion, but if the earliest of them has

of either the original of Bishop Richard's *actum*, or of anything purporting to be an *actum* of either Bishop William or Bishop Henry referring to Bishopstoke church now survives at Winchester College, though there are two other *acta* of the latter which are printed by Voss.

[19] Cf. F. Barlow, *The English Church 1066–1154*, London 1979, 212.

[20] According to the account of the foundation in College of Arms MS Vincent 28 two years and five months after the appointment of the first prior, i.e. c.1117 – cf. VCH *Surrey* II, 94; O. Manning and W. Bray, *The History and Antiquities of the county of Surrey*, 1st edn, 3 vols, London 1804–14, repr. 1974 with intro. by J. Simmons, I, 245.

[21] Knowles and Hadcock, 174.

[22] The text of the royal charter (*Regesta* II no. 1787) is printed in *Monasticon* VI, 244, i. The king grants the church of St Mary, Porchester, which he claims to have founded, and confirms William's gift of the manor of Candover from his demesne and two other hides of land purchased by the latter. Cf. Dickinson, 124 esp. n. 3, 126 on William de Ponte-de-l'Arch.

[23] *Ibid.*, 125–31.

[24] *Ibid.*, 120 n. 1.

[25] Below n. 34.

[26] The bishop confirms '... ecclesias de Porcestria et de Wimeringis quas donacione felicis memorie predecessoris nostri Willelmi episcopi canonice adepti estis ...' in two acts – Hampshire Record Office

any basis in fact it may well be that Blois was confirming donations of his predecessor made so close to his death that no charter of grant was ever issued. Blois was one of the witnesses to the royal charter of 1133: then, or earlier, would have been an appropriate moment to issue such a charter, rather than after the move to Southwick which the prior's style would imply, though if this were the case it is strange that the bishop's gifts are not mentioned in the royal charter. It is significant that the canons considered their house to have been founded 'in the time of Henry, brother of King Stephen'.[27]

Barlow's summing up of Giffard, '. . . after his eventual enthronement he seems to have played no great part in public affairs, but applied himself primarily to his diocese . . .',[28] would seem to be well merited. Where his *acta* as so far discovered do not show him directly supporting monasteries himself, from his own resources he is found intervening as a diocesan, confirming the grants of others, often after synodal judgements.[29] This is of course not really surprising, given the nature of the potential sources. Knowles, on the other hand, in his assessment of Giffard, was influenced by the chroniclers of the cathedral priory, with which Giffard certainly quarrelled in his early years, as the division of the resources of the see between bishop and cathedral priory inevitably lead to conflict.[30] The two surviving *acta* of Giffard in favour of St Swithun's are somewhat unusual in form, but probably reflect the precise nature of the quarrel more accurately than the priory chronicle written in the thirteenth century. It is probable, however, that only one *actum* is in fact genuine. In one of the two, which is in narrative form, it is stated that Bishop Wakelin originally divided the resources of the see equally between himself and the priory. His brother Symeon, the prior, not surprisingly, seems to have been happy with the arrangements before his departure in 1082 and conflict was avoided while the bishop was only diverting funds away from the convent for the support of his building projects. Disagreement, however, later arose over the patronage of the priory's churches which the narrative ascribes to the doing of Bishop Wakelin – 'Procedente tempore, favente eodem priore, usurpavit sibi ius patronatus ecclesiarum que pertinebant ad partem monachorum'.[31] This was probably a scribe embellishing later tradition wearing

---

MS 1M 54/1 fos 1r, 1v (the earliest of the three Southwick cartularies, the text of the second *actum* is damaged but can be recovered by reference to the text in the late fourteenth-century revision, MS 1M 54/3 where these *acta* of Bishop Henry appear at fo. 227r, respectively). The two *acta* are addressed to different priors, A[nselm] and Walter (prior from c.1152 – D. Knowles, C. N. L. Brooke and V. C. M. London, *The Heads of religious houses: England and Wales 940–1216*, Cambridge 1972, 184), who are both styled 'of Southwick', and one is manifestly a simple extension of the other. In both the plural form is used and 'Valete' rather than a list of witnesses provides the termination of the *actum*.

[27] Dickinson, 124, n. 3.
[28] Barlow, 78–9.
[29] As at Southwark concerning St Margaret's church noted above and with Carisbrooke (*The cartulary of Carisbrooke priory*, ed. S. F. Hockey, Isle of Wight Records Series 2, Isle of Wight County Record Office 1981, no. 15) Chertsey (*Chertsey abbey cartularies*, 2 vols, Surrey Record Society XII (1915–63), no. 45) and Colchester (*Cartularium monasterii sancti Johannis Baptiste de Colecestria*, ed. S. A. Moore, 2 vols, Roxburghe Club 1897, 78).
[30] D. Knowles, *The Monastic Order in England*, 2nd edn Cambridge 1963, 179.
[31] BL MS Additional 29436 fo. 26r printed from *inspeximus Registrum Johannis de Pontissara episcopi Wintoniensis a.d. MCMLXXXI–MCCCIV*, ed. C. Deedes, 2 vols, Canterbury and York Society 1911–24, 621–2.

rose-coloured spectacles; *ius patronatus*, the term used in this *actum*, is hardly appropriate terminology for this early in the twelfth century. The other *actum*, however, addressed to prior Ingulph, which records the return of seventeen churches to the priory is probably in no sense a fabrication.[32] It cannot be dated any more closely than the final three years of Giffard's episcopate, but might well be a death-bed retraction analogous to that which Roger of Salisbury made to Cirencester.[33] The bishop records that he had returned to prior Ingulph the churches which he had unjustly seised from them since the time of his enthronement.[34] The churches had clearly been used to provide for the needs of his *familia*, always a problem for a bishop of a monastic cathedral of course, since Giffard provided that those of his clerks who held these churches should continue to do so for the remainder of their lifetimes.[35] It is perhaps significant that the less trustworthy narrative *actum* enjoins upon Giffard's successors the duty of not diverting his church's resources away from his spiritual sons.[36] This is hardly likely to have been the product of an episcopal writing office. The high standing of Bishop Giffard in his later years, to which Knowles refers,[37] is probably the consequence of the *actum* addressed to Prior Ingulph.

Evidence for Blois supporting Cistercians would be interesting in view of St Bernard's opinion of him. Given the attitude to women shown by the Cistercians in their early years it would be even more unusual if it could be shown that Blois supported Cistercian women. This is not in fact the case, though a cursory examination of one surviving document might lead the unwary towards this impression. Blois' support for Giffard's foundation at Waverley has already been mentioned,[38] but it also would seem that he took the nuns of Wintney (Hants.), later acknowledged as a Cistercian house, under his protection at quite an early stage in his episcopate. Arguing that a small and poverty-stricken house of nuns which was later acknowledged as being Cistercian was necessarily of that order in

---

32 Ingulph was prior from c.1126 – Knowles, Brooke and London, 80. The priory chronicle says the dispute was about nine churches: *Annales Monastici*, II, 46.

33 Cf. *Regesta* III, no. 189 n; E. J. Kealey, *Roger of Salisbury, viceroy of England* Berkeley, Los Angeles and London 1972, App. 2 no. 27 (pp. 263–4). The chronicle says that peace was made in 1124 and that the bishop then issued a charter protected by anathema confirming the return of everything the monks had asked for – '... Hoc anno facta est concordia inter Willelmum Giffard et monachos, mediante rege ... redditque eis omnia interrogata et carta sua haec et alia multa sub anathematis vinculo confirmavit conventui possidenda ...': *Annales Monastici* II, 47. Only Bishop William's narrative *actum* explicitly mentions anathema among the penalties for transgression.

34 'Sciatis me reddidisse deo et beati Petro et Ingulpho priori et monachis quasdam ecclesias quas ab eis iniuste aliquando abstuleram sicut eos inveni saisitos quando ad episcopatum veni ...': BL MS Additional 29436 fo. 26v printed *Reg Pontissara*, 620–1.

35 '... tali consideratione ut clerici mei qui eas nunc tenent de iure et manu prioris eas teneant quamdiu vixerint, et talem redditum ei reddant qualem eo tempore reddebant eedem ecclesie. Post obitum vero eorum libere remaneant in manu prioris ...': *ibid.*

36 'Et ne aliqui successorum meorum, nec aliqui alii quicquam auferant ab eis de iure suo, malum pocius quam bonum exemplum sequendo, non attendentes, nomen patris et pastoris, magis diligant et benefaciant filiis adulterinis nepotibus et parentibus quam filiis spiritualibus quibus loco dei presunt et per quos fere omnia bona sua possident ...': BL MS Additional 29436 fo. 26r printed *Reg Pontissara*, 621–2.

37 'The later years were more peaceful and Giffard was in the habit of dining and taking his siesta with the monks; at the end he received the habit and died in the monks' infirmiary ...': Knowles, 179, building on *Annales Monastici* II, 48–9.

38 *Supra* p. 48.

the twelfth century is not the same thing of course, because so many poor nunneries later claimed to be Cistercian in order to claim the valuable privileges of that order with regard to tithes, but that Blois did take a house of a sort at Wintney under his protection seems reasonably certain. It has been customary to consider that Wintney came into existence late in the twelfth century.[39] However, on the charter rolls exists a royal *inspeximus* which, amongst other things, recites an earlier confirmation issued by William, prior of the cathedral priory of St Swithun in 1287. This document apparently narrated an *actum* of Bishop Godfrey de Lucy dated 18 December 1199 as well as one of Blois which is manifestly early in form.[40] Neither document provides any clue as to the order to which the nuns claimed to belong, they are described merely as 'nuns serving God in the church of St Mary Magdalen, Wintney'.

The tiny Benedictine nunnery of St Margaret, Ivinghoe (Bucks) also attracted the intervention of Blois. He issued a charter confirming his predecessor's gifts.[41] It has been suggested that Giffard was in fact the founder of Ivinghoe,[42] but neither Blois' *actum* nor the general confirmation issued by Becket[43] mention an actual charter issued by Giffard and it may well be that none was ever issued. Probably for this reason tradition, or at least that which Leland reported as tradition, held that Blois was the founder.[44] There is no other evidence for Giffard being involved with religious women, unlike his successor. It seems odd that the nuns should not claim some sort of relationship to the Bishops of Winchester, located as they were on a massive ancient estate of the see.[45] To Nuneaton, of the order of Fontrevault, in 1155x72 Blois issued a confirmation of Henry II's gift of the church of Chawton (Hants.), which was in his diocese.[46] It could be argued that because of Henry II's great interest in Fontrevault, these were family concerns. Of a similar date is a charter confirming a presentation to Catherington church.[47] The only other evidence for Blois intervening in the affairs of a nunnery is at Romsey and there the motive could also be said to be a family one, since from c.1155 his niece, King Stephen's daughter Mary was abbess there.[48] Blois was apparently responsible for building part of the convent.[49]

Family piety, or concern for monastic houses on the lands of the see would appear to be the primary motive for these bishops. Blois is also said to have founded two hospitals in the environs of Winchester. Concerning the first, dedicated to St Mary Magdalen, which was sited in the eastern suburbs, episcopal foundation has been suggested because the Mastership was in the Bishop's gift in the later Middle Ages. There is some doubt about Blois' involvement,[50] but the fact that rents

---

[39] Knowles and Hadcock, 277.
[40] PRO C53/124 memb. 30r cal *Cal. Chr Rolls 1327–41*, 394. The Blois *actum* is old-fashioned in form, having a complex *arenga*, elaborate anathema and the conclusion 'Amen' rather than the list of witnesses which was later customary.
[41] Greater London Record Office MS Acc 312/214.
[42] Knowles and Hadcock, 264.
[43] *English Episcopal Acta II: Canterbury 1162–90*, ed. C. R. Cheney, British Academy 1986, no. 16.
[44] VCH *Bucks* I, 353.
[45] Worth 20 hides in 1086 – *Domesday Book* I, 143d.
[46] BL MS Additional Roll 47398.
[47] BL MS Additional Charter 47855, copy on MS Additional Roll 47398.
[48] Knowles, Brooke and London, 219.
[49] VCH *Hants* II, 126.
[50] Knowles and Hadcock, 404 noting the conflicting views of R. M. Clay and Bishop Milner.

owed to the Hospital are recorded in the Survey of Winchester of 1148 would appear to be conclusive evidence of its existence in the middle of the twelfth century, though not, of course, of the bishop's involvement.[51] The same is not true of the more famous Hospital of St Cross. According to the first of his surviving charters to St Cross, Blois founded the Hospital to benefit his soul, those of his predecessors and the Kings of England.[52] His Hospital provided full care for thirteen inmates and food for a hundred more of the poor. To provide for these sizeable expenses he gave fifteen churches together with the tithe of his demesne in Waltham and various rents in the city of Winchester. Neither of his two charters to St Cross are from a particularly early stage in the Hospital's history: the one previously mentioned refers to confirmations by Popes Innocent and Lucius and is therefore unlikely to be from before c.1145, while the second, the grant of the newly rebuilt St Peter's church, Bishop's Waltham and its various appurtenances, must be later (in fact from after 1153 according to the witness list), since only the tithe of the bishop's demesne in Waltham is mentioned in the first charter.[53] There is some doubt about the actual foundation date of St Cross, various dates in the 1130s having been suggested,[54] but it is clear that the two surviving *acta* date from after it was handed over to the Hospitallers in 1151.[55] Later bishops were to contest this gift and at a stage in the dispute at the beginning of John's reign the Hospitallers claimed that Blois gave them St Cross and part of the endowment of their preceptory of Baddesley.[56] The former seems certainly to be true, but Blois' involvement in the donation of the manor of Godsfield to the Hospitallers would seem to be limited to his consent as feudal overlord to a donation by Walter de Audele.[57] While this point is not without interest, it shows that Blois' personal concern for the Hospitallers must not be overstressed, he seems merely to have handed his hospital to them as the proper persons to staff it.

It is in Blois' dealings with the ancient collegiate minsters of his diocese that the most interesting aspects of his religious patronage lie. In two of these he was dealing closely with the family possessions of the Redvers family, lords of the Isle of Wight. The surviving church of the first, Breamore, is used by architectural historians as the classic example of the cruciform Saxon minster. Baldwin de

---

[51] D. Keene, *Survey of Medieval Winchester*, Winchester Studies 2, Oxford 1985, 201.

[52] '. . . pro salute anime mee predecessorum meorum ac regum Anglie extra muros Wyntonie de novo institui . . .': BL MS Harley 1616 fo. 6v printed L. Voss, *Henrich von Blois, Bischof von Winchester*, Historiche Studien CCX, Berlin 1932, 157–8.

[53] The second charter – BL MS Harley 1616 fo. 9r, printed Voss, 159 – is attested by Ralph, archdeacon of Winchester and Robert, archdeacon of Surrey cf. J. Le Neve, *Fasti Ecclesiae Anglicanae 1066–1300*, (rev. edn), *II Monastic Cathedrals*, ed. D. E. Greenway, London 1971, 91–2.

[54] Knowles and Hadcock, 404. The earliest date (1132) is based on a letter from the Bishop to Pope Hadrian IV in which he claimed to have founded St Cross within three years of his consecration: *Arch. Journ.* LIX (1902), 356. This letter is transcribed from fo. 28r of the cartulary in the St Cross muniments, which I have yet to examine, by Baigent in BL MS Additional 39976 fo. 51r. The hospital must have been in existence by March 1138 when Innocent II issued a privilege in its favour – *Papsturkunden in England*, ed. W. Holtzmann, 3 vols, Abhandlungen der Gesellschaft der Wissenschaften in Göttingen, phil.-hist. Klasse, Berlin and Göttingen, 1930–52, III, no. 31 (full text); I, no. 19 (calendar).

[55] Knowles and Hadcock, 404; Bishop Henry's first charter is addressed to Raymond, the Master of the Hospital in Jerusalem.

[56] *Monasticon* VI, 808, xviii.

[57] BL MS Loans 29/59 fo. 6r; transcribed in BL MS Harley 6603 fo. 80v cf. Knowles and Hadcock, 303.

Redvers seems to have converted it to a priory for Augustinian canons in 1128x32.[58] Blois was not involved directly, but he seems to have sanctioned the gift of the church of Sopley to the new house.[59] The matter was complicated by the fact that Sopley lay in the *parochia* of the the ancient collegiate minster of Twynham. The gift of Sopley to Breamore was made by the de Stanton family, who claimed at that time to be the founders of Sopley church. In fact this honour probably belonged to Earl Godwin who before the Conquest gave a hide of land in Sopley to the church there, presumably on its foundation, or at least that is what Baldwin de Redvers said in his charter to Twynham of 1140x1.[60] During his period as papal legate (1139x43), Blois issued a general confirmation to Prior Robert of Breamore.[61] At about this time Hilary, the future bishop of Chichester, and Blois' trusted clerk, became Dean of Twynham.[62] Under its three Norman deans the Collegiate minster of Twynham had been transformed from 'a genuinely communal mother church, with tightly controlled dependents, to what was little more than a single, very rich living for a single clerk, assisted by hired chaplains'.[63] Probably in the short period before his elevation to the episcopate in 1147 and almost certainly before 1150, Hilary, however, seems to have tried to put the clock back. He vigorously asserted the rights of Twynham as the mother church of Sopley and obtained the assent of his bishop in synod.[64] In the 1150s the Bishop's attitudes seem to have changed. Twynham was converted into a house of regular canons and pastoral care in its *parochia* revolutionised with new-style resident vicars taking the place of chaplains sent from the mother church. The royal charter confirming this has been seen as spurious,[65] but the date of 1150 given in the bishop's narrative charter is probably near enough.[66] The reason for the change is clear enough, the evil of hereditary tenure, as we might expect from a reformer; unfortunately what is not quite clear is whether the canons were originally intended to serve the churches themselves.[67] While the surviving

---

[58] Dickinson, 123–4; Knowles and Hadcock, 149.

[59] PRO E328/383 cf. BL MS Cotton Tiberius D vi fo. 58v (printed Voss, 162): '. . . circa primordia promocionis nostre cum miles quidam Orricus nomine ecclesie de Soppeleia advocatum se diceret, et canonicos de Brummora in eadem conscribi postularet, nos ad presentationem eius, cum hoc verum non esset, per ignoranciam facti circumventi predictis canonicis ipsam ecclesiam assignavimus . . .'

[60] P. H. Hase, 'The mother churches of Hampshire' in *Minsters and parish churches: the local church in transition 950–1200*, ed. J. Blair, Oxford University Committee for Archaeology Monograph no. 17, 56.

[61] PRO E326/11280; printed T. Madox, *Formulare Anglicanum*, London 1702, no. LXVII.

[62] BL MS Cotton Tiberius D vi fo. 30v, trans. Hase, 60.

[63] *Ibid.*, 50.

[64] 'Sequenti vero tempore, cum bone memorie viro post Cicestrensi episcopo, decanatum Christi ecclesie assignassemus, querelam ipsius Christi ecclesie super iure ecclesie de Soppeleia, qua se iniuste spoliatam ab ecclesie Brummore dicebat postulant prefato Hillario in synodo Wyntoniensis ecclesie ordine judicario cognovimus et decidimus . . .': BL MS Cotton Tiberius D vi fo. 58v printed Voss, 162 (an account produced 1169x72). A second account – *ibid.* fo. 60r, printed Voss, 163–4 – in which the names of the *antiquissimi sacerdotum* present at the synod are listed, may well predate the death of Bishop Hilary in 1169.

[65] Knowles, Brooke and London, 159, n. 2 discussing *Regesta* III, no. 903.

[66] BL MS Cotton Tiberius D vi fo. 14v printed (and said to be from an ancient exemplar, rather than the cartulary) *Monasticon* VI, 305, vii.

[67] '. . . nullus de parentela eorum tanquam per hereditatem introducatur, sed fructus earum in usus canonicorum regularium redigantur et ipsi canonici regulares provideant qui ecclesias vel capellas honeste deserviant salvo iure presulis Wyntoniensis ecclesie . . .': *ibid.*

secular canons still lived, vicars were installed in their places, and in Christ Church itself, Robert, *capellanus*, took the place of Hutgredus, probably a chaplain doing duty for the dean, with a stipend of ten shillings, mortuary offerings up to the value of six marks a year and keep for himself, his horse and a servant.[68] The dependent churches too had similar arrangements made for them,[69] though the regular canons had considerable powers over the vicars who served their churches while the seculars still lived, including, apparrently that of removal.[70] Once the 'rectors' had died 'perpetual' vicars, as later canon lawyers would have described them, were to be instituted by Blois and his successors. Hase has suggested two phases for this fundamental organisational change: 1150x8 and 1161x70.[71] In changing the extent of the mother church's control over its *parochia*, and with it, *pari passu*, increasing the bishop's power over the pastoral affairs of his diocese, these changes were, as Hase says, revolutionary at the time, though later commonplace. In his promotion of the Augustinians Blois showed himself truly an apostle of the Reform.[72]

And yet he did, at the same time promote his own secular College, the sort of action which would be more expected from an eleventh-century lord. On the episcopal estate of Marwell, not far from Winchester itself, Blois set up a College for four secular priests. Because, however, their primary duty was to pray for the Kings of England and the bishops of Winchester; the College could be said to be one of the earliest chantries.[73] Blois provided £13 annually from his rents in Twyford, £4 went to each of the priests with the remaining £1 being spent on the College's church. Marwell could be said to be an expression of Blois' personal, and, in contemporary terms, very modern sense of piety.

The remaining English houses which appear to have benefitted from Blois' patronage are those with which he had a special relationship by virtue of being their head. Glastonbury, where his reputation was of the highest, St Martin-le-Grand in London and St Swithun's cathedral priory all fall into this category. Exceptions to this pattern are St Alban's, where his gifts were considerable,[74] Taunton, his predecessor's foundation, which was given Pipminster church,[75] and Hamble, the tiny Tironian house Giffard had also patronised,[76] which also benefitted, largely from the generosity of Walter, one of the bishop's clerks. St Peter's, Bishop's

---

[68] *Ibid.*, fo. 15r, printed Voss, 161–2.

[69] *Ibid.*

[70] '. . . in libera prioris et canonicorum disposicione retinendi et removendi': *ibid.*

[71] Hase, 57.

[72] Cf. Knowles, 290: '. . . as an ecclesiastical statesman he left his mark in England chiefly by throwing the door wide open to intercourse and appeals from this country to the curia, but in the evolution of ideas he is perhaps still more significant as being a Cluniac who held the full Gregorian conception of church government, but treated it as a political programme rather than as a moral ideal . . .'

[73] 'Noverit . . . quod ecclesiam de Merewell a fundamentis construxi et in honorem dei et beatorum martirum Stephani, Laurencii, Vincentii et Quintini consecravi . . . quatuor quoque sacerdotes Deo et sanctis eius ibidem perpetuo servituris pro regibus Anglie et episcopis Wynton' ceterisque benefactoribus et fidelibus Christi tam vivis quam defunctis oraturos constitui . . .': PRO C66/162 memb. 15r, cal. *Cal. Pat. Rolls 1324–7*, 114 and printed *Monasticon* VI, 1344, i (also printed, from the copy in Bishop Woodlock's register *Reg Woodlock*, 73).

[74] *Monasticon* II, 219.

[75] *Supra* n. 10.

[76] *Supra* p. 49.

Waltham was rebuilt in the 1150s just before it was given to Blois' own foundation of St Cross.[77] Before that Blois seems to have used it as the salary for members of his *familia*, first Walter and then Christopher.[78] Probably c.1155 he gave certain tithes in Bursledon to the monks and also gave them permission to build a chapel.[79] The rights of Bishop's Waltham church are protected in this charter which must predate the transfer to St Cross, for that charter confirms the right of the monks of Hamble to hold that chapel, while paying four shillings a year as a pension to the Hospital, as new rectors of Waltham.[80] Thus we know that Blois used this church, first as income for members of his *familia* and then finally to endow his own foundation just outside his cathedral city.

Title to the manor of Hayling had been disputed by the monks of Jumièges and those of the cathedral priory at Winchester continuously ever since the Conqueror gave the manor to Jumièges. The monks of St Swithun claimed that the Confessor's queen had given them the land, but permitted the *TRE* landholder Wulfweard to hold the estate during his life only. To their minds the Conqueror did not have the estate in his gift when Wulfweard finally died.[81] The dispute rumbled on for decades.[82] Blois, at the prompting of Innocent II, conceded his own rights and those of his cathedral priory in an *actum* which probably dates from c.1140.[83] It is interesting that in this *actum* Blois does not use the legatine style, though it comes from a period when he almost certainly was still legate. It may be significant that the recipient of this *actum* was definitely outside Henry's jurisdiction as legate. Another *actum* issued by Archibishop Theobald in 1143x7 suggests that the matter remained contentious despite Blois' charter.[84]

With the monks of his own cathedral there was no overt conflict as there had been under his predecessor. The record of his donations to the cathedral, mainly relics and other religious artefacts[85] would seem to confirm this. Nevertheless in his

---

[77] *Supra* p. 54.

[78] Walter is described as 'clericus meus' in Winchester College Muniment no. 10629; he only appears in one other witness list of a Blois *actum* – *ibid.* no. 10630, also in favour of Hamble. Christopher, on the other hand appears in four witness lists: Winchester College Muniments nos 10630 & 11835 (to Hamble), 11614 (in favour of Walter Ruffus) as well as Oxford, Queen's College Muniments Sherborne Monachorum no. 4 (to Monk Sherborne). It is significant that these are all original *acta*: so insignificant a member of the *familia* would often be omitted from cartulary copies.

[79] Winchester College Muniments no. 10629 [Hamble no. 5a] printed Voss, 165–6 and trans. Hase, 61.

[80] '. . . capella de Brixendona, quam monachi de Hamela de predicta domo hospitali tenere debent, solvendo inde prefate domui hospitali annuum censum, scilicet quattuor solidos . . .': BL MS Harley 1616 fo. 9r printed Voss, 159.

[81] *Domesday Book*, I, 43c cf. Sawyer, no. 1476 for the agreement between the cathedral and Wulfweard *temp.* Bishop Stigand.

[82] *Vid.* discussion in VCH *Hants* II, 216.

[83] *Chartes de l'abbaye de Jumièges*, ed. J-J. Vernier, 2 vols, Paris and Rouen 1916. no. LXIII. The attestation by Jocelin de Bohun as archdeacon of Winchester gives limiting dates of 1139x42, but the presence of the king and archbishop Theobald, coupled with Hilary, styled dean of Christ Church makes it unlikely to have been after the overt break between Henry and his brother, or indeed Stephen's capture in 1141.

[84] A. Saltman, *Theobald, archbishop of Canterbury*, London 1956, no. 138.

[85] E. Bishop, 'The gifts of Bishop Henry of Blois, abbat of Glastonbury to Winchester cathedral', *Downside Review* III (1884), 33–44, repr. in *idem, Liturgica Historica*, Oxford 1918, 392–401 cf. Rudborne's assessment of Bishop Henry written c.1440: 'Iste benignissimus presul Henricus in tantum dilexit suam ecclesiam quod omnia que habuit minima forent' and his list of gifts – 'Pedem sancti Agathe

acta to the cathedral priory the same seeds of simmering discontent are evident. Three of the five *acta* recorded in the cathedral cartularies probably date from the last years of Blois' long episcopate, one is explicitly dated in the last year of the bishop's life.[86] In each of these three documents the bishop returns things he unjustly took from them '. . . ideoque quecumque ab eis abstuli vel appropriavi omnia eis resignavi . . .' as one of the *acta* puts it.[87] The monks' right to the patronage of their churches was singled out for mention[88] and the profits of certain churches assigned for specific purposes, for example 'ecclesiam de Ellendune que ad libros conscribendos et organa reparanda . . .'[89] Even if these charters were the product of fertile monkish imagination it is significant that these were the evils of which Blois was thought to be guilty. Not all his donations to the monks were made in the last years of his life; one, addressed to Hugh the archdeacon granting the chapels on the manor of Chilcomb for the commemoration of benefactors is likely to date from the 1140s.[90] Knowles' summing up of Blois seems a little harsh – 'It is true that Henry was always an ecclesiastical statesman, and in later years an excellent bishop, but there is little trace of the specifically monastic. His gifts might well have been made by a Wakelin or a Giffard . . .'[91] – and perhaps influenced by Henry of Huntingdon's famous phrase 'novum quoddam monstrum ex integro et corrupto compositum, scilicet monachus et miles',[92] which Knowles describes as 'the familiar and bitter phrase . . .' which '. . . was at bottom true . . .'[93] Even the monks of Hyde, who had no reason to love the man who apparently caused the burning of their monastery and had plans to create a suffragan episcopal see within their walls, or more important out of their endowments, seem to have been able to go to him for episcopal services, though there seem to be no episcopal *acta* of Henry in their surviving cartularies. However, much as in the manner in which he dealt with the *parochia* of Twynham, Blois seems to have been careful to protect the rights of the ancient mother church of Alton, long a possession of New Minster, and its successor, the abbey of Hyde.[94] In c.1148, well after the destruction of the abbey Blois ruled in favour of Hyde in synod at Winchester in a case between the abbey and the monks of Waverley concerning the tithes of Neatham, stating that the Cistercians should pay 40 shillings a year to Hyde and presumably not be exempt as they would have

magnam crucem cum imaginibus de auro purissimo ad majus altare et alia ornamenta plurima que lingua non potest enarrare sue ecclesie contulit . . .': *Thomae Rudborne monachi Wintoniensis Historia major de fundatione et successione ecclesiae Wintoniensis*, in H. Wharton, ed. *Anglia Sacra*, 2 vols, London 1691 I, 285.

86 BL MS Additional 29436 fo. 27r; printed *Reg Pontissara*, 626–7, cal. *Chartulary of Winchester cathedral*, ed. A. W. Goodman, Winchester 1927, no. 3.

87 BL MS Additional 29436 fo. 29r, printed *Reg Pontissara*, 622–4 cal. *Ctl Winchester*, no. 7.

88 '. . . Preterea confirmo eis ius patronatus ecclesiarum maneriorum suorum sicut eos saisitos inveni, quando ad episcopatum veni . . .': BL MS Additional 29436 fo. 27r; printed *Reg Pontissara*, 624–6 cal. *Ctl Winchester*, no. 3.

89 *Ibid.*

90 BL MS Additional 29436 fo. 28r cal. *Ctl Winchester*, no. 5. Prior Geoffrey occ. 1139x53: *Fasti*, 88; Archdeacon Hugh du Puiset 1129x53: *ibid.*, 92.

91 Knowles, 287, n. 1.

92 Huntingdon, 315.

93 Knowles, 291.

94 New Minster had Alton by virtue of King Alfred's will – Sawyer, no. 1507.

claimed on the basis of papal privileges.[95] They also seem to have had a charter issued by him, now lost, but produced in court in 1205, which gave them the church of Binstead provided they paid the mother church of Alton five shillings a year.[96]

How typical were Bishops William and Henry when compared with their contemporaries? Were they atypical in their preferences for particular orders or particularly efficient diocesan administrators? Were they at all limited by the horizons of their own diocese in their choice of which house to patronise? These are all difficult questions to answer, primarily because in this context any form of statistical comparison is, by its very nature, fraught with potential danger. To simply compare surviving numbers of *acta* issued by bishops in different dioceses is likely to be slightly invalid, not only because the rate of destruction of monastic archives may have differed but also because of the differences between the two dioceses in size and nature. The length of individual episcopates will itself naturally affect any such statistics. Moreover, although the work of the British Academy Episcopal *acta* Committee will eventually remedy this situation, at the moment the number of exhaustive modern collections of *acta* to use as the basis of comparison is limited. This very study is of an interim nature.

However, given these considerable caveats it is possible to begin some form of classification.[97] The types of *acta* issued by twelfth-century bishops to monasteries would seem to fall into three main categories. First bishops might make direct grants from their own property in favour of particular houses. Second they might confirm the donations of others, either at the time of the grant or on a subsequent occasion. Finally a bishop might issue written instruments in the course of carrying out his episcopal functions, either as an ordinary in his own right, or, and increasingly so as the twelfth century went on, as a papal delegate. Any or all of these categories might be produced in favour of houses inside or outside the diocese, since spiritualities often came into the hands of distant monasteries. Moreover individual *acta* might very often contain both gifts by the bishops themselves and confirmation of those of others. Table 1 displays the available data for seven bishops classified in this manner. No account in this table is taken of multiple *acta*, or of multiple *acta* of the same type, surviving in favour of particular houses; for example, therefore, even though Henry of Blois issued at least five *acta* in favour of the monks of his cathedral St Swithun's counts merely as one house within the diocese of Winchester in the first two columns of this table, and also as one house in each of the third, fifth and seventh columns, because Blois

---

[95] '... quod ecclesia de Waverle persolvet ecclesie sancti Petri de Hyda singulis annis ad festivitatem sancti Michaelis quadraginta solidos pro supradicta decima hac sane condicione quod ecclesia de Hyda providebit capellanum familie de Netham ...': *Reg Wykeham* fos 224v–225r cal. *Wykeham's Register*, ed. T. F. Kirby, 2 vols, Hampshire Record Society 1896–9, II, 387. This charter is witnessed by Hugh, abbot of Chertsey, Geoffrey [III] prior of St Swithun's, Hugh [du Puiset], archdeacon [of Winchester] and Alard, prior of St Denis, [Southampton]. I owe this reference to Mr N. Vincent. Neatham was given by King Stephen to Waverley in 1140: *Regesta* III, no. 921.

[96] PRO KB26/65 memb. 1d printed *Curia Regis Rolls* III, 119.

[97] The following sections are based on my collection of Winchester *acta* to date compared with data culled from, respectively, M. G. Cheney, *Roger of Worcester*, Oxford 1980, A. Saltman, *Theobald, archbishop of Canterbury*, London 1956 and *English Episcopal Acta I: Lincoln 1067–1185*, ed. D. M. Smith, London 1980. It should be mentioned that it is known there are substantial additions to be made to the collection of acta printed in Saltman's *Theobald* and also that 'lost' *acta*, i.e. acts which are known to have existed, but are not now extant for one reason or another, are counted in these totals.

both made grants to them himself, confirmed others' donations and 'intervened' on their behalf. Necessarily, therefore, the figures in the third, fifth and seventh columns do not add up to the figure in the second column. No particular surprises emerge – as would have been expected the number of houses who were recipients of *acta* in the early part of the century is much lower than in the later part of the period under discussion. The Archbishop, no doubt because of his primatial position, seems to have been a much more fertile source of *acta*, particularly of those of a confirmatory nature. The relatively high number of recorded 'interventions' by the archbishop would also follow logically from his position as the highest ecclesiastical authority in the realm. Nevertheless it is clearly necessary to obtain some idea of the rate of survival of *acta* in relation to the length of episcopates in order to gauge the value of the statistics in Table 1. An attempt to provide this is given in Table 2, from which it appears that for the apparently most prolific of the bishops, Theobald, if each recipient house received its *acta* separately from others and also all at once, and if *acta* were always issued at regular intervals, the period of time between such issues would have been approximately ten weeks, compared with slightly over three years for the apparently least prolific, Robert Bloet. Of course this is a rather artificial form of comparison,[98] but a relative index, as in third column of Table 2, where Theobald's output is taken as providing a norm, shows that the three later bishops analysed – Theobald, Roger of Worcester and Robert de Chesney seem to have been broadly similar in the extent of their output, while the others, with the exception of Robert Bloet, again seem roughly alike. When the data in Table 1 is displayed in percentage form, as in Table 3, it shows up other more interesting points. The percentage of houses actually in the diocese of Canterbury who were recipients of Theobald's *acta* was very small (under 10%), hardly surprising given the size of the diocese and the archbishop's unique position, but the same is also true of Roger of Worcester (12%). In general it would be fair to say that houses outside their dioceses figured more significantly in the *acta* of the bishops of the latter portion of the period, with the exception of Robert de Chesney, whose diocese of Lincoln was simply so huge and which, in any case, had its own native order in the Gilbertines with whom Bishop Robert seems to have been particularly concerned. Moreover actual gifts seem to have formed a smaller proportion of the corpus of the *acta* of the bishops of the post-reform era. Again this would seem to fit in with what would be expected, since if bishops were more energetic administrators we would expect to see a higher proportion of 'confirmations' and 'interventions' recorded. This would appear to be the case with Henry of Blois' *acta* being split roughly equally between the three categories while of Robert de Chesney's output only some 10% was 'donations'.

  If an increasing preference of bishops for houses within their dioceses seems not to be apparent can it be said that any of these bishops favoured particular orders? It might perhaps be thought reasonable to expect for example Henry of Blois, a Cluniac himself, to favour houses of this type. The available *acta* seem not to support such contentions. For example, in the *acta* of Archbishop Theobald the

---

[98] However, the data seems roughly comparable with that for the diocese of Orléans where there were 21 documents which survive from the period 971–1096 (or 0.17 per year), 26 for 1096–1145 (or 0.53 per year), and 244 for 1146–1207 (or 4.0 per year). Figures quoted in C. Morris, *The Papal monarchy. The western church from 1050–1250*, Oxford 1989, 222, n. 32.

number of confirmations to Cistercian houses is extremely small, being only six out of eighty, some 7.5%. Of course this might reflect the poor rate of survival of Cistercian archives, or the lack of Cistercian houses in Kent, but, on the other hand, the same seems to be true of Roger of Worcester. Of the thirty-one houses in whose affairs he is known to have intervened, only one (3.2%) was Cistercian. The comparable figure for Archbishop Theobald is one out of fifty-three, i.e. 1.9%. It would seem that the Cistercians were either particularly unsollicitous of episcopal assistance, extremely unattractive as the recipients of episcopal bounty, or, alternatively, extremely bad at record keeping! Indeed the only one of these bishops of whose *acta* a significant proportion seem to have been directed to houses of the Cistercian order is William Giffard, and given the relatively small number of houses in favour of whom his *acta* survive and the fact that one of them was Waverley, the initial Cistercian house which he founded, these are hardly useful statistics! Perhaps more significant, given the massive increase in the number of houses of this order in the reign of Henry I, is the surprisingly low proportion of *acta* issued in favour of Augustinian houses. Only Henry of Blois with some 47% of his confirmations, seems to have issued more than approximately a fifth of each category of his *acta* to Augustinian houses. There are two possible explanations for this apparent abnormality. Because of his period of legatine jurisdiction Blois' confirmation may have acquired some of the kudos usually associated with that of the archbishop. That a descendant of the founder of Freiston priory (Benedictine, Lincs.), Alan de Creon, should think it appropriate that a charter granting three hides in *Crudeshale* to the monks of Freiston be addressed to Blois[99] suggests that this was the case. This charter does not refer to Henry as legate, but it seems reasonable to suggest that it dates from the period of his legation, or, a very outside possibility, from November 1136 x December 1138, that is the period between the death of Archbishop William and the election of Theobald, when Blois could, in some sense, be said to have the archbishop's place in the kingdom. Moreover, Henry himself, might well have gone and sought out business as legate. This display of enterprise may well in part be what caused Henry of Huntingdon to suggest that until Blois' time as legate papal jurisdiction had no place in England.[100] Only three Augustinian houses outside the diocese of Winchester have recorded 'confirmations' issued by Blois, and in all of these *acta* the legatine style is used; they presumably date from this period.[101] Finally, it may be that Blois' innovative decision to radically restructure the old minster system in his diocese, referred to above in discussion of Twynham, may have been part of the cause. That the diocese of Winchester, for various historical reasons, was more redolent with these survivals from a bygone age of pastoral organisation than others, may also have contributed to these figures. With such a small sample, and at the same time such considerable regional diversity, it is clear that any such interpretations can be little more than informed speculation.

---

[99] *Monasticon* IV, 125, iv.

[100] Huntingdon, 282.

[101] To Cirencester, (Marquess of Bath, Longleat House MS 38b pp. 19a, 19b printed Voss, *Henrich von Blois* pp. 172–3) Oseney (Bodl MS Dep Deeds Ch Ch O.881 printed *Facsimilies of early charters in Oxford Muniment rooms*, ed. H. E. Salter, Oxford 1929, 69) and St Frideswide's, Oxford (BL MS Cotton Vitellius E xv fo. 17r printed *Cartulary of Oseney Abbey*, ed. H. E. Salter, 6 vols, Oxford Historical Society 1929–36, II, 232).

It must remain not proven whether these bishops of Winchester were any the more attracted by one order or another. In any case, as Professor Brooke has emphasized,[102] to potential donors the perceptible differences between the various orders were probably slight. His example of King David I of Scotland, the founder of houses of four different orders,[103] makes the point that a lord with few economic constraints on his generosity would spread his spiritual bounty as widely as possible and gain a reputation accordingly. To both monk and canon equally the desire to achieve apostolic poverty was strong; they pursued their common aim in buildings which were fundamentally alike.[104] It is probably a mistake to identify specifically 'Augustinian' or 'Cistercian' religious practices: all the contemporary data point to the tremendous variety of both experience and aspirations within the orders themselves, and, in England, unlike Eastern Europe, there seems little evidence to support the contention that monks avoided and canons eschewed pastoral work. The story of the beginnings of Llanthony, cited by Professor Brooke,[105] was probably a common one: seekers of the desert, faced with the threat of large-scale royal patronage which would nullify their attempts to live in apostolic poverty, turned away from the traditional Benedictine observances and took up whichever of the newer rules was convenient. In 1103 Citeaux was unknown in England: Llanthony in consequence became an Augustinian house, a generation later it might just as easily have become Cistercian, whatever was in the minds of its patrons. It is manifest that bishops, and particularly bishops who were not themselves monks, would share many of the religious tastes of their peers: the same concerns about burial, the need to have one's name recorded in appropriate martyrilogies, the desire to leave behind fitting symbols of their social rise. To these feelings they would add a sense of duty, such as that which Anselm felt as St Augustine's successor,[106] and, perhaps, and this would be especially true for 'reformed' bishops, a greater realisation that the purpose of monasticism was changing, seeking to provide for the *opus dei* in a different, more 'modern', fashion. All these were stimuli engendering greater levels of spiritual investment. Moreover, bishops probably did not face the particular economic difficulties which applied to the holders of great fiefs. Their incomes continued to rise through the twelfth century, and so they did not need to feel that their spiritual responsibilities had been discharged by the pious generosity of their improvident predecessors because the stability of their estates was threatened to the same extent as did lay lords.[107] Why then did episcopal generosity to monks seemingly decline? In the Winchester context three particular considerations seem particularly relevant. First, because Winchester was a monastic cathedral, the splitting of episcopal and

---

[102] Brooke, 'Monk and canon', *passim*.
[103] *Ibid.*, 112.
[104] C. W. Bynum, *Jesus as mother: studies in the spirituality of the High Middle Ages*, Berkeley, Los Angeles and London 1982, 28; Brooke, 'Monk and canon', 118.
[105] *Ibid.*, 126.
[106] R. W. Southern, *St Anselm and his biographer. A study of monastic life and thought 1059–c.1130*, Cambridge 1963, 127–8.
[107] K. J. Stringer, *Earl David of Huntingdon 1152–1219*, Edinburgh 1985, 110; B. Harvey, *Westminster Abbey and its estates in the Middle Ages*, Oxford 1977, 63; E. Miller, *The abbey and bishopric of Ely*, Cambridge 1951, 94.

conventual revenues, which, as we have seen,[108] occasioned problems under both Giffard and Blois, probably fostered the notion that the see was already making considerable contributions to the monkish cause. Second, Blois particularly had his own projects on an international scale – for example his support of the financially ailing Cluny for a whole year from his own resources.[109] Finally the growth of episcopal governance, and the consequent need to finance the *familia* produced particular difficulties for a bishop of a monastic cathedral who had no prebends to dispense. As we have seen in the case of Waltham[110] the wealthier churches of the diocese needed to be used for the payment of the bishop's staff, and hence were unavailable to be used for the endowment of monasteries.

Perhaps the most interesting piece of patronage by these two bishops of Winchester is the foundation of the college at Marwell by Blois. This has been described as the earliest English chantry,[111] and while this is probably not entirely true,[112] that Blois should be concerned to provide for his soul in this way, suggests he was very up-to-date in his thinking. Like so many of his noble contemporaries Blois seems to have desired something more than the confraternity and association in the liturgy offered by the traditional monastery.[113] That the dedication of Marwell should be to four deacons, three of whom, Stephen, Lawrence and Vincent, had particular associations with the Roman church, suggests a connection with Blois' visits to Rome. However, there are no indications of date in the charter as it now survives, beyond perhaps the termination 'Amen', which would argue for a date earlier in his episcopate, rather than later.

As bishops of Winchester Giffard and Blois do not seem to have been particularly revolutionary in their monastic patronage, the latter at least not for the first fifteen years of his episcopate. They both supported fashionable monastic causes and took particular care that the churches on their demesnes were run according to the most up-to-date ideas. Blois, however, stands out, not just as the 'novum monstrum' which Henry of Huntingdon so bitingly condemned, but as a bishop with new ideas about episcopal administration. His reputation as an art connoisseur, which seemed so inexplicable to contemporaries, has formed no part of this paper, but it is symptomatic of the complexity of the man. We do well to remember that Henry II, no man of sentiment, felt it important to see him in his last hours. Clearly the king did not regard him as a super-annuated nonentity, even if he had been given up for dead.[114] The chronicler Diceto records Henry II's landing on 6 August

---

[108] *Supra* pp. 51–2, 58.
[109] *Monasticon Cluniacense Anglicanum, or Charters and Records illustrative of the English foundations of the abbey of Cluni from 1077–1534*, ed. G. F. Duckett, 2 vols, Lewes 1888, I, 80.
[110] *Supra* p. 57.
[111] In K. L. Wood-Legh, *Perpetual Chantries in Britain*, Cambridge 1965, 4.
[112] For example the chapel of St Martin in Northampton, the initial site of the Cluniac priory of St Andrew in the early years of the 12th century, could well have been a royal chantry – *vid.* M. J. Franklin, 'Minsters and parishes: Northamptonshire Studies', unpubl. Cambridge Ph.D. thesis 1982, 88 discussing VCH *Northants* III, 57, *Cal. Pat. Rolls 1348–50*, 247 and *Rotuli Hundredorum temp. Henr. III & Edw. I in turr' Lond' et in curiae receptae scaccarii Westm' asservati*, [ed. W. Illingworth], 2 vols, Record Commission, London 1812–18, II, 2.
[113] Cf. Morris, 288.
[114] The Pipe Roll for 1172 shows that the King was in possession of the revenues of the see from as early as 3 July 1171, even though Blois did not die until 8 August – H. E. Salter, 'The death of Henry of Blois, bishop of Winchester', *EHR* XXXVII (1922), 79–80. Salter suggests that the monks added

1171 and the king's charter to the monks of St Swithun confirming their manors to them at the bishop's request,[115] is dated on that day at Blois' palace.[116] He died only two days later.

APPENDIX OF TABLES

Table 1   Relationships with monastic houses within and without respective dioceses – using known surviving *acta*

BISHOP	Houses Total	in	Donation in	out	Confirm in	out	Intervention in	out
Henry of Blois	**40**	13	7	7	9	8	4	13
William Giffard	**14**	8	4	2	5	2	2	1
Roger of Worcester	**41**	5	1	2	4	14	4	27
Theobald	**111**	11	10	13	8	72	6	49
Robert Bloet	**9**	5	0	0	3	4	2	0
Alexander	**30**	22	6	0	19	7	6	2
Robert de Chesney	**69**	41	6	1	40	28	17	6

Table 2   Comparison of rate of survival of *acta* between certain bishops

BISHOP	Length of Episcopate (years)	Index *I* (years/no. of houses)	Relative Index (*I*/0.2)
Henry of Blois	42	1.05	5.25
William Giffard	22	1.57	7.85
Roger of Worcester	15	0.37	1.85
Theobald	22	0.2	**1**
Robert Bloet	29	3.22	16.1
Alexander	25	0.83	4.15
Robert de Chesney	18	0.26	1.3

a spurious incarnation date of 6 January 1172, *recte* 1171, as the given year of the bishop's consecration would imply, to Blois' final disposition to his monks (BL MS Additional 29436 fo. 27r) at a later date, presumably to give weight to his dispositions.

[115] *Reg Pontissara*, 628.

[116] *Radulfi de Diceto Lundoniensis opera historica*, ed. W. Stubbs, 2 vols, RS 1876, I, 347.

Table 3 Relationships with monastic houses within and without respective dioceses – expressed as a percentage of the number of known recipients of *acta*

BISHOP	Houses in	Donation in	Donation out	Confirm in	Confirm out	Intervention in	Intervention out
Henry of Blois	32.5	17.5	17.5	22.5	20	10	25
William Giffard	57.1	28.6	14.3	35.7	14.3	14.3	7
Roger of Worcester	12.2	2.4	4.9	9.8	34.1	9.8	7.1
Theobald	9.9	9.0	11.7	7.2	64.9	5.4	44.1
Robert Bloet	55.6	0	0	33.3	44.4	27.0	0
Alexander	73.3	20	0	63.3	23.3	20	6.7
Robert de Chesney	59.4	8.7	1.4	58	40.6	24.6	8.7

LIFE-GRANTS OF LAND AND THE DEVELOPMENT OF INHERITANCE IN ANGLO-NORMAN ENGLAND[1]

John Hudson

The heritability of land has been a key area in discussions of the emergence of Common Law. Together with security of tenure so long as services were rendered and freedom of alienation, it is seen as a vital feature of Common Law ownership. In order to illuminate the workings of succession and the development of inheritance, I shall analyse an attempt to *prevent* succession. In 1088, Abbot Herbert of Ramsey gave William Pecche the fraternity of the congregation and granted that he might have in his custody the land of Over in Cambridgeshire, for his own and the abbey's profit. After William's death and that of his current wife Alfwen, the land was to return to the abbot's hand.[2] Clearly the grant was intended to prevent succession by William's heirs! Nevertheless, the problems it produced were to last for a century and a half.[3]

The close analysis of individual cases from which broader conclusions may be drawn has distinct advantages as a way of writing legal history. Within disputes one can see norms and power interacting. Disputes may also reveal the existence of not one but several views of correct practice, conflict between which may underlie legal development. Moreover, it was at least partly within disputes that notions affecting, for example, land-holding were formulated. Sometimes these notions acted as important constraints on the arguments which participants put forward, sometimes they were made explicit, examined, contrasted.

In this paper, I begin by recounting in detail the case of Ramsey abbey, the Pecche family and the land of Over. Secondly I summarise existing views on the heritability of land in the Anglo-Norman period. Next I examine special provisions which controlled the actions of ecclesiastical lords. Finally I undertake my own analysis of the development of inheritance, with special reference to the dispute concerning Over. My main concern is with the reign of Henry I, but I shall range throughout the century after the Norman Conquest.

To begin with the case, and firstly the nature of the evidence. The 1088 agreement is preserved in the *Ramsey Chronicle*, as are two important documents of Henry I and two of Henry II.[4] However, the *Chronicle* supplies no narrative. Instead we

---

[1] I would like to thank the participants of the Conference for their comments on this paper, and especially Chris Lewis, whose exemplary parish history of Over has now been published in VCH *Cambs.*, ix 339–355.

[2] *Chronicon Abbatiae Rameseiensis*, ed. W. D. Macray, London 1886; RS vol. 83, 233. (Henceforth *Ramsey Chronicle*.)

[3] A brief account of the case is given in E. Miller & J. Hatcher, *Medieval England: Rural Society and Economic Change 1086–1348*, London 1978, 208.

[4] *Ramsey Chronicle*, 233, 225, 228, 296, 300 respectively.

rely partly on the Ramsey cartulary's reports of pleas in the 1220s and 1230s.[5] Obviously these may be biased, giving only memories of the twelfth century. Nevertheless, their story is compatible with the earlier evidence, and suggests what probably happened.

Ramsey was the main land-holder in Over, in 1086 having ten hides and three virgates out of a total of fifteen hides.[6] The lands had been given to the church by Aednoth, Bishop of Dorchester between 1034 and 1049.[7] Domesday Book records that 'this manor lies and always lay in the demesne of St Benedict's church.'[8] Then in 1088 came the agreement granting William Pecche and his wife Alfwen the land for their lives. Alfwen is described as 'his wife whom he has today', which suggests that the agreement was made on the day of their wedding. Her name may indicate that she was an Anglo-Saxon heiress, but nowhere in the dispute is a claim to Over derived through her. Rather, the grant seems to have been a new one, for which William immediately gave one mark of gold, and thereafter was to pay six pounds of pennies each year 'for the enjoyment of the land' ['pro usufructuario terrae']. A further payment of one hundred shillings or one mark of gold, 'pro anima sua', was linked to a promise of burial in the cemetery of Ramsey. After William and Alfwen's death, the land was to return to ['recedet'] the hand of the abbot, 'without any claim and contradiction, and as well stocked as . . . on the day mortal illness seizes Alfwen.' The witnesses included Alfgar the reeve, Turkill the steward, and two of the king's chaplains. One of the chaplains is called 'Rodulfus', and has been identified as Ranulf Flambard, whom Southern hints may have had some connection with Abbot Herbert. His presence could be mere chance or could represent a special effort to secure the terms of the charter.[9]

Despite the precautions, a dispute arose in the following reign, probably originating with a claim by William and Alfwen's heirs. From c.1109x1129 comes a charter of Henry I addressed to the bishop of Ely, the barons, justiciars, sheriffs and officers of Cambridgeshire, informing them of the decision of the king's court.[10] The document of 1088 seems to have played an important part, for Henry I's charter stated that

> It was witnessed and recognised in my presence by the barons of the honour of Ramsey and by a cirograph of the same church that William Pecche and Alfwen his wife were not to hold the land of Over from the fee of the abbot of Ramsey except in their own lives, by rendering six pounds thence each year, but after their deaths the land was to return to the demesne of the abbot and church without any claim.

Henry ordered that the church and abbot have the land in demesne, quit of all claims of William and Alfwen's heirs and posterity. Between 1123 and 1130, the

---

[5] *Cartularium Monasterii de Rameseia*, edd. W. H. Hart & P. A. Lyons, 3 vols, London 1884–93; RS vol. 79, i 123–7. (Henceforth *Ramsey Cartulary*.)

[6] *Domesday Book*, i 192b. See also the *Inquisitio Comitatus Cantabrigiensis*, VCH *Cambs.*, i 426.

[7] *Ramsey Chronicle*, 159. The late tenth-century holder of Over, Aethelstan Mannessone, had a wife and daughter both called Alfwen, *Ramsey Chronicle*, 59–61, 76; however, there is no reason to believe that they were related to Alfwen, wife of William Pecche.

[8] *Domesday Book*, i 192b.

[9] R. W. Southern, 'Ranulf Flambard', in his *Medieval Humanism and Other Studies*, Oxford 1970, 191.

[10] *Regesta*, ii no. 1629.

king confirmed all the lands which Abbot Rainald had brought into demesne since becoming abbot, and these specifically included Over.[11]

The claimant in the dispute is not named. The phrase 'William and Alfwen's heirs and posterity' could imply that it was a child of theirs: they may have had two sons, who died without surviving issue sometime after 1130.[12] Another candidate is William's son by his second marriage, Hamo, who certainly claimed the land at some point. In 1228 the abbot admitted that, despite the provision that William and Alfwen held only for life, after their deaths Hamo received the lands: 'since Hamo, his/their son, was on good terms with the king, at the king's own request it was permitted that he hold that land for all his life, thus that the service increased by twenty shillings.'[13] The reference to Hamo as 'filius suus' may imply the belief that he was William and Alfwen's son, in which case memories had grown confused. However, although Hamo was pardoned 28s. 7d. geld in Suffolk in 1129x30, his regaining the land through royal favour is hard to reconcile with the 1123x30 royal confirmation of Over to Ramsey.[14] Perhaps Henry I was promoting compromise, reconciling his general support for the abbey with personal favour for Hamo. Nevertheless, the most likely explanation is that the claim had been made by William's son or sons from his marriage to Alfwen, that it was successfully resisted by the abbey with the help of Henry I, but that when Hamo inherited William's other lands, he obtained a life-grant of Over with royal help, possibly from Stephen rather than Henry I.

Certainly Stephen appears not to have helped the abbey, which was unhappy with the arrangement. Weakness, or support for Hamo, could explain his non-intervention. Instead, at the end of the 1130s, the abbey looked to the Pope, Innocent II; his bull forbad 'that any man, against your wishes, may in any way claim for himself by right of succession, or bring any challenge or harm to you in the possession and place of Over, which is your very own.' However, the effect of the bull is unclear, and despite further papal aid for the abbey, the lands seem to have remained in Hamo's hands.[15] At some time before his death in 1178x1185, he enfeoffed his younger son Gilbert with the lands, who in turn temporarily granted them to his older brother, Geoffrey.[16] Meanwhile, the abbey continued to press its claim and in 1187 an arrangement was reached in Henry II's court at Clarendon: the land was granted to Geoffrey for life, whereafter it was to return to the demesne of the abbot and convent, 'with no retention or claim by the heirs of Geoffrey himself or by the posterity of Hamo Pecche.' Geoffrey swore that he would never waste the land, nor would he seek by any trick that the abbot or convent lose anything of the land or its appurtenances.[17] Crucial to the settlement seems to have been Henry I's charter of 1123x30, stating that the revenues of the lands which Abbot Rainald had brought back into the demesne should be divided between the building work on the church and its alms. Yet the dispute rolled on

---

[11] *Regesta*, ii no. 1686.
[12] GEC, x 332 fn. a.
[13] *Ramsey Cartulary*, i 124.
[14] *Magnum Rotulum Scaccarii, vel Rotulum Pipae, anno tricesimo-primo regni Henrici primi*, ed. J. Hunter, Record Commision, 1833, 99. (Henceforth *PR 31 HI*.)
[15] *Ramsey Cartulary*, ii 144 quoted, 136–7, 156.
[16] *Ramsey Cartulary*, i 124, 126; GEC, x 332–3.
[17] *Ramsey Chronicle*, 296, 300.

for another half century, only ending under Henry III when Gilbert's son Hamo unsuccessfully impleaded the abbey for the lands.[18]

The persistence with which both parties pursued their claims is in part explicable on economic grounds. Over was a potentially rich manor, on the edge of the fens. In 1086, Ramsey's ten hides and three virgates were valued at £8. In the 1270s, records of papal taxation reveal Over's value as £51.[19] Unfortunately intervening valuations are closely connected with the rent paid by the Pecches and conceal the extent to which the real value of the lands may have been increasing. The abbots probably saw potential revenue being lost as the Pecches extended their tenure at almost fixed rent. Perhaps if the abbots had been able to raise the rent substantially, they would have been willing to accept the Pecches as ever more productive tenants. As it was, the church sought to repossess the land, and the result was the long-running dispute revolving around succession claims.

Let us now, therefore, examine historians' views on the heritability of land in Anglo-Norman England, at least at those higher levels of society upon which analysis has concentrated and conclusions can be drawn. Maitland, with a note of caution, believed that 'the followers of the Conqueror who received great gifts of English lands held these lands heritably', and that tenure from mesne lords was similar: 'the *feoda* of the Norman reigns are indubitably hereditary.'[20] In general, this position has been maintained. It has been noted that 'the Normans came to England with well developed notions about inheritance' and that Anglo-Norman charters used inheritance language immediately it was appropriate. Furthermore, the descent of baronies, it is argued, shows that succession was customary.[21]

However, the bases of Maitland's views have been criticized by Thorne and Milsom, who argue that in the century after the Norman Conquest land was not heritable in the modern lawyer's strict sense.[22] They give no single definition of

[18] On the later stages of the dispute, see *Ramsey Cartulary*, i 123–7, ii 147, 368; *Ramsey Chronicle*, 323; *Rotuli Curia Regis. Rolls and Records of the Court held before the King's Justiciars or Justices*, ed. F. Palgrave, 2 vols, Record Commission, 1835, i 2, 87, ii 122; *Curia Regis Rolls*, HMSO, 1922-present, i 292, xiii no. 1141, xiv no. 194 (henceforth *CRR*); *Rotuli Chartarum in Turri Londinensi Asservati, 1199–1216*, ed. T. D. Hardy, Record Commission, 1837, 76; *Placitorum in Domo Capitulari Westmonasterii Asservatorum Abbreviatio. Richard I–Edward II*, Record Commission, 1811, 1; *Rotuli de Oblatis et Finibus in Turri Londinensi Asservati, Tempore Regis Johannis*, ed. T. D. Hardy, Record Commission, 1835, 17; *Rotuli Litterarum Clausarum in Turri Londinensi Asservati, 1204–1227*, ed. T. D. Hardy, 2 vols, Record Commission, 1833–1844, ii 149.
[19] *Domesday Book*, i 192b; J. A. Raftis, *The Estates of Ramsey Abbey*, Toronto 1957, 233. (Henceforth Raftis.)
[20] Sir Frederick Pollock and F. W. Maitland, *The History of English Law before the Time of Edward I*, 2 vols, second edn reissued with a new introduction and select bibliography by S. F. C. Milsom, Cambridge 1968, i 314–316. (Henceforth Pollock and Maitland.)
[21] See e.g. J. C. Holt, 'Feudal Society and the Family in Early Medieval England: II: Notions of Patrimony', *TRHS* 5th series 33, 1983, 193–220, quotation at 198. (Henceforth Holt, 'Notions of Patrimony') R. DeAragon, 'The Growth of Secure Inheritance in Anglo-Norman England', *Journal of Medieval History* 8, 1982, 381–391.
[22] S. E. Thorne, 'English Feudalism and Estates in Land', *Cambridge Law Journal* 75, 1959, 193–209; S. F. C. Milsom, *The Legal Framework of English Feudalism*, Cambridge 1976. (Henceforth Thorne, 'Estates in Land'; Milsom, *Legal Framework*.) See also R. C. Palmer, 'The Origins of Property in England', *Law and History Review* 3, 1985, 1–50. A. M. Honoré, 'Ownership', in *Oxford Essays in Jurisprudence*, ed. A. G. Guest, Oxford 1961, 107–147, provides a very useful legal introduction to notions of property.

heritability, but one version runs thus: if inheritance exists, 'when the ancestor dies, the heir is at once entitled under abstract rules of law and enters without anyone's authority.'[23] This definition implicitly distinguishes Common Law heritability from landholding in their postulated pre-inheritance world in three connected ways, relating to custom, thought, and seignorial authority.

Firstly, customary succession must not be automatically equated with heritability. Thus, according to Thorne, the fact that 'military tenancies often did pass from father to son, from ancestor to heir, ... does not necessarily imply heritability'.[24] What existed in the post-Conquest period was 'a fief held by successive tenants in return for service, each succeeding by gift. ... This devolution, it seems likely, was neither dictated by law nor accomplished by agreement between the parties. It was the result of expediency.'[25] At first, the heir's position may have been insecure. As time passed, repeated succession strengthened his claim against the lord, but such was still not true inheritance. 'The military fief was not heritable until about the year 1200'; previously 'its tenant held merely an estate for life.'[26]

The second implication is that such succession need not have involved abstract rules. Thorne seems to assume that there was little abstract thought on land-holding, whilst for Milsom such thinking could only emerge once the Angevin reforms brought jury trial to replace the old methods of proof, ordeal and oath: 'substantive law is the product of thinking about facts', and 'what takes a legal system beyond the mere classification of claims is the adoption of a mode of trial which allows the facts to come out. In England, the starting point was the introduction of jury processes.'[27]

Thirdly, both Thorne and Milsom hold that before the existence of true Common Law inheritance the heir only entered upon the tenement with the lord's authority.[28] This vital seignorial element in land-holding is hidden behind the sources because it was so central to men's lives and assumptions.[29] Thorne and Milsom's views are in part derived from Stenton's picture of the honour as a 'feudal state in miniature'.[30] According to Milsom, since the honour was autonomous, the essence of land-holding was not ownership – a proprietary right good against the world and enforceable by a sovereign authority – but the personal relationship, the mutual obligations, of man and lord. The only title that could exist to a tenement was that the lord had correctly seised his man with it. An heir had not a proprietary right but only a claim against his dead relative's lord. In such circumstances, succession might be usual but the lord still had discretion over regranting the decedent's lands. It was regular royal enforcement which transformed customary succession into strict inheritance by removing this element of discretion.[31]

[23] Milsom, *Legal Framework*, 154. Cf. M. Bloch, *Feudal Society*, tr. L. A. Manyon, 2 vols, London 1961, i 190. Bloch's comments in c. XIV of *Feudal Society* repay detailed attention from those interested in the development of heritability in England.

[24] Thorne, 'Estates in Land', 196

[25] Thorne, 'Estates in Land', 196–7.

[26] Thorne, 'Estates in Land', 195.

[27] Milsom, introduction to Pollock and Maitland, i lxvii.

[28] E.g. Thorne, 'Estates', 196–7; Milsom, *Legal Framework*, 41–2.

[29] Milsom, *Legal Framework*, 1, 7–8.

[30] F. M. Stenton, *The First Century of English Feudalism*, second edn, Oxford 1961, 51. (Henceforth Stenton).

[31] Milsom, *Legal Framework*, cc. 2 & 5.

Thorne and Milsom are more concerned with the underlying structure of land-holding than with the perceptions of people of the time. Their immensely stimulating work has forced a re-examination of many accepted positions. Yet too great neglect of stated perceptions is dangerous. Thorne may hold that feudal tenure in the Anglo-Norman period was, in modern legal terms, only a life estate, but men at the time did not see it thus. My own analysis concentrates more on contemporary perceptions and actions, whilst retaining the distinction between purely personal succession and strictly defined inheritance as a useful analytic tool.

Before entering into further detailed discussion of heritability, however, it must be stressed that land-holding in ecclesiastical honours may have differed from that in lay ones. Our concern here is not with the prelate's personal lands but with those of his church. Writing in 1920s, Galbraith accepted Maitland's position that fees held from laymen were heritable. However, he argued that in the late eleventh century the situation was different for church lands: 'there is evidence, I think, that life leases – whether military grants or grants at a rent – were the rule for whatever lands had been demesne (whether *de victu monachorum* or *de victu abbatis* or *episcopi*) before the Conquest.'[32]

Whenever dealing with early Anglo-Norman documents relating to gifts to laymen, one must remember that they are likely to record the exceptional rather than the normal.[33] The survival of written life-grants may hide an unrecorded majority of grants for unlimited terms made by ecclesiastics. Aware of their vulnerability against future claims by heirs of life-tenants, they used charters to reinforce their position. Fear of future claims ensured that these charters were preserved. However, churchmen were also aware of the importance of preserving long-term grants in the durable record of writing, and there are reasons to believe that the apparent emphasis on life-grants is not simply a product of the documentation.[34] Galbraith ascribed their prevalence amongst late eleventh-century ecclesiastical charters to conservative retention of pre-Conquest English practice. Yet life-grants were also made in pre-1066 Normandy, and given their continuing use on both sides of the Channel in the twelfth century, explanations other than Galbraith's seem preferable.[35]

---

[32] V. H. Galbraith, 'An Episcopal Land Grant of 1085', *EHR* xliv, 1929, 363; see also 353–4. The phrasing of Henry I's charter of 1109x29 to Ramsey, *Regesta*, ii no. 1629, '. . . in dominio ecclesie et abbatis', suggests that the division between the abbot and the convent's lands was not yet strict: cf. VCH. *Cambs.*, ix 343, Raftis, 38.

[33] See P. R. Hyams, 'Observations on the Charter as a Source of the History of the Early English Common Law,' forthcoming. Note also, for example, that lay charters from after 1150 rarely mention earlier documents, now lost. Conceivably such documents had already been lost by the second half of the twelfth century. However, this is improbable, since it would suggest that the laity did not greatly value records, in which case it seems unlikely that charters would have been produced in the first place.

[34] Note, for example, clauses emphasising the weakness of human memory, and the need to use writing to reinforce it. Such clauses already appeared in charters on both sides of the channel before 1066: see E. Zack Tabuteau, *Transfers of Property in Eleventh-Century Norman Law*, Chapel Hill 1988, 212–3, 218 on Normandy, (henceforth Tabuteau); F. M. Stenton, *Latin Charters of the Anglo-Saxon Period*, Oxford 1955, 77. On the post-Conquest period, M. T. Clanchy, *From Memory to Written Record*, London 1979, 116–120. Such clauses seem particularly appropriate for long-term grants.

[35] On pre-1066 Norman grants for life, see Tabuteau, 65–80. For twelfth-century English life-grants, see e.g. A. Saltman, *Theobald, Archbishop of Canterbury*, London 1956, 271, no. 44; *Early Yorkshire*

Church lords were supposed to be bound by canon law with regard to land-holding, as in other respects. The *Collectio Lanfranci* and later collections stated that 'it is in no way permitted for bishops to alienate the possessions of the church.'[36] The canons tend to concentrate on the duties of bishops, but such restrictions also applied to the heads of other churches. On their benediction, abbots swore to prevent future alienations and to resume past ones: the officiating bishop asked the abbot 'do you wish to gather the possessions of the church, previously unjustly dispersed, and conserve them for the use of the church, of the brothers and also the poor and of pilgrims?' The abbot replied 'I wish.'[37] Nevertheless, the outright prohibition of alienation was qualified in certain ways. Most importantly for this paper, the canons were particularly concerned with long-term alienations; less permanent ones might be permitted.[38] Thus both conformity to the canons and prudence encouraged churchmen to restrict the terms of their grants.

Was Galbraith therefore right to see life-grants as peculiar to church lordships? Certainly, charters of lay grantors provide little evidence of grants for life or lives.[39] One possibility is that the preponderance of such ecclesiastical grants merely reflects the production and survival of charters, and lay lords often made unwritten grants for life. *Glanvill*'s discussion of grants without livery of seisin, lasting only for the grantor's life-time, may indicate that short-term allocations were quite common.[40] Even before livery of seisin became vital for full alienation, temporary allocations may have involved less formality than a lasting gift.[41] If so, this, along with their short-term nature, may have decreased the chance of their being written down. Alternatively, lay lords may have had more discretion over regranting a dead tenant's lands, and hence did not need to make specific life-grants. However, the evidence suggests that lords rarely exercised such discretion, certainly not in the twelfth century.[42] Overall, the frequency of specific life-grants made by laymen, but not recorded in charters, must remain uncertain. The demands of canon law, together with the needs of self-protection,

---

Charters, vols i–iii, ed. W. Farrer, Edinburgh 1914–6; index to vols i–iii, edd. C. T. & E. M. Clay; vols iv–xii ed. C. T. Clay, Yorks. Archaeol. Soc. Record Ser. Extra Ser., 1935–1965, i no. 414. (Henceforth *EYC*.)

[36] Lanfranc's Collection: Cambridge, Trinity MS B 16 44, pp. 285–6; *Decretales Pseudo-Isidoriani*, ed. F. K. P. Hinschius, Leipzig 1863, 333. (Henceforth Hinschius.) Gratian, *Decretum*, C. x q. ii c. 1.

[37] *The Pontifical of Magdalen College*, ed. H. A. Wilson, Henry Bradshaw Soc., 39; London 1910, 81. See also *Statutes of Lincoln Cathedral*, edd. H. Bradshaw & C. Wordsworth, 3 vols, Cambridge 1897, ii 34–5 for similar oaths taken by bishop and deacon. *PR 31 HI*, 150 gives a remarkable echo of the abbot's oath: the abbot of.Westminster rendered account of 1000m. of silver 'ut bona Ecclesie sue que iniuste dispersa erant congregaret et congregata custodiret.'

[38] See especially Ivo of Chartres, *Decretum*, pars iii c. 183; also M. Cheney, 'Inalienability in mid-Twelfth Century England: Enforcement and Consequences', *Proceedings of the Sixth International Congress of Medieval Canon Law*, edd. S. Kuttner & K. Pennington, Monumenta Iuris Canonici, Ser. C, Subsidia vol. 7, Vatican City 1985, 470, 472 on fee farm. Other relaxations of the rule included pleas of necessity: Cambridge, Trinity ms. B 16 44, pp. 285–6, Hinschius, 332–3; Gratian, *Decretum*, C. x q. ii c. 1.

[39] For one, rather unusual, example, see D. Walker, 'Ralph son of Pichard', *BIHR* 33, 1960, 201.

[40] *Tractatus de Legibus et Consuetudinibus Regni Anglie qui Glanvilla vocatur*, ed. & tr. G. D. G. Hall, Edinburgh 1965, vii 1, pp. 69–70. (Henceforth *Glanvill* and chapter no., Hall and page no.)

[41] S. E. Thorne, 'Livery of Seisin', *Law Quarterly Review* lii, 1936, 345–364.

[42] See my D.Phil. thesis, 'Legal Aspects of Seignorial Control of Land in the Century after the Norman Conquest', Oxford 1988, esp. 123–137. (Henceforth Hudson.)

can probably explain not only the prevalence of life-grants amongst late eleventh-century ecclesiastical charters but also the greater proportion of ecclesiastical as opposed to lay charters recording life-grants in the twelfth century. As many church lords discovered, even such precautions were frequently not enough.

Drawing on the dispute concerning Over, then, what suggestions can be made concerning the development of inheritance in Anglo-Norman England? I divide my analysis into the three interconnected themes treated above when discussing Thorne and Milsom's definition of inheritance: custom, thought, and seignorial authority. I shall argue that at least in ecclesiastical honours the development towards inheritance had progressed further by 1135 than Thorne and Milsom would allow. The situation in lay honours is less clear because of the shortage of evidence. However, whilst bearing in mind the possible peculiarities of church practice discussed above, I shall suggest some similarities between lay and ecclesiastical lordships, and also point to further developments which strengthened the position of the aspiring heir even before the Angevin reforms.

Custom can be dealt with briefly. That, even in the late eleventh century, lords like Abbot Herbert of Ramsey took such care to prevent succession suggests that in other circumstances succession was common. Similarly, would so much effort have been expended on recording tenants' names in Domesday Book if men had really regarded succession as so insecure as to render the description of land-holding rapidly obsolete? I tend to think not. More generally, as time passed, simple long tenure by a family must have reinforced custom, since the very fact of succession strengthened future claims to succeed, reducing lords' discretion over regranting the lands: the very notion of *hereditas* pointed to future as well as past succession.[43] Moreover, land-holding was not regarded simply as a relationship between man and lord: a close relationship could exist between man and land, strengthening as the land remained in the family for an extended period. Thus heritability was occasionally identified with the land itself, apparently detached from the tenant's relationship with his lord: for example, Orderic wrote of the Fleming Gerbod's 'hereditary honour'.[44] During the Anglo-Norman period, such ideas must have greatly strengthened the claims of heirs to these lands.

On now to thought. Firstly, the Over case emphasises the importance of the actors' own perceptions. It suggests the possibility of the analysis of land-holding in terms of multiple views rather than a monolithic set of assumptions. The Over dispute may be analysed in terms of the competing views between the abbey and the Pecches. It is very possible that Hamo's sons, if not Hamo himself, saw themselves as pressing a valid hereditary claim: had not the land been in their family for a considerable time? Other cases show such claims meeting more favourable receptions than did the Pecches'. Although he was writing much later, Matthew Paris' account of a rather similar dispute involving the monastery of St Albans is based on a mid-twelfth century source, probably written by one closely participating in the abbey's legal affairs.[45] It again starts with a life-grant, by

---

43 Holt, 'Notions of Patrimony', 216–7.
44 Orderic, ii 260.
45 *Gesta Abbatum Monasterii Sancti Albani*, ed. H. T. Riley, 3 vols, London 1867–9; RS vol. 28d, i 63, 159–166. On the source, see R. Vaughan, *Matthew Paris*, Cambridge 1958, 182–3.

Abbot Paul to Peter de Valognes, in 1077x1093. The wood concerned, Northawe, was later given in turn to Peter's son and grandson for life. The grandson, Peter II, confessed as he was dying that his predecessors had not held hereditarily, and at his death Abbot Robert repossessed the wood. Peter, however, left a brother who was also called Robert. This Robert's claim was repeatedly refused by the abbot, so he obtained a writ from Henry II. After a struggle, Robert obtained possession, and only with great difficulty did the abbot finally get a royal judgement from Henry II in the abbey's favour. The abbey's troubles stemmed, at least in part, from the fact that some men believed that Peter's brother and heir Robert had a hereditary right to the land. In 1201, the jury decision in the famous Cockfield case gave the claimant hereditary title to two manors which had previously been in the family for three generations.[46] They had never been hereditary and the claimant's father had promised that at his death the manors would return to the convent without any claims from his heirs, yet the jury concluded that such long tenure constituted a fee farm. Thus by the beginning of the thirteenth century, some were taking the fact of succession as *sufficient* proof of heritability.

Attitudes might vary not only between lord and claimant or lord and jury but also, for example, between lords, according to circumstances. Thus, on occasion, ecclesiastical lords may not have been entirely against the succession of related tenants to a life tenement: the emphasis on life-tenure would be a strategy to indicate their residual control and satisfy their obligations under canon law.[47] Examination of the varieties of strategy and the underlying thought allow a more nuanced view of legal development.

Secondly, such disputes must have stimulated thinking on tenure, by laymen as well as ecclesiastics: it had to be established how the lands were held. The peculiarity of life-grants must have been stressed and at least implicitly contrasted with heritable grants. Settlements, probably including that of Ramsey and Hamo Pecche, brought this home particularly clearly by allowing the defeated party life-tenure. Such tenure contrasted with both the original hereditary claim and the long-term reversion to the victorious party.[48]

Thirdly, increasing use of documents may also have encouraged more precise thought about land-holding, and the role of documents in the dispute concerning Over is notable. The abbey was careful to write down and preserve the initial agreement. In Henry I's reign, Ramsey's case was proved not only by witness of the barons of the honour, but also by the cirograph drawn up in 1088.[49] Cases did not simply go to the general test of ordeal, battle, or oath. Rather, evidence was

---

[46] *The Chronicle of Jocelin of Brakelond*, ed. & tr. H. E. Butler, Edinburgh 1949, 58–9, 123–4, 138–9; *CRR*, i 430; *The Kalendar of Abbot Samson of Bury St Edmunds and related documents*, ed. R. H. C. Davis, Camden Soc. 3rd ser. lxxxiv, 1954, 127–8.

[47] See also Holt, 'Notions of Patrimony', 197, on the twelfth-century struggles over Cockfield: 'the picture is one of men of business fashioning a *modus vivendi* which both resolved differences and satisfied mutual interests.'

[48] See, for example, the case involving the Church of Marcham and lands at Garsington; *Chronicon Monasterii de Abingdon*, ed. J. Stevenson, 2 vols, London 1858; RS vol. 2, ii 40, 130–1, 166–8. (Henceforth *Abingdon Chronicle*.) The 1153 Treaty of Westminster proved to be an unusually successful example of such a settlement.

[49] *Regesta*, ii no. 1629.

brought and the facts came out. And since this was so, men must have been aware that clear expression of the terms of land-holding could be decisive.

Requirement for precision increased during the twelfth century. It can be seen in charters from the mid-century onwards, which reinforced life-grants with phrases such as 'only in his life-time, not by hereditary right.'[50] At the same time, the omission of inheritance language from a grant, and from the charter recording it, began seriously to jeopardize succession. Between 1154 and 1161 a claimant failed to obtain seisin of the Archbishop of Canterbury's manor of Wimbledon and Barnes since he could not show that the grant to his predecessors had mentioned inheritance or fee.[51] Conversely, once lords took the absence of inheritance language to justify denial of succession, the presence of inheritance language surely strengthened still more the heir's claim to succeed. Neither lord nor tenant could afford the terms of tenure to be vague.

I would therefore like to suggest that developments in thought concerning land-holding in the century after 1066 helped to prepare the way for inheritance, and more generally for abstract notions of ownership. Such abstract thinking might be seen as a practical side of the broader movements referred to as Gregorian Reform and the Twelfth-Century Renaissance. Thus the pressure of church reform, with its emphasis on the difference between church and lay land-holding, between succession by clerics to office and by laymen to family holdings, must have forced men to make distinctions, to concentrate on issues which would lead them to formulate abstract notions on land-holding.

It can be argued that certain conscious notions of tenures existed in this world, even if they did not exactly coincide with the set tenures of later Common Law.[52] The Domesday Survey must often have raised, implicitly or explicitly, the question 'how is the land held?' Within single charters of the late eleventh century, a contrast was drawn between holding in fee and holding in alms.[53] Grants for life were contrasted with grants to a man and his heirs, and cases turning on such points sharpened distinctions of tenures.

These ideas are particularly clearly illustrated by the royal charters granted to Reading Abbey in the first half of the twelfth century.[54] The lands of the church were its alms, and hence not to be permanently alienated, although they might be granted for rent: 'no-one is to hold anything from the possessions of the monastery of Reading *feodaliter absolutum*, but are to owe annual rent and service to the abbot and monks.' The phrase 'aliquid teneat feodaliter absolutum', it seems, would

[50] *EYC*, i no. 414.

[51] *Early Charters of the Cathedral Church of St Paul*, London, ed. M. Gibbs, Camden Soc. 3rd Ser. lviii, 1939, no. 163. By *Bracton*'s time, a grant had to be made to 'N. and his heirs' for it to be heritable. A grant to 'N.' was only for life. *Pollock and Maitland*, i 308; *Bracton's Note Book*, ed. F. W. Maitland, 3 vols, London 1887, iii 16–17, 248–9, 620, (= pleas nos 964, 1235, 1811).

[52] On later notions of tenure, see A. W. B. Simpson, *A History of the Land Law*, Oxford 1986, cc. 1 & 3. The development in the later eleventh and early twelfth centuries of abstract thinking on land-holding is apparent in the way in which the words *elemosina* and *feodum* are increasingly used not simply to describe pieces of land but also, in phrases such as *in elemosina* or *in feudo*, to describe how land is held; Hudson, 85–90, 99–104. On Norman usage, see J. Yver, 'Une Boutade de Guillaume le Conquérant: Note sur la Genèse de la Tenure en Aumône', in *Etudes d'Histoire du Droit Canonique, dédiées à Gabriel le Bras*, 2 vols, Paris 1965, i 784–6. (Henceforth Yver.)

[53] E.g. *Regesta*, i no. 338a. For a Norman example, Yver, i 788.

[54] *Reading Abbey Cartularies*, ed. B. R. Kemp, 2 vols, Camden Soc. 4th Ser. 31, 33, 1986, 1987, i nos 1, 8 (= *Regesta*, iii no. 675); see also no. 27.

attribute to the tenant a considerable right in the land. The logic of the contrasts in this charter, and surely more widely, can be seen as forcing men towards notions of heritability and ownership.

My last theme is seignorial authority. The dispute shows the various pressures on churches, and perhaps other lords, to allow succession. A claimant might use peaceful means, as Hamo Pecche exploited royal favour. On other occasions, lords may have lacked the force to prevent men from seizing lands which their predecessors had held only for life. Or a lord might be faced with an heir unwilling to leave his predecessor's land for which his claim had been rejected. Sometimes the relative power of lord and claimant must have been vital, and the lord compelled to accept the heir.

However, the Abbot of Ramsey did not passively succumb to such pressure. Rather, the case casts doubt on the very notion of the autonomous lordship. We see the church looking for outside help, taking matters of succession outside the honour. Sometimes, notably in Stephen's reign, the Pope was the primary source of aid, but for the development of inheritance the contacts with the king are particularly important. Why did the initial dispute go to Henry I? Surely it was a matter for the seignorial court: the claimant should have come to the lord and requested his inheritance. The lord would have refused, on the grounds that the claimant's father had only held for life. The court, it seems, would have backed their lord. Conceivably the claimant was already in possession or had seized the land and the abbot had looked to the king for support in ejecting him.

Alternatively, the claimant had sought royal help after his claim was refused. Certainly at some points during the dispute, it was not only the abbots who looked to the king for help, but also the Pecches. Claimants from other ecclesiastical lords also looked to the king. Another dispute concerning a life-tenure may suggest that Henry I could be interested in fairly minor succession cases.[55] Granta was a tenant of the Cathedral Priory of Bath. At his death, shortly before 1120, his son-in-law Modbert claimed that Granta had bequeathed him his holding in North Stoke. The priory countered that Granta had held only for life. Judgement went against Modbert, but what is notable is that he brought a royal writ in support of his case. There is no sign that he was a rich man, capable of buying royal support, nor that he had a special connection with the royal household. He seems simply to have turned to the king when he had trouble in obtaining what he regarded as his inheritance.

The strongest evidence for the regularity of Henry I's involvement in succession cases in ecclesiastical honours comes from a charter of St Mary's, York. Many of its grants lay down that no exchange will be given if the lands are lost, but this charter of 1122xc.1137 is unusually specific.[56] The church granted a messuage in Fossgate, which Richard Tortus had held of it, to Ougrim de Frisemareis and his heirs to hold in fee: 'if any heir of Richard Tortus can acquire that messuage of land *from the king* or deraign it against us or Ougrim and his heirs, we will not give an exchange.' Charters, chronicles and the 1130 Pipe Roll show us individual

---

[55] *Two Chartularies of the Priory of St Peter at Bath*, ed. W. Hunt, Somerset Record Soc. vii, 1893, 49–51. See also *Regesta*, iii no. 47.
[56] *EYC*, i no. 310.

instances of claimants obtaining Henry's help. This charter suggests that at least ecclesiastical lords sometimes expected disappointed claimants to do so, and modified their actions accordingly.

Thus we have seen that succession was common, that certain abstract notions of land-holding existed, and that Henry I became involved in succession cases in ecclesiastical honours. Certainly monasteries such as Ramsey had notably close ties to the king, but legal historians exclude ecclesiastical lordships at their peril.[57] In 1086, churches held about a quarter of the land in England.[58] Their judicial activities therefore must not be ignored. Indeed, church lordships may have been at the forefront of the development of the Common Law. Ecclesiastical lords seem often to have turned to Henry I for aid, and the forms in which this aid came often foreshadowed those which are generally regarded as becoming common under Henry II.[59] I would therefore suggest that by 1135, the practice of succession in ecclesiastical honours at least approached the definition of inheritance discussed above.

Were lay honours so very different from ecclesiatical ones? Certainly some ecclesiastical lords – whilst by no means timid, meek men – may not have had the strength to enforce their will on their vassals in the way a great baron did. Yet this must have been a problem for many lay lords as well. What of the lord who had a greater man as his vassal? Or had a vassal who could turn to some great man, his lord elsewhere, for aid in a dispute? The complexity of tenure ensured that the minor tenant might have a powerful backer.[60] Or he might be an office holder, with access to a royal or baronial patron. Such lords, impotent to enforce their own justice, would have been aware of how ecclesiastics acted in such circumstances. They were present at the county court which dealt with some of the relevant writs. They may even themselves have been victims of ecclesiastics armed with royal orders. Might they not have copied the ecclesiastics in obtaining royal help to compensate for their lack of personal strength? Claimants from lay honours might also look to the king. Thus the 1130 Pipe Roll recorded that Walter fitzOdo rendered account of £21. 13s. 4d. for justice ['pro recto'] about his inheritance from the Countess of Chester.[61]

I do not wish to suggest that there existed in Henry I's reign the regular application of royal justice of *Glanvill*'s time. However, I do think that lords and claimants, when deciding their actions, might have to take into account not only

---

[57] Milsom does not pay any explicit attention to ecclesiastical honours. This must in part stem from his reliance on Stenton, who explicitly concentrated on lay honours in his *First Century of English Feudalism*; see Stenton, vii–viii.

[58] D. C. Douglas, *William the Conqueror*, London 1964, 269.

[59] See, for example, the writs obtained by ecclesiastical lords in support of their demands for their dues: e.g. *Regesta*, ii nos 789, 1860a; these might be seen as precursors of the writ of customs and services.

[60] See 'Epistolae Fiscannenses: lettres d'amitié, de gouvernement et d'affaires', ed. J. Laporte, *Revue Mabillon* xi, 1953, 29–31, especially the statement concerning England on p. 30, 'locus iste autem tot dominis subiacet quot uicinis'; J. Boussard, *Le Gouvernement d'Henri II Plantagenêt*, Paris 1956, 33–62 provides a useful survey of English land-holding; D. B. Crouch, *The Beaumont Twins*, Cambridge 1986, 131–2, 138, and J. A. Green, 'Unity and Disunity in the Anglo-Norman State', *Historical Research* 63, 1989, 132 both suggest that the pattern of land-holding was more complex in England than Normandy.

[61] *PR 31 HI*, 114; see also William de Hotot's claim, *PR 31 HI*, 88.

personal obligations, the attitude of the honorial court, the force of custom and the relative strength of the various parties who might be drawn into the situation: they also had to consider the possible involvement of the king.

Thereafter, longer-term trends may have continued to shift the balance of power towards the claimant. To take one example, social change may have furthered the move towards inheritance by weakening seignorial control. At the time of Domesday, subinfeudation was limited. Many lords may have relied heavily on household knights to perform their military service. Such knights could help a lord enforce his will within the honour, especially since they might desire the reward of the land denied to an aspiring heir. The claimant to an ancestor's life-tenement thus faced many potential rivals.

Some historians have suggested that the meaning of the word *miles* changed during the late eleventh and twelfth centuries, being applied to men of greater status.[62] This could suggest the growth of a rank of men whom lords could not easily control. Moreover, the troubles of Stephen's reign may have accelerated such change. The treaties between the magnates during the last years of the reign had the reassertion of control over lesser men as one of their concerns.[63] Henry II may well have come to the throne at a time when men were particularly unwilling to take the decision of the honour as final. With the reassertion of peace, the disgruntled claimant could no longer fight, but he might turn to the king against his lord.

The *Cartae Baronum* of 1166 reveal enfeoffment at a stage of development far beyond that of 1086. Occasionally lords had tenants considerably more powerful than themselves.[64] Other lords had enfeoffed a large proportion of their lands to one vassal.[65] The *Cartae* repeatedly record lords, many ecclesiastical but some lay, who were unable to enforce their will on their tenants.[66] Moreover, the *Cartae* illuminate only the relations of king, tenant-in-chief and vassal. Subinfeudation would have had similar effects lower down the social scale. Such lords, incapable of bringing their tenants to justice, would surely have faced problems when a powerful claimant refused to leave his ancestor's life-tenement. Again the reaction might be to turn to the king for help, and indeed many of the *Cartae* read like pleas for aid.[67] Thus we see that seignorial authority must not be

---

[62] See S. Harvey, 'The Knight and the Knight's Fee in England', *Past and Present* 49, 1970, 3–43; R. A. Brown, 'The Status of the Norman Knight', in *War and Government in the Middle Ages*, edd. J. Gillingham & J. C. Holt, Cambridge 1984, 18–32.

[63] H. A. Cronne, *The Reign of Stephen 1135–54: Anarchy in England*, London 1970, 179–180.

[64] Outstanding examples of powerful sub-tenants include Geoffrey de Ver, *Liber Rubeus de Scaccario*, ed. H. Hall, 3 vols, London 1896; RS vol. 99, i 217, 226, 298, 352, 355; – see 274 for his tenancy in chief. (Henceforth *Red Book*). Ralph de Chahaines, who owed four knights in all, had Walter Giffard amongst his tenants, *Red Book*, i 218. See also William de Bosco, who was not a tenant in chief, but held of many lords: *Red Book*, i 203, 217, 291, 360, 362, 395, 397; he may well have been more powerful than, for example, Geoffrey de Valognes, from whom he held one knight, *Red Book*, i 349. Also the sub-tenancies held by Philip de Kyme, Red Book, i 375, 377, 381–3, 390, 416. On enfeoffment and seignorial power, see also S. Painter, *Studies in the History of the English Feudal Barony*, Baltimore 1943, 21–30.

[65] E.g. *Red Book*, i 219, 229.

[66] See especially the problems of the Earl of Warwick, *Red Book*, i 326–7; see also e.g. *Red Book*, i 196, 228, 243, 254 for lay lords, 200, 204, 251 for ecclesiastical lords.

[67] E.g. *Red Book*, i 251, 386, 415. It is surely to such weak lords that *Glanvill* referred when he stated that lords incapable of bringing tenants to justice concerning their services were to have a writ of customs and services; *Glanvill*, ix 1, Hall, p. 105, cf. Milsom, *Legal Framework*, 33.

assumed to be sovereign, in autonomous lordships; in practice, the difficulties of lords were important in involving the king in matters of succession, and hence were important in the development of inheritance.

To conclude. I have argued that the importance which at least ecclesiastics placed on life-grants can be taken to reinforce the common view that succession was otherwise normal in Anglo-Norman England. However, the phrase 'customary succession' can give too static a view of the situation before the Angevin reforms. If regular royal enforcement was required to bring inheritance according to strict rules into existence, in the century after 1066 various forces were already working in the same direction. I have suggested that life-grants indicate a degree of abstract thinking about land-holding, and that this affected laymen as well as ecclesiastics. There are signs that Henry I was frequently involved in disputes over succession, for example concerning life-grants, at least in church honours. On occasion, lords regulated their actions because of potential royal action. These arguments combine to suggest that considerable progress towards strictly-defined inheritance had been made by 1135.

We have also seen that the Pope became involved in the Over case during Stephen's reign, perhaps to fill the vacuum left by a weak king. Henry II did become involved in the dispute, but only in 1187. Even then the agreement made in his court did not prove decisive, and the litigation continued for another half century. This warns against equating the Angevin reforms with the complete and effective assertion of royal sovereign authority. As we discover more about the practice, as opposed to the aspirations, of royal justice under Henry II, we may again find the differences between his own and his grandfather's reign less dramatic than such phrases as 'the Angevin leap forward' would suggest.

The Idea of the Perfect Princess:
The *Life of St Margaret* in the Reign of Matilda II (1100–1118)*

Lois L. Huneycutt

Derek Baker's 1978 article, 'A Nursery of Saints: St Margaret of Scotland Revisited', provided a laudable recasting of the role of Queen Margaret (reigned 1070–1093) within the Scottish court and in the reform of the Scottish church.[1] But in the course of his argument, Baker opened up technical questions about the principal source concerning Margaret, the longer version of the *Life of St Margaret*. Specifically, Baker questioned whether the shorter version of the *Life*, which had until then been assumed to be an abridgement of the longer, might not be an independent earlier text. Pointing to what appear to be anachronisms and inconsistencies within the longer version, which has usually been dated between 1104 and 1107, Baker posited that this version might be an expansion from the earlier shorter *Life*, an expansion that ought in its present form to be tied to the canonization proceedings of c.1250.[2] But, because the evidence from the manuscripts themselves argues against Baker's hypothesis, what began as a plausible explanation for the many problems that surround the *Life* has only added to the already confused state of the scholarship surrounding the date, authorship, audience, and textual history of the *vita*.[3] My purpose here is to analyze the form and content of both versions of the *Life*. By comparing the contents of the text to other works written for Matilda, I will argue that the contents of the longer version tie it firmly to the reign of Margaret's daughter, Matilda II, queen to Henry I of England. I will also discuss the relationship of the available versions of the *Life*.

* I would like to thank Professors C. Warren Hollister, Jeffrey B. Russell, and especially Sharon A. Farmer (along with members of her graduate research seminar) of the University of California, Santa Barbara, for their assistance while this paper was being written. I would also like to thank the Department of History and the Graduate Division of the University for their financial assistance toward the preparation and presentation of this paper.

[1] In Derek Baker, ed., *Medieval Women*, Oxford 1978, 119–41.

[2] For the history of the cult and canonization of Margaret, see *Acta sanctorum*, Brussells 1643– , June 10, David Hugh Farmer, ed., *Oxford Dictionary of Saints*, Second edition, Oxford 1987, 283–4, and *Bibliotheca sanctorum*, 13 vols, Rome 1961–70, 8: 782–6.

[3] I will not resolve the problem of authorship here. Suffice it to say that the attribution to Turgot, the prior of Durham, is problematic and has been accepted only for lack of a better candidate. See Antonia Gransden, *Historical Writing in England c.550–c.1307*, 2 vols, London 1974–82, 1: 116, note 71. The earliest attribution to Turgot is in John of Fordun's fourteenth-century *Chronica gentis Scottorum*, ed. W. Skene, 2 vols, Edinburgh 1871–2. The manuscript of the longer version of the *vita* gives the name of the author only as 'T'.

There are two extant medieval manuscripts of the *Life*, one each of the long and short versions. The long version is found in British Library Cotton Tiberius Diii, a collection of saint's lives in a deluxe edition with colored initials. The manuscript has been variously dated from the last quarter of the twelfth century to the middle of the thirteenth, but the *incipit* of the *Life of St Margaret*, which mentions her translation, would seem to place the manuscript to the middle of the thirteenth century or later.[4] The manuscript of the shorter version of the *Life of St Margaret* is also at the British Library in Cotton Tiberius Ei. The shorter version consists of four folio pages and includes a table of Margaret's ancestry and her descendants at the foot of the final page. The genealogical table, which incorporates information about Margaret's ancestry from the text of the longer version, extends into the fourteenth century.[5] The final paragraph of the shorter *vita* contains an extract from Ailred of Rievaulx's *Genealogia rerum anglorum*, written 1153–4, which narrates an incident that took place at Henry I's Easter Court of 1105. Carl Horstman demonstrated that this manuscript, a collection of lives of British saints, was produced at St Alban's before 1396. The collection, which includes one hundred and fifty-six highly abbreviated lives, was compiled by John of Tynemouth in the first quarter of the fourteenth century. Horstmann indicated that John, a 'faithful recorder' rather than an original author, must have 'traversed all England' in search of materials for his collection, gathering information from earlier *vitae* as well as from the writings of Bede, William of Malmesbury, and Matthew Paris.[6]

John's manuscript was first printed in 1516 by Wynkyn de Worde, who added fifteen new lives to the collection he published under the title *Nova legenda angliae*. Surius used the *Life of St Margaret* from this collection as the basis for his own significantly revised version of the *Life*, which appeared in 1618. Baker, who had seen neither of the manuscripts, assumed that the *Life* as it appeared in Surius and in a nineteenth-century reprinting in Pinkerton's *Vitae antiquae sanctorum* was a reprinting, rather than a reworking, of the *Vita Margaretae* as it was written by John of Tynemouth. What Baker could not have known is that the John of Tynemouth manuscript and the Surius edition differ stylistically in many places, and where they do differ, the manuscript version is invariably closer to the longer version than is the Surius text. Thus, arguments concerning wording or style based on the printed text alone are invalid. I have appended a paragraph of the *Life* as it appears in each of the three versions in order to show typical changes between the long and short manuscripts and also Surius' changes from the shorter version as abbreviated by John of Tynemouth. Since the only known manuscript of the shorter version is in John's collection of highly abbreviated lives, there is little reason to assume that the *Vita Margaretae* represents an exception to John's pattern of collecting and excerpting from original sources.

---

[4] Hogsdon Hinde describe the manuscript as a 'folio volume on vellum, in double columns, of the latter part of the twelfth century', in Hinde, ed., *Symeonis Dunelmensis opera et collectanea I*, London 1868, lviii. The thirteenth-century provenance comes from William Levison, '*Conspectus codicum hagiographicorum*', in '*Passiones vitaeque sanctorum aevi Merovingici cum supplemento et appendice*' *MGH* 7, 600, entry number 283. Unless otherwise noted, I have accepted the punctuation of the *vita* as it appears in Papebroch's edition for *Acta sanctorum*.

[5] When quoting from the short version, I have adopted the punctuation of Surius as it appears in Pinkerton's *Vitae antiquae sanctorum qui habitaverunt in ea parte Britannia nunc vocata Scotia vel in ejus insulis*, London 1789, 303–70.

[6] See C. Horstmann, *Nova legenda angliae*, 2 vols, Oxford 1901, 1: lxi–lxiii.

Baker's primary objections to the traditional dating of the *Vita* were based on the contents rather than the style of the work. He proposed that the shorter text more accurately reflects the conditions of the late eleventh or early twelfth centuries than does the fuller version. He pointed out that the genealogical section in the long version stresses Margaret's relationship to Edward the Confessor, and Baker follows Frank Barlow in dating the cult of Edward to the 1130s and beyond.[7] He also argued that the writer's condescending attitude toward the unsophisticated Scottish court suggested a later date than the beginning of the twelfth century: 'there is no clear interface between the [long version] of the *Life* and reality, and it is from this mismatch, and the attempts to reconcile it, that problems arise.'[8] Baker then attempted to resolve some of these problems by speculating that the short version, which lacks the references to the Confessor and the problematic details of court life, was written in the period just after Margaret's death in 1093, and that the longer version, possibly begun as early as 1104, went through a succession of editorial additions before reaching the thirteenth-century form in which it now exists. He pointed to two passages that might bear out this possibility. The traditional dating for the *Life* is based on a passing reference to the uncorrupt body of St Cuthbert, whose tomb was opened in 1104. The *terminus ante quem* is the 1107 death of Edgar, King of Scotland, to whom the longer text refers as the 'son who now at present yet holds the kingdom after his father.'[9] The shorter version omits the reference to St Cuthbert and refers to Edgar as Margaret's son rather than as a reigning king. Thus, as Baker wrote,

> On this evidence it could be argued that the *Life* in its shorter version represents a text composed much earlier than usually assumed, after Margaret's death 16 November 1093 and before the summer of 1095 when Edgar was, probably, invested as king. Such a hypothesis, associated with a text which removes many of the difficulties of the longer version, is worth considering.[10]

In referring to the problems that arise when trying to match the *Life* to known historical events, Baker was responding to idiosyncracies in the text that have long exasperated historians, an exasperation perhaps most eloquently expressed by R. L. G. Ritchie: [the author's] 'mental vagueness, further dimmed by his rhetorical, perhaps meaningless Latin, reduces Scottish historians to despair. Despair, however, takes on different forms, ranging from tears to mirthless ribaldry or a dull, implacable resentment against author and subject alike – a strange fate to have befallen so good a man and so great a queen.'[11] And, while G. W. S. Barrow attributes the 'indifference to topographical detail and proper nouns of every sort' to the genre of early-medieval hagiography, Ritchie is more

---

[7] Baker, 121–2. See Barlow, *Vita Aedwardi*, 112–33, and Barlow, *Edward the Confessor*, Berkeley 1970, 14–23, 256–85.

[8] Baker, 129.

[9] 'Interea filus eius, qui post patrem regni gubernacula jam nunc in praesenti tenet.' Ailred of Rievaulx's account is evidently the first to supply Edgar's name. See Ailred, '*Genealogia regum anglorum*', J. P. Migne, ed. *Patrologia cursus completus, series latina*, 221 vols, 195: 711–38.

[10] Baker, 131.

[11] Ritchie, *The Normans in Scotland*, Edinburgh 1953, 397–8.

perspicacious as he tries to place the *vita* into a recognised literary genre: [the author] 'chose Hagiography and allowed himself an occasional excursus into Court Biography. . . . In Court Biography his error is literary; he leaves out nearly all the background and thus impinges on another genre, the Character Sketch, in which his error is to leave out the defects of his heroine's great qualities.'[12] Baker's speculative redating does appear to account neatly for some of the more bothersome aspects of the longer version of the *Life*, and on the surface his arguments are quite sound. Unfortunately, after the manuscript evidence is considered, Baker's hypothesis becomes less plausible, and the whole question of the dating and purpose of the *vita* must be reopened.

Neither the passage concerning Edgar nor the omission of the reference to the tomb of St Cuthbert provides convincing evidence for the priority of the shorter version. The reference in the shorter text to Edgar as Margaret's son, rather than as reigning king, would be the logical terminology for someone writing either before or after Edgar's reign. The passage about St Cuthbert occurs in a paragraph which is entirely omitted from the short version, a passage in which the author explains how he came to know the events that transpired at Margaret's deathbed. Although Baker is correct in pointing out the inconsistencies and problems in the longer version, the shorter version also contains inaccuracies and puzzling passages. For instance, it places Margaret's death 'quarto Idus Junii', which is the day of her translation in 1250 and not of her death in 1093. It contains a genealogy which places Margaret's natal family in Hungary at the court of King Solomon rather than King Stephen.

The most fundamental objection to Baker's proposed redating is that removing the longer version of the *Life* from the patronage of Queen Matilda renders many aspects of the text incomprehensible. The content of the longer version differs from that of the shorter in three main ways. First, the author refers to himself in the first person in the longer version, while the shorter text refers to the author in the third person. Second, the long version contains many non-hagiographic elements, such as descriptions of court life that do not appear in the shorter. The longer version also displays an ambiguous attitude to miracles concerning Margaret, an ambiguity that seems out of keeping with the hagiographical genre. The third textual difference is that the long version contains an extended section containing prologue, dedication and genealogy that is entirely missing from the shorter version. Analysis of these three categories indicates that the longer text does indeed belong to the reign of Matilda II.

I will begin with the first major difference, the author's reference to himself in the first person in the longer version as well as his narration of several conversations and incidents at court in which he played a part. He opens by reminding Matilda that she had entrusted the task of writing the *Life* to him because she had heard that 'I was privy to a great part of her [Margaret's] secrets'.[13] Later, he refers to himself as a former sacristan of the church of St Andrew.[14]

[12] Barrow, *The Kingdom of the Scots: Government, Church and Society from the Eleventh to the Fourteenth Century*, London 1973; and Ritchie, 398.

[13] 'Scilicet mihi praecipue in hoc credendum dicebatis, quem gratia magnae apud illam familiaritatis, magna ex parte secretorum illius conscium esse audieratis.'

[14] After a description of Margaret's foundation of the church of St Andrew and the precious liturgical objects it contained, the author writes 'quae tanto certius nosse poteram, quanto cuncta jubente regina ego ipse diutius ibidem servanda.'

The shorter version retains his description of the sacred objects Margaret gave to the church, while omitting the author's self-reference. The author inserts another personal note when he discusses Margaret's influence on Malcolm's religious practices, confessing that he considered Malcolm's exertion and compunction during prayer to be an occasion for marvelling at the 'great miracle of God's compassion' inasmuch as Malcolm was only a 'secular man'.[15] The author also notes that Margaret relied on him to watch over her and reprove her in secret whenever she had done anything wrong.[16] The short version, characteristically, puts the passage in the third person, 'for she used repeatedly to ask her Confessor, that whatever in her in word or deed he perceived worthy of reprimand, he should not hesitate to indicate it to her with a reprimand in secret.'[17] The same kind of change occurs repeatedly in the text. In the longer version, the author tells us that he came to know Margaret's outer self and inner conscience because she revealed herself to him, 'not because there was anything good in me, but because she used to think that there was.'[18] The short version omits that sentence, and opens the section with Margaret speaking to her 'confessor' about the welfare of her soul and the sweetness of eternal life.[19]

The author of the longer version becomes intensely involved in telling the story of Margaret's death, which takes the final seven paragraphs of the longer version, but the narrative is significantly condensed in the shorter text. There are two narrators in the longer version: the author, who leaves the action after a touching farewell, and a priest whom Margaret loved especially, and who later joined the author at the monastery at Durham where they frequently discussed the queen's final days. The shorter text does not mention the priest at all, and begins the story in the third person, even supplying the name of the presumed author: 'At length, having called her confessor, Turgot, afterwards prior of Durham, she began to relate her life.'[20] One more example of the personal detail included in the longer version will suffice, an example that contains a delightful illustration of the relationship between the king, the queen, and the author of the *Life*. Describing the queen's habit of pilfering coins, for charitable purposes, from the king's treasury, the author writes: 'And often, the king himself, although he knew, would pretend not to know. He greatly loved this sort of trick. Sometimes, seizing her hand with the coins, he used to joke that she was accused in court, leading her to me for justice.'[21] Like all other references to the author, this anecdote is omitted from the shorter text. It is difficult to see how these passages, which add to the charm and coherence of the longer version, could have been additions by another author, or

---

[15] 'Fateor, magnum misericordiae Dei mirabar miraculum, cum viderem interdum tantam orandi regis intentionem, tantam inter orandum in pectore viri saecularis compunctionem.'
[16] 'Unde crebro me rogabat, ut quidquid in ejus vel verbo, vel facto reprehendendum perviderem, id reprehens secreto illi indicare non dubitarem.'
[17] 'Crebro igitur Confessarium suum rogabat, ut quicquid in eius verbo vel facto reprehendendum cognosceret, id reprehens secreto illi non dubitaret.'
[18] 'Non quia bonum aliquid in me erat, sed quia inesse putaverat.'
[19] 'Quando enim illa de salute animae confessario suo, et de perhennis dulcitudine vitae. . . .'
[20] 'Vocato demum confessore suo Turgot, secundum priorem Dunelmiae, vita sua replicare coepit.'
[21] 'Et saepe quidem cum Rex ipse sciret, nescire tamen se simulans, hujusmodi furto plurimum delectabatur; nonnumquam vero manu illius cum nummis comprehensa, adductam, meo judicio, ream esse jocabatur.'

even why, if we assume a common author for both versions of the *Life*, these passages would not have been put into the first draft shortly after Margaret's death, when the author's memory would have been fresher. It is even more difficult to imagine why it would have been necessary for a thirteenth-century revisor to invent a first-person identity.

The second major difference between the long and short versions of the *Life* is that the longer includes many non-hagiographic elements such as personal anecdotes and details of court life – the detail that Ritchie called 'Court Biography'. An example of this kind of detail is the description of the artistic workshop that operated in Margaret's chambers. The short version does not mention any of the Queen's ladies, nor does it include the section describing the exemplary behavior of Margaret's children during mass – or even the extraordinary claim that the eight children never fought among themselves! Other references to the court servants and the relationship between the king and the queen are also omitted from the shorter version. The long version includes a passage referring to Margaret's habit of accepting 'gifts' from her retainers which she then distributed to the poor. The claim that Margaret civilised the barbaric Scottish court, effectively refuted by Baker, is downplayed in the shorter version. There is no mention of Margaret bringing in foreign merchants nor of her 'making the splendor of the royal palace more splendid for the king'. There is also no mention of her 'compelling the natives' of Scotland to wear more brightly colored clothing. All reference to her redecoration of the palace is omitted.

All of these omissions, which figure prominently in the longer version, combine to indicate that the longer version of the *Life* was indeed written for Matilda. She would have no doubt been interested in the anecdotal details about her mother's life at court and in the stories of her parents daily activities, and it is not easy to see how adding these descriptions of court life at a later date would have furthered a case for Margaret's sanctity.

The attitude of the author of the longer version about the one miracle in the *Life*, the rescue of Margaret's cherished Gospel Book after it had fallen into a river, also argues against a primarily hagiographic intent and certainly does nothing to suggest a growing cult around the queen. He is almost apologetic about the inclusion of this wonder, pointing out that miraculous signs are common to the good and the evil, but that pious works are exclusive to the good. He stresses that it is good behavior that can be imitated:

> Let us, I say, more worthily admire in Margaret deeds, which effected her sanctity, rather than portents, if she had done any, which showed such great sanctity to men. Let us more worthily admire in her, through whose zeal for justice, piety, compassion and charity we contemplate the deeds rather than the wonders of the ancient fathers.[22]

Nevertheless, he does include the Gospel Book story, and comparing his story and that in the short version to the independent text of a poem written in the flyleaf of the Gospel Book itself helps establish the relationship between the long and short

---

[22] 'Dignius, inquam miremur in Margareta facta, quae illam sanctam faciebant, quam signa, si aliqua fecisset, quae hominibus sanctam tantum ostenderent. Dignius illam obstupescamus in qua per justiciae, pietatis, misericordiae et caritatis studia, antiquorum Patrum facta magis quam signa consideramus.'

versions of the *Life*.[23] Although the miracle only occupies three lines in the short version, there are telling changes in the wording. According to John of Tynemouth's text, the book, having fallen into the water, remained inviolate for a day and a night, while the longer version only states that it was sought for a long time (*diu*) and recovered at length (*tandem*). The poem, which seems to have been written in Margaret's lifetime, relates only that the book was recovered 'post multa momenta'. If the longer version of the *Life of St Margaret* is to be associated with the thirteenth-century canonization proceedings, it seems strange that the writer chose to be less specific than the earlier writer about the time that the book spent under water. It is more likely the case that the miracle grew more miraculous over time, with 'many moments' turning into 'a long time' and finally becoming 'a day and a night'. The final difference between the long and the short versions provides the most compelling evidence for placing the *Life* in the reign of Matilda II. In the first paragraph of the five paragraph prologue and introduction, which is entirely missing from the short version, the author clearly identifies his purpose in composing the text:

> To Matilda, queen of the English. . . . You have requested that I should offer to you in writing an account of the way of life pleasing to God of your mother of blessed memory, which manner of living you have rather often heard lauded with the suitable praise of many people. . . . so that even though you little knew the outward appearance of your mother, you might have a full account of her virtues.[24]

Later, toward the end of the *Life*, the author shows that he considered himself to be a teacher to Matilda by repeating Margaret's last request to him: 'Be the caretaker of my sons and daughters. You shall teach them to fear and to love God, and you shall never cease from teaching them, and whenever you see whomever of them to be elevated to the summit of earthly dignity, you shall approach that one especially as a father and a teacher.'[25] He congratulated Matilda the queen for wanting not only to hear, but also to inspect continually in 'written down letters' (*impressam litteram*) the life of her mother the queen. The author's reluctance to discuss Margaret's miracle, and his stress on imitation of behavior rather than on divine intervention is explicable if he were indeed providing a didactic 'mirror for queens' rather than a hagiographic account. It is here that we need to consider the *vita* within the context of what is known about Matilda's reign, especially her ecclesiastical and literary patronage, for this may provide a key to understanding the purpose of the longer version of the *Life*.

---

[23] The book itself is now in the Bodleian library, Oxford, MS Latin liturgical f5. The poem appears on one of the introductory leaves. For a discussion of the dating, see the introduction to the facsimile edition, W. Forbes-Leith ed., *The Gospel Book of St Margaret: Being a Facsimile Reproduction of St Margaret's Copy of the Gospels Preserved in the Bodleian Library, Oxford*, Edinburgh 1896.

[24] 'Reginae Anglorum Mathildi. . . . Venerandae memoriae matris vestrae placitam Deo conversationem, quam consona multorum laude saepius praedicari audieratis, ut litteris traditam vobis offerrem, et postulando jussistis et jubendo postulastis. . . . ut quae faciem matris parum noveratis, virtutum ejus notitiam plenius habeatis.' Of course, many hagiographical prologues express a similar didactic intent in that the saint is to be an example to other Christians. See Michael Goodich, 'A Note on Sainthood in the Hagiographical Prologue', *History and Theory* 20, 1981, 168–74.

[25] 'Ut filiorum meorum ac filiarum curam habeas, amorem impendas, praecipue. Deum timere et amare doceas, at ab eis docendis numquam desistas: et cum in culmen terrenae dignitatis quemlibet ex eis exaltari videris, illius maxime pater et magister accedas.'

Even the historians who have deplored the lack of historicity in the *Life* have praised its literary qualities. Ritchie praised it as 'touching, in some ways beautiful', and David Knowles referred to it as 'simple but eloquent'.[26] Even Baker conceded that it is 'attractive' hagiography, while pointing out that it is not satisfactory in its portrayal of an active Scottish queen.[27] Ritchie concluded that the work 'unhappily defeats its own purpose' because 'clouds of incense obscure the central figure and leave King Malcolm and all others in a perhaps unmerited shade.'[28] These authors have raised crucial points. The long version of the *Life* is too worldly and personal to be pure hagiography, too muddled in detail to serve as a satisfactory biography. As others have pointed out, it does not even mention one of Margaret's most significant and far-reaching acts, her procurement of Canterbury monks from Lanfranc to colonise her new foundation at Dunfermline.[29] This work is clearly not intended to narrate, in strict detail, the life of a queen. Therefore, I would assert that it is best to take the author at his word and interpret the *vita* as a teaching text, a tool to present an image or a model to guide and serve as an *exemplum* for Matilda.

Caroline Bynum's 1980 article 'Did the Twelfth Century Discover the Individual?' provides a context for this interpretation of the text, an interpretation that accounts for most of the problems inherent in the longer version without relying on an improbable redating of the the text to the thirteenth century. Using religious groups, Bynum argued for a rethinking of the tendency to see the twelfth century as the age of the individual. She saw another new and important interest in the twelfth century, the interest in belonging to groups and filling roles. Authors of this period reflect 'an increasing sense both of choosing a specific role different from other roles, and of the necessity for that role to complement others and be of use to the whole.' And finally, Bynum stressed the importance of role models for this new mentality. Members of religious groups saw themselves both as following earlier models and as being models for others, teaching by word and by example.[30] I have elsewhere presented the case that the saint's lives, letters, coronation *ordines* and literary works written for queens and noble women during the period between c.1100–1150 show an increasing awareness in the secular realm of an abstract ideal of behaviour to be imitated.[31] Ecclesiastical writers both exalted and attempted to mold this image, at the same time sounding warnings lest the women who filled the office of queenship become inflated with pride or caught up in the splendor of the world.

The *Life of St Margaret* provides a model for Matilda to follow. The apparent problems concerning the longer version of the *Life* are resolved when we realise that it was intended neither as standard hagiography, straight biography, nor as a court history. Rather, as the text itself says, it was written as a didactic tool for

---

[26] Ritchie, 399, and Knowles, *The Monastic Order in England 943–1216*, second edition, Cambridge 1963, 170.

[27] Baker, 129.

[28] Ritchie, 399.

[29] See *Lanfranc's Letters*, 160.

[30] The essay, which first appeared in 1980, has been revised and reprinted in Bynum, *Jesus as Mother: Studies in the Spirituality of the High Middle Ages*, Berkeley 1982, 82–109.

[31] Lois L. Huneycutt, 'Images of High-Medieval Queenship', *The Haskins Society Journal: Studies in Medieval History* 1, 1989, 61–71.

Matilda, to instill in her an ideal of queenly behaviour, and to provide a pattern which she could follow in her daily activities. Matilda understood the message, even if modern historians have not. Matilda's conscious patterning of herself after the ideals presented in the *Life* helped her to become the 'good Queen Maud' of later legend.

In order to argue that Matilda did conform herself to an ideal represented in the *vita*, I will consider how the author presented Margaret's behaviour, and then discuss parallel incidents in the life of her daughter. Because Matilda (born c.1080) had been sent as a young child to the abbey of Romsey, to be educated by Margaret's sister, Christina, she would have had very little direct memory of her mother. She had remained in the convent, first at Romsey and later at Wilton, until the summer of 1093, when she was hastily removed by Malcolm, who objected to Christina's practice of dressing this valuable marriage-pawn in a nun's habit.[32] Matilda could have been taken back to Scotland for a short time between the late summer of 1093 and her parents death in November of that year, but this is only conjecture. The fact remains that the influence that Margaret had over Matilda was much more indirect than direct. When Matilda's actions are reviewed in comparison with the portrait of the 'perfect princess' in the *vita*, it seems apparent that this *vita* was an important conduit in shaping Matilda's image of the mother she had scarcely known. When Matilda acceded to the throne in 1100, England had been without a queen since the 1083 death of Matilda of Flanders, and the first Matilda had spent much of her reign in Normandy. There was no recent role-model for Matilda II, and it is logical that she would seek whatever advice she could on how to behave in her new position. The summary at the end of the sixth paragraph of the long version of the *vita* introduces the 'perfect princess' and her role in the court: 'All things which were fitting were carried out by order of the prudent queen; by her counsel the laws of the kingdom were put in order, divine religion was augmented by her industry, the people rejoiced in the prosperity of affairs.'[33]

There is no evidence that Margaret played an unusually active political role in Malcolm's kingdom, and the author is vague about her part in 'ordering the laws of the kingdom'. He depicts her regulating her people with guidance, busy among the 'tumult of lawsuits and the many-sided cares of the kingdom'.[34] She had enough of a household that she could send her servants to find which English captives were being treated more harshly than others so that she could pay their ransom. According to the *Life*, Margaret's primary political role was in church reform, and the author mentions the *crebra consilia* over which she presided, going to great detail in one case when Margaret is shown presiding over the passage of legislation concerning the Lenten fast, the annual Easter eucharist, the observance of the Sabbath, marriage practices, and the liturgy for the mass. Ritchie doubted whether these councils ever existed outside the mind of the author of the *vita*:

[32] See Eadmer, 121–6. For modern discussions of the events leading to Matilda's marriage to Henry, see Eleanor Searle, 'Women and the legitimisation of succession at the Norman Conquest', *ante* 3, 1980, 159–70, Richard W. Southern, *St Anselm and his Biographer: A Study of Monastic Life and Thought, 1059–c.1130*, Cambridge 1963, 188–90, and most recently, Sally N. Vaughn, *Anselm of Bec and Robert of Meulan: The Innocence of the Dove and the Wisdom of the Serpent*, Berkeley 1987, 276–9.
[33] 'Omnia quae decebant prudentis Reginae imperio agebantur: ejus consilio regni jura disponebantur, illius industria religio divina augebatur, rerum prosperitate populus laetabatur.'
[34] 'Inter causarum tumultus, inter multiplices regni curas.'

'Turgot seems to represent Margaret presiding over a church council, which would have been unprecedented in all Christendom, and must be dismissed as well-intended hyperbole'. He attributed this 'hyperbole' to the fact that the author was writing for Matilda, who was accustomed to sitting in on Henry's *curia regis*.[35] Perhaps Ritchie was premature in dismissing Margaret's role in the council. Matilda may have been following her mother's lead when she insisted on speaking in her own behalf at the council Anselm called to determine her eligibility for marriage in 1100.[36] Whatever the case with Margaret, the active role seemed natural to Matilda, who not only participated in Henry's council, but also chaired it in his absence.[37] The *vita*'s didactic message concerning the queen's duty to regulate and influence the laws of the kingdom is reflected in three other pieces of literature known to have been written for Matilda. An anonymous poem claims that Matilda persuaded Henry to pass better laws in England. Henry, referred to as 'Caesar', listened to the pleading of his queen and answered her petition by changing England's unjust laws.[38] Hildebert of Lavardin, the bishop of Le Mans, wrote to Matilda to praise her observance and upholding of the law.[39] Finally, the monk Benedeit, author of the *Anglo-Norman Voyage of St Brendan*, praised Matilda as the queen who helped to maintain peace in the kingdom.[40] The cumulative effect of this literature shows that Matilda, like her mother, was perceived as a peacemaker and as influencing the course of the kingdom. The author of the *Life of St Margaret* may have exaggerated Margaret's role in Malcolm's court in order to encourage Matilda in a more positive direction.

Margaret and Matilda could both claim to have 'augmented divine religion' in their respective kingdoms. The *Life* reports that Margaret immediately built a

[35] Ritchie, 397 and note five.

[36] Eadmer, 121–6.

[37] Francis West argues that Matilda's actions in the exchequer session of 1111 constitute the first example of a justiciar 'treating the administrative structure as the king would'. See West, *The Justiciarship in England*, Cambridge 1966, 14. For a contemporary designation of Matilda as 'vice-regent', see *Chronicon monasterii de Abingdon*, 2 vols, London 1858, 2: 97, 104.

[38] 'Vere consiliis excelebrata dei/ Quae simul Augusto legali foedere nupsit/ 'Lex injustiae rex bone cesset' ait/ Exaucivit eam Caesar, depressit iniquas/ leges suscepit publica cura bonas/ Fortunato viro mulier, vir coniuge felix/ Longaevus femma vivat uterque sua.' See André Boutemy, 'Notice sur le recueil poétique du manuscrit Cotton Vitellius A xii du British Museum', *Latomus* 1, 1937, 305. I am grateful to Dr Elisabeth van Houts for this reference and for discussing with me the usefulness of poetry as a historical source. See van Houts, 'Latin Poetry and the Anglo-Norman Court: the *Carmen de Hastingae proelio*', *Journal of Medieval History* 15, 1989, 39–62. Dr van Houts, who is preparing an edition of Robert of Torigni's *Gesta normannorum ducum*, which was written in the first third of the twelfth century, pointed out at the conference that Robert's chronicle makes reference to a life of Margaret or Matilda containing a genealogy that makes Matilda's relationship to the Anglo-Saxon kings clear. If the text to which Robert is referring is the *Vita Margaretae*, it can only be the long version, for this section is not included in the short version. See Dr Van Hout's forthcoming edition for Oxford Medieval Texts.

[39] *Patrologia latina* 171: 290.

[40] E. G. Waters, ed., *The Anglo-Norman Voyage of St Brendan by Benedeit*, Oxford 1928, xxiii–xxvi, 3. 'Par qui valdrat lei divine/ Par qui creistrat lei de terre/ E remandrat tante guerre/ Por les armes Henri lu rei/ Par le cunseil qui ert en tei.' The manuscripts of this poem vary in the dedication between Matilda and Henry's second queen, Adeliza of Louvain. Of the five manuscripts, four refer to Adeliza, but the oldest and most reliable attributes the poem to Matilda's patronage. After some hesitation, Waters pronounced in favour of Adeliza, but see R. L. G. Ritchie, 'The Date of the "Voyage of St Brendan" ', *Medium aevum* 14, 1960, 64–6 for a convincing argument placing the composition of the poem to Matilda's reign, and M. D. Legge, 'Letre' in Old French', *The Modern Language Review* 55, 1961, 333–4 for further arguments in favour of Matilda's patronage.

church in the place she had been married to Malcolm, even though that marriage supposedly had taken place by the urging of her family rather than by her own will. Margaret operated a kind of workshop within her quarters of the palace where her ladies worked at embroidering sacred vestments. Margaret's role as a mother is always uppermost in the author's mind, whether he is showing her teaching her husband and children *ejus hortatu et exemplo*, or in a more public sense as a maternal image for the kingdom at large.[41] Margaret fed little orphans with the spoons she herself used, so that 'the queen, who was honored by all the people, might on behalf of Christ fill the office of servant and most pious mother'.[42] The author emphasises her nurturing image: 'When she was proceeding or riding in public, crowds of widows and wretched orphans flocked toward the pious mother'.[43] Margaret took a special interest in paupers and pilgrims, setting up a hostel and providing a ferry service for pilgrims coming to St Andrews. The author concludes his praise with a comment on her generous spirit: 'Not only her things, but also her very self, if it were permitted, she would freely weigh out to the poor.'[44] Margaret is also praised for her close relationship with the Scottish hermits, who sometimes seem to have directed or been responsible for her charitable impulses.

Except for Margaret's unique role in presiding over church councils, Matilda's relationship to the church and churchmen in England was similar to her mother's in Scotland. With help and advice from Anselm, Matilda founded Holy Trinity Aldgate, one of the first houses of Augustinian canons in England.[45] She also gave numerous gifts to existing churches, and the language of some of Henry's donation charters indicate that his gifts were sometimes given at the suggestion of his queen.[46] Besides influencing Henry, Matilda took part in her son's religious training.[47] As with Margaret, Matilda was seen as a mother figure for the realm at large. The elderly Bishop Herbert of Norwich invoked this image when writing to Roger of Salisbury about a financial matter, claiming that 'out of her kindness, the queen has been a very mother to me'.[48] Anselm once reprimanded her for abuse of her ecclesiastical tenants by suggesting that she ought to be seen as a mother, a nurse, a kind mistress and a queen to the churches placed under her

---

[41] For the use of this phrase and the significance of teaching by both word and example among twelfth-century Cistercians, see Caroline Bynum, *Docere verbo et exemplo: An Aspect of Twelfth-Century Spirituality*, Missoula, 1978.

[42] 'Ita regina, quae ab omnibus populis honorabatur, pro Christi et ministrae et matris piissimae officio fungebatur.'

[43] 'Cum in publicum procederet vel equitaret, miserorum orphanorum, viduarum greges quasi ad matrem piisimam confluxerunt, quorum nulli ab ea sine consolatione abscesserunt.'

[44] 'Non solum sua, sed etiam seipsam si liceret, pauperi libenter impenderet.'

[45] See *Regesta* ii, entries 897, 898, 906 and 909. Also John C. Dickinson, *The Origins of the Austin Canons and their Introduction into England*, London 1950, as well as Gerald A. J. Hodgett, ed. *The Cartulary of Holy Trinity Aldgate*, London 1971.

[46] *Regesta* ii, entries 568 and 569. For the influence of wives in general, see Sharon A. Farmer, 'Persuasive Voices: Clerical Images of Medieval Wives', *Speculum* 61, 1986, 517–43.

[47] The records of Merton priory reveal that Matilda often visited the site where the priory was being built, bringing along her young son to play on the grounds so that he might be inspired by happy childhood memories to remain a lifelong patron of the new foundation. See M. L. Colker, 'Latin Texts Concerning Gilbert, Founder of Merton Priory', *Studia monastica* 12, 1970, 241–72.

[48] 'Ex sua misericordia, mihi facta est mater.' Robert Anstruther, ed. *Epistolae Heriberti de Losinga, primi episcopi Norwicensis*, 1846, repr. New York 1969, 50–2.

care.[49] Matilda's charitable influences were often directed toward the care of lepers, and she founded a hospital in Chichester and at least one in the London area to house them.[50] Her religious teachers were bishops rather than hermits, and she is known to have corresponded with, or received spiritual counsel from, a number of them, including Gundulph of Rochester, Ivo of Chartres, Marbod of Rennes, and the bishop of Rome himself, Pope Pascal II, as well as the aforementioned Herbert Losinga, Hildebert, and Anselm.[51] While there is no evidence that Matilda maintained an artistic workshop in the manner of her mother, she did commision and send liturgical objects to several of her correspondents, including Hildebert and Ivo.[52]

Both queens set examples in their personal piety as well as in their public acts of religious devotion. Margaret's humility and devotion to the church as well as her extreme asceticism are narrated in great detail within the *Life*. This kind of intense piety seemed intrinsically foreign to Matilda, who nevertheless participated in one dramatic incident, narrated by Ailred of Rievaulx and repeated by nearly every English chronicler in the following century.[53] During Henry's Easter court of 1105, David, Matilda's younger brother, entered her quarters and found her washing and kissing the feet of lepers. David warned her that should Henry find out where her lips had been, he would never want to touch them again. The pious Matilda replied that she was looking for the kisses of the heavenly king rather than and earthly one, and she bade David follow her example. This drew laughter rather than awe from the young prince, but the incident eventually served its purpose, finding its way into hagiography in John of Tynemouth's version of the *Life of St Margaret*.

The author of the *vita*, like Hildebert of Lavardin, implies that a good queen has some influence over the economic prosperity of the realm. The *Life* praises Margaret because she furthered commerce in the Scottish kingdom by starting a rage for foreign-made goods. Late in her reign, Hildebert praised Matilda for the long peace she had brought to the 'fierce land' of England, a peace that had allowed

---

49 'Ut ecclesiae Dei, quae sunt in vestra potestate, vos cognoscant ut matrem, ut nutricem, ut benignam dominam et reginam.' Francis Schmitt, ed., *Sancti Anselmi opera omnia*, five vols, Edinburgh 1946–61, 5: 284, letter 346.
50 Matilda's London foundation was at Holborn, and she may also have been a patron of the *leprosarium* of St James at Westminster. See Edward J. Kealey, *Medieval Medicus: A Social History of Anglo-Norman Medicine*, Baltimore 1981, 89–91. Also, M. J. Honeybourne, 'The Leper Hospitals of the London area', *Proceedings of the Middlesex Archaeological Society*, 1962, 4–61.
51 For Ivo of Chartres, see *Patrologia latina* 162: 125–6, 148–9 and 177. The correspondence of Hildebert and Marbod, both containing letters to the queen, is preserved in *Patrologia latina* 171. For Hildebert's poetry, see the *Patrologia* volume as well as the edition by A. Brian Scott, *Hildebertus carmina minora*, Leipzig 1969. Paschal's letters to the queen can be found in *Patrologia latina* 163 and in Schmitt, *S. Anselmi opera omnia*. For Gundulph, see the 'Vita Gundulphi', *Patrologia latina* 159: 830, and Marylou Ruud, 'Monks in the World: The Case of Gundulph of Rochester', *ante* 11, 1989, 245–60. In addition to letters of business, Herbert wrote a prayer and letter of spiritual counsel during what may have been Matilda's final illness. See Anstruther, ed., 33–7.
52 Both wrote to thank Matilda for gifts of liturgical objects. See *Patrologia latina* 171: 160–2 (Hildebert) and 162: 125–6, 148–9 (Ivo). The bronze candlesticks that Matilda had made for Hildebert may have been similar to the one that she gave to Cluny, which later prompted one of Bernard of Clairvaux's tirades against the lavish lifestyle of the Cluniacs. See Joan Evans, *Monastic Life at Cluny, 910–1157*, Oxford 1931, repr. 1968, 123, note two.
53 Ailred, 736.

England's natural prosperity to flourish.[54] The author of the *Life*, as well as authors of other literature addressed to Matilda, stressed the queen's duty to intercede with the king on behalf of the poor and oppressed. According to the *Life*, Margaret's persuasiveness was such that Malcolm, 'who perceived Christ truly to live in her heart, dreaded to displease that queen of venerable like in any manner, but rather he used to hasten to comply with her plans.'[55] Matilda too was often successful when she interceded with her husband. She persuaded Henry to restore to Anselm some of the Canterbury revenues confiscated during his exile, and when Pascal II failed to gain Henry's cooperation over investiture, he wrote to Matilda urging her forceful intervention.[56]

The ideals presented in the *Life of St Margaret* and reinforced in the other literature written for Matilda were reflected in her behaviour. And, although this behaviour could have arisen independently of the *vita*, Matilda's clear interest in her ancestry makes it likely that she did indeed commission and read the biography, then patterned herself after the mother presented so compellingly in the *Life*. Although I would agree with Baker that the genealogy of the longer version may well have been rewritten after 1107, the stress on Edward the Confessor is not *prima facie* absurd even at the earlier date. Most contemporary chroniclers described Matilda's lineage and her relationship to Edward, a tendency that is especially prominent among the English chroniclers.[57] When a son, William, was born in 1103 to Henry and Matilda, it was duly noted that he carried the bloodlines of both the old English kings and the new line of Norman conquerors. His birth was popularly believed to be the fulfillment of a deathbed prophecy of Edward's.[58] And, although the cult of Edward was not fully-developed at the beginning of the twelfth century, the 1102 opening of his tomb shows some interest in the possibility of his sanctity.[59] Matilda certainly displayed an interest in her West Saxon roots. She commissioned William of Malmesbury's *Gesta regum* and she requested and received a genealogical table of her ancestry from the monks at Malmesbury.[60] Finally, Matilda was buried at Westminster near the tombs of Edward and his wife Edith, her namesake.[61] Although the genealogy given by the author of the long version of the *Life* does rely heavily on Margaret's relationship to the Confessor, it should not be dismissed as simple anachronism.

---

[54] Scott, ed., 24: 'Anglia terra ferax/ tibi pax diuturna quietem/ multiplicem luxum merx opulenta dedit'.

[55] 'Ipsam tam venerabilis vitae Reginam, quoniam in ejus corde Christum veraciter habitare perspexerat, ille quomodo offendere formidabat; sed potius votis ejus et prudentibus consiliis celerius per omnia obedire properabat.'

[56] 'Memento quod dicit apostulus: salvabitur vir infidelis per mulierem fidelem. . . . argue, obsecra, increpa, ut et praefacturum episcopum in sede sua recipiat.' Schmitt, ed., 5: 292, letter 352. For the Canterbury revenues, see letters 320 and 321 between Anselm and the queen.

[57] See, for example, *ASC, sub anno* 1100, noting that Matilda was the daughter of both Malcolm and Margaret, King Edward's kinswoman, and thus of the 'rightful kingly line of England'.

[58] For example, William of Malmesbury, *De gestis regum*, 2: 495–6.

[59] Baker, 122. See also Barlow, ed., *Vita Aedwardi regis*, 114–15 and Barlow, *Edward the Confessor* 265–6.

[60] See E. Könsgen, 'Zwei unbekannte Briefe zu den Wilhelm von Malmesbury', *Deutsches Archiv für Erforschung des Mittelalters* 31, 1975, 204–14, and Rodney M. Thomson, 'William of Malmesbury as Historian and Man of Letters', *Journal of Ecclesiastical History* 29, 1978, 387–413.

[61] Orderic Vitalis reports that Matilda had been baptized 'Edith', a report uncorroborated by any other source, but which fits with the naming pattern of the other children of Malcolm and Margaret. Their five elder sons bore the names of Anglo-Saxon kings. See Orderic 6: 188.

Matilda's particular interest in her mother is well-attested in other contemporary sources, especially in the Latin poetry addressed to her. Elisabeth van Houts has collected eight poems by at least three different authors that were written for Matilda or as epitaphs shortly after her death.[62] All eight of these make some reference to Margaret. One of the anonymous poems typically stresses Matilda's noble origins:

> She was the daughter of a queen, the daughter of a king.
> Therefore, this woman is the glory of England,
> The glory of the kingdom.[63]

A second poem, perhaps written as an epitaph, laid the same emphasis on her lineage, describing Matilda as 'the daughter of a king, the daughter of a queen,/ Sprung from kings on both sides'.[64] A third poem, which has been attributed to the patronage of either Matilda II or her daughter the empress, is even more explicit in its message, describing its subject as having all things of her mother, who, although enclosed in her sepulchre, continued to illuminate the English realms with her merits.[65] Given the poems which stress Matilda's bloodline and the interest she herself showed in learning more of her ancestry, it does not seem surprising that she did commission 'a memorial of the mother she had scarcely known'.[66] Baker, arguing for the priority of the shorter version, suggested that if indeed Matilda was the patron of the *Life*, she would probably have not waited until 1104, fourteen years after her mother's death, to commision the work. That she evidently did so is probably related to the state of poverty in which she found herself immediately following the 1093 death of her parents. Because of the political upheaval in Scotland after Malcolm was killed, Matilda's siblings had fled to England, where they, along with Matilda, lived as refugees at the court of William Rufus.[67] Only after her marriage to Henry could Matilda afford to commission literary works and offer support to poets and musicians. Both versions of the *vita* refer to the author's special charge of watching over any of Margaret's sons or daughters who happened to 'reach the summit of earthly dignity', an inclusion which would have been a cruel irony anytime before Edgar's accession to the Scottish throne in 1095, but seems especially apposite after Matilda was crowned queen in 1100. The evidence suggests that Matilda did commission this life of her mother, and it is more likely that she did so in the period soon after her marriage and coronation that at any other time.

---

[62] Van Houts, 'Latin Poetry and the Anglo-Norman Court'. Three of the poems are from Hildebert, one from Marbod of Rennes, and four are anonymous.

[63] Boutemy, 105.

[64] Boutemy, 7, note 10.

[65] Scott, ed., 21–2. Scott attributes the poem to the patronage of Matilda II, but see van Houts for a summary of the arguments in favor of the Empress.

[66] Baker, 132–4.

[67] Matilda's actual whereabouts between 1093 and 1100 are unknown, but Anselm's letter to Osbert, the bishop of Salisbury in February 1094 reveals that he had asked the king if he had any objections before requesting Osbert to have Matilda returned to the monastery at Wilton. It seems certain that Matilda did not return. See Schmitt, ed., 4, 60–1, letter 177, and Walter Frölich, 'The Letters Omitted from Anselm's Collection of Letters', *ante* 6, 1984, 58–71.

From a comparison of the long and short manuscript versions of the *vita*, it is clear that no matter which preceded, one was derived from the other. Both structural and stylistic evidence argues for the priority of the longer version. Many of the sentences of the *Life* appear word for word in both texts, and although some incidents are significantly shortened in the condensed version, each unfolds in exactly the same order in both versions. In several places, the narrative in the shorter version lacks a necessary transition. For instance, the account of the Gospel Book miracle in the longer text follows a lengthy section describing Margaret's pious activities during Lent and the forty days before Christmas. The transitional paragraph, quoted above, explains that the reader should admire Margaret for these works which brought about her sanctity rather than the miracle that might display her sanctity.[68] In the short version, the miracle appears suddenly and without context at the end of the account of her Lenten austerities. This same kind of awkwardness occurs at several other places within the short text. At one point, the narrator discusses Margaret's influence over Malcolm and her insistence that he surround himself with a crowd of retainers whenever he appeared in public. The next sentence assures the reader than Margaret scorned all the pomp of the world by always thinking of the Day of Judgement.[69] The transitional sentences in the long version describe Margaret's reforms to make court life more elegant, pointing out, however, that 'she had done these things, not because she delighted in the honour of the world, but because she was compelled to carry out that which royal dignity demanded from her.' The author goes on to justify the use of costly ornaments as 'fitting for a queen' only then to show how Margaret repressed the swelling of pride in the pomp of the world.[70] In both these cases, the awkwardness in the short version, which is easily understood by reference to the missing portions of the longer version, is otherwise difficult to explain.

Although I have argued that the content of the long version of the *vita* corresponds with that of other literature being written for Matilda, its message does differ from that of the other literature in two respects. First, the author portrays Margaret as a highly literate woman, familiar with Scripture and the church fathers, able to hold her own in conferences and debates with the most learned men in the kingdom. This image would not have been foreign to Matilda, who quoted classical and patristic sources in her own letters, who participated in and presided over meetings of the *curia regis*, and who had willingly argued her eligibility for marriage before an episcopal council.[71] But while we do not see authors of the period condemning such activity in a queen, they more often tend to ignore it or to imagine that the queen is suffering great hardship in filling such a role. Hildebert once wrote to Matilda, who was acting vice-regally in Henry's absence, to urge her against despair at the absence of her lord, and Herbert of Norwich, who wrote about his financial woes, apologised for adding yet another burden onto the queen.[72] This kind of sentiment perhaps reached its zenith later in the century

---

[68] Above, p. 88.

[69] See appendix, paragraph II, for the text by John of Tynemouth.

[70] Appendix, paragraph I.

[71] Above, page 89. Matilda had at least a familiarity with some of the classical authors as revealed in one of her letters to Anselm in which she praises the archbishop by comparing him to Cicero, Quintilian, and Fronto as well as St Paul and the Latin fathers Jerome, Augustine, and Gregory the Great. Schmitt, ed., 5: 326–7, letter 384.

[72] Hildebert, *Patrologia latina* 171: 198. For Herbert, see Anstruther, ed., *Epistolae Heriberti*, 49.

when Bernard of Clairvaux wrote to the newly-widowed Queen Melisende of Jerusalem to console her at the death of her husband. In the process, he assured her that, despite the fragility of her sex, she could rule the kingdom of Jerusalem on her own, choosing to ignore the fact that she had already been doing so for over a decade.[73] The author of the *Life of St Margaret* explicitly approves of the queen's public role, at the same time reminding Matilda of the more important things in life when he writes of Margaret that 'I used to admire her application to sacred reading among the tumult of affairs and the many-sided cares of the kingdom.'[74] The author is also somewhat unusual in his approval of the lavish lifestyle enjoyed by royalty, for while other authors recognise that the upper-classes may live in luxury, he stresses the necessity of doing so, and approves of Margaret's conspicuous consumption, even pointing out that she was buried with the honour due to the office of queenship.[75] He is careful to praise Margaret because she always 'trampled these things in her mind like another Esther' and understood that she was but 'dust and ashes' under all her finery.[76] This author's acceptance can be contrasted to the more explicit warnings that other authors addressed to Matilda. One of Hildebert's poems advised Matilda to reflect on the fact that death, the great equaliser, would render the sceptre equal to the hoe, and Anselm admonished her to take care lest the 'glories of this world 'hinder her journey to the heavenly kingdom.'[77]

These warnings were evidently heeded, for later writers had much praise for Matilda's actions during her tenure as England's queen. Ailred of Rievaulx commemorated her as a 'second Esther', and by the thirteenth century, Matilda had become 'Good Queen Maud', remembered for her foundation of hospitals, monasteries, bridges and even a public toilet along the London wharves.[78] I believe that part of Matilda's success lies in her modelling of herself after the mother portrayed so attractively in the longer version of the *vita*. Obviously there

---

[73] Bruno Scott James, ed., *The Letters of Bernard of Clairvaux*, 346. See Hans Eberhard Mayer, 'Studies in the History of Queen Melisende of Jerusalem', *Dumbarton Oaks Papers* 26, 1970, 94–182, along with his recent qualifications on the problem of joint rule in *The Crusades*, Oxford 1988, 299 note 43.

[74] Above, p. 91.

[75] The author of the *Vita Eadwardi regis* reports that Queen Edith took special care to see that Edward was suitably dressed in a manner befitting his estate, which both the author and the king seemed reluctantly to accept. See *Vita Eadwardi*, 41–2.

[76] 'Omnia ornamenta velut ut altera Esther mente calcavit; seque sub gemmis et auro nihil aliud quam pulverem et cinerem consideravit.'

[77] Scott, ed., 2, and Schmitt, ed., 5: 284–5, letter 346.

[78] Ailred, 736. Robert of Gloucester and Matthew Paris were among the later authors who commemorated Matilda and contributed to her legend. Matthew Paris presents Matilda as a holy virgin, reluctant to marry the lustful Henry, but persuaded to do so for the good of the oppressed English people. After her death, many 'signs and miracles' occuring at her tomb proved that her spirit dwelt in heaven. See Frederic Madden, ed., *Historia minor*, London 1868, 3 vols, 1: 188–9, 201, 222. Robert of Gloucester always referred to Matilda as 'Mold the gode cuene', and particularly referred to her charitable works. See William Aldis Wright, ed., *The Metrical Chronicle of Robert of Gloucester*, 2 vols, London 1887, lines 6467–8, 7252–6 and 8936–83. There are some signs that a cult of sanctity had begun to form around the queen shortly after her death, and the Bollandists considered and rejected her claims to sainthood. See *Acta sanctorum*, May 1. William of Malmesbury is one of the earliest of the chroniclers to report 'signs' occuring at Matilda's tomb. See *De gestis regis*, 2: 495. For further references to Matilda's possible sanctity, see Barlow, *Edward the Confessor*, 270, note one.

For Matilda's practical charities, see VCH *Essex* 6: 59, Kealey, *Medieval Medicus*, 20, and Timothy Baker, *Medieval London*, New York 1970, 41.

was a conduit that carried the ideal of the 'perfect princess' from mother to daughter, and it is difficult to believe that the *vita* was not at least part of that conduit. The *Life of St Margaret*, used in the court of her daughter, Matilda II of England, created an ideal of the good queen who influenced her husband, the court, and the kingdom at large, and through Matilda, this text became an important element in the shaping of high-medieval queenship.

APPENDIX

I. Excerpt from the long version of the *Vita Margaretae* as it appears in British Library Cotton Tiberius Dii, fol. 182r (corresponding sections of paragraphs eleven and twelve of the *Acta sanctorum* version):

Obsequia etiam regis sublimora constituit, ut eum procendentum sive equitantem, multa cum grandi honore agmina constiparent; et hoc cum tanta censura, ut quocumque devenissent, nulli eorum cuiquam aliquid liceret rapere, nec rusticos aut pauperes quos libet modo quisquam illorum opprimere auderet vel laedere. Regalis quoque aulae ornamenta multiplicavit; ut non tantum diverso palliorum decore niteret, sed etiam auro argentoque domus tota resplenderet. Aut enim aurea vel argentea, ut deaurata sive deargentata fuerant vasa, quibus regi et regni proceribus dapes inferebantur et potus. Et haec quidem illa fecerat, non quia mundi honore delectabatur; sed quod regia dignitas ab ea exigebat, persolvere cogebatur. Nam cum pretioso ut reginam decebat cultu induta procederet, omnia ornamenta velut ut altera Esther mente calcavit; seque sub gemmis et auro nil aliud quoniam pulverem et cinerem consideravit. Denique in tanta celsitudine dignitatis, maximam semper habuit servandae curam humilitatis. Tanto enim facilius omnem ex mundali honore superbiae tumorem reprimebat, quanto fragilis vitae transitura conditio mentem illius numquam fugerat. Illius enim sententiae recordabatur, qui instabilis humanae vitae status sic describitur: Homo natus de muliere, brevi vivens tempore, repletur multis miseriis, qui quasi flos egreditur et conteritur, et fugit velut umbra, et numquam in eodem statu permanet. Illud quoque Beati Jacobi Apostoli semper in mente versabat; Quae est, inquit, vita nostra? Vapor est ad modicum patens, deinceps exterminabitur. Et quia, ut scriptura loquitur, Beatus homo qui semper est pavidus, tanto facilius peccata venerabilis regina devitabat, quanto tremens et pavens districtum judicii diem indesinenter ante mentis oculos sibi presentabat.

II. Excerpt from John of Tynemouth's version, British Library Cotton Tiberius Ei, vol. 2, fol. 11v:

Rege cum magno comitatu procedente familiares eius quosque tanta censura coercuit, ut nullus quicquam rapere, nec rusticos aut pauperes quoslibet opprimere vel laedere auderet. Tanto namque sancta regina facilius pompam omnem mundi contempsit, peccatorum maculam evasit, quanto tremens et pavens districtum judicii diem, ante mentis oculos sibi indesinenter praesentabat.

III. Excerpt from Surius' version of the *Vita Margaretae* as it appears in Pinkerton:

Rege cum magno comitatu aliquo proficiscente, omnes comites et satellites ejus tanta severitate coercuit, ut nullus quicquam rapere, nullus rusticos vel pauperes quoslibet laedere, vel opprimere auderet. Tanto autem facilius sancta regina omnem mundi pompam sprevit, et peccatorum evasit maculas, quanto majori cum tremore et pavore districtum judicii diem, ante mentis oculos sibi indesinenter repraesentabat.

THE GREAT TOWERS OF EARLY IRISH CASTLES

T. E. McNeill

The position of Ireland in Anglo-Norman studies, and indeed in the general later medieval period as a whole, tends to be as peripheral academically as it is geographically within Europe. Yet Ireland, although it might be a separate administrative unit from England, was never a separate political one. Institutionally there was always a very close link between the Lordship of Ireland and the Kingdom of England, in law or the structure of administration. The men who held the major lordships within Ireland in the twelfth and thirteenth centuries came from the lands of the king of England and often also held lands there as well as in Ireland. Throughout the same period, the English families of Ireland maintained close personal contacts with the aristocratic families of England (including what is now Wales), most obviously through the means of the marriage market. The 'separateness' of Ireland during the Middle Ages, and this could include the Gaelic world as well, can be overplayed: the fact that it is agreed to by both English and Irish nationalists should be sufficient to make it suspect. In castle studies, the most obvious and academically damaging consequence of this view was the exclusion of Ireland from *The History of the King's Works*.

The question of the building of castles in Ireland has a particular historical bent for the twenty-five years on either side of 1200, because it is closely connected with the nature and progress of the seizure of land by men from England. This process is termed an 'invasion' by historians, and it is very difficult to use any other word, but its nature needs to be defined more closely. It was not the same as the events of 1066, when a single, more or less unified, kingdom was overrun by a single invading group. Nor was it the same as the situation in Wales, where a whole series of individual lordships were set up and resulted in a long drawn out, piecemeal process of fighting to establish themselves over against the Welsh lordships they aimed to conquer. In Ireland the incoming English set up lordships quickly throughout the eastern and southern parts of the island. The lordships were large self-contained entities unlike the geographically tangled baronies of England, but it is important to stress the speed with which they were established. After the initial years, fighting in thirteenth-century Ireland was very much a matter for the parts west and north of the line between Cork and Carrickfergus, or between the English barons themselves.

There is no physical evidence that the incoming lords used the site of their aristocratic or royal Irish predecessors, and there is little or no literary evidence that they even used the same locations. As a result the English lords in Ireland were faced with the prospect of constructing a whole series of castles in which to live and from which they might administer their new lands. It is with these castles, assignable to the first two generations after the first arrival of the English in Ireland in 1169, or to the establishment of the lordships east of the Shannon, that this paper is concerned. The interest of the castles for the history of Ireland is in the indications of the style that the lords expected to live in and how the types of castle which they chose to build may tell us what they expected to need in their new lordships. Outside Ireland they are of interest as a group of castles erected on sites which apparently were unoccupied before, or whose previous buildings seem to have left no trace and had no influence. These were 'green field' sites for castles built by men who belonged to families of the first rank in the service of the English king. As such, they act in the same way as the castles associated with the conquest of England in 1066, as examples which may display the state of the art in the lands of the builders' origin.

Given the pressures of time and the probable difficulty of recruiting in Ireland the men capable of building castles for the new lords, it is only to be expected that many of the new structures appear to have been built mainly of timber and earth. Among these mottes predominate. The pattern of their building is not the subject of this paper, but has been considered in a recent article.[1] Instead I wish to concentrate on those castles, the capita of their baronies, where the lords concerned chose to build in stone from the first in almost all cases, rather than in less substantial materials. They are very much the minority of the castles of the period in Ireland. Not only do the honorial baronages seem to eschew stone building entirely, but nearly every lordship contains at least one example of an earthwork site located on a demesne manor of the lord himself. Along with the clear evidence[2] that the Justiciars of the 1210s accepted mottes as being first-rate military castles (Athlone, Roscrea, or Clones), this shows that the very fact of the choice of stone is a statement of the importance of the sites themselves, and of the status attached to it as material for the building of castles. We may conclude that earthworks may have been acceptable to a major baron as military structures, but that stonework was a sine qua non for a chief residence.

The best way of introducing the individuals who caused the stone castles of Ireland built before around 1225, is with a list of the surviving sites and their owners. This is arranged, very approximately because the dating evidence is distinctly uneven, in chronological order: those castles marked with an asterisk possess great towers (see Fig. 1).

*Trim	Hugh I de Lacy
*Carrickfergus	John de Courcy
*Nenagh	Theobald Walter
Carlingford	Hugh II de Lacy
*Adare	Geoffrey de Marisco
Dunamase	William I Marshal
*Dundrum	Hugh II de Lacy (?)
*Athlone	Royal
Dublin	Royal
Limerick	Royal
*Maynooth	Maurice fitz Gerald or Gerald fitz Maurice

---

[1] T. E. McNeill, 'Hibernia pacata et castellata', *Château Gaillard* 14, forthcoming.
[2] G. H. Orpen, 'Motes and Norman castles in Ireland' *EHR* 22, 1907, 452–5.

Round towers   •

Square towers   ■

Enclosures   o

CARRICKFERGUS

DUNDRUM

CLOGH
OUGHTER

CARLINGFORD

TRIM

CASTLE
KNOCK

MAYNOOTH

ATHLONE

LEIXLIP   DUBLIN

DUNAMASE

NENAGH

LIMERICK

ADARE

SHANID

KILTINANE

ARDFINNAN

DUNGARVAN

INCHIQUIN

0   80

K M

0   50

MILES

Fig. 1 Map of Ireland, showing early castles of stone

*Ardfinnan	Philip de Worcester
*Kiltinane	Philip de Worcester
*Dungarvan	Royal
*Inchiquin	Gerald fitz Maurice?
*Leixlip	Adam de Hereford?
*Castle Knock	Richard Tirel
*Shanid	William de Burgh or John fitz Thomas
*Clogh Oughter	William de Lacy??

We may distinguish, very crudely for they are not mutually exclusive, three groups among these men. Hugh I de Lacy and William Marshal were major barons outside Ireland, especially Hugh who was a considerable figure before he ever came to Ireland. Most of the names on the list are those with a background of royal service in their own careers (Philip de Worcester) or rather, perhaps, because of more illustrious relatives (Theobald Walter or William de Burgh). Compared to the rest, the Geraldines, perhaps, and John de Courcy, definitely, appear as men of lesser rank or connections; the only ones without experience and background which encompassed not only Britain but the Angevin lands as a whole.

The period concerned was one in which there was an intense interest in the design of castles. The interest tended to centre around the role and form of what had been the main element of castles of the earlier twelfth century, the great tower, in modern parlance the keep. Militarily, on the one hand, perhaps because of the vulnerability of square buildings to attack at their corners, there was a move to make the great towers round in plan. On the other, there were those who were building castles which had no great tower and which shifted the main effort of defence to the curtain wall. Deployment of archery skills required effective loops and the provision of flanking towers; the gate inevitably became the focus of attention. Domestically, the years around 1200 see a tendency for the lord to distance himself socially. Instead of the close proximity of his chamber to the general life of the castle, located in the hall, often bound into the single great tower, a lord was inclined to build a separate chamber block for himself and his intimate associates, away from the cameraderie of the hall. Again the role of the great tower was crucial, as indeed could be its plan; a square or rectangular tower was more suited to containing a hall and array of dependent rooms than a round one, while a round tower was well fitted to accommodating simply a pair of great and lesser chambers on two floors.

The castle builders in Ireland were well aware of these currents in design. Defensively there are examples of the replacement of the great tower by the curtain wall line. Dublin castle may well date from after the order of 1204.[3] There was clearly major work being undertaken in 1211–12 at Limerick, when £733. 16s. 11d. was spent on the fortification of the castle there.[4] In the north-east tower is a double loop with plunging slit. Both were royal castles from the first, while the royal works added the middle curtain at Carrickfergus between 1216 and 1224; it

---

[3] *Calendar of Documents relating to Ireland* I, no. 226.
[4] O. Davies and D. B. Quinn, 'The Irish Pipe Roll of 14 John', *Ulster Journal of Archaeology* 4 (supplement), 1941, 68.

is remarkable for the multiple arrow slits in the east tower.[5] These ideas were not confined to the royal works, however. Carlingford castle has no great tower, but the curtain is defended by two rows of loops to the north of the gate (the upper row have plunging slits) and a flanking tower to the south: the gate is placed between two rectangular towers set very close together. Dunamase has points in common: its main ward has a gatehouse somewhat the same as Carlingford's in plan; the outer ward is defended by loops with plunging slits; it is also set on a rock, but there may be a great tower at the top of the hill, although the remains are too fragmentary to tell.[6]

There are individual links visible between some of the castles concerned; the gatehouses of Dunamase and Carlingford have been mentioned. The south tower of Carlingford is splayed back from a rectangular plan at courtyard level to a half octagon at first floor; so too is the east gate tower at the De Lacy castle of Trim. The same arrangement is seen on the towers of the early curtain wall at the great De Lacy castle of Ludlow in Shropshire.[7] When there are differences between the castles, we cannot attribute it to ignorance of alternatives, but must assume that the man who commissioned the work was making a deliberate choice as to what sort of castle he wanted for his money. We should try to assess the reasoning that went into his choice, either in terms of the sort of life he intended to lead or of the defensive capability he thought he would require.

Carrickfergus serves as a good starting point; it is well preserved and has reasonable chronology, the inner ward and great tower dating certainly to the late twelfth century, and probably started in 1177 or 1178.[8] This first castle was small, and very much dominated by the great tower, roughly square and some 25 metres high, which took up approximately 25 per cent of the area enclosed within the castle, itself about 1200 square metres. The tower had three principal floors, of which the finest was the third, marked out by its fireplace and large windows. This was not the hall, however, for it was difficult of access from the courtyard and provided with only a single latrine (compared to the double one of the first, entry, floor), but was John de Courcy's chamber. The hall and probably the chapel were located in separate buildings in the courtyard, leaving the tower for the use of the lord and his immediate household. Defensively, the castle relied principally on its situation on a rock promontory projecting into the sea. Neither the curtain nor the gate had any elaboration or towers. The gate was set at the end of the promontory in a position which meant that any approach along the rock was outflanked by the great tower, but if an attacker approached across the sands exposed to the east at low tide, then the gate was in dead ground. This advantage to the attacker was increased by the fact that the windows of what was probably the hall opened through this vulnerable east flank of the curtain.

---

[5] T. E. McNeill, *Carrickfergus Castle* HMSO, 1981.

[6] There are no adequate descriptions of either Carlingford or Dunamase in print, although a full survey of the latter has just been undertaken by the Office of Public Works in Dublin. See H. G. Leask, *Irish Castles*, Dundalk, 2nd edn reprinted 1977, 61–3; H. G. Leask, 'Irish castles, 1180 to 1310', *Arch. Journ* 93, 1936, 192–4.

[7] D. F. Renn, ' "Chastel de Dynan", the first phases of Ludlow', R. Avent and J. Kenyon (eds), *Castles in Wales and the Marches*, Cardiff 1987, 55–73.

[8] McNeill, *Carrickfergus Castle*, 42.

Trim castle is the largest in Ireland and still dominated by its great tower, square in plan with four projecting side-towers, one on each wall. On a number of counts, the tower at Trim is not an easy building to discuss: its construction was halted and the existing structure roofed for a period half way through its building; the building has never been fully analysed, and indeed only the plan of one floor has been published;[9] the dating has never been clearly established. The plan of the great tower is of a square central block, with square side-towers projecting from each side. The central block of the tower is higher, by a storey, both above the surrounding ground level and the lowest floor of the projecting side-towers; it is likely that it was built over a mound, perhaps the motte referred to in 1172. The entrance to the tower is at first floor level in the east side-tower. The ground floor of the central block of the tower was divided, now by a wall which almost certainly replaced a primary wooden division running north and south, into two nearly equal-sized rooms, the western one of which has a fireplace which appears to be original. This floor and the two lowest ones of the projecting side-towers were at one point covered with a roof, a pause in building which is also marked by a change in the form of the windows. It is unlikely that there was ever any intention to leave the building as it was after the first phase of work. The side-towers were built higher than the ridge of the two roofs of the central block, while the door from the south-west stair would have led merely into a roof-space. Apart from the replacement of a timber division between the two rooms in the central block by a stone wall, the building as completed has every appearance of being built as it was planned, not with substantial new additions. After this pause, building was resumed to provide two more floors. The central block continued to be divided on the second floor, but on the third it was opened out into one very large room at least 10 metres square, with a fireplace in the centre of the south wall; neither of the second floor rooms were equipped with fireplaces. The second floor room of the east side-tower, over the entrance, was equipped as a chapel (figs 2–4).

The dating of Trim is far from being fixed but may be outlined here. The documentary references are firstly to the structure captured by the Irish in 1172, which was almost certainly an earth and timber one. The castle was taken by King John as part of his campaign of 1210, although the writs which he issued are recorded as being done, not at the castle, but at a meadow beside it; what this implies is unclear. The Liberty of Meath, and with it Trim castle, was seized by the King. In the 1211–12 Pipe Roll, £61. 6s. 7d. are recorded as being spent on unspecified works at Trim castle; from the amount involved this must be for masonry. In addition, the custodian only accounts for the farm of Trim for half of the relevant year; the other half may have been spent on works, to the extent of £60. 0s. 0d.[10] The most specific entry is for 22s. spent on a large horse from Dublin, sent to help strengthen the tower at Trim castle.[11] A later chronicle has the rather enigmatic statement that the castle of Trim was finished in 1220. In 1224, Walter de Lacy came over to Ireland to re-assert his power over his lands of Meath, which had been returned four years before, against his half-brother and others, as part of the general reinstatement of the Irish magnates deposed by John in 1210,

[9] Leask, *Irish castles*, 30–4.
[10] Davies and Quinn, 1941, 25, 37, 43.
[11] Davies and Quinn, 1941, 15: see the *Index and Corrigenda to the Pipe Roll of 14 John* published with the Index to volumes 1–6 of the *Ulster Journal of Archaeology*, p. 53.

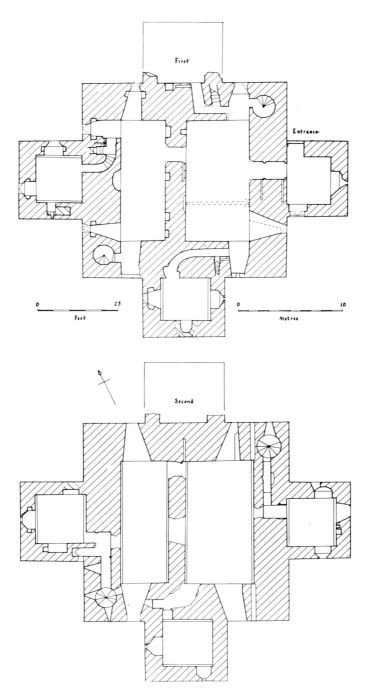

First

Entrance

Second

0   25
Feet

0   10
Metres

Fig. 2 Plan of the great tower at Trim, Co. Meath; first and second floors

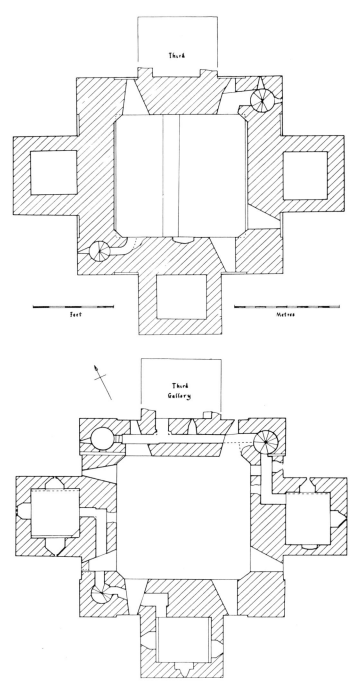

Third

Feet　　　　　　　　Metres

Third
Gallery

Fig. 3 Plan of the great tower at Trim, Co. Meath; third and gallery floors

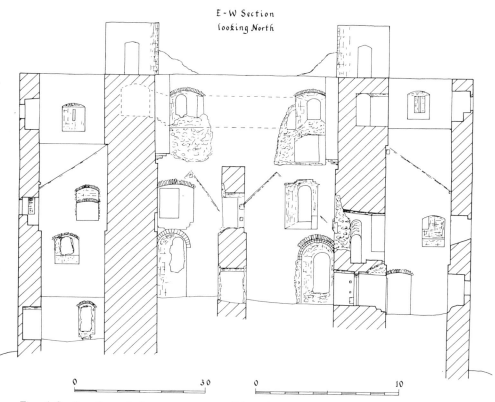

E - W Section
looking North

0   30   0   10

Fig. 4 Section through the great tower at Trim, showing the traces of the roofs of the first phase

which took place in the minority of Henry III. Walter, allied to the young William Marshal, besieged Trim castle for seven weeks, although we do not know how hard he pursued his siege. After he captured it, he held it as the caput of his lordship until his death in 1241.

Excavations at the base of the great tower showed that a secondary plinth had been added to it during a sequence of construction of rather flimsy buildings close to the tower.[12] This sequence seems to have ended with the cutting, or re-cutting, of a ditch around the tower. The pottery recovered showed that the plinth was added at a period when Ham Green ware from Bristol was current, but before local wares had come into use; the ditch was cut at a time for polychrome Saintonge ware to fall into the bottom. The excavator made the reasonable suggestion that the plinth was probably contemporary with the second phase of the tower, when it was completed to its full height. He was led to date the plinth to the middle of the thirteenth century, on the belief that this was the starting date for the currency of

---

[12] P. D. Sweetman, 'Archaeological excavations at Trim castle, Co. Meath' *Proceedings of the Royal Irish Academy* 78 (C), 1978, 127–98.

Ham Green ware; since then it can be shown to have been on sale in Ireland since the beginning of the century.[13] The polychrome at the base of the ditch must date to the end of the century, or a little later, so that the ditch, as it was found, can hardly have been dug before 1275.

A reasonable chronology of the great tower might be as follows. The first phase, with round rear arches to the windows, and quarter rolls on the arrises, should be of the twelfth century; it may date to the time of Hugh I de Lacy, who died in 1186. His sudden death and the minority of his heir, Walter, might have been the occasion for the makeshift roof over the first phase. The 1211–12 Pipe Roll specifically refers to work on the tower, which we can take as giving us a point during the continuation of phase 2 and the addition of the plinth, compatible with the finding of Ham Green ware. The reference to the completion of the castle in 1220 might be to the completion of the great tower.

If we analyse the aims of the great tower of Trim, the first question to consider is that of the relationship between the two phases. The overall plan of the tower and its internal arrangements do not seem to have been changed much, but still the number of rooms was doubled. When it was fitted up in the first phase, apparently on a temporary basis, the tower may have been arranged with a hall, equipped with a central hearth, in the eastern of the two large rooms in the central block and a great chamber, with a wall fireplace, in the smaller, western one. The eastern room was reached first, from the entrance in the east side-tower and gave access itself to rooms in the north and south side-towers. The western room of the central block gave access only to the western side-tower which was marked out as the only one with a latrine.

When the tower was heightened, this arrangement would no longer have been possible; the eastern room at entry level could no longer have had a central hearth because of the floors now running over it. Its internal arrangements were now complex, not to say confusing, and too elaborate to be considered in detail here. Perforce, we must simply pick out a few of the major features of the design. The third floor of the central block has the main room of the building, a splendid one extending over the whole block, with fine windows, a fireplace in the south wall, and possibly a latrine in the south-east angle. It is not, however, the centre of the circulation pattern of the building, but lies instead almost insulated from the rest of the rooms, access to the side-tower rooms being by way of a gallery at mezzanine floor level from the stairs not the main room. The second floor has the rooms of the central block similarly isolated; the stair closest to the entrance, the north-western one, giving access only to the chapel in the east side-tower at this level. None of the larger rooms is in fact easily reached from the outside, but instead they appear to be kept quite consciously as private or semi-private although clearly of high status; no hall but private chambers for the lord and his household.

These internal arrangements must be seen in conjunction with the remains of the outer courtyard, in particular with the north wall. Here there are four large windows at what was apparently originally first floor level, which pierce the curtain wall, albeit on the side facing the River Boyne. They served a building at least 20 metres long and clearly important. If the construction of the northern, apparently earlier, section of curtain walling goes with the second phase of the keep, and they

---

[13] C. J. Lynn, 'The excavation of Rathmullan' *Ulster Journal of Archaeology* 44–5, 1981–2, 113–14.

cannot be far apart in time, then the buildings must integrate. The obvious explanation is that after completion of the keep there was no hall there, so that one was built against the northern curtain. The great tower now was reserved for De Lacy and his household, with his great chamber on the third floor.

As a military structure, the great tower of Trim is remarkably weak, apart from the thickness of its walls. It has twelve exterior angles, although it is built on a gravel subsoil which would make mining relatively easy. The side-towers might have provided flanking fire, but there are no loops positioned to cover anything other than a minimum of ground. Excavation has also shown how the keep had buildings very close to it, at least on the south and west, making any clear field of fire impossible to achieve. The most glaring example of weakness is the entry. Not only is it a single door (with a double door to the central block emphasising the lack of strength into at least part of the building), but it was left uncovered by any flanking loop; this in spite of there being a mural passage (at second floor level) in the east wall of the central block which would have made such provision easy. Like Carrickfergus, but even more so, the great tower at Trim was designed for the occupation of the lord and his glorification, neither as a castle in itself, nor as a final strong point in case of siege.

Two other castles have been claimed as having great towers of the period: Adare and Maynooth.[14] Adare is interesting because there is an inner and an outer enclosure, with the alleged great tower in the inner. Punched dressing of the Carboniferous limestone voussoirs, typical of fifteenth-century workmanship in the west of Ireland, are to be seen on doors at both ground and first floor level on the tower: it may well be of that date. Irrespective of the date of the tower, it is interesting to note that the hall, undoubtedly dating to the time of Geoffrey de Marisco and the foundation of his lordship around 1200, is located by contrast in the outer enclosure, beside the simple gate. If the great tower and the hall were contemporary, then we can see that the tower excluded the main formal public building of the castle, and, if it was the main military strong point, then Geoffrey was prepared to sacrifice his hall in a siege.

Maynooth is a problem building, not least because it has seen both considerable later medieval rebuilding and drastic recent restoration. The ground floor has had a vault inserted which carried the weight of a stone arcade dividing the first floor. An internal scarcement and external change in the masonry about two thirds of the way up show that the whole of the upper parts are a later rebuilding or addition. As far as can be judged, however, the original tower was entered at first floor level into a single large room, perhaps divided by a timber arcade replaced later by the stone one, and with three tiny mural chambers; there is a probable latrine in the north wall. There is now no sign of any stair to an upper floor, either original or later, nor of how such a floor could have been supported. If we had to characterise its original use it would be as a first floor hall, and only that, with no provision for high-status attached chambers. The entrance is remarkable for its simplicity, although it has lost its forework.

The doyen of the round towers is that of Nenagh, the largest and best decorated, and also probably the most completely preserved.[15] There are two periods of

---

[14] Leask, *Irish castles*, 34–6.
[15] D. F. Gleeson and H. G. Leask, 'The castle and manor of Nenagh' *Journal of the Royal Society of Antiquaries of Ireland* 66, 1936, 247–69.

medieval masonry visible now, to which we will return, while the top storey and the site of the forework are nineteenth-century reconstructions. The tower was built astride the curtain wall of the castle. The entry to the tower was as usual at the first floor, which is equipped with two deeply plunging arrow loops facing the field outside the curtain wall, but is otherwise featureless. The second floor has a large fireplace, a window with window seats to the north, and a door leading either to the curtain wall-walk east of the tower, or to a latrine, or, indeed, to both. The second floor is reached by a spiral stair up from the first floor, which stops at that level. To go up to the third floor, there is a second, curving stair, rising up a passage in the thickness of the wall before changing to a spiral one half way. It opens from a window embrasure in the south wall of the second floor, whose rear arch is decorated with an elaborate chevron on the arris, of typical late Irish Romanesque sort.

It was clearly intended to make the original access to the third floor indirect by requiring the visitor to pass through the second floor before proceeding up. Whether it was meant to lead to a full third floor, rather than to the battlements, is not so clear. The addition of the third floor is marked by a slight change in the masonry, and the change in direction of the stair between the second and third floors, but more clearly by two other features. The corbel to support the main floor beam is inserted and has a complex thirteenth-century moulding, and the windows and fireplace of the third floor have segmental rear arches, attached shafts and capitals of earlier thirteenth-century date, in contrast to the second floor round arches and chevron ornament. The third floor may be an addition unintended in the original plan, resulting in a second grand room in the tower. The obvious chronology for this comes with the death of Theobald Walter I in 1206, which was followed by a hiatus until his heir, Theobald Walter II came of age in 1221, to whom we may attribute the addition of the third floor.

A small amount of money was accounted for in the 1211–12 Pipe Roll for work on the great tower at Dundrum, which must therefore have been in existence by then.[16] The same entry also refers to a small tower and to a (or the) hall. The present structure has been at least partially rebuilt at second floor level, but the rest is well preserved.[17] The first, entry floor is marked by two windows with window-seats, a large fireplace and a door like that at Nenagh leading out either to the curtain wall-walk, to a latrine or both; there is a double latrine in the curtain wall below it. The stair leading up from this floor to the second floor shows that it was intended from the first, and the chimney flue being built right to the top of the wall shows that more of what is there now is original than is attributed by the official publication, but the precise amount of the primary work remaining, or its original arrangements are unclear. Like Nenagh again, the stair was not reached directly from the entrance, but was placed across the room.

Dungarvan formed part of the royal demesne in Co. Waterford as defined by Henry II and there was certainly a castle there by 1215; thereafter it appears regularly among the listed royal castles of Ireland. None of this tells us what it appeared like at any time or when the present remains were built; these are in poor condition, having been used for a barracks until recently and now subject to

[16] Davies and Quinn, 1941, 59; *Corrigenda and Index*, 36.
[17] E. M. Jope (ed.), *An Archaeological Survey of Co. Down* HMSO, 1966, 207–11.

vandalism. They comprise three main elements. A twelve-sided stone enclosure, some thirty metres across, may represent the original nucleus of the castle: to it has perhaps been added a curtain wall with a large round tower at the south-western angle and a double towered gatehouse at the east. The tower has only loops on the ground floor, with an inserted vault; the first floor is now inaccessible but a survey done in the 1940s shows that it then appears to have had a fireplace, doors to the wall-walks and a possible latrine. The spiral stair is set in a projection at the junction of the tower and the south curtain wall.[18]

The other round great towers are readily summarised (Fig. 5); none have direct dating, or indeed, many original features. Kiltinane and Ardfinnan may date from after 1215 when lands there were granted to Philip of Worcester; both have semi-circular projections for the spiral stairs, like the quarter-round at Dungarvan. Traces are visible of the forework leading to the first floor entry at Kiltinane; one of the round-headed door jambs giving access to a mural passage on the first floor there has a fine Romanesque foliage carving as a chamfer stop. In both there are inserted later vaults with wicker-work centring. The first floor at Ardfinnan was not accessible on my visit. Also in the south of the country is the very ruined round great tower at Inchiquin, which still possesses a fireplace, small latrine and windows with window seats at first floor level.[19] The island site of Clogh Oughter displays remarkably few features apart from the first floor entry. Leixlip has also seen all its features replaced, either during the later middle ages or in more recent occupation. It seems to have been attached to a hall building.

It is unfortunately true that all three polygonal great towers, Athlone, Castle Knock and Shanid, are largely rebuilt (Athlone) or badly ruined. Athlone[20] is ten-sided, and to be dated to the 1210s: in 1211 a masonry tower at the castle fell, and in the 1211–12 Pipe Roll money was spent on the works at the castle in such quantity (£129. 12s. 0d.) as to be on stone work of some sort.[21] Both the others are set on mottes, in the case of Castle Knock a very large one. Both may be rather later than the 1225 end point of this paper as a result, especially Shanid whose motte is hardly likely to pre-date 1200 and would then need to consolidate before being fit to support a masonry structure. Castle Knock might date from after the years 1214–22, when repeated commands were issued for its destruction. It was a ten-sided tower, known mainly from a seventeenth-century drawing and now devoid of features diagnostic either of date or use. Shanid is round on the interior but polygonal on the exterior and equally lacking in features.

It is time to draw some generalities together, to see what the various towers, and the castles in which they were built, have in common. The best starting point is to consider them as military structures of the time. To be effective, we might expect a tower to display its strength in the thickness of its walls, the defence of its entry, or the firepower and aggression capable of being mounted either through arrow

[18] None of the remaining castles, except Inchiquin, have plans published or other than minimal descriptions. The only plan of Dungarvan was made by the Office of Public Works in Dublin in 1946 in connection with its use as a Garda barrack.

[19] P. J. Hartnett, 'Some Imokilly castles' *Journal of the Cork Historical and Archaeological Society* 50, 1946, 42–5.

[20] G. H. Orpen, 'Athlone castle' *Journal of the Royal Society of Antiquaries of Ireland* 37, 1907, 257–76.

[21] Davies and Quinn, 1941, 25.

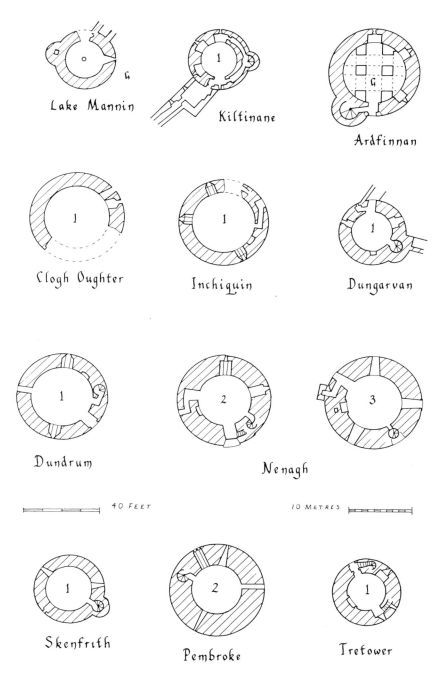

Lake Mannin

Kiltinane

Ardfinnan

Clogh Oughter

Inchiquin

Dungarvan

Dundrum

Nenagh

40 FEET

10 METRES

Skenfrith

Pembroke

Tretower

Fig. 5 Plans of the round great towers of Irish castles with Pembroke, Skenfrith and Tretower in Wales for comparison. G = ground floor; 1 = first floor, etc.

loops or from the wall head. We can take the great tower of Pembroke as a standard, in military as in domestic matters, with the analysis by Renn and King[22] as our basis for comparison; it was, after all, a building well known to all travellers to Ireland at the time.

Especially because they are built of rubble rather than ashlar, these in Ireland are not remarkable for the thickness of their walls, indeed rather the reverse. The actual figures (in metres) are as follows:

Nenagh	3.9
Carrickfergus	2.8/3.7
Trim	3.3
Shanid	3.0
Dungarvan	2.8
Dundrum	2.6
Maynooth	2.5
Castle Knock	2.5
Inchiquin	2.4
Clogh Oughter	2.4
Ardfinnan	2.2
Kiltinane	2.2
Leixlip	2.0
Adare	1.8

These compare with examples such as the following:

Dover	7.5
Pembroke	4.6
Newcastle on Tyne	4.3
Conisbrough	3.6
Orford	2.75
Brecon[23]	2.0–2.5

The defence of the entrance to a tower depended on a forework (at Pembroke possibly, and at other sites definitely), leading to a moveable bridge in front of the door, and then a door closed by a strong drawbar. This arrangement can be seen at Carrickfergus, where there are two doors in the entrance passage. At Nenagh and at Kiltinane there are the remains of the forework but the details have gone. Against the (relative) strength of Carrickfergus must be put the weakness of the tower of Trim, with no sign of a forework, other than the east side-tower which also contained the chapel above the entry level. Trim also displays a lack of any provision for archery loops in the tower walls, in spite of the presence of mural passages and of turrents ideal to use for flanking fire; the weakness of this in the case of the entrance has already been noted. Only at Nenagh tower do we see the

[22] D. F. Renn, 'The donjon at Pembroke castle' *Transactions of the Ancient Monument Society* 15, 1968, 35–48. D. J. C. King, 'Pembroke castle' *Archaeologia Cambrensis* 127, 1978, 75–121.
[23] D. F. Renn, 'The round keeps of the Brecon region' *Archaeologia Cambrensis* 110, 1961, 129–43.

provision of plunging arrow loops, which would be essential for the control of the base of the tower. A note of caution must be struck here: although their presence at Nenagh and at Carlingford and at Dunamase in the outer curtain and particularly in the south-east gate at Trim shows that they were known in Ireland by 1200 or soon after, it is just possible that both the towers of Carrickfergus and Trim were built before this. This will not do for the bulk of the towers, however. We are lacking the wall tops of most of the towers; only at Trim and Carrickfergus, or possibly at Dundrum, can we see the battlement level. At these towers, however, there is no evidence of anything other than of simple merlons and embrasures; no sign of hoarding, let alone the elaboration of the parapet at Pembroke.

For the domestic accommodation, the crucial question is that of the identification of the great hall, and then of the chambers and any specialised rooms such as the chapel. The great hall was the social pivot of the castle, its main raison d'être: to function at all it had to be large and capable of accommodating many people; it had also to be easily accessible from the courtyard, because it was essentially a public room. Its importance and social functions were shown in the quality of the masonry, especially the doors and windows, which were often equipped with window-seats. It needed a fireplace or central hearth and a latrine, often a double one, was also essential. As the centre of the castle's social life, it is to be expected that the hall will stand at the head of the internal communications to the other parts of the castle, although without the elaboration of the later thirteenth century and beyond. The chambers, especially the principal one, are denoted by their fireplaces and good quality masonry details, and usually by a single latrine. Chapels are, of course, to be recognised by their provision of ritual features, such as piscinae.

The only case where it is likely that a hall might have been incorporated in any of the towers we have looked at is the first phase of the great tower at Trim. This is based only on the fact that the largest room in the tower was one reached first after the entry floor in the east side-tower; if it was the hall, it was replaced in the second phase. The largest room in the second phase was the one on the third floor, covering the whole of the main block of the tower, but it cannot have functioned as the great hall of the castle. It was too remote, reached up one of two spiral stairs in opposing corners of the tower, neither of them convenient to the entrance. At Nenagh there was something of the same arrangement. The entry floor is plain and from it a stair rose to the more elaborately decorated and equipped second floor; this is a narrow spiral unsuitable for the numbers that Theobald Walter might be expected to entertain in his great hall. A second stair leads from the second floor to the third floor, as it was intended to before the interruption of the building programme, so that we know that a third floor was part of the original scheme. It was reached indirectly, via the second floor room, whose occupants could thus control access to it, and therefore ensure its privacy. As completed in the second building phase, this third floor room was a fine one and clearly meant for high status occupation. At Carrickfergus, the other site where the tower is more or less complete as built, the arrangement was: entry floor, public and low status; second floor for the inner household, and third floor John de Courcy's private chamber; the great hall was in the courtyard outside.

These three towers were apparently reserved for the lord and his household alone, and excluded the larger crowds of the great hall. In each case there was a floor between the entry level and the third floor. The third floor in the case of both Trim and Carrickfergus was the best room in the tower; in Nenagh as it was completed it was so also. At Nenagh and Carrickfergus the third floor seems to have been a single large chamber for the lord, with an outer chamber on the second floor. The greater size and elaboration of Trim shows in the subdivision of the first and second floors, and in the creation of a core of relatively reserved rooms of which the third floor one was clearly pre-eminent. Both this and the arrangement of the side-towers, seem to give evidence that Hugh or Walter de Lacy not only provided for his own accommodation but also provided individual rooms for the staff of his household. This may explain the presence of the chapel at Trim, uniquely among the great towers if Ireland.

Of the smaller and less well preserved round towers, that of Dundrum castle is the most important here. The entry floor, in common with Kiltinane and Inchiquin at least, has an elaborate fireplace, high quality windows and access to a latrine. Apart from the rather awkward shape of the circular room, this could have been intended as the hall of the castle. The 1211–12 Pipe Roll entry, however, seems to make it clear that the hall and the great tower were two different buildings. Again the second floor was clearly a fine one at Kiltinane at least, and there were clearly originally second floors at the other two. These may have been for private chambers, like the third floors of the three bigger towers, giving a similar outer and inner chamber arrangement at all towers. The difference with the smaller towers was that the entry floor was the outer chamber, rather than a plain, lower-status, outer (guard?) room. The corollary to this is provided by the tower of Maynooth, which has been heightened, of course. This, because of its simple plan of a single room at first floor level, should be considered as a first-floor hall building, detached from any chamber it might serve. Throughout we can see the separation of the hall and the chamber in these towers.

As evidence of the new lords' intentions in Ireland during the first generation of their lordships, the most striking thing is the very existence of these towers. The choice of masonry rather than timber and earth for their new capita shows their confidence that their lordships were here to stay. Not only were the towers a notice of intention to remain by their builders, but they also show that they were intent on putting resources into their enterprise early on, in the confidence that they would soon draw them out again. The second message that they seem to have been built to proclaim is the emphasis on the social pre-eminence of the lord, rather than on his defensive strength in war; the castles seem to reflect political rather than military power and concerns, if it is legitimate to make such a distinction. With the benefit of hindsight, we know that the social and political structure of the Irish inhibited them from developing the skills in war that would have made these castles as vulnerable to a rebellion by the native inhabitants in combination with other Irish lords. The English lords had neither second sight, however, nor were they sociologists. Their readiness to put up expensive great towers which were both weak in themselves and which left major elements of their castles, such as the hall, outside them says much for their confidence and conviction that they did not face an internal military threat to their power. In this, they are the counterpart of the pattern of building that we see in the earthwork castles.[24] These are deployed for military purposes to guard the frontiers of the lordships, above all those which faced the power of Cenel Eoghain and their allies of Breifne or Arghialla.

---

[24] T. E. McNeill, *Château Gaillard*, forthcoming.

The towers that we have considered set a pattern for the later castles of Ireland. This is immediately evidenced by the fact that it has been impossible to give a firm closing date for this paper and exclude all sites after it. Lake Mannin is a castle with a single round great tower, smaller than but essentially similar to the others that we have discussed. It must date to after the occupation of Connacht in the years after 1235: nor can we be sure of the earlier dating of Dungarvan or Kiltinane. The middle of the thirteenth century in Ireland was marked by the development in Ireland of the 'towered keeps' (as Leask called them) such as Ferns, Carlow or Lea in Leinster. In Connacht the smallest castles consist of hall-houses, essentially free-standing stone blocks dominated internally by their first-floor hall, but often with a second floor above. In larger castles of enclosure, such as Athenry and Dunmore in Co. Galway, or Greencastle in Co. Down, the first floor hall dominates the whole castle, and is surely meant to do so. Here, as with the 'towered keeps' perhaps, the hall and the chamber are quite separate so that much of the similarity is purely that of external appearance rather than of detailed continuity of function, but this is itself valid. It is a version of the continuing love of the lords of the middle ages for the great tower to dominate their castles, in the thirteenth century from Wakefield tower in London to Flint in Wales on through the fourteenth and fifteenth centuries. Keeps these were not, in the sense of the essentially complete castles of the twelfth century; they were above all for the accommodation of the lord and his immediate inner household. From this point of view the great towers of the period around 1200 in Ireland are of considerable interest for they represent clear evidence of precisely this transition at an early stage. The elaboration of Trim in particular looks forward to the complex planning of the later thirteenth century.

This rejection of the all embracing keep in favour of the private tower of lordship is part of a tradition common to the aristocracy of Europe, well evidenced because of the need in Ireland to build new sites. This and the way that it seems to lead on to a particular emphasis in later generations does however immediately pose the question of the sources of this trend. Where did the ideas and masons come from to build these towers, for they were not there in Ireland when the English came? There are hints, such as the similarities of Trim and Carlingford with Ludlow, or the royal works at Limerick or Carrickfergus and their double or triple loops. The most obvious apparent direct stimulus is between Nenagh and Pembroke. Both appear to act as progenitors of the popularity of the round great tower in their respective countries. The first point to be made is that if we follow this link up, we must date the great tower of Pembroke to the late twelfth century, and certainly before 1207, and rule out the likelihood of it belonging to the end of William Marshal I's career, between 1211 and 1219.

Nenagh and Pembroke are alike in that they are both most impressive round towers, but beyond that they are as much dissimilar as similar. The differences are reflected in the differences between the other round towers of Wales and Ireland as well. In Ireland the first (or with Nenagh and Pembroke the second) floors are quite clearly designed with the comfort of the lord as a major priority: they have fireplaces, latrines and relatively large windows. Their walls tend perhaps to be thinner in proportion to their size. The emphasis on their use as the lord's chamber is rather clearer in Ireland. In these circumstances, it is perhaps better not to see the one as imitated from the other, but that both are reflections of the same idea. It is interesting that it has not been possible to show any close relationships between the castles of William Marshal or his sons in Wales and Ireland, either in overall planning or in details such as the loops which Knight has studied.[25] The east gate house at Trim may provide us with a pointer. It has no parallel in the British Isles but it has in France, at Coudray-Salbart at least.[26] Round great towers were popular in France in the twelfth century when they were unknown in England. Here we recall the Angevin experience of the early English lords in Ireland. The difference of emphasis that we see in their castles, and those of their descendants may not be evidence of their isolation from the mainstream of European castle design, but rather that they reflect some French ideas rather than English ones.

[25] J. Knight, 'The road to Harlech', in R. Avent and J. Kenyon (eds), *Castles in Wales and the Marches*, Cardiff 1987, 75–88.
[26] P. E. Curnow, 'Some developments in military architecture c.1200: Le Coudray-Salbart' *ante* 2, 1979, 42–62.

THE CHARTERS OF HENRY II: WHAT ARE THE CRITERIA FOR AUTHENTICITY?

Richard Mortimer

Henry II's charters have not lacked their historians. Aspects of the subject have been dealt with in considerable detail: Delisle and Berger, and Van Caenegem have subjected the diplomatic to formal analysis; T. A. M. Bishop, in a remarkable palaeographical achievement, has identified the hands of a large number of scribes in Henry's service and assigned a large proportion of the surviving originals to them.[1] But Delisle and Berger's great *Recueil des Actes de Henri II ... concernant les Provinces Françaises et les Affaires de France* is limited as the title states, though they interpreted their brief widely, including a good deal of English material place-dated in France; and Bishop's *Scriptores Regis* naturally concentrates on the chancery scribes, while Van Caenegem is concerned with one type of document only. A view of the whole has never been attempted, for one obvious reason: the mountain that has to be climbed first is the collection of all Henry's *acta*. Such a collection is in progress, and I was fortunate enough to work on it under Professor Holt for a number of years.[2] Until it can be regarded as finished, and has been examined, general statements on diplomatic will be premature, and I am not going to try for a view of the whole now. Nevertheless historians continue to ask questions, the commonest being, of course, 'Is this charter genuine?' It may still be worth an attempt to examine the complexities that lie behind this question, using only the considerable quantity of material already in print.

Any examination of a body of charters must begin by looking at the originals, and it is these that I shall be concerned with. By an original I mean, for the moment, a single sheet of parchment with a document running in the name of Henry II on one side of it, and which could have been written in the twelfth century. I have included 402 such documents in the calculations which follow; it is quite likely that there are more awaiting discovery, but unlikely that they will be very numerous as all the obvious repositories have been explored.[3] As for the total surviving *acta*

---

[1] L. Delisle and E. Berger, *Recueil des Actes de Henri II Roi d'Angleterre et Duc de Normandie concernant les Provinces françaises et les Affaires de France*, 3 vols, Paris 1909–20; T. A. M. Bishop, *Scriptores Regis*, Oxford 1961; R. C. Van Caenegem, *Royal Writs in England from the Conquest to Glanvill*, Selden Soc. lxxvii, 1959. My thanks are due to Professor J. C. Holt and members of the Battle Conference and the Oxford medieval history seminar for their comments, and to John Moore for help with basic numeracy; but final responsibility for both opinions and numbers is mine.

[2] J. C. Holt, 'The Acta of Henry II and Richard I of England 1154–1199: the Archive and its Historical Implications', in *Fotografische Sammlungen mittelalterlicher Urkunden in Europa*, ed. Peter Rück, Sigmaringen 1989, 137–40, describes progress to date.

[3] J. C. Holt and Richard Mortimer, *Acta of Henry II and Richard I: Hand-List of Documents surviving in the Original in Repositories in the United Kingdom*, List and Index Society Special Series vol. 21,

of Henry II, as of October 1988 the number was already approaching 3,000 with many likely sources still uncleared. So the proportion of originals to copies stands at approximately 1 to 7. This will probably decrease, perhaps to 1 to 10; I think it means that the originals provide a fair basis for discussing the whole corpus of surviving *acta*, though in this paper I shall only be concerned with the originals.

How can we detect forgeries among the originals? Let us begin by examining a number of commonly used criteria, firstly script. Does script provide a criterion of authenticity? Bishop has examined the originals in order to identify the scribes, and has succeeded in assigning a remarkable number of the originals. Those hands which write documents for a number of beneficiaries he identifies as chancery scribes: in some cases it is possible to follow individual careers, and in some even the name of the scribe is known. In contrast to Delisle, his conclusion is that there was no 'generic official script'.[4] And of course it is precisely the variations and eccentricities which permit the identification of individuals.

What about regular diplomatic formulae? Van Caenegem has traced the evolution of the standardised common law writs originating procedure under the various Assizes from the earlier 'shapeless instruments of government'.[5] There was a process of hardening, of crystallization at work, in one area of business. Since this was the direction of change in writs, it comes as no surprise to find that the total of identifiable consistent features in charters and writ-charters is very small, and not sufficient to work as a guarantee of authenticity. The royal style, the use or omission of 'Dei Gratia', which was introduced in 1172–3, are standardized; the king uses the first person singular; the witnesses are in the ablative absolute, are arranged in a rough order of rank, and never completed by 'et multis aliis'; there is a place date. This is about all.[6] As far as the formulae themselves are concerned, the apparent similarities in phrasing are in fact only similarities. Individual scribes appear to achieve consistency in these details in their own work: thus Stephen of Fougères, alias Scribe XXXVI, uses *et omnibus hominibus (et fidelibus suis)* in the address clause, while Scribe XL uses *ministris et omnibus fidelibus*, and XXXV *et omnibus ministris et fidelibus*. Such personal idiosyncracies enable Bishop to attribute a cartulary text to Scribe XL.[7] These minor variations are just what would need to be absent if formulae were to be effective as a criterion of authenticity. But in fact it is hard to see how formulae could ever have worked as a criterion of authenticity: if they were perfectly standardized, nothing would be easier to forge, while if they were kept varying, how could anyone keep track of the genuine variations?

So apart from a very basic framework the phrasing of documents is of no help to us. But phraseology could only be a criterion of authenticity if chancery production was, and as far as I know nobody, certainly not Delisle or Bishop, has ever argued that chancery production was essential for authenticity in Henry II's reign. Non-chancery scribes could be those permanently employed by the beneficiaries – even one of the beneficiaries, if a member of an ecclesiastical corporation – or a casually employed local scribe who happened to be the only

1986, lists and gives details of the known British material to date of publication; Bishop, *Scriptores*, also lists those known in France, of which details can be found in *Recueil*.

[4] Bishop, 12; compare *Recueil* i, 147.

[5] Van Caenegem, 167.

[6] Bishop, 18–20.

[7] Bishop, 21.

person available at the time. The work of such scribes could easily show oddities in diplomatic and sealing.

It would be absurd to adopt criteria of authenticity more stringent than those used by contemporaries, and the main contemporary criterion was the seal. It was the addition of the seal to the parchment that gave it authenticity, as any number of sealing clauses in the private charters of the period make clear. A story from the Battle chronicle will serve to make the point about royal charters too. In 1155 many of the greater ecclesiastics were obtaining royal confirmations of their lands and privileges, among them the abbot of Battle, then in the middle of the long wrangle with the bishops of Chichester about their exemption. The bishop heard that Battle's extensive privileges were about to be confirmed, and enlisted the archbishop on his side. The archbishop urged the king not to allow any privileges contrary to the rights of Canterbury or Chichester. He understood that the abbot possessed charters conferring such privileges. 'He earnestly asked that the king might nullify this with the royal authority, or that the abbot's charter go without the royal seal until it had been revised by his advice . . .' The king agreed, called the chancellor and forbade the abbot's charter 'to be confirmed by the royal seal.' The story continues with the abbot persuading the king to order the sealing, the bishop coming up at a near run to object, and the king finally deputing the archbishop, the bishop, the abbot and the chancellor to sort the matter out between themselves. Should they prove unable to reach agreement 'the abbot's charter should be taken into the chancellor's custody in the king's chapel until the king could decide what was to be done about it', which is what in fact happened.[8] As well as the importance of sealing, this story demonstrates that in 1155 the chapel was the chancellor's headquarters and repository.

The obvious difficulty with the seal as a criterion of authenticity useful to us is that the majority of surviving originals have no remaining seal attached, and comparatively few even of surviving seals offer a complete impression. And clearly the criterion cannot be extended to the majority of acta surviving in copies. There is a further, almost equally obvious problem: seals too can be forged. Walter Map has a story of a man who made an absolutely perfect copy of the king's seal by taking an impression in pitch and then casting it in copper. The king sentenced him to be hanged, but reprieved him on the sight of the man's good and virtuous brother grieving.[9] True or not, the story shows that contemporaries were quite prepared to believe that seals could be forged, though unfortunately the story doesn't say how the forger was detected. Pierre Chaplais's conclusion, after studying the seals and original charters of Henry I, was that seals cannot be used as proof of genuineness – the criticism of the seal has to take account of the authenticity of the document.[10]

What about the witnesses? Surely the purpose of adding a list of witnesses was so that the parties in a lawsuit would know whom to vouch to warranty. In the nature of the human condition the witness list was a wasting asset, as everyone must have been aware, if only from lawsuits involving the charters of earlier kings. But

[8] *Battle Chronicle*, 155–9.
[9] Walter Map, *De Nugis Curialium, Courtiers' Trifles*, ed. and trans. M. R. James, revised by C. N. L. Brooke and R. A. B. Mynors, Oxford 1983, 494.
[10] Pierre Chaplais, 'The Seals and Original Charters of Henry I', EHR 75, 1960, 260–75, repr. in Pierre Chaplais, *Essays in Medieval Diplomacy and Administration*, Hambledon Press, 1981.

another Battle story makes it clear that the document itself could be treated as sufficient evidence. This is the famous Barnhorn suit, in which the monks produced charters to prove their rights against Gilbert de Baillol. Gilbert tried various ploys to impugn the charters: first that he didn't see the seals of his ancestors on them, which drew the comment from Richard de Luci, the justiciar, that it had not been the custom in the past for every petty knight to have a seal – unfair comment, as Gilbert's ancestors were more prominent than de Luci's.[11] He then tried to cast doubt on a confirmation of Henry I – which, as Professor Holt has recently shown, was quite possibly a forgery.[12] 'The king then took the charter and the seal of his grandfather King Henry into his own hands and, turning to Gilbert, replied "By God's eyes, if you could prove this charter false, you would make me a profit of £1,000 in England" '. He went on to say that if the monks had that kind of title to Clarendon itself, where they then were, he would have to give it to them. 'Turning to the abbot and his entourage, the king said "Go, take counsel, and consider together whether there is anything on which you would rather rely than on this charter. But for the present I do not think you will look for further proof" .' The abbot took the hint, and after consultation they declared that 'they did not place their reliance in anything else besides the charter, that they demanded neither more nor less than what was in the charter, and that they awaited the judgement of the royal court on the matter. Their adversary had nothing to say; he neither dared nor could impugn the genuineness of the charter, because he could prove nothing.' Judgement was in favour of the monks, and the king himself ordered sealed letters to be sent to the local justiciars of Sussex.[13]

This often-quoted story has a number of points of interest for us: the chronicler describes no attempt to call the witnesses of the charter, or to ascertain whether any of them was still alive, or even to see who they were. We are at the beginning of Henry II's reign, when his court contained many people whose memories went far back into Henry I's reign – Robert, earl of Leicester, for example – so it would not be by any means impossible for the witnesses to be alive, or even present. But the charter itself was good enough for Henry II, and thus for the sensible abbot. The story also shows the value of documentation in a dispute: their adversary was speechless, he could prove nothing – and if indeed the charter was a forgery it shows how useful that could be. Equally, if contradictory charters of the same king were produced by the two sides in a dispute, the much-praised wheels of Henry II's justice shuddered to a halt. Jocelin of Brakelond describes a trial before Henry between Abbot Samson of Bury and the archbishop of Canterbury, Baldwin, concerning the rights of the monks of Canterbury in a manor of theirs which lay within the 8½ Hundreds, the franchise of St Edmunds. 'The charters of both churches were read aloud by the parties. And our lord the king replied, "These charters are of the same age, and both were issued by the same King Edward. I know not what to say save that the charters contradict each other" '. The abbot, who had previously ensured that he had seisin by organising an armed raid on the Canterbury property, then offered to put his case to a jury of the two counties, Norfolk and Suffolk. The archbishop refused, saying that the men of those parts

[11] See R. Mortimer, *ante* viii, 182 n. 24, 184.
[12] J. C. Holt, 'More Battle Forgeries', *East Anglian and Other Studies Presented to Barbara Dodwell*, ed. M. Barber, P. McNulty and P. Noble, Reading Medieval Studies xi, 1985, 75–86, esp. 78–9.
[13] *Battle Chronicle*, 214–19.

had a great love for St Edmund, and the abbot had too much power there. 'The king, however, was angry and rose in indignation, and said as he departed, "Let him take who can!" And so the matter was postponed, and the suit is still unjudged.'[14]

There are two ways in which witnesses might be held to condemn a charter of Henry II. Firstly they might present chronological inconsistencies, one being dead before another, a bishop, was consecrated, for example. After the middle of the twelfth century I think we are no longer in a world where an existing document can be brought out to receive the authentication of a passing dignitary, one way in which an anachronistic witness list may be consistent with a genuine charter. But in fact I know of no original of Henry II which has such an inconsistency. The other possibility is that the date of the witness list might be inconsistent with 'Dei Gratia' in the royal style, but in such cases as this Bishop cites a number of instances in which documents from the first half of the reign were renewed later, by known chancery scribes, copying out the old witness list but adding the new royal style, thus producing a perfectly genuine document with a glaring diplomatic inconsistency.[15]

Where does all this leave us? Are there no criteria for authenticity? I think it would be salutary to be intellectually prepared for the possibility, and I would certainly prefer that situation to having documents dismissed as 'forgeries' on insufficient grounds. The most usual proceeding, though, is not to rely on any one criterion, but to look at several at once – script, diplomatic, witness list, seal if any: but I fail to see how the adoption of several inadequate criteria can produce more certainty than just one of them. Of course absolute certainty is not something any historian can aspire to; diplomatic, as has been said, is not an exact science.[16] Which must mean that we can never certainly condemn a document as a forgery. Not that forgery did not exist: the number of amercements on the Pipe Rolls for tampering with writs is sufficient evidence of what went on, and that malefactors could be detected to the satisfaction of some contemporaries, while Glanvill records severe penalties for falsification of royal charters.[17] Forgery existed, but we can never be sure when we are confronted with it. If we cannot be absolute, how far can we be tentative? Is it possible to discern regularities or suggestive patterns among the surviving originals? Can we establish limits of variation? Instead of asking 'How can we detect forgeries', let us try asking, 'What is a genuine document?' What is especially needed is to find out as much as possible about the circumstances of production, both of those by chancery scribes, and especially, of the others. Let us begin by going back to the question of chancery and non-chancery production.

Can any pattern be discerned in the use of chancery scribes, or others, by certain types of beneficiary? Table 1 plots the incidence of scribes against certain types of document and beneficiary. Before discussing it, a word about my choice of categories: by general confirmation I mean both the brief confirmation in general

[14] *The Chronicle of Jocelin of Brakelond*, ed. and trans. H. E. Butler, Nelson 1949, 51–2.
[15] Bishop, 35.
[16] Simon Keynes, *The Diplomas of Aethelred the Unready*, Cambridge 1980, 13.
[17] Van Caenegem, 170. *Tractatus de Legibus et Consuetudinibus Regni Angliae*, ed. G. D. G. Hall, Nelson 1965, 176–7; see also *Battle Chronicle*, 243, and the cases cited in C. N. L. Brooke, 'Approaches to medieval forgery', *Journal of the Society of Archivists* iii no. 8, 1968, 377–8.

terms and the lengthy type which rehearses specific grants, often naming the donor. Specific confirmations include both confirmations of single grants, and of more than one grant where that clearly comprises a small proportion of the endowment. 'Writs' are a category not susceptible of precise definition, but include all orders to do or to refrain from doing something; I include letters conferring protection. The lay and urban categories are self-explanatory, and do not include writs. 'England ' and 'France' represent the whereabouts of the archive in which the document has survived, and is thus not quite the same as a division between English and French beneficiaries. But few or no documents for English beneficiaries have survived in France, while those in England for French beneficiaries usually relate to English lands or dependencies and are best seen in an English context. We may note as a preliminary one feature revealed by the table: the poor rate of survival in France of documents for lay beneficiaries. This might appear to be the result of a lack of incentive to keep titles deriving from a defunct regime after the Capetian conquest, or even a lack of interest in acquiring such documents in the first place, though churches were not deterred from obtaining and keeping 'Plantagenet' deeds. Perhaps it just reflects the superiority of ecclesiastical record keeping in the twelfth century.

That said, a number of points emerge clearly from Table 1. Laymen and towns overwhelmingly used chancery scribes, who also wrote a large majority of writs. The only type of document of which unidentified scribes write a majority, and then quite a considerable majority, is the general confirmation to a church. There is an obvious explanation for this: laymen and towns would not have been in such a good position to write their own documents as ecclesiastical institutions which had scriptoria – in other words, the general confirmations are beneficiary products. But there is then a contrast with the specific confirmations for churches, which are largely chancery products. How can we discover what lies behind this difference? We could begin by asking if date is a factor.

Table 2 arranges chancery and non-chancery products into dating groups distinguished by the introduction of Dei Gratia in the royal style in 1172–3. It shows that in overall totals documents from the first half of the reign outnumber those from the second half by roughly two to one; but non-chancery products from the first half of the reign outnumber later ones by more like three to one. To put it another way, non-chancery productions comprise 33% of early documents, but only 23% of later ones. So even allowing for the greater number of early documents, non-chancery production becomes less common later in the reign. It is particularly noticeable in the category of writs. Non-cancellarial writs are fairly unusual, as Table 1 revealed; we can now see that they are overwhelmingly early too. Returning to the general confirmations, Table 2 reveals an interesting discrepancy in date between cancellarial and non-cancellarial: the great majority of non-cancellarial general confirmations are early, while chancery products are concentrated later in the reign. This presents an unmistakeable drift towards chancery production, in the only category of documents where non-chancery production predominates. The specific confirmations show the same general tendency, with chancery products outnumbering others in the later period by even more than they do in the earlier period, but with a much higher number of chancery products early on. The number of non-cancellarial specific confirmations in the later period in France is apparently anomalous, but the absolute number concerned is small, and non-chancery pieces are still handsomely outnumbered by chancery

Table 1   Distribution of Documents by type

	Chancery scribes	Unid. scribes	Rough Proportion
A. General confirmations to churches			
England	12	40	
France	13	14	
Total	25	54	1 : 2
B. Specific confirmations to churches			
England	54	27	
France	30	9	
Total	84	36	2.3 : 1
C. Writs			
England	90	22	
France	20	6	
Total	110	28	4 : 1
D. Confirmations to towns			
England	14	2	7 : 1
France	—	—	
E. Confirmations, grants to laymen			
England	42	3	
France	3	1	
Total	45	4	11 : 1
Overall total	278	124	2.25 : 1

ones in the later period. The more we look at the distribution, the more the main anomaly is revealed as the early non-chancery general confirmations.

Examining the distribution by date helps to define the problem. Early in the reign, while writs and specific confirmations were generally written by chancery scribes, general confirmations were written outside the chancery, probably by the beneficiaries. The explanation probably lies in the way these documents were constructed. An obvious question to ask of a charter of Henry II which confirms an immense list of possessions is, how did the king know what to confirm? There was no central land register, of course. How did he avoid giving the beneficiaries title to possessions to which they had no right? Perhaps part of the answer is that the title conferred by the confirmation was conditional. This may be the effect of the word *rationabilis* or *rationabiliter*, which is often applied – *omnes rationabiles donationes*, which perhaps means 'given in due form'. But the best answer is provided by a further Battle story, which demonstrates that the validity of a confirmation was normally dependent on supporting evidence. The monks were anxious about a charter of William the Conqueror now decayed with age, and requested Henry to renew it. The king in person dictated (*dictavit*) a new clause, 'Since I have inspected the charter of William my ancestor, in which were contained the aforesaid liberties, etc', to replace the clause 'as the charter of so-and-so testifies'. The difference, the king himself explained, was that with the usual

Table 2   Distribution of Documents by date

		1154×73	*1172×89*	*Rough Proportion*
Non-Chancery products				
General confirmations to churches				
	England	27	9	
	France	10	4	
Specific confirmations to churches				
	England	22	5	
	France	1	8	
Writs	England	19	3	
	France	6	—	
Towns, laymen				
	England	3	1	
	France	—	1	
Total		88	31	3 : 1
Chancery products				
General confirmations to churches				
	England	3	9	
	France	4	9	
Specific confirmations to churches				
	England	33	21	
	France	15	15	
Writs	England	75	15	
	France	12	8	
Towns, laymen				
	England	34	22	
	France	2	1	
Total		178	100	1.7 : 1
Overall total		266	131	2 : 1

Note: there are also 5 undatable non-chancery documents, of which 4 are general confirmations for English churches and 1 is for a laymen.

phrase the charters referred to would be needed as evidence, and the object of the present exercise was to obviate the need for the Conqueror's decayed charter.[18] The clause *sicut carte donatorum testantur*, or with royal foundations *antecessorum meorum*, is quite common. In other words the confirmations were constructed from and intended to be supported by information supplied by the beneficiary, who probably brought along the charters to prove their right. And it seems they might well bring along a draft or a fair copy of the desired result as well. Given that the

[18] *Battle Chronicle*, 311–3.

information and the evidence were supplied by the beneficiary, what would it matter whose scribe actually wrote the document? This was the point at which missing earlier documents would need to be created, or existing ones recopied with improvements.[19] As long as they convinced contemporaries, they would give rise to a genuine confirmation. It was not necessary to forge a charter of the reigning king, if the documents which lay behind it could be made to say what was required. Thus a perfectly genuine document can confirm rights supported by spurious charters, just as a spurious document can confirm genuine rights. So the genuineness of a confirmation is quite independent of the genuineness of what it confirms; which means that a Henry II confirmation is not to be condemned as a forgery, or regarded as interpolated, because some of the items it confirms can be shown to have been controversial at just that period, or based on suspicious charters. Nor is a Henry II charter to be condemned if it was written outside the chancery and follows the beneficiary's diplomatic practices rather than the chancery's.

In all probability specific confirmations were based on the beneficiary's information too, so the same remarks on genuineness apply to them, though many more of them were written by royal scribes. More than anything, perhaps, it was a simple matter of convenience and time saving: the longer the document, the more helpful to have it ready for quick sealing. And there was probably a cost factor too, as we shall see.

The possibility that charters of Henry II may have been forged later in the middle ages to support confirmations of later kings takes us into a rather different set of problems. Within a generation of Henry's death the normal type of royal confirmation was the *inspeximus*, in which existing charters were recited verbatim. Typically the greater churches have a series of such documents, spread over perhaps three centuries, preserved on the chancery enrolments and sometimes in the original too. While it was presumably necessary to produce the charters for the first inspeximus, and charters not previously inspected could be introduced at any stage, the impression created is that by far the commonest tactic was to present an existing inspeximus, or a number of them, when the next inspection was required. The inspeximus of a former king would thus obviate the need to produce the original. Or would it? There has been very little study of the inspeximus and the chancery enrolments, given their great importance in the transmission of early charters – Anglo-Saxon and Anglo-Norman as well as those of Henry II. Was the enrolment made from the original or from the engrossment? Did the chancery itself operate any tests for authenticity? What led the possessors of charters to have them inspected, and what factors governed their choice of those to be inspected? Was it possible to forge a charter, get it inspected, and then destroy the forgery, relying afterwards on the perfectly genuine inspeximus? Whatever the answers to these questions, which open an interesting and neglected field of enquiry, they will not seriously affect conclusions based on the study of the twelfth century originals, being much more relevant to the discussion of those surviving in copies.

To return to the twelfth century, it is interesting to see who writes their own writs. They are nearly all for great ecclesiastical institutions: 2 for Ely, 2 for Lincoln, both by an identified Lincoln scribe, 2 for Lire, 3 for Ramsey, one by an

---

[19] See Marjorie Chibnall, 'Forgery in narrative charters', *Fälschungen im Mittelalter*, Monumenta Germaniae Historica, Schriften 33, iv, Hanover 1988, 332, 344–6.

identified Ramsey scribe; but by far the biggest beneficiary is the archbishop and cathedral priory of Canterbury.[20] The total is 11, and 4 of them are by an identified scribe, Bishop's scribe XIV whose known career began in the Chancery under Henry I, but who in Stephen's reign went over to Matilda before entering the service of Archbishop Theobald, many of whose acta he wrote. All these Canterbury writs date from the first half of the reign. The position of Canterbury is very noticeable among the general confirmations too. It has some of the most extraordinary documents to run in the name of Henry II, having, as Bishop put it, 'a special interest in procuring or fabricating multiplicate originals', and a tradition of large bilingual charters, Latin and English.[21] Canterbury had a quadruplicate bilingual document of Henry I, of which three survive, all by chancery hands; of Henry II, by whose reign such things are as far as I know confined to Canterbury, it has a quintuplicate bilingual document, all of them by chancery hands and four still sealed.[22] It also has another quadruplicate, though only in one language, all four sealed, two by chancery scribes, one possibly a Christ Church hand, and one, according to Bishop, a bad imitation of one of the chancery hands.[23] Some Canterbury documents struck Henry himself as rank forgeries when they were read out to him near the end of his reign: he 'swore magnificently' on hearing the first, continued to do so on hearing the second, 'touching his eyes and banging his neck', and continued to rage while no less than seven charters were read out to him.[24] If quite such lavish and odd products mark Canterbury out, it is not alone in having multiple copies: others survive for Durham, also quadruplicates, all by unidentified scribes, and Lincoln, triplicates, two by chancery scribes, also Salisbury, Mont St Michel, Fontevrault, St Etienne Caen, and other places.[25] The reason for making multiples is clear, and the invaluable Battle chronicle spells it out: after the decayed William I charter had been renewed, the new charter was executed in triplicate, all identical, all sealed: 'for the monastery's estates lie at some distance from the monastery, and if ever for some reason one, or even two of the three were taken elsewhere, one of them at least would now always be at hand in the monastery.'[26]

A quick way of producing a valid copy would be to seal the draft which perhaps the beneficiary brought along. Delisle has an instance of a document by a beneficiary's scribe to which the witness list and place date have been added in a different hand and ink.[27] Or alternatively the draft could be retained in the beneficiary's archive, to the confusion of later historians: I suspect this is what happened with a Henry II charter for Cluny, and with a supposed charter of Stephen for Cluny, which is full of crossings-out and interlineations; the editors of *Regesta* iii regard this as a 'pretended original', but I'm not at all sure it's pretending.[28] If

[20] Holt and Mortimer nos 92, 96 (Ely), 160, 165 (Lincoln), 226, 234, 240 (Ramsey), 43, 49, 52A, 53, 56, 59, 61 (Canterbury), 44–7 (Canterbury by scribe XIV – Bishop nos 110, 115–16, 122); *Recueil* nos CCCLVI, CCCXXXI (Lire).

[21] Bishop, 34.

[22] Bishop, 34; Holt and Mortimer no. 41.

[23] Holt and Mortimer no. 67, Bishop nos 108 (Christ Church hand), 292 (bad imitation).

[24] *Epistolae Cantuarienses*, ed. W. Stubbs, RS 1865, 221 – I owe this reference to Professor Christopher Holdsworth.

[25] Holt and Mortimer nos 88, 161, 164, 178, 262; *Recueil* CCXXXVIII, CLIV, XXXVI.

[26] *Battle Chronicle*, 311–13.

[27] *Recueil* i, 280–1.

[28] *Recueil* XLIX; *Regesta* iii, no. 444, compare R. Mortimer, 'The Baynards of Baynard's Castle', in

this was the case with confirmations it was even more so with writs, and a number of writs exist in multiple copies, presumably, as Bishop suggested, for production to officials in different places at the same time, and as a precaution against wear and tear. There are also identically worded writs for the same beneficiary made out to different addressees, those ordering freedom from toll being quite commonly executed in multiples in this form.[29]

Now when charters are being executed in several copies, by different scribes simultaneously or one scribe serially, the proper names need not be spelt in the same way in each copy, nor is it impossible that minor textual variations may creep in. The effect of this is to undermine the concept of 'the original' as a unique physical object. It is not necessary to suppose that every surviving later transcription of a document, each with its own variants, derives from a single authoritative ancestor: they could derive from a group of siblings, closely related but all subtly different.

A concrete instance of the production of multiples is provided by a letter from the register of Master David of London.[30] The story goes as follows. Master David, sent by Gilbert Foliot to appeal to Rome against Becket's excommunication of him in 1169, succeeded brilliantly, the pope in a letter even saying that it was David who persuaded him to grant Bishop Gilbert absolution. Returning armed with testimonials and recommendations for benefices, David was assigned an annual pension of £20 by the king from the archdeaconry of Oxfordshire in the vacant bishopric of Lincoln; Gilbert Foliot also gave him a pension of £10 a year. David was then sent on an embassy to Becket – we are now in 1170 – and the archbishop took the opportunity to upbraid Master David about his pension from the king (*durissimam mihi retulit controversiam*), presumably, as Z. N. Brooke suggested, because Becket rejected the king's right to dispose of the revenues of a vacant see. This alarmed David for the security of his tenure, and he persuaded the king to assign his £20 pension elsewhere, on the king's own income. This was to be £15 paid by Rannulf de Broc (a man with a lurid future in 1170) from the hundred of Godalming; and £5 paid to the king annually by the bishop of London. The written orders needed to achieve this transaction were as follows:

(1) a confirmation of the transaction by the king
(2) another confirmation of Gilbert Foliot's gift of a pension
(3) an order to Henry the young king to confirm both the above in identical terms (*per similes suas*)
(4) a writ to Rannulf de Broc to pay the £15 without demanding further written proof from David
(5) a writ to the bishop to pay the £5 to David, which writ David himself took to the bishop
(6) a writ to the sheriffs of Middlesex telling them to cease demanding the £5 from the bishop

Studies in Medieval History presented to R. Allen Brown, ed. C. Harper-Bill, C. Holdsworth and J. L. Nelson, Boydell Press 1989, 244 and n. 9. See also Bishop, 33.
[29] Bishop, 34–5.
[30] Z. N. Brooke, 'The Register of Master David of London, and the Part he Played in the Becket Crisis', in *Essays in History presented to Reginald Lane Poole*, ed. H. W. C. Davis, Oxford 1927, 237–41.

(7) a writ to the barons of the exchequer telling them to allow £15 to
Rannulf and £5 to the bishop from what they would normally be
expected to account for – in other words a writ of *computate*.

David then tells his correspondent that he is having copies of the writ of
computate and the writ to Rannulf sealed as a precaution against them being queried
– *transcriptum illius, et transcriptum eius quod mittitur Rannulfo, ad cautelam ne
quandoque malignari possint sigillari feci* – which he wanted kept by the addressee
of the letter with his other charters. This should be done as quickly as possible,
sparing neither trouble nor expense, and Richard of Ilchester and Geoffrey Ridel
were writing to William de St John and Thomas the *sigillarius* (who is otherwise
unknown) telling them to get on with it (*ut curent hec expedite fieri*).
   There is much of interest in this story, and I will not attempt to discuss it all.
He does in fact say 'copy' – *transcriptum* – as in this instance one piece of
parchment for each order must have had priority in time, but the *transcripta* must
be of equal authority or there would be no point in having them. It is interesting
to see that it could take some time to have copies made: so they are not necessarily
the product of one occasion. We might even speculate who the witnesses to the
copies would have been – those to the 'original', presumably, even if one had died
in the meantime; would Richard of Ilchester and Geoffrey Ridel have been added
to the list, since their authority was behind the copy? But the most obvious feature
of Master David's story is the sheer quantity of parchment-work produced by the
royal administration in the course of the transaction, none of which has survived,
though the effect can be traced on the Pipe Rolls. Historians have always been
aware that what survives is the tip of an iceberg, but attempts to quantify the
amount of internal secretarial work run into serious difficulties. Bishop says he
counted some 300 references to writs on the Pipe Roll of 31 Henry I,[31] and for
what the figures are worth I have found 149 references on the the roll for 1161–2
when Henry was in France, 109 on that for 1163–4 when he was in England, and
175 on the 1182–3 roll when he was in France. The difficulty is to know how many
writs each of these entries represents: many of them take the form '*et in perdon'
per br' regis*', to *a* so much, to *b* so much, to *c* so much, so that one cannot tell
from the grammar whether the writ was singular or plural; there could have been
one writ covering them all, one each, or some unguessable combination of the two.
Then there is the matter of the writs, of which Glanvill gives us the texts, which
initiated legal proceedings under the assizes, and of which little or nothing has
survived, and the large quantity of orders, which we know about from Pipe Roll
references, concerning routine matters such as transporting treasure, restocking
manors, victualling castles, arranging Channel passages for royal servants and so
on. But the point about the internal secretarial work is not so much that it was
onerous, though it surely was, as that it existed at all. There is a class of document
having no beneficiary outside the royal administrative system; so there was no
alternative to a nucleus of royal scribes for writing them. This is a point to
remember when comparing Henry II's government with that of other contemporary
princes.
   The chancery as an institution has not been ignored by historians, and I am not
going to try to say everything that could be said about it under Henry II, which

31 Bishop, 32.

would in any case be very premature. I shall just point out what appear to me to be a few salient relevant features. Firstly, it didn't work for nothing; the beneficiary had to pay, over and above whatever bargain he may have had to make with the king himself. We even have a scale of charges: in 1199, after John's coronation, at Hubert Walter's instance, the charges were put back to what they had been in King Henry's day.[32] (There is no need to doubt that the prices represent those charged at least at some time in Henry's reign, which after all was only ten years earlier.) For a charter of new enfeoffment, a mark of gold or 10 marks for the chancellor, a mark of silver each for the vicechancellor and the 'protonotharius', and 5s for the wax; for a simple confirmation with nothing new inserted, a mark for the chancellor, a 'bisancius' each for the vicechancellor and the protonotary, 1s for the wax; for a 'simple protection', 2s. This also gives us a glimpse of one way the chancery categorized its products, probably reflecting the work involved. And it shows that the chancellorship was an office of profit.

. The first and best known of Henry's chancellors was of course Thomas Becket. Up to his resignation in 1162 he was very active; he witnessed an enormous number of documents, and he was no doubt ultimately responsible for their production. But William fitz Stephen, in his life of Becket, makes it clear that Becket's activities were many and various: the chancellor 'has custody of the seal ... He is in charge of the order and arrangement of the royal chapel. He takes into his keeping all vacant archbishoprics, bishoprics, abbeys, and baronies that fall into the king's hands. He takes his seat in all the king's councils ... Everything is signed by the hand of his clerk who bears the royal seal, and everything is ordered by the counsel of the chancellor'.[33] The biographer goes on to describe Becket's embassy to Paris, and his military exploits on the Toulouse campaign. Of course Becket as chancellor was a great deal more than Henry's chief clerk; the work of document production was carried out by subordinates – the vice-chancellor and 'protonotarius' of the price-list. This makes it comprehensible that Becket had no titular successor until 1173: for over ten years there was no chancellor at all. That the office was a source of profit explains how the other two chancellors, Ralph de Warneville and Geoffrey the king's son, came to be appointed, and how they left so little mark on Henry's acta. The office of chancellor was not actually necessary, and after Becket Henry may have doubted whether it was desirable in quite that form.

What we know of the personnel and working methods of the chancery has to be pieced together from scraps of information, and deduced from the documents themselves. Bishop pointed out how some individual scribes achieve some consistency of formulation in their own work.[34] This could be, as he suggests, because the scribes themselves were responsible for the details of composition. But there are indications that dictation was a common method of composition – perhaps even the normal method in the twelfth century [35]. William fitz Stephen describes himself as a *dictator* in the chancery under Thomas Becket.[36] One of the *Epistolae*

---

[32] Printed in T. Rymer, *Foedera* i, 75–6.
[33] *Materials for the History of Thomas Becket*, ed. J. C. Robertson and J. B. Sheppard, RS 1875–1885, iii, 18.
[34] Bishop, 20.
[35] M. Clanchy, *From Memory to Written Record*, 97.
[36] *Mats. Becket* iii, 1.

Cantuarienses relates a vivid episode illustrating a number of points about document production. It is a letter of a monk of Canterbury cathedral priory, writing to his convent in February 1189 about the stage reached in the interminable dispute between the monks and the archbishop resulting from Archbishop Baldwin's intention to found a college of secular canons.[37] Brother R, bringing letters from Rome, had caught up with the king at Le Mans: the archbishop was there too. Having plucked up the courage to tell the king that a certain someone was attempting to destroy the church, Brother R relates that the king swore that he would take good care of the honour and profit of the church of Canterbury. Later he summoned the archbishop, through Hubert Walter, dean of York, and Roger the almoner, and they agreed that the king should write to the cathedral priory. The dean dictated the letter (*decanus dictavit litteras*), in the presence and hearing of Brother R, who had the letter sealed (*et ego feci illas sigillare*). The actual writing cannot have taken place in the archbishop's presence, because when he heard what had happened he rushed to the court wanting to see the letter. He sent Hubert Walter and Peter of Blois to the chancery (*ad cancellariam*), and they broke the king's seal. (It must have been a letter close.) When the archbishop came in, he said to the dean, ' "*oportet quedam deponere et quedam apponere*", ("some things will have to be got rid of, and others added"). To which I said, "You can add what you like, but I won't take the letter" (*Talia potestis apponere quod litteras non feram*). Angrily the archbishop replied, "You certainly won't! I will take it", and he went to the chamber (*thalamus*), and added three clauses. Coming out again, he made two letters, giving one to me and keeping the other. *Nullo modo* will I send you this letter', continues Brother R, 'without forewarning you.'

Perhaps not every actum of Henry II includes unauthorised interpolations by the archbishop of Canterbury, but the story shows how the apparently formal matter of document production can actually be the stuff of politics and intrigue. It also shows how letters could be produced without the principals being present, or even knowing exactly what they contained. It would be interesting to know who the witnesses to that document were. It was dictated by Hubert Walter.

If dictation was frequently used, and multiple originals by different hands do suggest dictation, scribal consistency in formulae could be explained by the dictator's consistency, plus a stable dictator-scribe relationship. Bishop suggested that some scribes might have been personally dependent on senior members of the chancery, though the evidence is inconclusive; the 1199 price list does not mention the scribe, who presumably received any payments through one of the seniors.[38] But it seems likely that they were all ultimately dependents of the chancellor, at least under Becket. In the first years of Henry's reign there was a group of 4 very similar scribes at work,[39] two of whom produced copies of the quintuplicate bilingual document for Canterbury, while another, scribe XIV, is an identified Canterbury and former chancery scribe. We know that Henry turned to Archbishop Theobald to recommend a candidate for the chancellorship – Becket, says William fitz Stephen, was appointed *commendatione et obtentu archiepiscopi*.[40] If the king

[37] *Epistolae Cantuarienses*, 544–5.
[38] Bishop, 27.
[39] Bishop scribes XXVIII, XXX, XXXI, XXXII.
[40] *Mats. Becket* iii, 17.

got his chancellor from Canterbury, it would be only natural for Becket to take some of his scribes from there, one of them, scribe XIV, what one might call an old chancery hand. In working for the king they joined at least 2 scribes who had been working for Henry as duke of Normandy.[41]

Once working for the king, there is no reason to suppose that scribes led institutionally static lives. The Pipe Roll of 31 Henry I was written by Bishop's scribe VIII, who may have left the chancery at that stage; scribe XLIV, who wrote a surviving original of Henry and another of Richard I, also wrote 2 chancellor's rolls in the 1180s.[42] The Dialogue of the Exchequer explains that the clerk in charge of the king's scriptorium has to find scribes for the chancellor's roll, for writs made in the exchequer and summonses.[43] But not all the writing in the exchequer was carried out by chancery clerks: the treasurer had scribes too, who wrote what appear to have been estreat rolls while the exchequer was in session, and it was the treasurer's scribe who wrote the treasurer's roll itself.[44] But writing was necessary at many points in the machinery of government; for instance, the Dialogue refers to rolls of the justices in eyre (*minores perambulantium iudicum rotuli*), which were excerpted by the treasurer's scribes.[45] The chancery cannot have had anything like a monopoly of the writing business. The chancellor's scribes are engaged on several types of business in various places, but as we have seen they hadn't even a monopoly of what they chiefly did, though their proportion of it was growing in Henry II's reign. There are treasurer's scribes doing other things, and clearly there are still other groups: sheriffs had clerks too. Perhaps government in the twelfth century is best conceived of as a series of households, linked but semi-independent, with a certain amount of staff mobility – I feel we tend to exaggerate its degree of centralisation, under the influence perhaps of the Dialogue of the Exchequer, and of 20th century assumptions. Document production was fluid, informal and subject to many pressures; genuine documents can contain many kinds of oddity occasioned by the circumstances under which they were produced.

Are there limits to the acceptable oddities? To go back to the beginning, Bishop suggested a very few ground rules, a 'general average' for chancery productions, to which beneficiary scribes often conform, but not always. Now if, as I suspect, diplomatic oddities correlate with beneficiary, or at least non-chancery, production (and this is only a suspicion subject to confirmation when the collection of *acta* is finished), then we can expect to find the oddities concentrated in certain types of document – general confirmations to churches, early specific confirmations, and some early writs to churches; and if oddities are found there, they should not occasion surprise. But this is still not to say that oddities occurring elsewhere invalidate a charter. The effect of these rambling thoughts has been to stand the normal process of criticism on its head – they suggest looking, not for reasons to reject, but for reasons to include. The criteria of authenticity are not strong enough

---

[41] Bishop scribes XXIII, XXIV.

[42] Bishop, 29.

[43] *Dialogus de Scaccario*, ed. C. Johnson, Nelson 1950, 26. The Chancellor's Rolls were, and continued to be, written in typical Pipe Roll hands, which by John's reign were very different from those used in chancery documents; but this did not preclude chancery scribes from writing them and using chancery hand in other documents, a point made by Professor Holt.

[44] *Dialogus*, 29–31, 70.

[45] *Dialogus*, 70.

for us to reject with confidence. When confronted with a diplomatically odd Henry II document therefore, I suggest the best approach is to think that it might be genuine and to try to imagine how it came about. And if that fails, suspend judgement.

NORMANDY OR BRITTANY?
A CONFLICT OF INTERESTS AT MONT SAINT MICHEL
(966–1035)[1]

Cassandra Potts

On 7 February 966, Lothar, King of France, issued a charter on behalf of Mont Saint Michel which has traditionally been seen to mark the beginning of Norman dominance over the reformed Benedictine community.[2] The document, which survives as an interpolated pseudo-original from the mid-eleventh century, states that Richard I of Normandy restored *in melius* the place called Mont Saint Michel. With Pope John XIII and the archbishop of Rouen, he then requested that King Lothar confirm its reformation, a petition which the king willingly granted. Although the editors of the charter accept the essential content of Lothar's confirmation, John XIII's role in the reform of the abbey should most likely be discounted, since the scribe's purpose in redrafting the charter a century later was

[1] The research presented in this article was supported by a Fulbright Grant, an International Doctoral Research Fellowship from the Social Science Research Council, a Gilbert Chinard Scholarship from the Institut Français de Washington, and a Humanities Research Grant from the University of California, Santa Barbara. I owe special thanks to M. Jean-Luc Leservoisier, the conservator of the *fonds ancien* at Avranches, who very kindly made it possible for me to work on the cartulary of Mont Saint Michel while the library was closed for renovation. I am also very grateful to Dr Katharin Mack for her helpful comments and suggestions on an earlier draft.
[2] *Recueil des actes de Lothaire et de Louis V, rois de France (954–987)*, ed. Louis Halphen and Ferdinand Lot, Paris 1908, 53–7, no. 24. In 1891, Ferdinand Lot argued that the refoundation of Mont Saint Michel should be seen in the context of the peace of Gisors, which he dated to 966 rather than 965, and he consequently redated Lothar's charter to 967 in order to have it follow the settlement of peace. When Lot and Halphen published Lothar's charter seventeen years later, however, they chose the earlier date for the refoundation. See below, note 56. Ferdinand Lot, *Les derniers Carolingiens, Lothaire, Louis V, Charles de Lorraine, 954–991*, 2nd edn, Paris 1975, appendix viii, 346–57. On the history of the refoundation of Mont Saint Michel, see collected articles in the *Millénaire monastique du Mont Saint-Michel*, 2 vols, Paris 1966, in particular: Jean Laporte, 'L'Abbaye du Mont Saint-Michel aux Xe et XIe siècles' i, 53–80. Also see: René Herval, 'L'Abbaye du Mont-Saint-Michel', in *La Normandie Bénédictine au temps de Guillaume le Conquérant (XIe siècle)*, Lille 1967, 117–36; J. J. G. Alexander, *Norman Illumination at Mont St Michel, 966–1100*, Oxford 1970, 1–21. For more general studies on the recovery of monasticism in Normandy, see: Jean Laporte, 'Les origines du monachisme dans la province de Rouen', *Revue Mabillon* xxxi, 1941, 1–41, 49–68; Jean-François Lemarignier, *Etude sur les privilèges d'exemption et de juridiction ecclésiastique des abbayes normandes*, Paris 1937; Lucien Musset, 'Les abbayes normandes au Moyen Age: position de quelques problèmes' in *Les abbayes de Normandie, actes du XIIIe congrès des sociétés historiques et archéologiques de Normandie*, Rouen 1979, pp. 14–26; Lucien Musset, 'Monachisme d'époque franque et monachisme d'époque ducale en Normandie: le problème de la continuité' in *Aspects du monachisme en Normandie (IVe–XVIIIe siècles): Actes du Colloque Scientifique de l'Année des Abbayes Normandes'*, ed. Lucien Musset, Paris 1982, pp. 55–74.

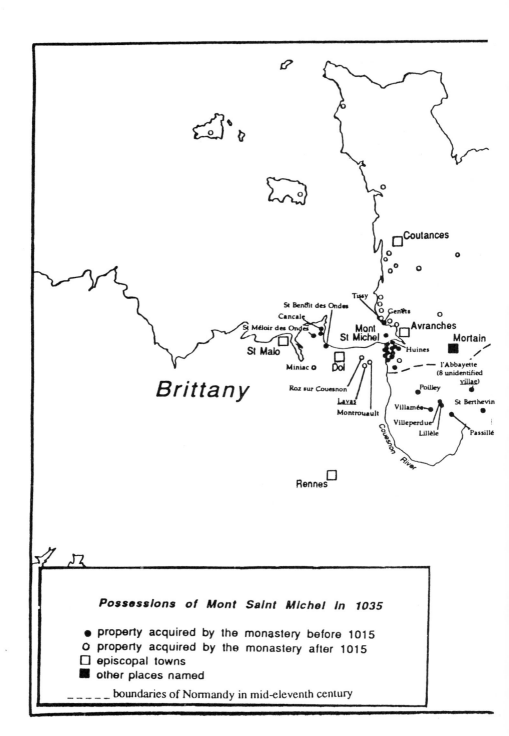

Coutances

Tissy
St Benoît des Ondes
Cancale
St Méloir des Ondes
Genêts
Mont
St Michel
Avranches
Mortain
St Malo
Huines
Miniac
Dol
l'Abbayette
(8 unidentified
villae)
Roz sur Couesnon
Poilley
Brittany
Lavas
Villamée
St Berthevin
Montrouault
Villeperdue
Lillèle
Passillé

Couesnon River

Rennes

Possessions of Mont Saint Michel in 1035

- ● property acquired by the monastery before 1015
- ○ property acquired by the monastery after 1015
- ☐ episcopal towns
- ■ other places named
- _ _ _ _ _ boundaries of Normandy in mid-eleventh century

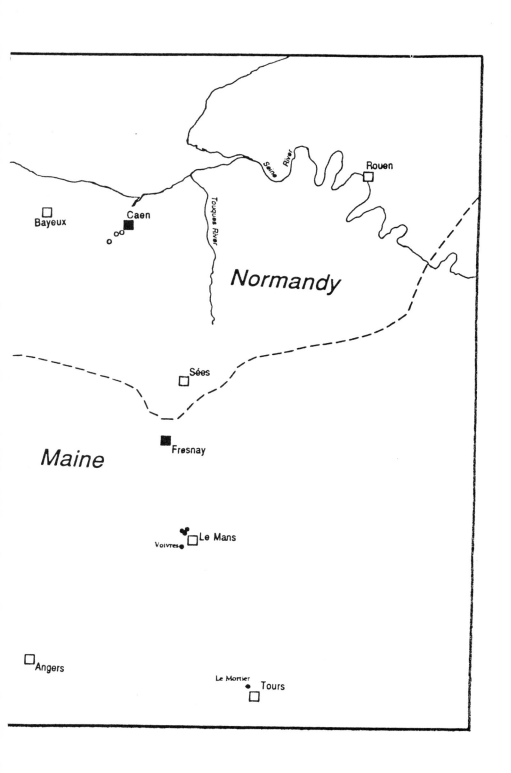

Bayeux

Caen

Seine River

Rouen

Touques River

Normandy

Sées

Fresnay

Maine

Voivres ● □ Le Mans

Angers

Le Mortier ● □ Tours

to include a forged bull from this pope promising free abbatial elections.[3]

Lothar's confirmation, if it can be trusted, represents the earliest surviving evidence of Norman involvement in the refoundation of Mont Saint Michel. It gives no indication, however, that Duke Richard I or his archbishop actually appealed directly to Lothar; it merely says that their request 'came to our ears'.[4] No attestation list reveals who was present at the time of the confirmation, and the only signator of the document was the king himself. Jean Laporte, in fact, suggests that Maynard, the Flemish reformer whom Richard I sent from Saint Wandrille to rule the Mont, should receive credit for gaining Lothar's consent rather than Richard I or the archbishop.[5] The earliest extant Norman charter concerning the abbey was drawn up in 1009.[6] For over forty years after the traditional date of the refoundation of Mont Saint Michel, therefore, the record sources are silent regarding Norman involvement in the community's future.

No contemporary narrative sources help to fill in the picture, although Dudo of Saint Quentin, writing during the first decades of the eleventh century, briefly describes Richard I's construction of monastic buildings and the gathering of monks at the Mont.[7] The fullest description of the community's reformation is found in the *Introductio monachorum*, composed during the second half of the eleventh century.[8] Thoroughly Norman in its outlook and bias, the *Introductio* dwells on the corruption and decadence of the canons whom the Benedictines replaced, and extolls the generosity of Richard I, describing his frequent gifts and visits to the community. This account of the refoundation of Mont Saint Michel also places importance on Pope John XIII's alleged bull and the freedom of elections which

---

[3] The editors suggest that the monks destroyed a genuine tenth-century document when they concocted the extant act a century later. Two charters actually survive from the eleventh century, one which is interpolated, and another, which Lot and Halphen consider the first attempt at falsification, in which the papal bull follows the act, rather than being interpolated. On this charter, also see: Lemarignier, *Etude*, 29, n. 10.

[4] Halphen, *Recueil*, 56: 'Pro cujus perpetuo roboramine atque stabilitate, domni prefati papae necnon et memorati marchisi atque Hugonis, sanctae Rotomagensis aeclesiae archiepiscopi, ad cujus diocesim pertinet jamdictus locus, nostras devenit ad aures petitio id ipsum nostro perpetuo manendum roborare fulcimine.'

[5] Laporte, 'Abbaye', 61. Jean-François Lemarignier, *Recherches sur l'hommage en marche et les frontières féodales*, Lille 1945, 68, n. 165. Lemarignier makes the point that the case was certainly unusual, in that Mont Saint Michel was the only monastery which lay in the lands of what would be later Normandy to receive a royal confirmation of its refoundation.

[6] Fauroux no. 12. For a description and analysis of the written sources on Mont Saint Michel, see: Jacques Hourlier, 'Les sources écrites de l'histoire montoise antérieure à 966' in *Millénaire* ii, 121–32.

[7] Dudo, 290: 'In Monte namque maritimo, refluae lunari dispositione inundationis gurgite undique secus circumdato, delubrum mirae amplitudinis, spatiosaque monachilis habitationis moenia construxit: ibique monachos, sub aerumnosa theoricae vitae palaestra, normalibus celebris itineris decretis astrictos, Christo coegit famulari.' The most comprehensive study of Dudo's *De moribus* remains: Henri Prentout, *Etude critique sur Dudon de Saint-Quentin et son histoire des premiers ducs normands*, Mémoires de l'Académie Nationale des Sciences, Arts et Belles-Lettres de Caen, 1915. More recently, see: Eleanor Searle, 'Fact and Pattern in Heroic History: Dudo of Saint-Quentin', *Viator* xv, 1984, 75–86; Eleanor Searle, *Predatory Kinship and the Creation of Norman Power, 840–1066*, Berkeley 1988, especially 61–7; Elisabeth van Houts, 'The *Gesta Normannorum Ducum*: a history without an end', *ante* iii, 1981, 106–18; Gerda Huisman, 'Notes on the Manuscript Tradition of Dudo of St. Quentin's *Gesta Normannorum*', *ante* vi, 1984, 122–36.

[8] *Introductio monachorum et miracula insigniora* in Thomas Le Roy, *Livre des curieuses recherches du Mont-Sainct-Michel*, ed. Eugène de Robillard de Beaurepaire, Mémoires de la Société des Antiquaires de Normandie xxix, 1876, Appendix III, 864–92. I would like to thank Dr Elisabeth van Houts for providing me with a copy of this edition.

it purports to guarantee, an emphasis which somewhat undermines confidence in the *Introductio*'s veracity.[9]

Although written a century after the event, the *Introductio monachorum* has led historians to see Mont Saint Michel mainly in the context of the Norman realm. Thus, Jean Laporte ascribes the reform of the abbey in part to the need of the Norman dukes to have a secure base for the reconquest of Brittany, and Jean-François Lemarignier describes the monks at the Mont, 'at the front rank of Norman pioneers at the border of Brittany'.[10] Jacques Dubois presents a survey of the dependencies of Mont Saint Michel across France *circa* 1200, and concludes that 'the most important domains were given by the dukes of Normandy or members of their family'.[11] Although true by the end of the twelfth century, this had not always been the case. As David Bates points out, Breton and Manceaux lords were the first to endow Mont Saint Michel after 966.[12] There is no reason to believe, moreover, that the view of Brittany as a land for the Norman dukes to reconquer existed before Dudo wove his tale of the Norman past. Indeed, it was by no means a foregone conclusion in the tenth century that the Norman duchy would even include Mont Saint Michel. That it did has led historians to minimize the difficulty of the monks' position and the complexity of their response in a society disrupted and fragmented by the Viking invasions.

Several books which have appeared recently reinforce the need to reconsider Mont Saint Michel's position in the tenth and early eleventh centuries. On one hand, Constance Bouchard's study of the nobility and church in eleventh and twelfth century Burgundy, and Penelope Johnson's monograph on the abbey of La Trinité, Vendôme both encourage historians to view monastic communities in their social context; from the point of view of the monks and their neighbors.[13] Emily Zack Tabuteau's detailed work on Norman property law also offers much insight into the specific agreements and compromises between monks and laymen in early Normandy.[14] Likewise, Stephen White in his study on the *laudatio parentum* and Barbara Rosenwein in her latest book on Cluniac property stress the role of abbeys as local institutions – their relations with the communities outside the abbey walls and the role of land as a bond which united the lay and monastic worlds.[15] The emphasis of these scholars on the significance of monasteries in local society encourages a reevaluation of Mont Saint Michel's situation in the period of the

[9] M. Lelegard, 'Saint Aubert' in *Millénaire* i, 29–52, suggests that the *Introductio* might have been composed by Renouf of Bayeux, abbot of the Mont from c.1055 to 1085. His suggestion is strengthened by the correspondence in dates between Renouf's abbacy and the fabrication of Pope John XIII's bull. Also see: Jacques Hourlier, 'Le Mont Saint-Michel avant 966' in *Millénaire* i, 13–28; Hourlier, 'Les sources,' 128–9.

[10] Jean Laporte, 'Gérard de Brogne à Saint-Wandrille et à Saint-Riquier' *Revue Bénédictine* lxx, 1960, 142–66, at 164; Lemarignier, *Hommage*, 68.

[11] Jacques Dubois, 'Les dépendances de l'abbaye du Mont Saint-Michel et la vie monastique dans les prieurés' in *Millénaire* i, 619–76, at 650.

[12] David Bates, *Normandy Before 1066*, London 1982, 33.

[13] Constance Brittain Bouchard, *Sword, Miter, and Cloister: Nobility and the Church in Burgundy, 980–1198*, Ithaca 1987; Penelope D. Johnson, *Prayer, Patronage, and Power: The Abbey of la Trinité, Vendôme, 1032–1187*, New York 1981.

[14] Emily Zack Tabuteau, *Transfers of Property in Eleventh-Century Norman Law*, Chapel Hill 1988.

[15] Stephen D. White, *Custom, Kinship, and Gifts to Saints: The Laudatio Parentum in Western France, 1050–1150*, Chapel Hill 1988; Barbara H. Rosenwein, *To Be the Neighbor of Saint Peter: The Social Meaning of Cluny's Property, 909–1049*, Ithaca 1989.

Norman settlement, from the point of view of the monks struggling to retain lost lands, to secure new holdings, and to maintain the *amicitia* of their neighbors, rival territorial princes frequently at odds with each other. Legal and monastic historians, therefore, urge a fresh look at the Mont's recovery from the perspective of the monks themselves.

From the point of view of the Vikings of Rouen, on the other hand, the traditional view of Mont Saint Michel's reform needs to be reconsidered in light of Eleanor Searle's recent model of Norman expansion. While most historians would concur with David Bates that 'the territory of Normandy was forged by the aggressive wars of its tenth-century rulers,' Searle disagrees.[16] 'No reliable evidence,' she warns, 'invites us to think that "Normandy" was created in the tenth century at all, in the sense that regional leaders recognized a chieftain with authority over them all.'[17] In her eyes, the west long remained separate even after the tenth century, 'under its own local leaders, playing little part in the polity that gradually coalesced around Rouen'.[18] Searle also challenges the assumption that the Normans embraced Frankish institutions and traditions; she claims instead to find in Dudo 'evidence of Norman fear of the Franks and Norman hostility to all that was Frankish, and an anxious realization of their own disunity'.[19] Searle's assessment of the attitude and authority of the Normans of Rouen, therefore, raises the possibility that hindsight has coloured the standard view of Richard I's intentions when he refounded Mont Saint Michel as well as his ability effectively to champion this community.

The refoundation and subsequent early history of the monastery of Mont Saint Michel, therefore, needs reevaluation – first, in light of the abbey itself, as a community of monks with urgent, immediate responsibilities to neighboring communities and lordships, and second, in light of the Rouen Normans, by no means destined to control the Mont, and perhaps hardly in a position to do so for generations after the abbey's official refoundation. These two lines of inquiry, the local ties of the monks and the political range of Rouen, converge in the early 1030s when the Mont found itself in the middle of a quarrel between two cousins, Robert the Magnificent of Normandy and Alan III of Rennes. At the center of this dispute and caught between conflicting loyalties, the Mont demonstrates well the predicament of an abbey whose patrimony cut across frontiers and alliances still forming in the wake of the Viking invasions.

Those frontiers were by no means fixed and certain. Although evident to the editors of *Neustria Pia* and *Gallia Christiana* that Mont Saint Michel stood *in confinio Britonum ac Normannorum*, it would not necessarily have been as clear to the inhabitants of the monastery in the tenth and eleventh centuries just where the boundaries between these two realms might lie.[20] In fact, the *Annales de Saint-Bertin* report that Charles the Bald had ceded the Avranchin and Cotentin in

---

[16] Bates, xiv.

[17] Searle, *Predatory Kinship*, 69–70. For the background to the question of Norman expansion in the tenth century, see: John LePatourel, *The Norman Empire* (Oxford, 1976), pp. 4–15; Karl Ferdinand Werner, 'Quelques observations au sujet des débuts du "duché" de Normandie', in *Droit privé et institutions régionales: Etudes historiques offertes à Jean Yver* (Paris, 1976), pp. 691–709; Lucien Musset, 'Naissance de la Normandie (Ve–XIe siècles)', in *Histoire de la Normandie* (Toulouse, 1970), pp. 75–130.

[18] Searle, *Predatory Kinship*, 103–4.

[19] Searle, *Predatory Kinship*, 5.

[20] *Neustria Pia*, ed. A. du Monstier, Rouen 1663, 371; *Gallia Christiana* xi, Paris 1874, 510.

867 to his *fidelis*, the Breton ruler Salomon – perhaps, as Wendy Davies has recently suggested, in order to gain Breton support against the Vikings.[21] Then in 933, according to Flodoard, King Ralph granted Rollo's son William Longsword 'the land of the Bretons situated on the seacoast,' presumably those same *pagi* which Salomon had received some sixty years earlier.[22] Thus the Mont, along with the Avranchin and the Cotentin, officially passed from the Bretons to the Normans of the Seine in 933. It is important to realize, however, that these grants involved lands no longer under royal control; their goal was primarily to direct Breton and Norse aggression away from the Ile de France.[23]

Royal concessions, as limited as the royal resources, were of less concern to the Mont than the immediate conditions of the territory in which the monks lived and held property. Unfortunately, no Mont Saint Michel *acta* survive from the pre-Viking period, and only one charter exists in which lands explicitly described as having been lost during the Viking invasions were regained.[24] It is not possible, therefore, to reconstruct the patrimony of the monastery before the disruption wrought by the Norsemen. Indeed, very little at all is known about the early community at Mont Saint Michel. The primary source of information is the *Revelatio ecclesiae Sancti Michaelis*, dating perhaps from the ninth century, which describes the environs of the Mont, the visions which the archangel Michael sent Saint Autbert, bishop of Avranches, the subsequent construction of a sanctuary around 708, and Autbert's acquisition of relics from Mont Gargan.[25] A final section states that Autbert also established twelve clerics to serve the church, and gave the villages of Genêts and Huisnes to them from his diocese.[26]

Noting that the *Revelatio* calls the men whom Autbert established at Mont Saint Michel *clerici*, rather than *monachi* or *canonici*, Jacques Hourlier suggests that the Mont was inhabited before 966 by non-Benedictine monks, most likely practicing a Breton form of asceticism, rather than the decadent canons portrayed by the later *Introductio monachorum*.[27] Hourlier's argument rests on the assumption that the *Revelatio* author, following the reforms of Benedict of Aniane and Louis the Pious, hesitated to call non-Benedictines 'monks.' The evidence is too slim to confirm Hourlier's theory, but the fact that the single known head of the Mont between

---

[21] *Annales de Saint Bertin*, ed. F. Grat, J. Vielliard, S. Clémencet, Paris 1964, 137; Wendy Davies, *Small Worlds: The Village Community in Early Medieval Brittany*, Berkeley 1988, 19–20.

[22] *Annales de Flodoard*, ed. Philippe Lauer, Paris 1906, 55: 'Willelmus, princeps Nordmannorum, eidem regi se committit; cui etiam rex dat terram Brittonum in ora maritima sitam.'

[23] Searle, 'Frankish Rivalries', 208–9, has aptly described the king's grant to William Longsword in 933 as being as idle as the grant of Brittany and Nantes to the Vikings of the Loire in the 920s. She notes that no one came to the aid of the Loire Vikings when the Bretons returned to drive them out in 937.

[24] *Cartulaire de Saint-Michel de l'Abbayette, prieuré de l'Abbaye du Mont-Saint-Michel*, ed. Bertrand de Broussillon, Paris 1894, 9–12, no. 1.

[25] *Revelatio ecclesiae Sancti Michaelis* in Le Roy, Appendix II, 856–63. The earliest copy of the *Revelatio* which exists (Bibl. Avranches, MS 211, fols 156r–210v) was transcribed by the monk Hervardus between 990 and 1015. For a description of MS 211 and other work by Hervardus, see: Alexander, 224–7; François Avril, 'La décoration des manuscrits au Mont Saint-Michel (XIe–XIIe siècles)' in *Millénaire* ii, 203–38, at 204–5. Hourlier, 'Sources écrites,' 124–8, dates the *Revelatio* to the second half of the ninth century.

[26] Hourlier, 'Sources écrites,' 125–8, considers this last section an appendix added to the ninth-century text in the mid-tenth century. However, I consider it likely that the gifts attributed to Aubert in the *Revelatio* were indeed among the community's earliest possessions. I am grateful to Dr Elisabeth van Houts for her comments on this subject.

[27] Hourlier, 'Le Mont', 22–8.

Autbert, in the early eighth century, and Maynard, in the second half of the tenth century, is *abbas* Phinimontius, *brito*, c.865, strengthens his case.[28] And certainly, the author of the *Introductio*, by depicting Mont Saint Michel's previous inhabitants as resisting reform, intent only on feasting, hunting, and other pleasures, followed a convention which Benedictines often employed to denigrate the communities they supplanted.[29] Indeed, in this case the author may have had a double axe to grind, since in his eyes the virtuous Benedictines had come from upper Normandy.

But all this rests on very little. The first three centuries of religious life at the Mont must, unfortunately, remain shrouded in mystery. For the ninth and tenth centuries, it can only be said with some assurance that the territory in the vicinity of Mont Saint Michel sustained many hardships from conflicts between Bretons, Franks and Vikings; and that whoever held the Mont would have suffered from the prolonged disruption. In the ninth century, Breton leaders alternated between alliance and enmity toward the Franks, as it suited their interests and intrigues.[30] In the early tenth century, the ravages of the Vikings forced many Bretons to flee into France or across the channel. When they returned in the 930s, rallied by Alan Barbetorte and backed by King Athelstan of England, they took their vengeance in blood.[31] But even after Alan had 'driven the Vikings out of all the Breton region' – undoubtedly an overstatement coming from the *Chronicle of Nantes* – peace did not follow the Breton homecoming.[32] Before Alan's death in mid-century, internal rivalry between houses, in particular between the counts of Nantes and Rennes, undermined hope for security in this region.[33] Outside intervention further exacerbated tensions, as the counts of Anjou and Blois-Chartres attempted to profit from Brittany's disunity, and Vikings, especially those who had settled on the Loire, continued to make raids on Breton lands.[34]

It is doubtful that Breton lords would have cared – if they had even known – that the king had given their lands in the Cotentin and Avranchin to the Vikings of Rouen in 933. Rosamond McKitterick's appraisal, that 'the Bretons simply lost control over this region in the early years of the tenth century, and the Cotentin Vikings moved in', probably more closely reflects the practical reality of the

[28] *Descriptiones Terrae Sanctae*, ed. Titus Tobler, Leipzig 1874, 97–8.

[29] *Introductio*, 868. For a comparable example of canons with lands along a sensitive frontier, charged with decadence to justify reform, see: Francis X. Hartigan, 'Reform of the Collegiate Clergy in the Eleventh Century: The Case of Saint-Nicholas at Poitiers', *Studies in Medieval Culture* vi–vii, 1976, 55–62. On this subject more generally, see: Lucien Musset, 'Recherches sur les Communautés de Clercs Séculiers en Normandie au XIe siècle', *Bulletin de la Société des Antiquaires de Normandie* lv, 1961, 5–38; Jacques Dubois, 'Les moines dans la société du moyen âge (950–1350)' in *Histoire monastique en France au XIIe siècle*, London 1982, ch. 2, 5–37 (originally published in *Revue d'histoire de l'église de France* lx, 1974, 5–37).

[30] Davies, 7–28; Searle, *Predatory Kinship*, 27–33.

[31] Flodoard, 63; *La Chronique de Nantes*, ed. René Merlet, Paris 1896, 87–91.

[32] *Nantes*, 88: 'donec Alanus Barbetorta, Alani Magni nepos, surrexit et hos Normannos ab omni regione Britannica et a fluvio Ligeris, qui illis erat nutrimentum magnum, omnino depulsos dejecit.' Since Flodoard, 94, reports that Northmen attacked Brittany and captured Dol in 944, the *Chronicle of Nantes* must have overestimated Alan's success.

[33] Flodoard, 94, discusses discord between Berenger, count of Rennes, and Alan Barbetorte. Also see: Lemarignier, *Hommage*, 116; Arthur de la Borderie, *Essai sur la géographie féodale de la Bretagne*, Rennes 1889, 1–5; Guy Devailly, 'Les dépendances bretonnes des abbayes Normandes (Xe–XIII siècles)', in *Aspects du monachism*, 115–24.

[34] *Nantes*, 110–120; Richer, *Histoire de France (888–995)*, ed. Robert Latouche, 2nd edn, Paris 1964, ii, 278–97; Olivier Guillot, *Le comte d'Anjou et son entourage au XIe siècle*, Paris 1972, i, 8–12.

situation.[35] The report of Bretons and Vikings vying for lands as far east as Caen, however, argues against an easy advance during the first half of the tenth century.[36] Around mid-century, the emergence of Harold, Viking leader of Bayeux, must have quashed whatever Breton ambitions remained in the Bessin.[37] To the north of the Mont, toponymic evidence shows Scandinavian settlement heaviest along the west coast, from Granville to Cherbourg.[38] And Michel de Bouard's excavations at La Hague Dike, by confirming the Scandinavian origin of this rampart, point to an entrenched Viking camp at the western tip of the Cherbourg peninsula.[39] Those Scandinavians who settled in the Cotentin, as well as those in the Bessin, would have had scant reason to consider the Vikings of Rouen as their overlords; the royal grants which declared these areas for the house of Rollo would have carried as little meaning for rival Vikings as for Bretons. It was up to the Normans of Rouen to collect.

The monks who accompanied Maynard to Mont Saint Michel in 966 or thereabouts, would have encountered a challenging situation. Far from their protector in Rouen, bereft of property, in a contested area, they were not in an enviable position – located, like the monks of Redon to their south, on a border area, which lacked stability.[40] It is also possible that the house suffered, at least initially, from internal dissension, divided between the newcomers, perhaps around thirty monks, and the previous inhabitants of the Mont, whether monks or canons.[41] However, since Bretons continued to enter the monastery in the

---

[35] Rosamond McKitterick, *The Frankish Kingdoms under the Carolingians, 751–987*, London 1983, 245.

[36] Flodoard, 50, n. 5; Prentout, *Etude critique*, 284–91. Lauer and Prentout both discuss the account Pierre le Baud composed at the beginning of the sixteenth century of the Battle of Caen in 931 (*Histoire de Bretagne*, Paris 1638). Prentout points out that toponymic studies indicate a Breton, as well as Viking, presence in the Bessin.

[37] Flodoard, 98, speaks of 'Hagroldus Nordmannus qui Baiocis preerat.' In the history of William of Jumièges, 41, he receives the exalted but erroneous identity of 'Heroldus Danorum rex.' For a discussion of this chieftain, see Henri Prentout, *Essai sur les origines et la fondation du duché de Normandie*, Paris 1911, 241–5; Bates, 13, 34; Searle, *Predatory Kinship*, 286, n. 13.

[38] Jean Adigard des Gautries, 'Les noms de lieux de la Manche attestés entre 911 et 1066', *Annales de Normandie* i, 1951, 9–44. Also see Map 4 in Bates, 267; François de Beaurepaire, 'Les noms d'Anglo-Saxons contenus dans la toponymie normande', *Annales de Normandie* x, 1960, 307–16; François de Beaurepaire, 'Quelques finales anglo-saxonnes dans la toponymie normande' xiii, 1963, 219–36. Beaurepaire notes that Anglo-Saxon elements in Norman placenames indicate the immigration of Vikings who had spent time in England.

[39] Michel de Bouard, 'La Hague, camp retranché des Vikings?', *Annales de Normandie* iii, 1953, 3–14; Michel de Bouard, 'Le Hague-Dike', *Cahiers Archéologiques: Fin de l'Antiquité et Moyen Age* viii, 1956, 117–45; Michel de Bouard, 'A propos de la datation du Hague-Dike', *Annales de Normandie* xiv, 1964, 270–1.

[40] Davies, 27–28. Mont Saint Michel's situation is also analogous to that of La Trinité, Vendôme, whose ties reached beyond Vendôme into Blois, Tours, Anjou and Beaugency. See Johnson, 97–8.

[41] Le Roy, 281–3, who cites a lost cartulary, the *Livre Blanc*, as one of his sources, numbers the group sent from Rouen to the Mont at thirty monks, including Maynard. On Le Roy and his history of Mont Saint Michel, see: F. Vandenbroucke, 'Dom Jean Huynes et Dom Thomas Le Roy, Historiens Mauristes du Mont Saint-Michel' in *Millénaire* ii, 155–67. A list of monks, alive and dead, dated 996 to 1008, indicates that about fifty monks belonged to the community under the second abbot. Denis Gremont and Frère Donnat, 'Fleury, le Mont Saint-Michel et l'Angleterre à la fin du Xe et au début du XIe siècle à propos du manuscrit d'Orléans no. 127 (105)' in *Millénaire* i, 751–93. Gremont and Donnat present the list on p. 783. On this list, also see: Claude Simonnet, 'L'enluminure dans les manuscrits normands' in *Trésors des abbayes normandes*, Rouen 1979, 103–62, at 104–5. The *Introductio* certainly expects its readers to believe that the pre-existing community on the Mont was

eleventh century, the community apparently soon reconciled Breton and Norman elements.[42]

As the map of Mont Saint Michel's possessions in 1035 illustrates, the community gained as much or more property in Brittany and Maine, as in Normandy, during the early years between its refoundation and the reign of William the Conqueror. That is, at least, the story that the surviving charters tell. The rich *fonds* of Mont Saint Michel were gutted during the Second World War, and consequently any study of Mont Saint Michel's patrimony during the tenth and early eleventh century must rely on the twelfth-century cartulary at Avranches, copies of charters which survive at other archives, and various *acta* which were edited before the war.[43] The cartulary was compiled during the abbacy of Robert of Torigny (1154–1186), who would not have been inclined to overlook the generosity of Normans when he had the grants and agreements of Breton and Manceaux lords recorded.[44] Indeed, the Norman bias of the cartulary is apparent in its organization, which places charters of Richard II, Gunnor, Robert the Magnificent, and William the Conqueror all before benefactions from other sources, several of which predate the Norman acts.[45] This arrangement, nevertheless, can not hide the fact that over forty years elapsed after Mont Saint Michel's refoundation before it received a landed endowment from the counts of Rouen. In the meantime, the monks had developed ties elsewhere.

hostile to Benedictine reform, but evidence indicates that the two groups coexisted: Lelegard, 51–2; Dubois, 'Les moines', 17.

[42] Among the several eleventh-century Bretons who joined the community, one lord from the diocese of Dol, Tréhan of Saint Broladre, entered too hastily, believing his death imminent. When he recovered his health, Tréhan returned his habit to the monks and resumed secular life, generously endowing the Mont. Tréhan's history is known through charters in the cartulary of Mont Saint Michel (Bibl. Avranches, MS 210, fols 44r–v; 74r–v), and is summarised by Guillotin de Corson, *Pouillé Historique de l'Archevêché de Rennes*, Rennes 1881, ii, 527–30; Dubois, 'Les dépendances', 643–644; Dubois, 'Les moines', 30.

[43] I will limit citations to printed editions, except when published versions differ significantly from the cartulary or archive copies. Professor Lucien Musset had planned to publish an edition of the Mont Saint Michel cartulary, but unfortunately he has had to abandon the project. I am very grateful for his help with these materials, and I would also like to thank Dr David Bates and Dr Simon Keynes for their unflagging assistance through the diplomatic sources. For a description of the cartulary (hereafter cited as Bibl. Avranches, MS 210), see: François Burckard, 'Chartes, cartulaires et archives des abbayes' in *Trésors*, 59–83, at 75; Michel Bourgeois-Lechartier, 'A la recherche du scriptorium de l'abbaye du Mont Saint-Michel' in *Millénaire* ii, 171–202.

[44] On Robert of Torigny, see: André Dufief, 'La vie monastique au Mont Saint-Michel pendant le XIIe siècle (1085–1186)' in *Millénaire* i, 81–126, especially, 101–26; Raymonde Foreville, 'Robert de Torigni et "Clio" ', in *Millénaire* ii, 141–53; Marjorie Chibnall, 'Orderic Vitalis and Robert of Torigni' in *Millénaire* ii, 133–9.

[45] The cartulary begins with a copy of the *Revelatio* (fols 5r–10r), followed by a copy of the *Introductio monachorum* (fols 10r–17r), which is followed by a copy of Pope John XII's forged bull (fols 17r–18r), and a copy of King Lothar's charter of 966 (fols 18v–19r). A picture of Richard II appears on fol 19v, which is followed by: Fauroux no. 49 (fols 20r–22v); Fauroux no. 47 (fols 22v–23r); a picture of Gunnor (fol. 23v); Fauroux no. 17 (fols 24r–25r); a picture of Robert the Magnificent (fol. 25v); Fauroux no. 73 (fols 26r–27v); Fauroux 148 (fols 27v–29r); Fauroux no. 111 (fols 29v–30r); Fauroux 110 (fols 30r–31r); Fauroux no. 133 (fols 31r–32r); Fauroux no. 76 (fol. 32v); *Regesta* no. 208 (fols 33r–34v). The charters which follow fol. 34v, are arranged fairly haphazardly, although the *acta* of certain priories tend to be grouped together. These charters range in date from the tenth century to the twelfth, and describe possessions throughout France, Italy, and England. Given Robert of Torigny's loyalties, the placement of Norman ducal charters foremost is understandable, but it nevertheless obscures the monastery's debt to non-Norman patrons during the early years after its refoundation.

Thirteen years after King Lothar's confirmation of the monastery's reformation, Conan, count of Rennes, presented the next extant charter in favor of the Mont, dated 990. Issued from Rennes, the act explains that abbot Maynard had sent two members of the community as *legatores* to Conan in Dol, to approve his donation of four *villae* south-east of the Mont: Villamée, Lillèle, Passillé, and Villeperdue.[46] This was only the first known of many gifts from the counts of Rennes. In addition to his father's gifts, Conan's son Geoffrey granted several important properties to the Mont along the western side of the bay: the vill of Cancale, with its adjacent port, the church of Saint Méloir des Ondes, and the vill of Saint Benoît des Ondes, with all its pertaining lands.[47] Geoffrey's son Alan III was also a generous benefactor of the Mont, coming to the monastery to confirm his father's gifts and add his own, which included the vill of Roz sur Couesnon with the surrounding marsh, and Montrouault with half a mill. When one of his men entered the community as a monk, Alan also granted the land of *Lavas* with its mill, which that man had held.[48] Both Conan and Geoffrey, moreover, chose to be buried at the Mont.[49] The most reasonable conclusion from their actions, as Bates suggests, is that the counts of Rennes intended Mont Saint Michel to become their family monastery and mausoleum.[50]

For three generations, therefore, the counts of Rennes posed as benefactors of Mont Saint Michel. And the lands which they gave gained in importance, so that by 1200, Villamée, Montrouault and Saint Méloir had developed into priories.[51] Other Breton lords followed the lead of the counts of Rennes, endowing and entering into transactions with the Mont. An individual named Grallon, for example, mortgaged his church at Poilley to Mont Saint Michel for four pounds of *denarii* sometime before 1009.[52] Later, probably because he could not clear the mortgage, Grallon simply gave the church to the abbey, and his wife offered the monks a cloak of very high quality. In exchange, the Mont was to provide them refuge in the event of war, and, should Grallon and his sons go into battle, they were to receive two horses, which they were to return intact. The monks, a later agreement reveals, did not live up to their end of the bargain regarding the horses,

[46] Although this charter survives in several modern copies, it does not appear in Bibl. Avranches MS 210. Copies exist at: BN, n. acq. fr. 21821, fol. 138r–v and BN, n. acq. fr. 21821, fol. 139r–v; BN, MS lat. 5430A, 48–49; BN, MS lat. 10072, fol. 3r; BN, coll. Moreau xvi, fols 141r–143r. These copies differ in several respects from the version edited by Hyacinthe Morice, *Mémoires pour servir de preuves à l'histoire ecclésiastique et civile de Bretagne* i, Paris 1742, 350–1. I am following Dubois, 'Les dépendances', 643, on the identification of these placenames.

[47] Geoffrey's gifts are known only through a charter of his son: Bibl. Avranches MS 210, fols 40r–42r. This charter also appears in BN, n. acq. fr. 21815, fol. 225r–v; BN, coll. Moreau xxi, 70r–74v; BN, coll. Moreau xxi, 76r–79v. It is edited by Morice, 379–81, but his version departs from the cartulary and the BN texts, especially with regard to placenames. Dubois, 'Les dépendances', identifies *Cancavena* and *Semmeler* as Cancale and Saint Méloir des Ondes. François de Beaurepaire, 'Toponymie et évolution du peuplement sur le pourtour de la baie du Mont Saint-Michel' in *Millénaire*, ii, 49–72, at 58, identifies *Landeguethoi* as Saint Benoît des Ondes.

[48] Bibl. Avranches 210, fol. 40r–42r. Corson, 524, identifies *villa Bohel* as Roz sur Couesnon; Dubois, 'Les dépendances', 644, identifies *Mons Rohalt* as Montrouault; *Lavas* is unidentified, but it is located in commune of Pleine-Fougères.

[49] *Gallia* xi, 514; Le Roy, 288.

[50] Bates, 70.

[51] Dubois, 'Les dépendances', 660.

[52] Bibl. Avranches MS 210, fols 47r–48r; BN, MS lat. 5430A, 49–50 and 170–171; BN, coll. Moreau xl, fols 196r–197v and 231r–232v. The contents of this charter are summarised by Laporte, 'Abbaye', 73; Tabuteau, 51.

so Grallon's sons resumed possession of the church. They returned it in the late 1020s, however, in exchange for eight pounds of *denarii* and a confirmation that they could still find refuge at the monastery should war break out.[53] This example of Mont Saint Michel's relations with Grallon and his sons affirms that lay involvement with the monks could go far beyond pious gifts *ad succurrendum*. Indeed, it would be difficult to ask for a better illustration of Mont Saint Michel's role in local Breton society over two generations. Later examples indicate that the monastery continued to offer refuge to Bretons in times of war through the eleventh century, and that it enlisted Breton protection of its own estates as well.[54]

Guy Devailly, however, attaches long-range political goals to Breton patronage, noting that the counts endowed the Mont during the decades in which they sought the support of the Norman dukes against their rivals, the counts of Nantes.[55] While political and spiritual interests could certainly go hand in hand, the evidence that Conan sought an alliance with Richard I is very slim.[56] If Norse allies did support Rennes during the first battle of Conquéreuil against the counts of Nantes and Anjou in 982, they were probably from the Viking settlements on the Loire rather than the Seine.[57] This seems at least to have been Richer's assumption, since he makes it clear that the Vikings supporting Conan in the second battle of Conquéreuil ten years later came from the Loire.[58] As for Geoffrey, who did ally with the Rouen Normans, if he had sought to win their lord's favor through monastic patronage a gift to Fécamp or Saint Ouen in upper Normandy, one imagines, would have been more persuasive.

But quite simply, their generosity to Mont Saint Michel needs no elaborate explanations. To the counts of Rennes, and to their men, the Mont was a nearby community in an area where, as Devailly himself explains, monasteries were few and poor.[59] It is not surprising that they turned their favour toward this house; to ascribe Breton patronage to political incentive and intention to influence a third

---

[53] Bibl. Avranches, MS 210, fols 47r–48r: '... et si necessitas WERRE nobis evenerit, habeamus refugium ad sanctam Michaelem.'

[54] Bibl. Avranches, MS 210, fols 44r–v show that after Tréhan of Saint Broladre had hastily withdrawn from the monastery, he still retained the right to stay at the Mont in case of war, where he would receive daily as much bread and wine as one monk. Fol. 73v describes an agreement whereby Mont Saint Michel would come to the aid of Breton lord if he were captured – the monks' assistance would be commensurate with the value of the land in Brittany which he had given them ('de eodem adjutorio secundum hoc quod terra valebit et justum fuerit'). One charter, which is not in MS 210 but was copied by G. de Beausse (Arch. Calvados, F 5276, i), describes an individual named Rivallon, 'a most noble leader of Brittany', agreeing to protect Mont Saint Michel's possessions at Pontorson, in exchange for spiritual benefits of the abbey. This charter, unfortunately, cannot be dated with assurance, but it is known from another (*Abbayette*, no. 5) that Abbot Suppo entrusted Breton property to a Rivallon between 1033–1048. I would like to thank Dr Marjorie Chibnall for her comments on Beausse's copy of Rivallon's charter.

[55] Devailly, 118–22.

[56] Lot, *Les derniers Carolingians*, 110 and appendix viii, 346–57. Lot argues that Richard I's war in the 960s against Theobald of Blois-Chartres concerned affairs in Brittany, but the story in *Nantes*, 111–12, of the 'palus magnus, in ore Ligeris fixus, metum Normannis faciens', only makes sense if the Vikings who attacked Nantes in 960 were based on the Loire rather than the Seine. I tend to agree with P. Chesnel, *Le Cotentin et L'Avranchin sous les ducs de Normandie (911–1204)*, Caen 1912, 82–3, that Richard I seems not to have launched any important expeditions against Brittany.

[57] *Nantes*, 118–19.

[58] Richer ii, 280–3: 'Ad alterum vero per Ligerim classes Piratarum adhibet', and note 1, 282. Latouche doubts the truth of Richer's inclusion of Loire Vikings.

[59] Devailly, 116.

party introduces unnecessary complexity into the situation. Was Rolland, a monk of Mont Saint Michel, chosen to be bishop of Dol at the beginning of the eleventh century in order to please Richard II?[60] It seems unlikely. Moreover, Bretons continued to visit the community, endow it, and seek its prayers and protection, regardless of the state of affairs between Rennes and Rouen. To the counts of Rennes, as well as to other Bretons in the vicinity, the community would have represented a major landlord and a religious center – not a Norman outpost filled with Norman pioneers.

Brittany was not the only area outside of the boundaries of later Normandy in which the Mont acquired property. As the map of its possessions in 1035 indicates, the monks also gained interests south-east of the abbey. One of the earliest extant charters to the Mont after its refoundation is a grant from Mayeul abbot of Cluny, in which he presents to the monks lands in the *villa* of Le Mortier, just outside of Tours.[61] A condition was written into the agreement that they would hold this property only 'as long as the monks live according to the rule of Saint Benedict'.[62] This extra clause was perhaps deemed critical in the case of the Mont, especially if Hourlier's thesis regarding the non-Benedictine character of the original community holds true. And as Mayeul's refusal to send monks to Fécamp indicates, his confidence in monastic reforms in the lands of former Neustria was not generally high.[63]

Le Mortier was the abbey's most distant holding before 1035. The remainder of its lands to the south-east lay in the county of Maine, a principality which had emerged in the tenth century. It was in this area that abbot Maynard's successor Maynard II (991–1009) requested that former lands lost during the Viking incursions be restored, namely eight *villae* which became the core foundation for the priory of l'Abbayette.[64] The concession was made by a certain Yves, whose references to his parents, Fulk and Rothair, and his uncles, Bishop Seinfroi and William, have caused a great deal of consternation among genealogists of the Bellême clan. Both Bertrand de Broussillon and Geoffrey White finally abandoned the attempt to fit him into the family, and Jacques Boussard has remained cautious about including him.[65] But, placing the question of Yves' identity aside, the

[60] *Gallia* xiv, 1044.

[61] Bibl. Avranches, MS 210, fol. 55r–v. The date of this act poses some difficulty, since it claims to be written in the forty-first year of King Lothar's reign, which would be 994, yet Mayeul, who appears as abbot in the text, was no longer active after 991. Dubois, 'Les dépendances', 640–1, discusses this problem.

[62] Bibl. Avranches, MS 210, fol. 55r–v: '... ut quam diu ipsi monachi secundum regulam sancti Benedicti regulariter vixerint, teneant, et possideant.' Since this charter is entitled 'de vineis Turonis' in the cartulary, it can be concluded that the monks had planted vineyards on these lands near Tours by the mid-twelfth century.

[63] Lemarignier, *Etude*, 30–1, n. 18.

[64] See above, note 24.

[65] Henry Renault du Motey, *Origines de la Normandie et du duché d'Alençon*, Paris 1920, 119–20, 301, accepts that Yves benefactor of Mont Saint Michel is the same as Yves I of Bellême. This view is shared by Jean Laporte, 'Les séries abbatiale et priorale du Mont Saint-Michel' in *Millénaire*, i, 267–81, at 271. Laporte does not cite Broussillon's edition, which appeared in the last century, but instead refers to the folio number in Bibl. Avranches, MS 210 for this act (fols 50r–51r); his date 'après 1004', is incorrect. Broussillon, in his introduction to *Abbayette*, 3, disassociates Yves of l'Abbayette from the Bellême family. Geoffrey White, 'The First House of Bellême', *TRHS* xxii, 1940, 67–95, in appendix B, 91–5, concurs, 'It is necessary to abandon the attempt to make the founder of l'Abbayette a member of the House of Bellême.' Jacques Boussard, 'La seigneurie de Bellême aux Xe et XIe siècles'

charter does indicate Maynard II's willingness to travel some distance to recover the monastery's properties, since the act, issued from Fresnay and dated by Broussillon to 997, describes him approaching Yves with this request, and it bears the abbot's cross.[66]

Maynard's efforts were well-rewarded. The priory of l'Abbayette, some forty-two kilometers from Mont Saint Michel, became an important overnight stop for pilgrims on their way to the Mont, and it attracted many gifts from its neighbors.[67] On occasion, the same piece of property could be the subject of a series of transactions. For example, a short time after he had sought out Yves, Maynard approached an individual named Guy, requesting that he sell Mont Saint Michel two-thirds of the church of Saint Berthevin, south-east of l'Abbayette, which his parents had mortgaged to the abbey.[68] Guy admitted that he had taken the property, along with various other *beneficii*, after the death of his parents, and he agreed to sell them back to the monks.[69] Then, about fifteen years later, Guy's son-in-law made the same agreement, to sell two-thirds of the church of Saint Berthevin to Mont Saint Michel, thereby demonstrating that it had again been appropriated by the family.[70] The son-in-law settled for an annual fee of eight *denarii*, to be received at the feast of Saint Denis, and the monks proceeded to acquire several other churches in the vicinity in the course of the eleventh and twelfth centuries.[71]

The advantage of a compromise settlement, such as Guy's son-in-law's, meant that neither party was left empty-handed. As Constance Bouchard has discussed, relations between monks and a specific family could be very tricky over generations, since the sons and heirs would often contest a gift of their ancestors. And yet, those same sons were the ones most likely to endow the monastery themselves further down the line, since patronage to a certain abbey tended to run in the family.[72] The monks would not wish to alienate the family members of a benefactor, instead preferring mutual concession to confrontation. Stephen White's work on Marmoutier's disputes has shown the importance of compromise and reciprocation in assuring the security of agreements.[73] And most recently, Barbara Rosenwein has discussed how land, given and taken over generations, forged a continuing chain of relationships between the monks and a lay family; appropriation should not simply be seen in the context of lay rapacity.[74] The

---

in *Mélanges d'histoire du moyen âge dédiés à la mémoire de Louis Halphen*, Paris 1951, 43–54, at 45, n. 2 discusses the charter directly, but comes to no definite conclusion, only suggesting that Yves the benefactor of Mont Saint Michel might have been the nephew of Yves of Bellême or the nephew of the wife of Yves of Bellême.

66 Broussillon, *Abbayette*, no. 1, has also published a facsimile of the original charter.

67 *Abbayette*, 5; Broussillon also edits the subsequent gifts to this priory in *Abbayette*. Dubois, 'Les dépendances', 653, argues that Mont Saint Michel priories were not established as stopping places for pilgrims; nevertheless, they could serve that function.

68 *Abbayette*, no. 2. Dubois, 'Les dépendances', 642, identifies the church of *Centrannis* as Saint Berthevin.

69 Unfortunately, the charter does not quote the price.

70 *Abbayette*, no. 3.

71 Dubois, 'Les dépendances', 643.

72 Bouchard, 150–2; 209–17

73 Stephen D. White, ' "Pactum . . . Legem Vincit et Amor Judicium" The Settlement of Disputes by Compromise in Eleventh-Century Western France', *The American Journal of Legal History* xxii, 1978, 281–308.

74 Rosenwein, 49–77.

church of Saint Berthevin, as Rosenwein would point out, was the focus of an ongoing relationship between the monks of Mont Saint Michel and one family, an association initiated by Guy's parents, which set the stage for later acquisitions and relations in this area during the eleventh and twelfth centuries.[75]

Mont Saint Michel also acquired considerable interests in the area around Le Mans, especially during the reign of Count Hugh III, from 992 to 1015.[76] Thus Ralph, vicomte of Maine, gave a close of vineyards outside Le Mans to the monks around 994,[77] and Count Hugh added four more vineyards[78] and three mills[79] to their possessions in the area between 995 and 1015. Ralph's charter makes it clear that he had journeyed to the abbey himself with his wife and son, and while there, made his offering on the altar of Saint Michael. On his return, he secured Hugh's consent and ordered that the charter be written. Count Hugh's grant of three mills took place at the request of Hugh son of Hebrannus, who held them of the count, on the condition that this Hugh son of Hebrannus would be paid by the monks three *solidi* each year at the festival of Saint John the Baptist. It is difficult to gauge the value of coin in this society, but Wendy Davies places three *solidi* as the value of an ox in ninth-century Brittany, and Lucien Musset rates horses in early eleventh-century Normandy from two or three pounds up to ten – ten pounds for a 'cheval de luxe'.[80] Three *solidi* would therefore seem a low price for three mills, which suggests that the money, delivered each year by the monks to Hugh son of Hebrannus, had at least as much symbolic significance as monetary.

A similar conclusion should be derived regarding the eight *denarii* which Guy's son-in-law received annually for giving up his claim to the church of Saint Berthevin; eight *denarii* was worth about the price of a pig, according to Davies, and Grallon's charter indicates that a church could be worth a great deal more.[81] The money these men received from the monks, no doubt publicly, on a certain feast day would have reaffirmed each year their relationship with the monastery. It assured the recipient that he was still associated with the original transaction, and thereby included in the spiritual benefits enjoyed by patrons of the Mont. Moreover, it reminded the lay community of these facts as well, enhancing his prestige and perhaps prompting more gifts from his neighbors.

These examples make it clear that it would be a mistake to view the monks at Mont Saint Michel as passive recipients of non-Norman patronage. They sought out patrons beyond the duchy and the monks were persistent in keeping the property they acquired and maintaining relationships they entered with laymen. Once they established a foothold in one area, the monks endeavored to accumulate more lands nearby. For instance, in 1014 Abbot Hildebert (1009–1023) approached the

---

[75] Dubois, ' Les dépendances', 642–3, describes later possessions in the neighborhood of Saint Berthevin.

[76] Robert Latouche, *Histoire du comté du Maine pendant le Xe et le XIe siècle*, Paris 1910, 14–21. Latouche also presents a catalogue of acts of the counts of Maine, which summarises their gifts to Mont Saint Michel, 140–2.

[77] *Cartulaire de Saint-Victeur au Mans*, ed. Bertrand de Broussillon, Paris 1895, no. 1.

[78] *Saint-Victeur au Mans*, no. 2.

[79] *Saint-Victeur au Mans*, no. 3.

[80] Davies, 57; Lucien Musset, 'La vie économique de l'abbaye de Fécamp sous l'abbatiat de Jean de Ravenne (1028–1078)' in *L'Abbaye Bénédictine de Fécamp: ouvrage scientifique du XIIIe centenaire* i, Fécamp 1959, 67–79, 345–9, at 71.

[81] Davies, 57.

generous Hugh III of Maine, expressly asking that he donate or sell at a just price land in the vicinity of property which they had already received.[82] The count agreed to give the monks the land of Voivres, a bit south-west of Le Mans, and he came personally to the Mont to place this gift on the altar. The monastery's holdings around Le Mans continued to grow. Sometime between 1033–1040, Mont Saint Michel received more vineyards in the area,[83] and in 1040, the monks gained a former monastery, Saint Victeur, which then flourished as a priory of the Mont.[84]

The accumulation of lands in a given area, followed by the establishment of a nearby priory, was a pattern common among monasteries. Penelope Johnson describes a similar tendency, for example, in the development of La Trinité, Vendôme's property.[85] Obviously, there were administrative advantages in having a priory in the midst of their lands to watch over the tenants and collect revenues.[86] It is important to note, however, that in the case of Mont Saint Michel, the first priories, indeed, the first seeds of its patrimony were planted outside of Normandy. The view from the Mont, therefore, would have naturally been oriented more toward its holdings and its commitments in Brittany and Maine, than toward Rouen, at least through the first decade of the eleventh century.

This was especially the case because Mont Saint Michel's ecclesiastical ties with Rouen were very weak during this period. Although the *Revelatio* acknowleged Autbert, bishop of Avranches, as the monastery's original founder, and the Mont stood technically within the boundaries of the archdiocese of Rouen, the Viking invasions had broken the ecclesiastical chain of command, and the west was slowest to recover. Episcopal lists in the *Gallia Christiana* for the diocese of Avranches show a gap for over a century, from 862 to 990,[87] and the cathedral church of Avranches did not regain its lands until Duke Richard II's reign.[88] The diocese of Coutances, we are told, was 'devoid of Christians' in the ninth and tenth centuries, the church 'crushed by pagan thieves and the pollution of idolatry'.[89] Although later writers no doubt indulged in hyperbole, the residence of five bishops of Coutances in a row at Rouen, from Rollo's time until 1025, attests to the disruption of ecclesiastical life in the west. In 1025, Bishop Herbert braved a return to the

---

[82] *Saint-Victeur au Mans*, no. 4: 'Adiit sepe nostram presentiam Heldebertus abbas . . . et aliqui sub eo degentes monachi, petentes ut in vicino earum rerum quas in pago Cenomannico tam a nobis quam etiam ab aliis possident, aliquam bene utilem terram vel precio quanto dignum esset eis venderem, vel . . . donarem.'

[83] *Saint-Victeur au Mans*, no. 5; *Abbayette*, no. 4.

[84] *Saint-Victeur au Mans*, nos 6 and 7; *Gallia* xi, instrumenta 106–7. Dubois, 'Les moines', 32–3, discusses three different versions of this charter.

[85] Johnson, 53.

[86] Dubois, 'Les dépendances', 659–60.

[87] *Gallia* xi, 474. Between bishops Waltbert and Norgod, the *Gallia Christiana* editors write: 'Aliquot adhuc praesulum Abrincensium nomenclatura seculo toto deficit.'

[88] Fauroux 24, n. 24, from pancarte, c.1060–1066.

[89] 'De statu hujus (Constantiensis) ecclesiae ab anno 836 ad 1093', in *Gallia* xi, instrumenta 217–24, at 217. On this source, see: John Le Patourel, 'Geoffrey of Montbray, Bishop of Coutances, *EHR* lix, 1944, 129–61, specifically, 130–9. The traditional story of the sufferings of the church of Coutances during the Viking invasions is indeed one of gloom and doom. See, for example: E. A. Pigeon, *Histoire de la cathédrale de Coutances*, Coutances 1876, 16–34; René Toustain de Billy, *Histoire ecclésiastique du diocèse de Coutances*, Rouen 1874, i, 91–116. Some revision of this extreme view is in order. Musset, 'Monachisme d'époque franque', 67–71, has shown that even in the Cotentin the memory of ruined abbeys remained intact.

diocese, but both he and his successor held out half-way into their see, in the naturally fortified town of St Lô.[90]

Mont Saint Michel's charters indicate that the ecclesiastical hierarchy of Rouen played little role in the abbey's affairs before the second decade of the eleventh century. The first charter which the archbishop, or any bishop within Rouen's archdiocese, attested dates *circa* 1015.[91] The bishops of Brittany and Maine, meanwhile, had witnessed and confirmed several of the Mont's *acta* by this time.[92] The monastic map of Normandy also accentuates Mont Saint Michel's distance from Rouen during the first decades of the eleventh century. By 1025, eight monasteries had been founded or refounded in the lands by then called Normandy, but only Mont Saint Michel stood west of the Touques river.[93] This contrast cannot be seen as a legacy of pre-Viking conditions, since over twenty monasteries had existed beyond the Touques before the invasions.[94] The distribution of monastic property during the first three decades of the eleventh century reinforces the Mont's isolation, since the vast majority of lands which other houses held were located in upper Normandy or along the Seine.[95] All of Mont Saint Michel's Norman property, on the other hand, as late as the accession of William the Conqueror, fell west of Caen.

No charters recall any gifts to Mont Saint Michel by Richard I; even Dudo does not elaborate beyond the initial restoration. Only one source, the partisan *Introductio monachorum*, states that Richard I endowed or even later visited the monastery on the Mont which he had restored, and this information is offered only in the broadest sense, devoid of specific example.[96] From the point of view of Rouen, Mont Saint Michel remained far off in the distance for over forty years, while Richard I and Richard II were preoccupied with affairs closer to home. Finally, there appeared in 1009 the first indication after the Mont's refoundation that the Norman duke intended to assert his authority over this community, when Richard II relieved Maynard II of his position as abbot and replaced him with Hildebert, taking the unusual precaution of having a charter drawn up to confirm the appointment.[97] Laporte argues that the formality of the 1009 charter 'leads readily to the conclusion that it's goal was to impose on the monks an abbot whom they did not want'.[98] After almost half a century, it would not be surprising for the monks to resist Richard II's intervention, and their desire to elect an abbot freely remained a point of contention between the monks of Mont Saint Michel and the counts of Rouen into the twelfth century.[99]

Richard II's decision to assume an active role at Mont Saint Michel occurred subsequent to his alliance with Geoffrey, count of Rennes, a pact of friendship and

[90] 'De statu', 217–18.
[91] Fauroux no. 16
[92] BN, n. acq. fr. 21821, fol. 138r–v; Bibl Avranches, MS 210, fols 47r–48r; *Abbayette*, nos 1, 2; *Saint Victeur au Mans*, no. 4.
[93] See Map 11, in Bates, 274.
[94] Laporte, 'Les origines', pp. 25–41.
[95] This statement is based on research which I presented at the 64th Annual Meeting of the Medieval Academy of America, April 1989.
[96] *Introductio*, 870: '. . . ecclesias, villas, cuncta que necessaria monachis pro eorum voto concessit, sic que gaudens a loco discessit.'
[97] Fauroux no. 12.
[98] Laporte, 'Abbaye', 67.
[99] Laporte, 'Abbaye', 76–80; Dufief, 81–101.

aid sealed by their double marriage to each other's sister. According to William of Jumièges, the wedding, appropriately enough, took place at Mont Saint Michel.[100] In 1008, Count Geoffrey left on a pilgrimage from which he never returned, and his two sons were raised in the court of their uncle, Richard II. It was therefore in the absence of the count of Rennes – indeed, just one year after Geoffrey's departure, that Richard II decided it was time to take the upper hand in the affairs of the monks at Mont Saint Michel. Richard's charter justifies Maynard's replacement on the grounds that he was too old to perform his duties any longer, but Laporte suggests that Maynard no longer enjoyed the favour of the Norman duke.[101] The timing of the abbot's deposition lends credence to Laporte's suggestion; Richard may well have chosen to act in 1009 precisely because the count of Rennes was out of the picture.

It was also in this context, during the years while Count Geoffrey's heirs remained under the guardianship of the Norman duke, that Dudo composed his work. Brittany, according to Dudo, had been under Norman authority from the origins of the duchy, and the chronicler describes William Longsword invading the Breton territory to suppress a rebellion.[102] Thus the view of Brittany as a land to reconquer was conceived, and Dudo has the Bretons crushed under Longsword's righteous fury, begging the Norman leader to regard them as 'a conscientious lord regards his wayward servants'.[103] As Chesnel and Prentout concluded long ago, Dudo tailored his account of the Norman past to please his audience; his description of Brittany's subjugation to Rouen was no doubt a reflection of the political ambitions of Richard II, rather than an accurate appraisal of any raids William Longsword might have launched against the Bretons.[104] There is, however, no reason to deny the possibility of Rollo or William Longsword attacking the Breton coast. The *Chronicle of Nantes* very clearly identifies the diabolical Vikings who arrived from Rouen by boat and 'devastated all Brittany' in 919, joining their brothers from the Loire in the rampage.[105] The Rouen Normans would have come to Brittany, however, not on a campaign of reconquest as Dudo paints it, but with the same ruthless opportunism as they struck the Beauvaisis and the Amiénois.[106]

---

[100] Jumièges, 77–8, 88–9. Lemarignier, *Hommage*, 116–17, following Arthur de La Borderie and Jacques Flach, dates the alliance between the counts of Rennes and Rouen to 996. David Douglas, 'Some Problems of Early Norman Chronology', *EHR* cclvi, 1950, 289–303 discusses the dates of the two sets of marriages.

[101] Fauroux no. 12: '... pastoralis et enim curam sollicitudinis quam idem memorabilis senex proficere nequit viribus propriis, subrogati sibi laudabiliter exposcit complere adjutorio fratris.' Laporte, 'Abbaye', 69.

[102] Dudo, 183–5.

[103] Dudo, 185: 'Videntes autem Berengerus et Alannus caeterique Britones, quod non sufficerent nec praevalerent adversus Willelmum, miserunt ad eum verbis deprecativis legatum: "Patri tuo obedienter servivimus, tibique incumbentes famulari cupimus. Ne despicias nos, quaesumus, neque abomineris servitium nostrum ullatenus; sed respice nos, ut servos offensos pius dominus." '

[104] Chesnel, 71–4; Prentout, *Origines*, 184–6.

[105] *Nantes*, 81, and 82, n. 1: 'Tunc ipsi Normanni, viri diabolici crudelissimique et perversi homines, primum Franciam aggredientes, totam provinciam Rothomagensium in dominicatu suo retinuerunt et Karolo stulto abstulerunt. Deinde, cum ingenti navium classe per mare Oceanum navigantes, totam Britanniam devastarunt.' Also see Searle, *Predatory Kinship*, 71.

[106] Flodoard, 29–30. The medallion or coin found at Mont Saint Michel, with the legend that reads + VVILEIM DV + IRB, seems too ambiguous to accept as corroboration to Dudo's version. Michael Dolley and Jacques Yvon, 'A Group of Tenth-Century Coins Found at Mont-Saint-Michel', *The British Numismatic Journal* xl, 1971, 1–12; Searle, 'Frankish Rivalries', 209.

The *Introductio monachorum* borrows Dudo's account of unfaithful Bretons rebelling against their proper Norman lords, and it also accepts his assertion that Rollo endowed Mont Saint Michel immediately after his conversion to Christianity.[107] Historians have generally regarded Dudo's description of Rollo's patronage to the Mont with suspicion, especially given the limits of the Viking lord's authority.[108] However, the contention that William Longsword gave the monastery lands, which a charter of Richard II purports to return, is usually accepted at face value.[109] Yet, as Searle has pointed out, Longsword's benefaction would necessarily predate the refoundation; the lands described in the act, moreover, a cluster of *villulae* just south of the Mont, had most likely pertained to the community in pre-Viking days.[110] Searle does not dismiss the possibility that Longsword might have confirmed the community's lands, but the scenario seems improbable. One imagines that the inhabitants of the Mont, most likely Bretons themselves, would have been more inclined to flee from William Longsword and his band raiding the Breton shores than ask him for favours. Moreover, the charter itself does not inspire confidence, since Longsword's alleged gifts are immediately followed by a reference to Pope John XIII's forged bull.[111]

The earliest Norman benefactor of Mont Saint Michel, of whom we can be certain, was not a son of Rollo's line at all, but rather a wife.[112] In 1015 Richard II made it known that the Duchess Gunnor gave the monks at the Mont two allods southwest of Caen which she had received in dower from her husband, Richard I.[113] Gunnor's role in the restoration of the church of Coutances attests to her commitment to the recovery of ecclesiastical life in the west.[114] And Gunnor, coming from the Cotentin, would have been more likely than her husband to be familiar with the Mont, its history as a place of religion, and its spectacular location. Searle has described Richard I's union with Gunnor as an opportunity for the Norman leader from Rouen to unite his family in kinship with Gunnor's.[115] It is possible to see his refoundation of Mont Saint Michel in a similar light. By

---

[107] *Introductio*, 866–7; Dudo, 170–1.

[108] Prentout, *Etude*, 198–200; David Douglas, 'Rollo of Normandy', *EHR* lvii, 1942, 417–36, at 433; Laporte, 'Abbaye', 55, suggests that it might be more than just a legend.

[109] Fauroux no. 49; Bates, 12; Laporte, 'Abbaye', 56; Hourlier, 'Le Mont', 26–7, bases his argument for the redating of the last section of the *Revelatio* on this reference to William Longsword's gifts.

[110] Searle, *Predatory Kinship*, 76–7.

[111] Lemarignier, *Etude*, 75, n. 46, appendix vi, 264–6.

[112] Fauroux no. 17.

[113] Bretteville sur Odon and Domjean. Searle, *Predatory Kinship*, 295, n. 7, suggests the the charter, the earliest copy of which dates from the twelfth century, might have confused dower and dowry. It is also possible that Richard I gave Gunnor lands in the Bessin over which he had a theoretical claim, but in an area where her family in fact had practical control – thus, the marriage portion would represent an amicable solution. This is no more than speculation, but the subsequent gift of these lands to Mont Saint Michel would then have been most appropriate. In any event, as Searle notes, the grant of these properties indicates that the Normans from Rouen toward the end of the tenth century possessed lands in central Normandy. Henri Navel, 'Les Vavassories du Mont-Saint-Michel à Bretteville-sur-Odon et Verson (Calvados)', *Bulletin de la Société des Antiquaires de la Normandie* xlv, 1937, 137–65, and Robert Carabie, *La propriété foncière dans le très ancièn droit normand (XIe–XIIIe siècles)*, Caen 1943, i, 25–145, have subjected the properties of Bretteville and Verson (given to Mont Saint Michel by Richard II, Fauroux no. 47) to careful analysis. They argue that these possessions attest to the continuity of domainal institutions, under different masters, from the Carolingian to the Norman ducal period.

[114] 'De statu', 218; Fauroux, 406, no. 214.

[115] Searle, *Predatory Kinship*, 61–7; 87–90; 124–5.

sending Benedictine monks from upper Normandy to the Mont, perhaps at Gunnor's prompting, Richard I laid a cornerstone for his realm. It was a tentative step, neither inevitable nor definitive. As with his alliance with Gunnor's people, there was no assurance of success. It would therefore be more accurate to view Richard I's implantation of Benedictine monks at Mont Saint Michel as a signal of his aspirations, rather than his dominance, over this monastery.

Mont Saint Michel's only other Norman patron around 1015 was a Robert, *comes*, most likely the first count of Mortain, who granted the monastery his allod of Tissy, just north of the Mont.[116] This Robert appears to have been either the natural son or the son-in-law of Richard I, since Robert's son is identified as Richard II's nephew.[117] The count of Rouen probably hoped that Robert's presence at Mortain would help secure this corner of the province, but the earliest counts of Mortain proved unreliable at best. Robert is said to have seized several properties from the Mont, those same *villulae* which the monks claimed to have received from William Longsword, and his son Richard fled to England after having become embroiled in a conspiracy against Richard II.[118] William Werlenc, who might have been another son of Robert count of Mortain, was summarily deprived of the county by William the Conqueror, and replaced by the duke's half-brother circa 1055.[119] If Richard I had intended the count of Mortain to bolster his authority in the west, the brace proved unsteady for over half a century.

In the years following his confirmation of Robert of Mortain's donation of Tissy, Richard II added a nearby *villa* to Mont Saint Michel's holdings in the Bessin, and gave the community several lands along the west coast; he also reconfirmed Gunnor's gifts.[120] If Richard I had granted Mont Saint Michel any property in the past, one would expect Richard II to have sanctioned his father's benefactions, at least when he confirmed his mother's gifts to the Mont. But no mention is made of Richard I providing any lands to the community he reformed. His apparent failure to endow the monks with property, however, should not be taken as indifference to the revival of monastic life. The reign of Richard I witnessed the restoration of Fécamp, Saint Wandrille, and Saint Ouen, as well as Mont Saint Michel, and the duke himself was generous toward the upper Norman abbeys, as well as toward his new foundation of Saint Taurin. Moreover, his request to Mayeul of Cluny to send some monks to reform Fécamp underlines Richard's commitment to the quality of monastic life as well. It also argues strongly that this son of William Longsword was not hostile to all that was Frankish.

[116] Fauroux 16.

[117] 'Vita Gauzlini abbatis Floriacensis von Andreas von Fleury' in *Neues Archiv der Gesellschaft für ältere deutsche Geschichtskunde*, 1878, rpt. Hanover 1981, 3, 356; Gremont and Donnat, 787–90. Some confusion exists over the earliest counts of Mortain which I address in my dissertation. For background on this problem, see: Jacques Boussard, 'Le comté de Mortain au XIe siècle', *Moyen Age* lviii, 1952, 253–79; David Douglas, 'The Earliest Norman Counts', *EHR* cclx, 1946, 129–56; Lucien Musset, 'Aux origines de la féodalité normande: l'installation par les ducs de leurs vassaux normands et bretons dans le comté d'Avranches (XIe siècle)', *Revue historique de droit français et étranger* xxix, 1951, 150.

[118] Fauroux 49; *Vita Gauzlini*, 356.

[119] Orderic, ii, 312; Orderic, iv, 98; Orderic, *Jumièges*, interpolations, 171–3; Searle, *Predatory Kinship*, 222–5, William's half brother, Robert of Mortain, proved a stauncher ally to both the duke and the monastery of Mont Saint Michel, claiming in one charter, in fact, to have carried Saint Michael's banner into battle. *The Cartulary of St. Michael's Mount*, ed. P. L. Hull, Torquay 1962, 3–4, no. 3. I would like to thank Dr David Crouch for bringing this reference to my attention.

[120] Fauroux nos 47, 49.

Instead, Richard I's want of patronage toward Mont Saint Michel suggests that whatever theoretical rights he claimed as count, his effective power circa 966 had not stretched so far from Rouen. For Richard II, on the other hand, thanks to the increased stability of his rule, his mother's connections, his alliance with the count of Rennes, and the latter's convenient departure on pilgrimage, the monastery on the Mont appeared within range of more active intervention, as attested by his appointment of Hildebert and his subsequent benefactions. The sequence of abbots, however, becomes muddled and uncertain after Hildebert's reign. The *Annales of Mont Saint Michel* contradict each other regarding the order and even the existence of certain abbots.[121] The most likely chain of events is that when Hildebert died in 1023, the monks elected a successor, whom the duke rejected. Instead, Richard II placed Thierry, abbot of Jumièges, in charge of the community, perhaps as *custos*. And the monks, in reaction, chose the monk Almod from Maine as their head. During Almod's abbacy Mont Saint Michel stood in precarious balance between Brittany and Normandy.[122]

The only source for Robert the Magnificent's Breton war in the 1030s is William of Jumièges, and his account is not impartial. Jumièges echoes Dudo in describing Alan III, count Geoffrey's heir, carried away with arrogance, renouncing the service he owed the duke.[123] David Bates has placed this conflict in the context of Duke Robert's struggles against 'the erosion of the Norman frontier'.[124] But from the point of view of Brittany, it could have been seen as an effort by Alan of Rennes to assume his father's inheritance and resist Norman encroachment. The castle of Chérrueix, which Robert constructed during this conflict, lay within later Breton territory, so the Couesnon river was not necessarily seen as a clear demarcation between the two realms. Both princes no doubt intended to seize whatever territory they could; both would have sought to hold the abbey in peril of the sea.

As Bates points out, Mont Saint Michel's allegiance during this conflict apparently lay with the house of Rennes.[125] In 1030 Count Alan came to the Mont to confirm his father's donations and add gifts of his own.[126] The monastery also received four more villages south-west of Dol during this period.[127] And in 1032, Almod approached Count Alan, requesting that he restore two churches and some property which had been usurped in the disruption.[128] These were timely benefactions of Breton property from the Breton lord. Moreover, Duke Robert's actions immediately after the war confirm where the Mont's loyalties had lain: after receiving Alan's homage at the Mont, he sent Almod packing up north to Cerisy

---

[121] Laporte, 'Les séries', 271–3.

[122] H. Chanteux, 'L'abbé Thierry et les églises de Jumièges, du Mont-Saint-Michel et de Bernay', *Bulletin Monumental* xcviii, 1939, 67–72.

[123] Jumièges, pp. 105–6: 'Britannorum quoque comes Alanus, proterviae fastu elatus, a ducis Rodberti servitio se surripere pertinaciter est aggressus.'

[124] Bates, 69.

[125] Bates, 70–1.

[126] See above, note 48.

[127] Bibl. Avranches, MS 210, fols 45r–46r; BN, nouv. acq. fr. 21815, fols 226v–227r. Morice, 361–2, provides an extremely condensed copy of this act. See Laporte, 'Abbaye', 73; Michel Mollat, 'La seigneurie maritime du Mont Saint-Michel', in *Millénaire* ii, 73–88, at 76. Three of the villages were in the parish of Miniac: *Tretgkented*, *Kaibesgel* and *Ros*; the other, in that of Mothoon: *Kainotker*. I have not been able to locate the latter parish.

[128] Bibl. Avranches, MS 210, fols 46r–47r; BN, coll. Moreau xxi, fols 207r–209r and fols 212r–214r. Morice, 372–373, presents a condensed version of this charter.

and placed on the Mont a new abbot, Suppo, whom he deemed more trustworthy.[129] Robert then granted the Mont several properties in the Cotentin, strengthening its ties to Normandy.[130]

Almod's readiness to ally with the count of Rennes would have no doubt been influenced by Alan III's assistance to the count of Maine, Herbert Wakedog, against Fulk Nerra and the bishop of Le Mans in 1027.[131] But more important was the fact that the community had, in the sixty-odd years since its refoundation, developed stronger ties and interests in Brittany and Maine, than in Normandy. Bates hastens to explain that Mont Saint Michel's motives for allying with Alan were not 'so blatantly treacherous as they at first sight appear'.[132] And he notes the depredation of the church, for which Robert's early years as duke are notorius, to explain why the monks might have been moved to choose Alan's side. But their choice needs no explanation. Grallon's charter indicates that Breton lords had found refuge at the Mont in time of war as early as the reign of Maynard, and they continued to do so, as the actions of Grallon's sons and others attest. Seen both in the context of the immediate local concerns of the community, and from the point of view of Rouen, still more distant than Rennes in the third decade of the eleventh century, the Mont's alliance with Alan III made sense.

Joseph Lynch has recently demonstrated that 'it was simply a matter of prudence on the part of a religious house to obtain or to retain the *amicitia*, the formal friendship, of its important neighbors.'[133] When disputes occurred between neighbors, however, conflicting loyalties could place a monastery in an awkward position. The view of the monks of Mont Saint Michel as 'Norman pioneers at the borders of Brittany' does them disservice, by oversimplifying their situation and underestimating their achievement. It also implies the need to explain their apparent lapse in loyalty during the Breton wars of Robert the Magnificent. Instead, we should see the monks at the Mont in their own context, endeavoring to fulfill complex social and spiritual commitments which crossed constantly shifting political and territorial boundaries. Lucien Musset has described Mont Saint Michel as an exception among Norman abbeys: the only community which did not shake off its ties to distant lands in the course of the eleventh century.[134] Its ability to maintain a far-flung network of lands and relations attests to the enduring prestige of the abbey on the Mont, as well as its unique position within the eventual boundaries of the Norman realm.

---

[129] Suppo, a disciple of William of Dijon, enriched the monastery with relics, books and ornaments, but the monks nevertheless accused him of squandering the monastery's possessions. In 1048, perhaps after having sided against the duke during the rebellion in 1047, Suppo abandoned Mont Saint Michel and returned to Italy. *Neustria Pia*, 384–5; *Gallia* xi, 515; Laporte, 'Les séries', 273–4; Laporte, 'Abbaye', 74–6; Alexander, 11–13; Bates, 82.

[130] Fauroux nos 65, 73, 76.

[131] Latouche, pp. 24, 28, n. 3.

[132] Bates, 70–1.

[133] Joseph H. Lynch, 'Monastic Recruitment in the Eleventh and Twelfth Centuries: Some Social and Economic Considerations', *The American Benedictine Review* xxvi, 1975, 425–47, at 439–40.

[134] Lucien Musset, 'Les destins de la propriété monastique durant les invasions normandes (IXe–XIe siècles): l'exemple de Jumièges' in *Jumièges: Congrès scientifique du XIIIe centenaire*, Rouen 1955, i, 49–55, at 55.

FROM THEGNAGE TO BARONY:
SAKE AND SOKE, TITLE, AND TENANTS-IN-CHIEF[1]

David Roffe

1066 is deservedly the most memorable date in English history, for the Norman Conquest saw a political revolution of unparalleled speed and completeness. Within nine years of the Battle of Hastings both local and national government was firmly in the hands of the conquerors, and the English aristocracy had been all but entirely dispossessed. So much is undisputed by historians, but controversy still surrounds the extent of the social, economic, and tenurial changes that accompanied the Norman settlement. The continuing importance of pre-Conquest laws, however, has never been doubted. Twelfth-century compilations like the Leges Henrici Primi (1114–1118) and the Laws of Edward the Confessor (1115–1150), along with the copying and preservation of early codes, attest to interest in native legislation and the development of its forms and concepts.[2] The most important of these concepts was sake and soke, toll and team. The term sake and soke is first found in a diploma of 956 whereby King Eadwy granted the estate of Southwell (Notts) and its soke to the archbishop of York, and thereafter it is commonly found in charters and writs.[3] Toll has a longer history, but coupled with team it only appears in the reign of Cnut and is almost invariably linked with sake and soke.[4] The whole phrase is common in Domesday Book, and throughout much of the twelfth century the liberties that it conferred were an essential, if increasingly automatic, component of grants in hereditary fee.

The rights have specifically jurisdictional connotations. Their association with infangentheof, that is the summary judgement of hand-taken thieves, indicates that the privileges were concerned with the rights and profits of the processes of law and the legal sale of goods.[5] Such dues were considered to be essentially regalian by 1066, and in the unshired areas of the North, they effectively constituted an earl's share or shire. Elsewhere in the country, by contrast, although sake and soke conferred the king's two pennies, the context was clearly not *haute justice*: at least forty-nine individuals enjoyed the franchise over their estates in Yorkshire, Lincolnshire, Nottinghamshire, Derbyshire, and Rutland before 1066, but the lands to which they gave title did not constitute separate wapentakes either in 1086 or

---

[1] I would like to thank Dr Ann Williams and Dr Trevor Foulds for their comments on an early draft of this paper. Both helped me to clarify my ideas and drew my attention to a number of useful references.
[2] *Leges Henrici Primi*, ed. L. J. Downer, Oxford 1972; *Die Gesetze der Angelsachsen*, ed. F. Liebermann, Halle 1903–16, i, 529–669.
[3] P. H. Sawyer, *Anglo-Saxon Charters: an Annotated List and Bibliography*, London 1968, no. 659; *Anglo-Saxon Writs*, ed. F. E. Harmer, Manchester 1952, 74–6.
[4] Sawyer, *Charters*, no. 1423; *Writs*, 77–8.
[5] F. W. Maitland, *Domesday Book and Beyond*, Cambridge 1897, 97; F. M. Stenton, *Types of Manorial Structure in the Northern Danelaw*, Oxford 1910, 78–81.

subsequently.[6] On the contrary, such immunists, or their successors, regularly paid suit to the wapentake court for their lands. Peterborough Abbey, for example, held Collingham (Notts) with sake and soke in 1066, but still paid suit of court to the bishop of Lincoln's wapentake of Newark every two weeks in the thirteenth century, while the abbot of Burton, similarly privileged in Mickleover, Little Over, Findern, and Potlock (Derbys), attended the wapentake of Litchurch each month in c.1115.[7]

Sake and soke was confined to the holder's estate and was more akin to what was later known as leet jurisdiction. Thus, the archbishop of York not only enjoyed sake and soke with the king's two pennies, but also the earl's third; nevertheless a panel of lawmen from York declared in c.1100 that, although the men of the archbishop were free of the public courts, the bailiff of each manor made suit on their behalf.[8] Market rights were likewise confined to the estate, and in effect, sake and soke, toll and team conferred an intrinsic hundred or wapentake which was subject to the supervision of the king's agents in the shire.[9] The immunist himself, however, remained in a special relationship with the king. In the Laws of Cnut (1027–1034) the heriot of the king's thegn 'who has his soc' is sharply contrasted with that of the mean or median thegn, and the very same distinction is explicit in Domesday Book.[10] It is stated in a preamble to the Yorkshire folios that those who had sake and soke, toll and team in 1066 made their forfeitures to no one but the king and earl, and in Staffordshire an Alric is said to have held land 'cum soca taini regis'. Accordingly, it would appear that it was exclusively they who were king's thegns.[11]

This relationship not only survived the Conquest, but was one of the fundamental bonds of Anglo-Norman society, for it informed the concept of barony. In the late twelfth and thirteenth centuries tenure *per baroniam* was distinguished by a number of characteristics. First, although it could be held in parage, the barony had an identity as a group of fees regardless of the descent of the lordship. As a consequence, it rendered services and dues to the king as a unit and, unlike the tenement held by knight service, was legally indivisible. Second, its lord paid a relief at the will of the king, subsequently fixed at a hundred pounds, as opposed to a relief of five pounds for an ordinary estate. Third, a single manor was designated as a *caput* and could not be divided between collateral heirs. Finally, the baron was exempt from juries and was only amerced before the king's council.[12] By this time the rationale of the form had been forgotten, and its imposition was merely a matter of record. However, as Reid has shown, in origin the essential feature of barony was sake and soke, and it was the close relationship

---

[6] DB i, 280c, 298c, 337a; N. D. Hurnard, 'The Anglo-Norman Franchises', *EHR* 64, (1949), 298–327.

[7] *Documents Relating to the Manor and Soke of Newark-on-Trent*, ed. M. W. Barley, Nottingham 1956, 27, 42; 'The Burton Abbey Twelfth-Century Surveys', ed. C. G. O. Bridgeman, *Collections for a History of Staffordshire*, William Salt Archaeological Society, 1916, 231.

[8] *Visitations and Memorials of Southwell Minster*, ed. A. F. Leach, London 1891, 192.

[9] *Gesetze* i, 647.

[10] *Gesetze* i, 358.

[11] DB i, 249d, 298c; R. R. Reid, 'Barony and Thanage', *EHR* 35, (1920), 170–1. For the *taini regis* of Domesday Book, see below note 93.

[12] *The Treatise on the Laws and Customs of England Commonly Called Glanvill*, ed. G. D. W. Hall, London 1965, 108; *Henrici de Bracton de Legibus et Consuetudinibus Angliae*, ed. T. Twiss, London 1878, i, 8; ii, 39.

between crown and tenant-in-chief that this entailed that characterised the tenure.[13]

Both king's thegn and baron, then, were, in the words of the Laws of Cnut, 'nigh to the king', and there can be no doubt that conceptually there is a direct relationship between pre- and post-Conquest usage.[14] The Leges Henrici Primi specifically equates king's baron with king's thegn, and in the far North where Norman penetration was late, the equation is underpinned by a degree of direct continuity of tenure.[15] The barony of Bywell in Northumberland, for example, was merely the shire of Bywell, a multiple estate which dates to at least the ninth century, under a different lord; drengage remained the normal mode of tenure until enfeoffment in the mid twelfth century.[16] More usually, however, it is supposed that there was only functional as opposed to tenurial continuity. Stenton, for example, argued that sake and soke were the sort of liberties that baronage entailed, and that the two concepts were effectively independent since the Conquest saw the advent of a new order in which feudalism replaced the more personal bonds of English society. Homage and fealty became the essential relationships of a world in which military service was not a public duty but a condition of clientage and tenure.[17]

This view has not gone entirely unchallenged. In the last twenty-five years there has been a vigorous debate about the nature and origins of the *servitia debita* of the twelfth century. No consensus has yet emerged on whether they were English or Norman. Until recently, however, all have agreed on the reality of a tenurial revolution after 1066. King's thegn and baron were as chalk and cheese.[18] It is this assumption that is examined in this paper. Much of the evidence employed in the argument is drawn from the Domesday account of the East Midlands and the North, for the inclusion of numerous *obiter dicta* and a systematic record of the proceedings that arose from the enquiry (the *clamores*), illuminate the nature of tenure in an unparalleled fashion. Thus, a study of the tenurial context of sake and soke indicates that almost all the essential characteristics of tenure by barony were present before the Conquest in extended bookland estates. Evidence for other areas of the country is not always as explicit, but there are indications in Domesday Book and near contemporary charters and law codes that this was not a peculiarity of the

---

[13] Reid, 170–1. Reid's analysis has been critised on the grounds that the tenure of sake and soke was never the test of barony in the thirteenth century (I. J. Sanders, *Feudal Military Service in England*, Oxford 1956, 6–8). However, it was the 'nighness' to the king which conferred the especial status of barony. From the late eleventh century franchises were being created within honours, but the tenure of jurisdiction within that context did not forge a direct relationship with the crown.

[14] *Gesetze* i, 358.

[15] *Leges Henrici*, 35.1a, 41.1b, 80.9b, 87.5.

[16] J. E. A. Jolliffe, 'Northumbrian Institutions', *EHR* 41, (1926), 34–5; D. R. Roffe, 'The History of Whittonstall', *Excavations at Whittonstall 1970–1*, ed. C. M. Mahany, forthcoming.

[17] F. M. Stenton, *The First Century of English Feudalism 1066–1166*, Oxford 1932, 102 and n.

[18] E. John, *Land Tenure in Early England*, Leicester 1960, 140–61; J. Gillingham, 'The Introduction of Knight Service into England', *ante* iv, 1982, 53–64; J. C. Holt, 'The Introduction of Knight Service into England', *ante* vi, 1984, 89–106; C. W. Hollister, J. C. Holt, 'Two Comments on the Problem of Continuity in Anglo-Norman Feudalism', *Economic History Review*, 2nd ser., 16, (1963–4), 104–13; S. Harvey, 'The Knight and the Knight's Fee in England', *Past and Present* 49, (1970), 3–43.

Danelaw, and it is argued that Norman tenants-in-chief were generally heirs to such bookland estates and that their territorial interests, and the franchises they enjoyed therein, were directly derived from them. The granting of honours, then, hardly constituted a tenurial revolution, but it is concluded that the emergence of an honourial baronage marked a real departure in landholding, for it saw the creation of similar liberties in a feudal context beyond the direct control of the crown.

The pre-Conquest identity of some fees as aggregates of estates has long been recognised, but the novelty of honours as institutions was first generally questioned in detailed research on Nottinghamshire and Lincolnshire.[19] The case for continuity, however, has been most ambitiously stated by Professor Peter Sawyer. In his paper '1066–1086: A Tenurial Revolution?' he adduced evidence to suggest that the compiler of Domesday Book consistently omitted reference to pre-Conquest overlords. Nevertheless, it was they rather than the tenant recorded in the text who conferred title on the Norman tenant-in-chief, and by and large the honour in 1086 therefore had a pre-Conquest identity.[20] This analysis was subsequently criticised at this conference in 1986 by Dr Robin Fleming. She conceded that some Norman lords, like Gilbert de Ghent and Count Alan of Brittany, succeeded to the lands of a single pre-Conquest *antecessor*, but asserted that these were grants made early in the reign of William when Norman control of the country was less than complete. Dismissing Sawyer's evidence as insignificant in extent and probably exceptional, she discounted the possibility of extensive overlordship before the Conquest and employed a computer analysis to demonstrate that fees were generally composite. She concluded that most were locally based and had their origins in the specific grant of land by the king in the aftermath of conquest without regard to English title.[21]

The two papers have excited much comment, but to my mind they both miss the point. Although ostensibly concerned with continuity of tenure between 1066 and 1086, both in fact describe the mechanism of land transfer from English lord to Norman tenant-in-chief to the exclusion of tenurial relationships. To prove that an honour was composed of lands held by a single English overlord does not preclude a tenurial revolution if nebulous bonds of soke and commendation within the estate were replaced by enfeoffment for military service. Likewise, changes in lordship do not necessarily imply a revolution in the mode of landholding. In the early eleventh century there were considerable upheavals in patterns of tenure in the aftermath of Cnut's conquest of England, but, although new forms emerged, there was no wholesale abandonment of traditional tenurial relationships.[22] The problem of continuity, then, cannot be resolved by simply looking at title, but must be examined in legal and tenurial terms.

It is perhaps hazardous to make generalisation about English landholding. But it can be stated at the outset that the evidence for pre-Conquest overlordship in Domesday Book and contemporary sources is overwhelming. The fact is implicit

---

[19] D. R. Roffe, 'Norman Tenants-in-Chief and their Pre-Conquest Predecessors in Nottinghamshire', *History in the Making*, ed. S. N. Mastoris, Nottingham 1984; D. R. Roffe, 'Nottinghamshire and the North: a Domesday Study', unpublished Ph.D. thesis, Leicester University 1987, chapters 4 and 5.
[20] P. H. Sawyer, '1066–1086: A Tenurial Revolution?', *Domesday Book: a Reassessment*, ed. P. H. Sawyer, London 1985, 71–85.
[21] R. Fleming, 'Domesday Book and the Tenurial Revolution', *ante* ix, 1986, 87–102.
[22] K. Mack, 'Changing Thegns: Cnut's Conquest and the English Aristocracy', *Albion* 16, (1984), 375–87.

in law codes, for, since king's thegns forfeited to the king and earl alone, it can be assumed that mean thegns generally did not. Indeed, numerous passages in Domesday Book indicate that they were in the soke of those who held with sake and soke, and many more entries demonstrate that the soke of one estate was often attached to another.[23] The relationship implied is most apparent in ecclesiastical estates which were held by laenage before the Conquest. Those of the bishop of Worcester are the best documented both in the Great Survey and pre-Conquest charters, but others can often be detected.[24] In Huntingdonshire, for example, it is clear from subsidary evidence in the *clamores* that the TRE holders of monastic lands were all lessees.[25] It is true, however, that, with the exception of Circuits III (Cambridgeshire, Bedfordshire, Hertfordshire, Buckinghamshire, and Middlesex) and VII (Norfolk, Suffolk, and Essex), there is little explicit notice of dependence in secular contexts in Domesday Book. In Circuit VI (Yorkshire, Derbyshire, Nottinghamshire, Lincolnshire, and Huntingdonshire) a few references are found. Karli, for example, held land in Billingborough (Lincs) from Ralph the Staller, and Wulfbert was the lord of Farthegn, Alwine, and Tonni at Appleton (Yorks).[26] Elsewhere there are only sporadic notices of dependence of this kind, and many hundreds of thegns are said to have held freely or to have been able to leave with their lands.

Fleming is clearly wrong to place so much stress upon these characteristics of the Domesday record. As Sawyer and others have shown, the significance of holding *libere* and with the right to sell is far from obvious, and there are far more indications of overlordship than she is willing to allow.[27] Thus, numerous references are found to TRE holders of land who were said not to have held from a certain lord. In Derbyshire, for example, Gilbert de Ghent held two carucates of land in Shipley which had been held by Brown and Odincar in 1066. His title was apparently challenged for the sworn men stated that the land had not belonged to Ulf Fenisc, Gilbert's predecessor, in 1066, but that the two thegns so held it that they could grant or sell to whom they would.[28] His title was presumably invalid in this instance, but it can surely be concluded that Odincar and possibly Brown were tenants in those places in the East Midlands in which Gilbert's title to their land went unchallenged.[29]

Many such references greatly increase the number of overt indications of overlordship in the East Midlands and the North, and others are afforded by the disparities between the text and satellite material. The most considerable body of evidence, however, is found in the forms and conventions of the text. Calligraphic devices are the most subtle. The Exchequer Domesday is a business document, and

---

[23] G. Black, D. R. Roffe, *The Nottinghamshire Domesday: a Reader's Guide*, Nottingham 1986, 21. See, for example, DB i, 336a, 336d, 375a, 375c, 376b.
[24] A. Williams, 'Introduction to the Worcestershire Domesday', *The Worcestershire Domesday*, eds A. Williams, R. W. H. Erskine, London 1989, 24–6; John, 80–139.
[25] D. R. Roffe, 'An Introduction to the Huntingdonshire Domesday', *The Huntingdonshire Domesday*, eds A. Williams, R. W. H. Erskine, London 1989, 8–10.
[26] DB i, 377b, 329a, 374a.
[27] Sawyer, '1066–1086', 78–80; C. Stephenson, 'Commendation and Related Problems in Domesday Book', *EHR* 59, (1944), 289–310; A. Williams, 'An Introduction to the Gloucestershire Domesday', *The Gloucestershire Domesday*, eds A. Williams, R. W. H. Erskine, London 1989, 18.
[28] DB i, 277d.
[29] DB i, 355c.

it is generally appreciated that, despite a shakey start with the Yorkshire folios, the scribe exhibited consummate skill in the editing and abbreviation of his sources.[30] However, his expertise as a draughtsman is less often recognised. Information is as frequently conveyed by the layout of the text and letter forms as explicit record. Thus, in Circuit VI manorial entries are distinguished from dependent holdings by a distinctive treatment of initial letters and place-names, and variations often indicate a subordinate status. Leofnoth's manor in Oakham (Rutland), for example, has the same form as a berewick or sokeland entry and was apparently a dependency of Queen Edith's fee in the same vill. The relationship is only otherwise articulated in a note at the end of the account which records the dimensions of 'the whole manor'.[31]

In other circuits similar devices are found, although they have remained largely uninvestigated, and differences in status are emphasised by variations in diplomatic. In Circuits I (Kent, Sussex, Surrey, Hampshire, and Berkshire), II (Wiltshire, Dorset, Somerset, Devon, and Cornwall), III, and IV (Leicestershire, Warwickshire, Northamptonshire, and Oxfordshire), for example, entries relating to principal manors are of the form 'The Count [Alan] holds *MUNDEN* [Herts]. It defends itself for 7½ hides and 1 virgate ... Edeva the Fair held this manor', The account of dependent land, by contrast, begins with a formula something like 'In Reed [Herts] Alfward holds ... Thorbern, Edeva's man, held this land [TRE]', and the dichotomy in status is emphasised by the distinctive use of terms such as *terra* as opposed to *manerium*.[32]

A more obvious sign of dependence is the multiple-manor entry. Like the estates of ten thegns in Eaton (Notts), manors are frequently described together in single entries throughout the text.[33] The form has usually been seen as a convenient scribal device for the enrolment of a number of small holdings or as evidence of post-Conquest amalgamation of estates.[34] Neither explanation, however, is satisfactory. Small estates in the same settlement were by no means always described together, and the several estates of grouped entries, such as the two manors in Radcliffe-on-Trent (Notts), were often separately managed in 1086 and throughout the Middle Ages.[35] Rather there are grounds for believing that multiple-manor entries relate to groups of estates held from an overlord. Thus, although each of the thegns named often had his own hall, the holdings still had a common identity. Ligulfr and Northmann, for example, had two manors in Bulmer and Stittenham (Yorks), but sokeland in Hutton, Welburn, Ganthorpe, and Terrington was said to belong to 'this manor'. Furthermore, there was one assessment TRE, and only one farm was paid in 1066.[36] The identity of their lord is not recorded, but that of other groups, most regularly in Lincolnshire, is sometimes explicit in the text.

---

[30] D. R. Roffe, 'Domesday Book and Northern Society: a Reassessment', *EHR* 105 (1990), 320–8; H. R. Loyn, 'A General Introduction to Domesday Book', *Domesday Book Studies*, eds A. Williams, R. W. H. Erskine, London 1987, 3–14.

[31] Black and Roffe, *Nottinghamshire Domesday*, 16; DB i, 293b.

[32] Roffe, 'Domesday Book and Northern Society', 322–3.

[33] DB i, 284d.

[34] Stenton, *Types of Manorial Structure*, 52; R. W. Finn, *The Making and Limitations of the Yorkshire Domesday*, York 1972, 8; Black and Roffe, *Nottinghamshire Domesday*, 22.

[35] See for example, DB i, 285a, 285b, 285d, 288a.

[36] DB i, 306a

The incidence of such entries was largely determined by the structure of local government, for manors were only grouped in the text where they were situated in the same vill: a manor in Hagworthingham (Lincs) was subtracted from one group in Mumby since it was in another twelve-carucate hundred and enrolled elsewhere.[37] But in like wise a single TRE value for two or more manors indicates an extended group, and others are frequently suggested by irregularities in the order of entries. In Drew de Beurere's lands in Lincolnshire, for example, an otherwise regular wapentake sequence is disrupted to enter the manor of Normanby between three estates in Barrow-on-Humber. In the normal course of events only dependent sokeland is enrolled with the manorial *caput* in this way. The anomaly therefore suggests dependence, and indeed in this instance the fact is explicit, for the three brothers who held the land were clearly tenants of Earl Morcar in Barrow since the value of their manor is appended to his fee.[38]

All of these devices illustrate the widespread importance of overlordship before the Conquest. Nevertheless, it is evident that it was not the intention of the commissioners to record its incidence, for the fact was largely irrelevant to the purpose of the enquiry. That the information was available is clear. A thegnage is recorded in the Inquisitio Eliensis account of Bluntisham (Hunts), for example, but the Exchequer scribe enrolled the land as demesne without comment.[39] Generally overlordship is only noted when germane to estate management in 1086. Thus, outside of Circuits III and VII, explicit notice of dependence is only found where it brought one tenant-in-chief into a tenurial relationship with another, while the occurrence of multiple manor entries merely reflects a continuing tenurial nexus at the time of the survey. Domesday Book was not a register of title, but a record of the value of lands to the king and his tenants-in-chief. The TRE tenant was therefore recorded in preference to his lord because, as the one liable to the discharge of the geld, it was he who identified the royal dues owed from the estate in the records of the shire.

The evidence for pre-Conquest overlordship, then, is considerable if largely unexplored, and, despite the reticence of Domesday Book, the nature of the relationships implied can therefore be described in some detail. Sawyer argued that *commendatio* and *soca* were the essence of the bond between lord and tenant. He has rightly pointed out that simple commendation was a relatively weak tenurial bond. for, although many tenants-in-chief held and claimed land purely on the basis of that relationship, it did not legally confer title. Thus, after the Conquest a freeman commended himself to Ranulf Peverel's predecessor, but he did not give him his land in Vange (Ess), and Wulfwine cilt was said to be a man of Earl Harold, but his land in Hail Weston (Hunts) was a manor on its own and did not belong to the earl's manor of Kimbolton.[40] It is almost certainly to this freedom of commendation that the numerous references to holding *libere* and the like relate. Rights to land were a different and far more weighty matter; Wulfric, Tovi, and Leofwin held three manors in Windrush (Gloucs) and were free to go with their land. Nevertheless, it is clear from a second entry that their estates were in fact

---

[37] DB i, 348d; D. R. Roffe, 'The Lincolnshire Hundred', *Landscape History* 3, (1981), 30–3; Roffe, 'Nottinghamshire and the North', 85–6.
[38] DB i, 360b.
[39] *Inquisitio Comitatus Cantabrigiensis ... Subjicitur Inquisitio Eliensis*, ed. N. E. S. A. Hamilton, London 1876, 166; DB i, 204a.
[40] DB ii, 71b; DB i, 208a.

held from a certain Bolle who conferred title upon the church of Winchcombe.[41]

Sawyer equated this interest in the land itself with *soca*, but failed to explore the content of the concept.[42] Soke has usually been understood to refer to the rights of jurisdiction and has thus been seen as a relatively loose bond between lord and man; beyond the forfeitures and the receipt of amercements, it conferred no interest in land itself.[43] However, it is clear that the term was not confined to this specific meaning. In itself soke appears to have articulated nothing more than a relationship in which customary dues were rendered; it could refer to a whole host of dues from the render of a quitrent from an acre of land on the one hand, to the regalian rights of the king in the shire on the other.[44] As such, it was often annoyingly vague in the eleventh century: the North Riding of Lindsey declared that Count Alan's predecessor had the soke of Eiric's land in Tealby (Lincs), but they knew not of what kind.[45]

Such a comment is enough to inspire despair. However, an important and widespread use of the term soke is apparent in Domesday Book. In a large number of sokeland entries in the North, and their equivalent in the rest of the country, the soke *qua* jurisdiction of an estate, hereafter designated as *soca*, was held by one lord, but the land itself was in the tenure of another. The interest that the latter, the landlord, enjoyed was articulated by the term *terra*, 'land', or *consuetudines*, 'customs', and, consistently contrasted with simple *soca*, it referred to actual tenure both before and after the Conquest.[46] Nigel Fossard, for example, held five parcels of land in Yorkshire in succession to three named individuals, but the *soca* belonged to Conisborough which had been held by Earl Harold in 1066, and in Feltwell (Norf) the abbot of Ely had thirty-four sokemen with all customs TRE and six freemen with *soca* and commendation only.[47]

The nature of the dues implied is not explicit in the text; references to ploughing are common, but otherwise they are largely unspecified. It is clear from both pre- and post-Conquest charter evidence and twelfth-century estate surveys, however, that a number of renders were involved. The foundation charter of Blyth Priory indicates that other labour services like sowing, hay-making, reaping, and repair of the lord's hall and mill were owed.[48] More importantly, however, there was a financial tribute and/or a render in kind. It was this due that constituted the essence of the customs, and was of considerable value.[49] In the soke of Oswaldbeck (Notts) it seems to have accounted for all the monetary issues of the land, for the twenty shillings in customs that twenty-two sokemen in Leverton rendered in 1066 seem to represent the value that is appended to all the other parcels of land in the soke.[50] In origin, the payment was almost certainly a commuted food rent or farm. A probably authentic late tenth- or early eleventh-century grant of land to

[41] DB i, 165d, 170c.
[42] Sawyer, '1066–1086', 80–1.
[43] Stenton, *Types of Manorial Structure*, 1–55.
[44] DB i, 376b, 375b; C. A. Joy, 'Sokeright', unpublished thesis, Leeds University 1974, 70–77.
[45] DB i, 376a.
[46] Stephenson, 305–9; A. K. G. Kristensen, 'Danelaw Institutions and Danish Society in the Viking Age', *Medieval Scandinavia* 8, (1975), 74–85; E. M. Demarest, 'Consuetudo Regis', *EHR* 42, (1927), 161–79.
[47] DB i, 373d; DB ii, 213b.
[48] Stenton, *Types of Manorial Structure*, 22–8, 92–4.
[49] Stenton, *Types of Manorial Structure*, 33–7.
[50] DB i, 281c.

Ramsey Abbey in Hickling and Kinoulton (Notts) specifies a heavy render in kind, but at the time of Domesday there is no suggestion of anything other than a money rent.[51]

In aggregate these dues were considerable, and, supplemented by even heavier tributes from villeins, it is unlikely that they could be unilaterally withdrawn by the villagers. Thus, in the hundred of Oswaldlow (Worcs) the men of the church of Worcester could not keep back *consuetudines* except by the will of the bishop, and it is clear that in the Danelaw the freedom of the sokeman was similarly circumscribed.[52] *Terra*, then, as opposed to *soca qua* jurisdiction, evidently constituted the essential identity of the manor. The right of some lords may well have been confined to precisely this interest. The archbishop of York, for example, probably did not enjoy the rights of jurisdiction over his manor of Laneham (Notts) until it was granted to him by a writ of 1060x65; nevertheless, he still derived a profit from his soke *qua* land.[53] But *soca* and *terra* were by no means always held by different lords, and there is a considerable body of evidence to demonstrate that their liberties were then known as sake and soke.

With specifically jurisdictional referents, sake and soke is normally held to be synonymous with *soca*.[54] It is, however, with but few exceptions, consistently contrasted with simple jurisdiction in Circuit VI and elsewhere.[55] Of Alfred's claim to two bovates of land in the hundred of Huttoft (Lincs), for example, the South Riding of Lindsey declared that 'he ought to have one with sake and soke and the other is his in like wise, but Earl Hugh has the *soca* in Greetham'.[56] This dichotomy is reflected in the near contemporary Instituta Cnuti (1095–1150) where 'the king's thegn who has his soc' of the Laws of Cnut is glossed as *liberalis*

---

[51] Stenton, *Types of Manorial Structure*, 37–8.

[52] DB i, 172c. The freedom of sokemen has been exaggerated. Some at least of the twelfth-century charters adduced as evidence for an independent peasantry were subsequently confirmed by their lords, suggesting that they were not such free agents as supposed. See, for example, F. M. Stenton, *The Free Peasantry of the Danelaw*, Oxford 1969, and *Documents Illustrative of the Social and Economic History of the Danelaw*, London 1920, where no. 118 of the one is confirmed by the lord in no. 538 of the other. Moreover, their services were akin to those of the dependent thegnlands of Ely (Stephenson, 297n, 308n).

[53] *Writs*, no. 119.

[54] Maitland, 84; F. M. Stenton, 'Introduction', *The Lincolnshire Domesday and Lindsey Survey*, eds C. W. Foster, T. Longley, Horncastle 1924, xxxvii, xxxix.

[55] Roffe, 'Nottinghamshire', 104–7. There are apparently two exceptions in Circuit VI (DB i, 375c, 376c). In both cases, a Norman tenant-in-chief merely claimed soke over land, even though his predecessor had enjoyed sake and soke in the estate. It was on the basis of these two solitary entries that Stenton postulated the identity of the terms sake and soke, and soke (*Lincolnshire Domesday*, xxxvii). As they stand, both are highly exceptional and cannot be easily reconciled with the usage found throughout the rest of the circuit. However, it may be supposed that there was some unrecorded transaction which conferred rights to land between 1066 and 1086, or that the scribe was simply in error. Given the similarity of the terms, and the fact that the compiler must have had far more information in front of him concerning the liberties than appears in the text, confusion would not be surprising. Indeed, it can sometimes be directly observed. In a Lincolnshire *clamores* entry relating to Osbournby, the curious term *soca et soca* appears (DB i, 377c). This is clearly nonsense, and the editors have emended the text to *saca et soca*. However, it is clearly *soca* alone which is intended for the liberty entitled Ralf Pagenel to a horse from the land when he went to war. Such rights are always expressed in terms of *soca* (see, for example, DB i, 357c). Likewise, the statement that Countess Godiva had sake and soke over Newark *Wapentake* (Notts) is not only illogical, but also patently untrue since the abbey of Peterborough had the same liberties in Collingham within the same wapentake (DB i, 280c).

[56] DB i, 375b.

hominis qui consuetudines suas habet.[57] But the distinction was clearly not a post-Conquest innovation, for in 1086 it was scrupulously observed in the determination of title. Thus, Guy de Craon, for example, sued for six bovates of land in Gosberton (Lincs) which had been held by Athelstan his predecessor, but he was unsuccessful in his suit because Ralph the Staller, Count Alan's predecessor, had had sake and soke over the land.[58] Sake and soke clearly expressed the concept of full rights – *terra* and *soca* – as opposed to the limited dues conferred by the latter. Its application to title is therefore comprehensible: in precluding all claims on land, including the king's two pennies, the term is indicative of and synonymous with tenure by book.[59]

In Circuit VI where the holders of sake and soke, toll and team are listed the extent of such land can be readily determined. Some king's thegns, like Athelstan, held vast tracts, but many seem to have had only modest holdings. However, it is clear that their bookland was far more extensive than Domesday Book indicates. Harold the Staller, Fyach, and Azor son of Sualeva, Ulf Fenisc, and Countess Ælfeva had sake and soke, toll and team in Lincolnshire, Yorkshire, and Nottinghamshire and Derbyshire respectively. Their names, however, do not appear in the text, and it is clear that their lands were held by tenants.[60] Robert Malet, for example, claimed soke in Ingoldsby (Lincs) through his predecessor Azor son of Sualeva rather than Godwin the tenant of his manor.[61] The relationship, however, was not one of mere jurisdiction; several other references demonstrate that *terra* was also reserved. Siward, for example, held the manor of Scrivelsby (Lincs) with inland in Coningsby and Wilksby, and sokeland in Mareham-upon-the-Hill. His lord Achi retained the soke in his estate of Thornton, however, and apparently also enjoyed residual rights in the land since he conferred title to the manor on Robert the Steward: where the nexus was purely jurisdiction the land was either enrolled in the *breve* of another tenant-in-chief or in the lands of the thegns.[62] More explicitly, Count Alan had title to *terra* in Billingborough (Lincs) not by right of Karli the tenant but Ralph the Staller who had sake and soke.[63] The king's thegn, then, clearly enjoyed full rights over large groups of dependent manors.

These extended bookland estates shared many of the characteristics of those held by barony. Both the Worcestershire and Berkshire Domesdays suggest that the lord alone was personally summoned to the fyrd and, like the baron, he was responsible for the discharge of the military service assessed on the estate by his tenants.[64] Tewkesbury (Gloucs), along with its dependent lands and manors which could not be withdrawn from the head manor, is specifically said to have been quit of royal

[57] *Gesetze* i, 359; Reid, 172.
[58] DB i, 377d.
[59] The equation is explicit in the Laws of Cnut and the Leges Henrici, for it is stated in both that bookland was forfeited to the king alone (*Gesetze* i, 316–19; *Leges Henrici*, c.12). In Worcestershire sake and soke was 'rendered', that is, the dues that *soca* and *terra* involved were rendered by tenants to their lord. In East Anglia sake and soke specifically refers to jurisdiction, but is almost always coupled with *consuetudines*.
[60] DB i, 280c, 298c, 337a.
[61] DB i, 377b.
[62] DB i, 363b, 375c. The tenure of *soca* alone did not confer title to land.
[63] DB i, 377c.
[64] DB i, 172a, 56c.

service except for the service of its lord.[65] As Dr Abels has argued, bookland was a precarious tenure in this respect, but otherwise it was hereditary and its lord had free disposal of it.[66] Nevertheless, in terms of the services due, the estate was probably indivisible. Thus, in Lincolnshire, for example, Siwate, Fenchel, Alnod, and Aschil had divided their father Godwin's booklands between them 'share and share alike', but they held in parage as far as service towards the king was concerned.[67] Furthermore, a few references are found to capital manors; Doddington Pigot (Lincs) and Northwick (Worcs) are each described as *capitale manerium*, and the tenure of sake and soke, toll and team by Countess Godiva in Newark, Alfsi son of Kaskin in Worksop (Notts), Gamall in Cottingham, and Copsi in Cuxwold (Yorks) before the Conquest hint at several others.[68] Evidence for the reliefs that were owed is more equivocal. They were certainly rendered to the king, for in Yorkshire, Nottinghamshire, and Derbyshire it is stated that thegns with more than six manors gave eight pounds. Lesser thegns paid two pounds to the earl or sheriff.[69] Elsewhere higher reliefs were paid, but both pre- and post-Conquest law codes indicate that fixed sums were normally levied.[70]

The relationship between these estates and post-Conquest honours can be directly observed. At the outset it is clear that not all Norman fees were directly derived from pre-Conquest estates and franchises. The king could and did grant lands by writ or otherwise which cut across earlier rights; Beverley minster, for example, had the right to soke in the East Riding of Yorkshire by the seal of the king, and some fees may well have had their origin in a number of such grants.[71] The evidence for many castleries, like those in Sussex, is superficially impressive, and other fees were probably created for a specific and local purpose. The lands of Heppo the Arblaster in Lincolnshire, for example, were probably all ministerial tenements, for they were held by sergeancy in the twelfth century and appear to have no pre-Conquest identity.[72] But most of the suits recorded in the *clamores*, *invasiones*, and *terre occupate* sections of Domesday Book and Exon suggest that the transfer of land by writ was unusual. The procedure apparently precluded all claim on land. Thus, in Lincolnshire, for example, Gilbert de Ghent had legal title to soke in Stainfield and Apley and all were agreed on the fact. Nevertheless, William de Percy had seisin by gift of the king and that was the end of the matter.[73] And yet, despite the unequivocal authority of writ, in 99 per cent of cases title to land and dues was not claimed as of the grant of the king but by right of a predecessor.

Almost without exception these predecessors can be shown to have have had sake and soke where evidence is available. Indeed, it may well have been generally

---

[65] DB i, 163b–163d.

[66] R. Abels, 'Bookland and Fyrd Service in Late Anglo-Saxon England', *ante* vii, 1985, 1–18.

[67] DB i, 375c, 376a.

[68] DB i, 377a, 173c, 280c, 298c. Scottlethorpe in Lincolnshire was converted from an ordinary to a chief manor in the reign of William, and a thegn who was 'head of a manor' is noted in Cropwell Butler in Nottinghamshire (DB i, 367b, 291b).

[69] DB i, 280c, 298c.

[70] See *Gesetze* i, 358–9, for example.

[71] DB i, 373c, 374a.

[72] DB i, 369a; *Rotuli Hundredorum*, ed. W. Illingworth, London 1812–18, i, 252a, 304b; *Book of Fees*, PRO, London 1920–31, 180; *Calendar of Inquisitions Post Mortem* i, 72, 216; ii, 245; vii, 450.

[73] DB i, 375c.

assumed that title was derived from a king's thegn, for in Little Domesday we read of an *antecessor cum saca et soca sua*.[74] Further, it is evident that it was not just their demesne estates to which they gave title in 1086. The repeated plea in the West Country that one manor did not belong to another indicates that groups of estates were normally transferred *en bloc*, and patterns of pre-Conquest land tenure that are apparent in post-Conquest fees illustrates that the process was general.[75] As Fleming argues, it is possible that the widely scattered lands of the same individual that pass to a number of tenants-in-chief may point to grants of land in a locality without regard to tenure.[76] But it is usually closely grouped parcels of land which are so divided. In a handful of adjoining vills in south Kesteven (Lincs), for example, Offram's estates in Dowsby, Keisby, Southorpe, and Avethorpe passed to Guy de Craon and Alfred of Lincoln, while he himself retained Kirkby Underwood as a tenant of the same Alfred and further manors in Dowsby, Keisby, and Little Lavington as a king's thegn.[77] Such distributions are ubiquitous and can hardly indicate locality as the criterion of transfer, and individual grants would presuppose a survey which was equally as comprehensive as Domesday Book itself. Rather, the pattern must attest to pre-existing relationships.

It seems likely, then, that the grant of a manor by right of a predecessor conferred title to all of those manors which were dependent upon it. Henry de Ferrers, for example, probably claimed his lands in Derbyshire through the tenure of Ednaston, Doveridge, and Brailsford where he enjoyed sake and soke.[78] The process was generally understood, and exceptions may well be consistently and carefully noted. Thus, in Thurstan son of Rolf's fee in Somerset various small estates are said to have been added to the lands of Alfwold and we can conclude that the manors which are ascribed to other tenants without comment were held from this his predecessor, and in Suffolk it is noted that land did not belong to the honour of Geoffrey de Mandeville's predecessor Asgar (*non est de honore Ansgari*).[79] Elsewhere, as in Willoughby in the Marsh (Lincs), and Fenton, and Clarborough (Notts), it is just laconically stated that land was held with sake and soke and presumably therefore had a pre-Conquest identity distinct from that of the bulk of the fee.[80]

With such minor exceptions, it follows that many honours had decidedly pre-Conquest characteristics. Indeed, throughout the North there is a marked tendency for the demesne manors of king's thegns to remain in the hands of tenants-in-chief, and over three-quarters of honourial courts in the later Middle Ages met in manors which were held with sake and soke, toll and team in 1066. The pre-Conquest identity of the groups of estates which owed services to them is most apparent where the presence of an overlord is explicit. Gilbert de Ghent, for example, succeeded to the lands of Ulf Fenisc and the manors which were ascribed to others were held from this predecessor. In the Leicestershire folios this is the norm, for it appears that it is only the predecessor who is regularly named in the text. Where the tenant is noticed, however, as is the norm elsewhere, the English identity of

---

[74] DB ii, 118a.
[75] *Domesday Book* iv, 457ff.
[76] Fleming, 96–9.
[77] DB i, 358c, 367b, 368a, 368b, 370c, 371a.
[78] DB i, 280c.
[79] DB ii, 412c.
[80] DB i, 355b, 286c, 287a. Many small parcels of bookland like this may have been held by tenants-in-chief simply because no one else claimed them.

the fee is less obvious. The honour of Tickhill is a case in point. Roger de Bully succeeded to the lands of at least a hundred named individuals in north Nottinghamshire and South Yorkshire, and his fee has the appearance of a post-Conquest castlery.[81] However, pre-Conquest overlordship apparently belies the form of the Domesday account, for the honour was endowed with impressive privileges of an apparently early form. *Tolenea*, throughtoll, was reserved to Tickhill (Yorks) from before 1088 when part of the banlieu was granted to the priory of Blyth (Notts) on its foundation, and tithes were owed from much of the honour to the royal free chapel of Tickhill from at least 1148.[82] Both liberties hint at the importance of Tickhill and Blyth as royal or comital centres before the Conquest – indeed, Earl Edwin had a hall at nearby Laughton-en-le-Morthen (Yorks)[83] – and a detailed examination of the Domesday account and later documentation adds weight to the argument. Numerous multiple-manor entries attest to the presence of overlordship and some elements of the honour interlock with larger estates and thereby suggest a common origin for whole groups of manors. Roger's lands in the wapentake of Oswaldbeck (Notts), for example, are situated in the same vills as the royal soke of Oswaldbeck, and a local jury in the thirteenth century maintained that the king had formerly held the whole complex.[84] No firm conclusions can be drawn from such tantalising detail, but it can be suggested that part, probably even most, of Roger's honour was derived from the interests of the pre-Conquest earl.

Many honours of this kind may have encompassed quite ancient groups of estates. Ralph fitzHubert, for example, seems to have been heir to a large number of the early eleventh-century estates of Wulfric Spot through his predecessors Leofric and Leofnoth.[85] It cannot be concluded from this, however, that each honour had a single pre-Conquest identity. Sawyer assumes, or leaves the reader to assume, that such is in fact the case.[86] But in reality there were often significant changes. First, it is clear that some tenants-in-chief had more than one predecessor. Walter de Aincurt, for example, seems to have had right to the various estates of Tori, Swein cilt, and Heming, and in Lincolnshire the lands of two of these are separately enrolled.[87] The use of blank lines in the text to define groups of manors and repetition of hundredal or wapentake order often point to a number of *antecessores* and identifies the estates which they held.[88] Second, all the estates of the same antecessor throughout the country did not always pass to the same tenant-in-chief. Pre-Conquest tenurial relationships were often responsible. Beorhtric son of Ælfgar, for example, was a king's thegn, but he appears to have held land from the bishop of Worcester in Barley and Bushley (Worcs), and the estates were

[81] Stenton, *First Century*, 62; Fleming, 96–9.
[82] Stenton, *Types of Manorial Structure*, 92–3; *The Registrum Antiquissimum of the Cathedral Church of Lincoln* i, ed. C. W. Foster, Lincoln 1927, 62, 211; *Calendar of Documents Preserved in France ... 918–1206*, ed. J. H. Round, London 1899, nos 61, 62; J. H. Denton, *English Royal Free Chapels 1100–1300*, Manchester 1970, 115. For a full discussion of the institution, see Roffe, 'Nottinghamshire', 185–90.
[83] DB i, 319a.
[84] *Rotuli Hundredorum* ii, 300b–1a.
[85] DB i, 277a–277c; P. H. Sawyer, *The Charters of Burton Abbey*, Oxford 1979, 53–6.
[86] Sawyer, '1066–1086'.
[87] DB i, 288c–289a, 361a–361b.
[88] Roffe, 'Nottinghamshire', Appendix 2.

retained by the church after the Conquest.[89] As in the twelfth century, political influence and support was bought by the grant of land to important local personages.[90] However, what can be perceived as a thegn's demesne manors and the tenanted, as opposed to commended estates which were dependent upon them, usually seem to have passed to a single tenant-in-chief. With the exception of illegal seizures, it is generally only in the transfer of royal and comital estates that individual interests were divided. Tosti/Morcar's estates in Lincolnshire, for example, were retained by the king, but those in the vicinity of Nottingham were granted to William Peverel.[91]

In the East Midlands the division of comital estates may well reflect pre-Conquest patterns of tenure, for the region was subject to the claims of rival earldoms in the reign of Edward the Confessor.[92] But there can be no doubt that the redistribution of bookland estates, both by division and amalgamation, was immediately related to post-Conquest political and strategic concerns. However, the degree of discontinuity should not be overstressed. It was probably no different in kind or extent from tenurial upheavals of the first half of the eleventh century and was almost certainly belied by the survival of existing tenurial nexus and relationships. As we have seen, king's thegns had full rights over the estates of lesser thegns before the Conquest. In Yorkshire many of these subordinate holdings were apparently ministerial. The lands of the so-called *taini regis*, for example, are explicitly assigned to the royal demesne in the Summary and a parallel entry suggests that a further 332 manors which were postscriptally appended to the king's *breve* were thegnages. Indeed, in the North the lesser thegns paid the same relief as the drengs of Twix Ribble and Mersey and their status may have been very similar.[93] The incidence of forinsec services south of the Humber does not preclude similar tenures elsewhere; drengs are found in Kent and radknights in the West Midlands, while the common record of renders from manorial commodities like the mill indicates the reservation of dues to the overlord throughout the country. But something akin to laenage was probably more common in the south since the rights to *terra* in the form of sokeland were attached to the thegn's hall.[94]

In both types of tenure the nature of renders and services owed to the booklord are rarely explicit, but the main outlines are clear. All tenants were in the soke of their lord, who presumably stood surety for them, and paid suit to his court. Some TRE drengages, like Wharram Percy (Yorks), were later held by sergeancies in the feudal army and may therefore have owed military services; various entries in the Lincolnshire Domesday hint at similar military obligations and escort duties and the like are found elsewhere.[95] Domesday Book, however, suggests that all, if only notionally, rendered a farm to their overlord. Throughout the country *valuit* figures, the value of estates in 1066, are generally expressed in round sums and

[89] DB i, 173b; Williams, 'Worcestershire', 23.
[90] Harvey, 6–7.
[91] DB i, 337a, 337c, 338a, 338b, 338c, 280a, 287c.
[92] Roffe, 'Nottinghamshire', 256–60.
[93] DB i, 269d, 298d. Although called the king's thegns, these individuals did not have their 'soc' and must therefore be distinguished from the holders of bookland. They were in fact the king's mean thegns and are hereafter referred to as *taini regis* to distinguish them from the more privileged *ministri*.
[94] Stenton, *First Century*, 145–7; Roffe, 'Domesday Book and Northern Society', 328–33.
[95] D. R. Roffe, 'Wharram Percy', forthcoming; DB i, 354a, 357c, 361a, 366b, 368a, 375c, 377c.

are clearly conventional. Occasionally they are explicitly called renders.[96] It is unlikely, however, that they represent a farm that was paid by the villagers to the tenant, for villeins, freemen, and sokemen appear to have rendered their services and tributes, often in kind, directly to the manorial hall, and, as is clear in Little Domesday, these can often be shown to be different from the value of an estate.[97] On the contrary, the render that the queen's soke of Rutland made to the crown appears to have been the sum total of the value of the manors in the liberty, not all of which were held by Queen Edith, and elsewhere the recipient of the sums is occasionally explicit.[98] In Osmaston by Derby (Derbys), for example, the value of the estate was divided in the ratio of two to one between the king and Henry de Ferrers in 1086.[99] Henry was apparently heir to the earl's share, and the render was therefore almost certainly of pre-Conquest origin, for the earldom was in the king's hands for much of William's reign. Within this context, the attachment of the value of one manor to another becomes immediately comprehensible: the 'valuation' of a manor was a sum that went out of the estate and was a farm that was paid to the overlord.

The terms of subtenancy after the Conquest were generally not markedly different. By the second half of the twelfth century most tenanted manors were held in hereditary fee by knight service. However, although each tenant-in-chief was probably responsible for a *servitium debitum* in 1086, it is doubtful that such a radical change in the nature of tenure was far advanced at the time of Domesday. First of all, it is clear that many pre-Conquest families continued to hold their estates. In almost every county a number of tenements in the hands of *taini regis* were held by the same individuals in both 1066 and 1086, and many others passed to sons and heirs. However, they were only the ones who held of the king, and many more can be identified. In some *breves* there are one or two lesser thegns who survived the Conquest to hold their manors of a tenant-in-chief. But Domesday Book probably hides many others, for subtenants are only erratically recorded in the text. Colle, for example, held Youlgreave (Derbys) in 1066, and no tenant is recorded at the time of the survey, but in the twelfth century the manor was held by Colle's grandson.[100] Likewise, the Cromwell family was enfeoffed in Nuthall and Toton (Notts) which had been held by their ancestor Aldene before the Conquest.[101] Many other subtenants may have been sons of TRE holders, for a large proportion of tenants in 1086 had English or Anglo-Scandinavian names. In Nottinghamshire, for example, some 40 per cent were apparently of native stock.[102]

All of these continued to hold their lands under much the same conditions as before the Conquest. References are occasionally found to tenure in thegnage and in the Nottinghamshire folios many are specifically distinguished from the foreign tenants, for they are said to 'have their land under', or 'hold from', as opposed to

---

[96] Commonly in the *terra regis*.

[97] Demarest, 161–5.

[98] T. Cain, 'An Introduction to the Rutland Domesday', *The Northamptonshire and Rutland Domesday*, eds A. Williams, R. W. H. Erskine, London 1987, 26–7.

[99] DB i, 275d.

[100] DB i, 275c; *Monasticon Anglicanum*, eds J. Caley, H. Ellis, B. Bandinell, London 1817–30, vi, 468.

[101] DB i, 287c, 287d; *Documents Relating to Newark-on-Trent*, xxx.

[102] Roffe, 'Nottinghamshire', 95.

being 'men of', the tenants-in-chief.[103] Further, a high proportion of the estates emerged in the thirteenth century as socages or sergeancies. In Yorkshire, for example, whole groups of manors were held by various personal services and several characteristics of tenure suggest that many more estates were of this kind.[104] Thus, large numbers of military fees were primarily assessed in carucates, and feudal dues were calculated by set formulas: in Holderness, fourteen and sixteen carucates to the knight fee was the norm, while ten, twelve, and twenty-four are found elsewhere.[105] Feudalism was just a thin veneer: ministerial tenure was apparently the essence of these manors, and it is likely that they had their ultimate origin in pre-Conquest thegnages and drengages.[106]

By far the majority of recorded subtenants, however, were newcomers. Nevertheless, it must be doubted that many held under radically different terms. The evidence is most unequivocal in ecclesiastical estates. In the lands of the bishop of Worcester, for example, Normans seem to have held laenages on exactly the same terms as their English predecessors; Westminster and Hereford charters indicate that grants of land were non-hereditary; and again at Ely there was no enfeoffment since the *servitium debitum* was discharged by household knights.[107] But there are indications that this was also the norm in lay estates. As late as 1166 not all barons had enfeoffed enough knights to cover their *servitium debitum*, but nevertheless, it is clear that many of their estates were still tenanted. Brailsford (Derbys), for example, was in the tenure of Elfin in 1086, but it was not until c.1140 that it was granted in hereditary fee;[108] the land was presumably only held for a life or term of lives before this date, although the family may have had a presumptive right to the estate. Precarious tenure of this kind is in fact reflected in post-Conquest legal treatises. In the Leis Willelme (1090-1135) the vavassour is contrasted with the *baro* and appears to represent the lesser thegn, while in the Leges Eadwardi Confessoris (1115-1150) the knight was apparently in the frankpledge of his lord who had sake and soke, and right was done in his court instead of that of the hundred or wapentake.[109] Military service was still essentially personal and was performed by the household knight or by tenants under the terms which they could best negotiate.[110]

103 F. M. Stenton, 'Introduction to the Nottinghamshire Domesday', VCH *Notts* i, ed. W. Page, London 1906, 230; Roffe, 'Nottinghamshire', 95–7.

104 J. Campbell, 'Some Agents and Agencies of the Late Anglo-Saxon State', *Domesday Studies*, ed. J. C. Holt, Woodbridge 1987, 210–13.

105 Roffe, 'Wharram Percy'; C. W. Hollister, *The Military Organisation of Norman England*, Oxford 1965, 48; *Early Yorkshire Charters* i, ed. W. Farrer, Edinburgh 1914, 172; North Yorkshire Record Office, Outfac 125; *Charters of the Honour of Mowbray*, ed. D. E. Greenway, London 1972, xxxviii, nos 366–7, 374.

106 Roffe, 'Wharram Percy'; *Mowbray*, xxxix, xl.

107 DB i, 172c; *Westminster Abbey Charters 1066–c.1214*, ed. E. Mason, London 1988, 108–9; V. H. Galbraith, 'An Episcopal Land-Grant of 1085', *EHR* 44, (1929), 353–72; E. Miller, *The Abbey and Bishopric of Ely*, Cambridge 1951, 67–8.

108 S. P. H. Stathern, 'The Brailsfords', *Journal of the Derbyshire Archaeological and Natural History Society* 59, (1938), 67–8; *The Red Book of the Exchequer*, ed. H. Hall, London 1896, 338. For Yorkshire examples, see D. Michelmore, M. L. Faull, S. Moorhouse, *West Yorkshire: an Archaeological Survey to AD1500*, Wakefield 1981, 243.

109 *Gesetze* i, 507, 647; Stenton, *First Century*, 141. For a discussion of the emergence of hereditary fees, see S. E. Thorne, 'English Feudalism and Estates in Land', *Cambridge Law Journal*, 1959, 193–209.

110 M. Chibnall, *Anglo-Norman England*, Oxford 1986, 28–34; E. King, 'The Peterborough "Descriptio Militum" (Henry I)', *EHR* 84, (1969), 94–5.

The greatest indication of continuity, however, lay in renders due from the estate itself. Every manor had a value in 1086, and this was still a sum which went out of the estate. Thus, the value of Onibury (Salop) in 1086 was the annual rent that Roger de Lacy agreed to pay the bishop of Hereford for the estate in the previous year, and the ten shillings at which Ticknall and Stanton by Newhall (Derbys) were valued was the rent that two tenants paid to Burton Abbey in the early twelfth century.[111] Indeed, the sums are again sometimes called renders. In Worcestershire, for example, it is explicitly stated that the sheriff rendered sums from each of the king's manors, and the income that the king derived from his estates in the county (which is noted in the account of the city of Worcester) is within a few shillings of the sum total of the renders and values (the *reddit* and *valet* figures) recorded in his *breve*.[112] It is clear that, although the sums owed often changed dramatically, the tenant-in-chief levied the same farm from the manors of his honour, both demesne and tenanted, which had been collected by his predecessor in 1066.

It is evident, then, that baronies represent pre-Conquest estates in both form and composition. Some embraced two or three pre-Conquest bookland estates, and all, with but few exceptions, were subject to new lords. But in its essentials the honour was a pre-Conquest institution. One detailed example will have to suffice to illustrate the point. The honour of Peverel of Nottingham extended into the shires of Bedford, Buckingham, Northampton, Leicester, Nottingham, and Derby. Title in the southern Danelaw and Leicestershire was derived from Countess Gytha and her husband Earl Ralph of Hereford who, as Dr Ann Williams has shown, was the earl of the East Midlands.[113] The Derbyshire estates had been held by sundry *taini regis* before the Conquest, and after 1086 they were supplemented by the royal manors which William Peverel held in custody at the time of Domesday.[114] Encircling the borough of Nottingham in an all but unbroken block, the Nottinghamshire estates had descended to William from a large number of individuals and appear to constitute a castlery.[115] The complex, however, had a decidedly pre-Conquest identity. Eleven of the named tenants in 1086, representing at least eight individuals, had English or Anglo-Scandinavian names, and many of the pre-Conquest tenures survived. Wulfnoth, for example, held one bovate of land in thegnage in 1086, and others are said to 'hold from' or 'under' William.[116] The absence of specifically Norman forms is accompanied by evidence of pre-Conquest unity in the estates. Watnall and Bulwell formed an extended group of manors, and, along with eight multiple manor entries, thereby imply the presence of an overlord. No such is named, but it was apparently Gytha, for she held the comital manor of Clifton.

[111] Galbraith, 'Episcopal Land-Grant', 357; DB i, 252b; 'Burton Abbey Surveys', 240; DB i, 273b, 274b.

[112] DB i, 172a–172c. The sheriff of Worcester is said to have rendered £123 4s from the king's estates, while the total of the *reddit* and *valet* figures in the king's *breve* is £124 6s. Kinver (Staffs) appears to have rendered in Worcestershire, but Trodebrigge and Clent (Worcs) in Staffordshire.

[113] A. Williams, 'The King's Nephew: the Family and Career of Ralph, Earl of Hereford', *Studies in Medieval History Presented to R. Allen Brown*, eds C. Harper-Bill, C. J. Holdsworth, J. L. Nelson, Woodbridge 1989, 327–44.

[114] DB i, 276b, 272d–273a.

[115] DB i, 287b–288b.

[116] DB i, 287c.

This was not the *caput* of the fee, however, for the honourial court was held at Nottingham in St James' chapel in Moothallgate, the present Friar Lane, within an estate which had been held by Earl Tosti before the Conquest.[117] Gytha's relationship to him is not clear to me, but it would seem that William Peverel's ultimate predecessor was the earl. It is likely, then, that Tosti had controlled a large number of estates from his hall in Nottingham. Clifton was probably held in demesne, along with Newbound and Lenton which Tosti's successor Earl Morcar enjoyed in 1066.[118] The rest were in the tenure of his thegns; it was probably to them, *inter alios*, that a writ of 1060x1065 addressed to Earl Tosti's thegns in Yorkshire and Nottinghamshire was directed.[119] This pattern of tenure is consistent with the strategic importance of the borough of Nottingham. As early as 920 Edward the Elder recognised the need to secure the Trent crossing when he built a second borough to the south of the river in West Bridgford which was a member of the manor of Clifton in 1066.[120] The necessity to control the approaches to Nottingham was no less vital in the eleventh century; the distribution of the earl's estate no doubt reflected earlier arrangements, and it is likely that William Peverel was heir to them as constable of the castle.

It is not possible to examine the relationship between William Peverel's *servitium debitum* and the military services due from the pre-Conquest estate. In 1166 sixty and a half knights were owed, but little is known about the emergence of the honourial fees.[121] Most of the English families certainly seem to have been successful in establishing themselves. Some of their estates emerged as sergeancies, and in the others it may be supposed that there was a gradual transition from *laen* to *feudum* such as Dr Ann Williams has described in the lands of Shaftesbury Abbey.[122] Within this sort of context the question of the origin of quotas is probably largely otiose. Regardless of whether there was a five-hide or six-carucate system before the Conquest, the responsibility of the booklord for the service due from his demesne and tenanted lands must in practice have always implied that the service performed was a matter of negotiation between him and the king or the earl. After the Conquest no less a system applied, and the obligations of the tenant-in-chief's predecessors may well have been the starting point for the determination of quotas since they were directly related to the new lord's resources.

The grant of honours to Norman tenants-in-chief, then, cannot be said to constitute a radical change in land tenure. Barony was derived from bookright and in many, probably most, instances there was direct continuity of tenure and service. In this context it is meaningless to talk of a tenurial revolution between 1066 and 1086. Nevertheless, a revolution of sorts was underway. By the thirteenth century the origins of barony had been forgotten and its incidence could only be determined by appeal to record and usage. Many of the characteristics of the tenure, notably the possession of sake and soke, were exhibited by fees which were not held *per*

[117] W. Stevenson, A. Stapleton, *The Religious Foundations of Old Nottingham* i, Nottingham 1895, 50; D. Crook, ' "Moothallgate" and the Venue of the Nottinghamshire County Court in the Thirteenth Century', *Transactions of the Thoroton Society* 88, (1984), 99–102; DB i, 280a.
[118] DB i, 287c.
[119] *Writs*, no. 119.
[120] *ASC*, 67. Wilford, equally a member of the manor of Clifton, has also been suggested as a possible site (J. Haslam, 'The Second Burh of Nottingham', *Landscape History* 9, (1987), 45–51).
[121] *Red Book of the Exchequer*, 344.
[122] A. Williams, 'The Knights of Shaftesbury Abbey', *ante* viii, 1986, 214–32.

baroniam and the fact effectively precluded a definition of the form. The evident confusion is significant, for it attests to radical changes within honours which were afoot in the reign of William. By the early twelfth century the tenant-in-chief had a group of knights around him who acted as an entourage of advisors. These tenants, the honourial barons, are contrasted with the common knights, and it would appear that they held their lands in hereditary fee.[123] The chronology of enfeoffment is not clear, for documentation is lacking. But some knights, like those of Peterborough Abbey, may have had full rights to their lands from the time that they were settled on them, and the essential composition of the honourial baronage may have already been established by the time of Domesday. In the honour of Peverel, for example, most of the tenants held small fees, but ten individuals had title to a number of estates. Their successors in the twelfth and thirteenth centuries were the great mesne tenants of the honour, and it seems likely that they already occupied a pre-eminent position in the honour in 1086.[124]

The use of the term *baro* in seigneurial charters to refer to such tenants is instructive. It was no doubt coined by analogy with the tenant-in-chief's relationship with the king, but in very real terms it also described exactly the same type of tenure. It is apparently to the honourial baron that the Leges Henrici refers in describing the jurisdictional rights of vavassours. It is stated that those 'who hold free lands shall have the pleas where the punishment is payment of the *wite* or *wergeld* in respect of their own men and on their own land and in respect of the men of other lords if they are seized in the act of committing the offence and are charged with it'.[125] This is sake and soke and infangentheof, and the few charters of enfeoffment that survive illustrate that they enjoyed all the other essential rights to which the king's thegn was entitled. In addition to the grant of the rights of justice, the estate was conferred *in feudo et hereditate*, that is, it was to be held hereditarily as opposed to a life or term of lives; and the new lord, for such we can now call him, was to hold *in nemoribus et in planis, in villa et vico, et campis et pratis, in aquis et omnibus locis*, or words to that effect, that is he was endowed with all the rights which Domesday Book calls *terra*.[126] The *feudum* has all the

---

[123] Stenton, *First Century*, 96–7.

[124] *Ibid.*, 97–99.

[125] *Leges Henrici*, 27.1.

[126] Stenton, *First Century*, Appendix nos 25–7, 29, 30, 39; *The Charters of the Anglo-Norman Earls of Chester, c.1071–1237*, ed. G. Barraclough, Gloucester 1988, nos 35, 40, 43, 56, 66, 67, 69–71, 80, 89; *Early Yorkshire Charters* i, 35, 413; iv, 18; D. C. Douglas, 'A Charter of Enfeoffment under William the Conqueror', *EHR* 42, (1927), 245–7; *Mowbray*, nos 350, 355, 359, 363–4, 371, 377, 400. Not all the charters consulted exhibit every formula. Seventeen out of twenty-nine grants were made with sake and soke, and the liberties are hinted at in a further four in which land was held 'with all liberties', 'in fee', or 'with the reservation of the king's six forfeitures'; twenty-three were to be held hereditarily; and twenty were specifically conveyed with appurtenances in fields and the like. This pattern is to be contrasted with the few surviving leases for life, usually drawn up in chirographs, in which no mention is made of such terms (*Westminster Charters*, nos 236, 237, 247; *Chester Charters*, no. 15; *Mowbray*, no. 375). Grants in fee farm occupy a position between these two extremes. The early ones tend to be drawn up in the form of a chirograph and rarely mention rights of jurisdiction. By the 1140s, however, charters take over, and sake and soke and grants of *consuetudines* and appurtenances become more common (*Westminster Charters* nos 241–2, 246, 262–3, 267, 269, 271; *Chester Charters*, nos 86, 111; *Early Yorkshire Charters* i, 291, 344, 409; ii, 300; iii, 29). The diplomatic of private charters in the second half of the twelfth century is beyond the scope of this study, but it can be noted that grants with sake and soke seem to become rarer in some collections. The change may reflect the growing expectation of a hereditary right to seisin in all tenements (Chibnall, 173).

attributes of bookland. Indeed, there are even echoes of pre-Conquest diplomatic in the charters which grant land in fee, for the phrase *in nemoribus et in campis* seems to represent the English *on wudu and on felda* of Anglo-Saxon writs and charters.[127] The honourial *baro* was a king's thegn in all but name.

The context, however, was different. The grant of sake and soke was a royal prerogative, and bookland was forfeited to the king alone. Some mesne fees may have had pre-Conquest antecedents, although I have noticed no convincing examples of such continuity. But after the Conquest this direct link was threatened, for they were held by fealty and homage of the tenant-in-chief. In effect bookland estates were being created over which the king had no direct control. The development of a feudalism of a Continental type which the process implies was inimical to the rights of an English king, and William can have had little enthusiasm to encourage its growth in England. In response he probably attempted to assert the rights of the crown, for early enfeoffments in hereditary fee may well have been subject to royal sanction; Abbot Baldwin of Bury St Edmund's sought the permission of William before enfeoffing Peter his knight, and in Herefordshire even Earl William apparently did not have a free hand.[128] But the process was inexorable, and by necessity other expedients had to be adopted. It was probably in the course of the Domesday enquiry that the extent of the threat came to light, and the demand of allegiance from the honourial barony at Salisbury in 1086 can perhaps be seen as a direct consequence. It was the creation of an honourial barony which was probably the most revolutionary result of the Conquest in the context of tenure, and the challenge which its emergence introduced was to be a preoccupation of royal government throughout the next century.

The import of this paper has been continuity, but, paradoxically, not continuity without change. It is to oversimplify a complex social, economic, and political reality to argue for revolution without context, on the one hand, or continuity within stasis on the other. Inevitably the Norman Conquest saw the introduction of new ideas, but they were applied to an already vital society; it was existing forms and conventions which were shaped to the desires and needs of a conquering king and a new aristocracy. Thus, it has been argued that, as institutions, honours were directly related to pre-Conquest groups of estates in both legal form and tenurial constitution. Nevertheless, we have identified changes in the amalgamation of extended bookland estates and the dissection of comital fees. Tenurial relationships generally remained much the same after the Conquest as before, but renders were modified and services changed. Only in the creation of an honourial baronage does there seem to have been a change that would merit the epithet of revolutionary. But even here it was largely English law and customs which articulated change. Thegnage and barony were not so much as chalk and cheese as mild and mature cheddar.

---

127 See, for example, *Writs*, 91, 431n. A writ issued by Gospatric in favour of Thorfynn mac Thore in 1041x1055 refers to a grant made 'on weald, on freyð, on heyninga, ⁊ æt ællum ðyngan þeo bȳ eorðe bænand ⁊ ðoeronðer' (*Writs*, no. 121). The extant copy, however, is a thirteenth-century rework of a poorly understood original.
128 Douglas, 245–7; C. Lewis, 'The Norman Settlement of Herefordshire under William I', *ante* vii, 1985, 199, 212. In the case of Peter, however, the king may have been concerned that *his* man was becoming the man of another lord.

SECURING THE NORTH:
INVASION AND THE STRATEGY OF DEFENCE
IN TWELFTH-CENTURY ANGLO-SCOTTISH WARFARE

Matthew Strickland

The northern border of the Anglo-Norman kingdom presented the Norman and Angevin kings with one of the most significant problems of defence outside Normandy and the Vexin. Unlike Wales, whose fragmented polity of petty warring kingdoms restricted the nature of aggression largely to guerilla warfare within its own boundaries, sporadic revolt and the harrying of marcher lordships, Scotland confronted the rulers of England with a kingdom increasingly unified, and increasingly adopting Norman social, political and military institutions.[1] The Scots were consistently able to field large armies and carry war far beyond the frontier into England. Though much weaker than her southern neighbour in wealth, manpower and military technology, Scotland exploited the political and strategic embarrassments of the English kings to the full. It is far from accidental that the two principal periods of Scottish aggression in the twelfth century should correspond to the civil war of Stephen's reign and the great revolt of 1173–4 against Henry II. It was the war of 1173–4 which first revealed the full strategic potential of the 'Auld Alliance' with France, of such fundamental importance to future Anglo-Scottish affairs.[2]

Anglo-Scottish relations were not, of course, on a constant war footing. Indeed, the twelfth century saw sustained periods of peaceful and even harmonious co-existence.[3] Yet to emphasize the disparity between such lengthy periods of *de facto* peace that existed between 1093 and 1136, 1154–1173, and 1174–1209 and the comparatively brief periods of war is to run the risk of distortion by hindsight. For to contemporaries, the political *status quo* was always potentially volatile, and the Scottish kings' claim to Cumbria and Northumbria provided a constant *casus*

---

[1] For general discussions of these developments see R. L. G. Ritchie, *The Normans in Scotland* (Edinburgh, 1954); A. A. M. Duncan, *Scotland: The Making of the Kingdom* (Edinburgh, 1975); G. W. S. Barrow, *The Anglo-Norman Era in Scottish History* (Oxford, 1980); G. W. S. Barrow, *Kingship and Unity: Scotland 1000–1306* (London, 1981).

[2] William the Lion's alliance with France in 1173–4 formed part of a wider coalition centred on the Young King, to whom William had sworn homage and fealty. It was the culmination, however, of several years of shared Franco-Scottish antipathy against Henry II (Duncan, 227–9). The fullest contemporary description of the alliance and its diplomatic background is furnished by Jordan Fantosme (*Jordan Fantosme's Chronicle*, ed. and trans. R. C. Johnston (Oxford, 1981), hereafter Fantosme), ll. 242–458. Fantosme clearly regarded Louis VII as the prime mover in enlisting the support of the Scots king for the allied cause.

[3] For general surveys of Anglo-Scottish relations in this period see Ritchie, *passim*; Duncan, 216–55; W. L. Warren, *Henry II* (London, 1973), 169–87; A. O. Anderson, 'Anglo-Scottish Relations from Constantine II to William', *Scottish Historical Review* xli (1963), 1–20.

belli.[4] The threat of invasion was never too distant, the problems of defence remained ever present.

I propose to approach the subject of Anglo-Norman defence of the northern border principally through a study of the campaigns of 1138 and 1173–4, which represented the most serious incursions by a Scottish army into England during the twelfth century, and in particular to examine two closely connected themes. The first is the role of the castle in defence and its relationship to the operations of the English field army. The second is the circumstances in which pitched battle was offered, denied or joined. A major trend in recent medieval military historiography has been to stress – and rightly so – the caution and reluctance of commanders to engage in full-scale battle unless circumstances weighed heavily in their favour.[5] The majority of this work, however, has concerned either warfare between the rulers of the principalities of north-west France, where opposing forces were of a similar nature, or warfare in the Latin East, where armies might enjoy at least the potential for being evenly matched. By contrast, Anglo-Scottish warfare presents us with a theatre of war in which there was a permanent and decisive military imbalance in favour of the southern kingdom. A sophisticated and professional Anglo-Norman military elite confronted the hybrid forces of a tribal amalgam bolstered by a small core of newly planted feudal settlers, mercenaries and Franco-Norman adventurers.[6] The composition of the Scottish armies, the paucity of defensive equipment among the native infantry and in particular their lack of a powerful cavalry arm profoundly affected the strategy of the respective armies. On the one hand, Anglo-Norman commanders consistently sought to exploit this disparity, and in so doing displayed considerably less reluctance about offering battle than their counterparts in other theatres of war. On the other, the Scots sought to avoid full-scale engagements wherever possible. For them, the caution in committing troops to battle displayed by many contemporary commanders was not a choice, but a necessity. The disastrous outcome of the one major engagement where the Scots had assumed the offensive, that of the Standard in 1138, only served to highlight these dictates and emphasize the wisdom of non-engagement.

Any discussion of border defence must, of course, begin with the castle. It was one of Allen Brown's central contentions that we must view the castle as a multi-functional unit; as an administrative centre, as a base for offensive as much as defensive operations, and above all as a seigneurial residence.[7] The following observations will, I hope, only serve to reinforce these views, but given that the needs of defence were integral to the conception of the castle, it is worth using the

---

4 On the nature of these claims see Duncan, 216–55. Cf. also M. O. Anderson, 'Lothian and the Early Scottish Kings', *Scottish Historical Review* xxxix (1960), 98–112.

5 See in particular R. C. Smail, *Crusading Warfare, 1097–1193* (Cambridge, 1956), especially 138–204; J. Bradbury, 'Battles in England and Normandy, 1066–1154', *ante* vi, 1984, 1–12; J. Gillingham, 'Richard I and the Science of War in the Middle Ages', *War and Government in the Middle Ages*, ed. J. Gillingham and J. C. Holt (Woodbridge, 1984), 78–91; J. Gillingham, 'War and Chivalry in the History of William the Marshal', *Thirteenth-Century England II. Proceedings of the Newcastle upon Tyne Conference, 1987*, ed. P. R. Cross and S. D. Lloyd (1988), 1–13; J. Gillingham, 'William the Bastard at War', *Studies in Medieval History Presented to R. Allen Brown*, ed. C. Harper-Bill, C. J. Holdsworth and J. L. Nelson (Woodbridge, 1989), 141–158.

6 Below, 190–4.

7 R. A. Brown, *English Castles* (London, 3rd edn, 1976), particularly 172–213.

Anglo-Scottish evidence as a case study to examine the function of the castle in frontier defence.

Scottish attacks on England were invariably heralded by assaults on castles such as Wark, Carlisle or Norham, and the narrative sources give the firm impression that these frontier fortresses, supported by others further behind the border, formed the primary element of defence.[8] Jordan Fantosme, for example, devotes much of his poem to the heroic defence of Wark, Carlisle, Alnwick, Prudhoe and Newcastle by Henry II's castellans.[9] Looking, moreover, at a map plotting the location and density of castles in Cumbria, Northumberland and Yorkshire it is tempting to suppose the existence of a castle 'network' and to speak in terms of 'defence in depth'. Professor John Beeler, indeed, took such a notion to its extremes by suggesting that the majority of early Norman castles in England, both royal and baronial, had been sited according to some coherent strategic masterplan, designed principally by William I, in order to meet the needs of national defence.[10] It is not my intention here to discuss Beeler's thesis in detail. Professor Hollister has already provided a balanced critique, which accepts elements of a planned defence, such as the rapes of Sussex or the three great earldoms of the Welsh marches, yet rejects 'the idea of a national – an *English* – system of defensive strongholds against some foreign invader'.[11]

For the Northern march, Beeler is surely right to point to the significance of the fact, first observed by Hunter-Blair, that of the fifteen Northumbrian baronies eight had castles prior to 1189, but seven did not.[12] This suggests that castle distribution, far from being the result of indiscriminate building, might be profoundly affected by royal policy on the licensing of castles.[13] But one must not

---

[8] Hence in 1136, David had seized the fortresses of Carlisle, Wark, Alnwick, Norham and Newcastle (Richard of Hexham, *De gestis regis Stephani et de bello Standardi* (hereafter Richard of Hexham), ed. J. Raine, *The Priory of Hexham, its Chroniclers, Endowments and Annals*, 2 vols (Surtees Society, xliv, 1868) (I, 63–10), 72; John of Hexham, *Historia Johannis, prioris Haugustadensis ecclesiae* (hereafter John of Hexham), ed. J. Raine, *The Priory of Hexham, its Chroniclers, Endowments and Annals*, 2 vols (Surtees Society, xliv, 1868) (I, 107–72), 114; Huntingdon, 258). The Scots retained Carlisle throughout Stephen's reign until Henry forced its restoration by Malcolm IV. Its recapture was one of William the Lion's chief goals, and he laid siege to it in both 1173 and 1174 (Fantosme ll. 609–24, 645–68; *Gesta regis Henrici secundi Benedicti abbatis*, ed. W. Stubbs, 2 vols (RS, 1867), 65. Because of its location, Wark frequently bore the brunt of initial Scottish assaults. In January 1138, William fitzDuncan led an unsuccessful dawn attack on Wark, which was followed shortly by an investment by David's main army (Richard of Hexham, 77; John of Hexham, 115). Wark was William's first target in 1173, and he besieged it again in 1174 (Fantosme ll. 477–81). Jordan Fantosme considered attacks on Wark as so synonymous with the declaration of war that on William the Lion's decision to invade England in 1173, he notes that among the Scots, 'You could hear many shouts of: "Let us go and capture the castle of Wark in England!" – no need to go far to hear them' (Fantosme ll. 461–2).
[9] Fantosme ll. 477–688, 1143–1446, 1475–1708.
[10] J. H. Beeler, 'Castles and Strategy in Norman and Early Angevin England', *Speculum* xxxi (1956), 581–601.
[11] C. W. Hollister, *The Military Organization of Norman England* (Oxford, 1965), 161–6.
[12] Beeler, 'Castles and Strategy', 592; C. H. Hunter-Blair, 'The Early Castles of Northumberland', *Archaeologia Aeliana*, fourth series, xxii (1944), 119.
[13] On royal castle policy see R. A. Brown, 'Royal Castle Building in England, 1154–1216', *EHR* lxx (1955), 353–98; R. A. Brown, 'A List of Castles, 1154–1216', *EHR* lxxiv (1959), 249–89. On the closely related subject of rendability see C. L. H. Coulson, 'Rendability and Castellation in Medieval France', *Château Gaillard* vi (1972), 59–67; C. L. H. Coulson, 'Fortress Policy in Capetian Tradition and Angevin Practice: Aspects of the Conquest of Normandy by Philip II', *ante* vi, 1984, 13–38; C. L. H. Coulson, 'The Impact of Bouvines upon the Fortress Policy of Philip Augustus', *Studies . . . Presented to R. Allen Brown*, 71–80.

confuse such a royal policy of castle-building, licensing or appropriation of baronial castles with the existence of a co-ordinated network of castles operating in war as a defensive entity. For it is highly questionable whether the majority of northern border castles were ever conceived of as a coherent grouping, with each forming an integral link in a carefully planned chain. Not only did the border itself fluctuate significantly during this period, particularly in the north-western marches,[14] but also the castles themselves were constructed piecemeal over an extended period of time. Thus, for example, Newcastle was begun in 1080, Carlisle in 1092, but Norham as late as 1121.[15]

Whether designed as a coherent system or not, moreover, the vagaries of political allegiance would have severely disrupted any such inter-dependence. For in both 1138 and 1173–4, the collusion of baronial elements with the Scots ensured the neutrality or even the active support of the garrisons of strategically important castles. Hence in 1138, Eustace fitz John, who held the castles of Alnwick and Malton, sided with David I.[16] His defection would have also brought the great fortress of Bamburgh into the Scottish ambit had not King Stephen earlier removed it from his custody.[17] As it was, Eustace's garrison of Malton sallied out and burned several villages in the vicinity while the English forces were engaged with the Scots at the battle of the Standard.[18] In 1173–4, treachery weakened the northern defences still further. The position of the bishop of Durham, Hugh du Puiset, was at best ambivalent in 1173, and his *de facto* neutrality ensured that the episcopal castles of Norham and Durham, two of the most important defences of north-east Northumbria, offered the Scots no resistance.[19] By 1174, he was regarded as being openly in league with William the Lion.[20] His castle of

---

[14] For the changes in the border see G. W. S. Barrow, 'The Anglo-Scottish Border', *The Kingdom of the Scots. Government, Church and Society from the Eleventh to the Fourteenth Century* (London, 1973), 139–61.

[15] *Symeonis monachi opera omnia* (hereafter Simeon), ed. T. Arnold, 2 vols (RS, 1882–5), II, 211; *ASC* 'E' 1092; Simeon, II, 260.

[16] Richard of Hexham, 84, who notes how he 'had long secretly favoured the king of Scotland'; John of Hexham, 118. Eustace had been an intimate of Henry I (*Gesta Stephani*, ed. and trans. K. Potter, with an introduction by R. H. C. Davis (Oxford, 1973), 54–5, xxviii–xxix; *Relatio venerabilis Aelredi, abbatis Rievallensis, de Standardo* (hereafter *Relatio*, ed. R. Howlett, *Chronicles and Memorials of the Reigns of Stephen, Henry II and Richard* I, III (RS, 1886), 191.

[17] John of Hexham, 118. Ailred, *Relatio*, 191, says that it was in retaliation for the seizure of Bamburgh that Eustace sided with Stephen, but it seems more likely that Stephen's move had been prompted by suspicions of treason well before.

[18] Richard of Hexham, 93–4. Eustace himself fought with David at the Standard against the English (*Relatio*, 191).

[19] Ralph of Diceto noted that William the Lion invaded in 1173, '*per fines itaque episcopi Dunolmensis securum transitum habens*' (*Radulfi de Diceto decani Lundoniensis opera historica* (hereafter Diceto), ed. W. Stubbs, 2 vols (RS, 1876), I, 376). In the same campaign, Jordan Fantosme has William say: 'There is none to stand in my path – who is there to fear? The bishop of Durham – behold his messenger – writes to me that he has no stomach for war, and that I shall have nought to complain of in the way of interference from him or his forces' (Fantosme ll. 532–6). It was du Puiset, however, who was responsible for purchasing a truce with William from 13 January until the end of March, 1174 (*Gesta Henrici* I, 64). For a detailed discussion of the bishop's role in the war of 1173–4 see G. V. Scammell, *Hugh du Puiset, Bishop of Durham* (Cambridge, 1956), 35–43.

[20] Fantosme ll. 1597–8, where Jordan has the bishop of Winchester tell Henry II that ' ''he is hand in glove with King William'' '. Du Puiset had summoned 500 Flemings and forty French knights under the command of his nephew, Hugh, count of Bar, but their arrival in Northumbria coincided with William's capture at Alnwick. The bishop thus dismissed his Flemings but placed the French knights in Northallerton (*Gesta Henrici* I, 67).

Northallerton formed part of a rebel enclave in Yorkshire in conjunction with Roger de Mowbray's castles of Thirsk, Malzeard and Kinard Ferry in Axholme.[21] Equally dangerous was the possession of the castle and honour of Huntingdon by William the Lion's younger brother David, who in 1174 conducted successful forays against the royalist garrisons of the south midlands.[22] It is impossible to see how an effective castle 'system' could have operated under such conditions.

Indeed, an analysis of the campaigns of 1138 and 1173–4 strongly suggests that far from acting as a cohesive network, castles in times of war operated largely as independent, self-contained units. Hence in 1138, David I had been able to isolate first Norham then Wark, taking both castles without interference from other northern garrisons.[23] Similarly, Brough, Appleby, Liddell and Harbottle fell to William the Lion in 1174 without any recorded attempts at relief by neighbouring castellans.[24] The previous year, William had been able to advance in turn on Wark, Alnwick, Warkworth, Newcastle, Prudhoe and Carlisle without encountering any co-ordinated resistance.[25] Rather, each garrison came to individual terms with William, and where castellans were granted conditional respite, they seem to have sent for aid not to adjacent fortresses but much further south to the justiciar, Richard de Lucy.[26] It was only when William was withdrawing north in both 1173 and 1174 that some of the Northumbrian castellans swelled the ranks of the English field army in giving pursuit.[27] In short, there is little evidence for sustained tactical co-ordination or even extensive communication between the garrisons of the Cumbrian or Northumbrian castles.

Still more striking, however, is the impression that several castles in the marches were unprepared for war when it came. In 1138, the bishop of Durham earned censure for not having fortified Norham as the times required, despite its having fallen to the Scots only two years previously.[28] In 1173, the garrisons of both

---

[21] *Gesta Henrici* I, 48, 64; Diceto, I, 379, 384–5.

[22] *Gesta Henrici* I, 48; Fantosme ll. 1107–31. For the role of Earl David in the war of 1173–4 see K. J. Stringer, *Earl David of Huntingdon, 1152–1219. A Study in Anglo-Scottish History* (Edinburgh 1985), 19–29.

[23] Richard of Hexham, 82–3, 84, 94–5, 99–100; John of Hexham, 117–8.

[24] *Gesta Henrici* I, 65; Fantosme ll. 1457–1506.

[25] Fantosme ll. 477–668.

[26] Fantosme ll. 500–15, 538–43. The castellan of Wark, Roger de Stuteville, is made to say that he will either 'send missives sealed with wax' to the king or 'cross the sea' to Normandy to seek aid from Henry II in person (Fantosme ll. 501, 511–12). It is probable, however, that this is more of a literary device to highlight the personal and immediate nature of de Stuteville's loyalty to the king, and that in reality he would have dealt directly with the justiciar. Jordan subsequently implies that Roger went south but did not leave England ('*alad en Englettere*', l. 526), a view supported by the fact that he succeeded in levying a relief force and returning to Wark within forty days (Fantosme ll. 525–9). Whatever the source of de Stuteville's relieving army, it was clearly not raised from the Northumbrian garrisons. In 1174, it was to Richard de Lucy that Robert de Vaux first appealed for aid when granted respite by William the Lion (Fantosme ll. 1507–13).

[27] Fantosme ll. 759–62, 1710–15.

[28] Richard of Hexham, 83, '*quia non pro sua opportunitate et temporis necessitate castrum suum muniverat*'. It seems certain, however, that unlike his later successor Hugh du Puiset, Bishop Geoffrey was not in collusion with the Scots. For when Norham had fallen, David offered to return it to the bishop and make reparation for any damage inflicted if he would abandon Stephen and swear fealty to David. Geoffrey refused and Norham was consequently demolished. Such lack of foresight seems to have been surprisingly common. Cf. below n. 33. Similarly, the author of the *Gesta Stephani* attempted to explain Henry of Blois' lack of support for his brother following Stephen's capture at Lincoln in 1141 in terms of inadequate logistical planning. Describing the dilemma in which Blois found himself, the *Gesta* noted

Wark and Alnwick did not feel themselves strong enough to resist William the Lion without petitioning him for respite to seek reinforcements.[29] In the same year, the defences of Warkworth were felt to be so inadequate that its custodian, Roger fitzRichard, abandoned it and fell back on Newcastle.[30] In 1174, the castle of Appleby was found virtually undefended when attacked by William the Lion, that of Brough inadequately garrisoned despite the precedent of the previous year's hostilities.[31] In certain cases, such negligence might smack of treachery – the castellan of Appleby, Gospatric fitzHorm, and the few who comprised his garrison were amerced by Henry II after the war[32] – but more significantly, such evidence suggests that not all castles were deemed to be defensible in a full-scale war.[33] Warkworth doubtless had continued to act as a fortified seigneurial residence and to be employed for the administrative functions of lordship, yet in 1173 was considered indefensible against a major Scottish invasion.[34] By contrast, other

that 'it was most difficult to support the king's cause and restore it to its former flourishing condition, above all because he had not provisioned or garrisoned his castles sufficiently enough' (*Gesta Stephani*, 118–9).

[29] Fantosme ll. 500–1, 510–15; 541–4, 555–8. Jordan noted of Roger de Stuteville, the castellan of Wark, that 'he realized that the force at his command was not going to help him at all against the army of the Scots that presses hard on them' (Fantosme ll. 484–5). By contrast, once Roger succeeded in using his respite to bring back a larger force, 'he was able to tell the king of Scotland that he was free to attack him with his Flemings and that he will confidently await them' (*ibid.* ll. 527–9).

[30] Fantosme ll. 561–4, where Jordan notes 'for the castle, its wall and embankment are feeble; Roger fitzRichard, a valiant knight, had had it in ward, but he could not defend it'. That Warkworth was deemed indefensible despite having a stone curtain by 1173 further suggests that only the strongest of the border castles were adjudged capable of resisting a major attack. Given this, the construction of the stone *enceinte* would seem to have as much to do with seigneurial status and the display of wealth as purely defensive concerns. These defences, and a stone hall, may have been erected by Earl Henry after his possession of Northumberland from 1139 (Hunter-Blair, 'Early Castles', 129–31; C. H. Hunter-Blair and H. L. Honeyman, *Warkworth Castle* (Department of the Environment Official Handbook, twelfth impression, 1977), 5–6.

[31] Fantosme ll. 1457–62, 1475–1506. See also below, n.32.

[32] *PR 22 Henry II*, 119–20. It is perhaps no coincidence that the entry concerning the amercement of the garrison of Appleby is followed by the recording of a debt of thirty marks owed by one William fitzWilliam, '*ut habeat duellum versus Gospatric filius Orm*' (*PR 22 Henry II*, 121). Nevertheless, the entry for Appleby supports Jordan's insistence that the castle was surrendered merely through cowardice and inadequate manning rather than treachery (Fantosme ll. 1458–62). Gospatric was amerced 500 marks '*quia reddidit castellum regis de Appelbi regi Scottorum*', but that many others were fined for being '*ad consilium reddendi castri*' suggests that the decision to capitulate was taken by the garrison as a whole. Only one man in the entry for the county, a Udard de Brougham, was unequivocally amerced '*quia fuit cum inimicis regis*' and there is no reason to assume his connection with the garrison of Appleby. The Pipe Roll entry also clearly shows that Gospatric's 'garrison' consisted only of domestic officers or civilians; among those fined for their counsel of despair were William *dispensator*, William *clericus* of Appleby, Robert the steward of Hugh de Moreville, two cooks, a miller, a tailor, an embroiderer (*plumarius*) and a mercerer.

[33] This conclusion is supported by several other examples of the same phenomenon in other theatres of war. Hence the *Gesta Stephani* notes how in 1136 Alured, son of Judhael of Totnes, became one of the sworn allies of Baldwin de Redvers against Stephen. 'But as he had a castle that was ruinous and weak, and inadequately fortified for the protection of his followers, he left it completely empty and ungarrisoned'. The castle was probably Barnstable (*Gesta Stephani*, 36–7, 36 n. 1). In 1142, the Empress's forces had fortified Cirencester, but on his arrival there, Stephen was able to raze it to the ground 'finding the castle empty because the garrison had stolen away' (*Gesta Stephani*, 92). In 1173, Henry II was able to take Breteuil, since Robert of Leicester had fled to Louis VII, leaving his fortress '*sine custodia*' (*Gesta Henrici* I, 51).

[34] For a complementary discussion in an Irish context of certain castles appearing primarily as fortified residences rather than major fortresses, see T. E. McNeill, 'Great Towers in Irish Castles, c.1175–1225', above pp. 99–118.

major fortresses such as Newcastle, Wark and Norham had had considerable amounts of money expended on them in the years prior to 1173.[35] In this context, it may be significant that we hear nothing from the chroniclers of the smaller baronial castles of the area such as Bothal, Bolam, Wooler, Bellingham, Gunnerton or Haltwhistle. Clearly, the modest scale of their defences was not designed to resist large-scale Scottish incursions, being capable of defence only against the smallest of raiding parties.[36] By the same token, whether they were abandoned or defended in times of invasion, such fortified residences offered the Scots little strategic gain. Rather, both David and William the Lion concentrated their main efforts against a smaller number of key strongholds.

Added to such considerations was the fundamental fact that castles, no matter how densely sited or how individually strong, could not in themselves halt the incursions of an invading army. Indeed, one of the most striking features of Anglo-Scottish warfare in the late eleventh and twelfth centuries was the ease with which the Scots could repeatedly harry the northern counties and even penetrate significant distances into England. In 1070, Malcolm Canmore had laid waste the whole of Teesdale and Cleveland, and in 1079 he ravaged up to the Tyne.[37] Though in 1091 he only reached Durham before being repulsed, he had still managed to inflict considerable damage in Northumbria.[38] Malcolm's invasions came, of course, at a period when Norman control of the north, with its concomitant castle-building, was only in its first stages of consolidation, but the inability to prevent widespread harrying holds equally true of the major Anglo-Saxon defences such as Durham and Bamburgh.[39] Scottish kings, moreover, could achieve similar degrees of penetration even after the proliferation of castles north of the Humber. Hence on failing to take Wark in January 1138, David marched south and devastated as far as the Tyne without opposition.[40] He invaded again

---

[35] Thus in the financial year 1167-8, Henry II spent £120 19s 6d on Newcastle and £30 on Bamburgh. Between 1171-3 a further £439 6s 8d was expended on Newcastle. Expenditure of £425 between 1170-3, followed by a further £44 16s 6d in 1173-4, saw the construction of the great tower at Bowes. Just over £382 was spent on Wark between 1157-1161, reflecting a period of particularly strained Anglo-Scottish relations. Further behind the border, Scarborough seems to have been high on Henry's priorities, with £589 15s 8d being spent on it between 1158-1164, and a further £57 1s 3d in 1167-8. These sums are all calculated from the tables of royal expenditure on castles compiled by Brown, 'Royal Castle Building', particularly 379-80. Exact sums are unavailable for Norham, but on Henry II's orders Hugh du Puiset rebuilt the castle constructed by Rannulf Flambard and destroyed by the Scots in 1138, adding a great keep and a stone curtain in the years prior to 1173 (Simeon, I, 168; Hunter-Blair, 'Early Castles', 138-141; C. H. Hunter-Blair and H. L. Honeyman, *Norham Castle* (Department of the Environment Official Handbook, sixth impression 1978), 5-6).

[36] Hunter-Blair, 'Early Castles', 121-2, 146-8, 160-4.

[37] Simeon, II, 190-1; *ASC* 'E', 1097. In 1061, Malcolm had harried Tostig's earldom of Northumbria and had laid waste Lindisfarne (Simeon, II, 174-5).

[38] *ASC* 'E', 1091; Huntingdon, 216; Worcester, II, 28; *De miraculis et translationibus sancti Cuthberti* in Simeon, II, 338-40.

[39] Thus when Malcolm II invaded Northumbria, probably c.1006, the ageing Earl Waltheof shut himself up in Bamburgh while the Scots blockaded Durham. The Scots were defeated only when Waltheof's son, Uhtred, led a combined force of Northumbrians and the men of York against them in battle (*De obsessione Dunelmi* in Simeon, I, 215-6). In 1039, by contrast, the defenders of Durham sallied out and routed the Scottish besiegers under King Duncan (Simeon, I, 90-1).

[40] Richard of Hexham, 77-9. One section of the army crossed the Tyne and 'slew innumerable folk in the desert places, and ravaged in the same manner the most part of the land of St Cuthbert toward the west' (Richard of Hexham, 79). John of Hexham, 115-17, noted that a massacre of civilians occurred at Tanfield, south of the Tyne.

after Easter, and was able to ravage the eastern seaboard as far as Durham.[41] He invaded a third time that year in September, and was only halted at Northallerton in Yorkshire where the English army had stood its ground.[42] Prior to this engagement, his Galwegians had devastated Cumbria and penetrated as far as Clitheroe in Lancashire.[43] Similarly, in both 1173 and 1174, William the Lion was able to circumvent the major Northumbrian and Cumbrian fortresses and ravage at will until compelled to retire by the arrival of the Anglo-Norman field army.[44] Like the Germans with the Maginot line, the Scots could simply go round the main English castles if they so chose.

It is often remarked that an invading commander was loath to leave pockets of enemy resistance in his rear. Castle garrisons might sally out and either engage the enemy force or disrupt lines of communication. Thus in 1138, knights had sallied out from Wark, attacked David's supply train and engaged the retinue of Earl Henry, killing some and taking others for ransom.[45] Yet in practice – at least in this theatre of war – such forays were rare occurrences. No similar sallies by any other garrison against the Scots are recorded either in 1138 or 1173–4.[46] Robert de Vaux, the castellan of Carlisle, joined in chasing William the Lion back across the border in 1173, but this was only on the arrival of a large relief force under Richard de Lucy.[47] And yet one of the principal mechanisms of the castle was to act as a fortified base from which knights could control the countryside.[48]

Two principal reasons account for the lack of such offensive action by castle garrisons. First, a wise invading commander might detach a section of his army to invest a potentially disruptive garrison while his main army plundered and burnt. Hence in 1138, the majority of David's army laid siege to Norham while his nephew, William fitzDuncan, led the Galwegians and other units on a great harrying raid into Yorkshire and Lancashire.[49] Shortly afterwards, having failed to take Wark by storm a second time, David entrusted its blockade to two of his leading men while he led his army past Bamburgh and Mitford to the Tyne, laying waste all in his path.[50] The inability of Wark's garrison to replenish its supplies by foraging led to its eventual surrender through starvation.[51] In 1174, having

---

[41] Richard of Hexham, 81–2; John of Hexham, 117.

[42] Richard of Hexham, 84–90.

[43] John of Hexham, 117; Richard of Hexham, 82.

[44] Fantosme ll. 477–758, 1139–1507, 1634–1826; *Gesta Henrici* I, 64–7; William of Newburgh, *Historia rerum anglicarum* (hereafter Newburgh), ed. R. Howlett, *Chronicles and Memorials of the Reigns of Stephen, Henry II and Richard I* (RS, 1884) (I, 1–408, II, 409–53), 177, 181–5.

[45] Richard of Hexham, 84; John of Hexham, 117–18.

[46] I have discounted the rash foray of the '*juvenes*' of Hexham against a Scottish thegn and his band in 1138, when a group of young men rushed out and slew the leader of a foraging party which they believed intended to despoil Hexham abbey. The Scots army nearly destroyed the town in reprisal, but were prevented from so doing by William fitzDuncan, David's nephew and leader of the advance guard (John of Hexham, 115–16). This incident was clearly not an effective sally executed by knights from a fortified base.

[47] Fantosme ll. 759–62.

[48] Brown, *English Castles*, 172–3, 198–9.

[49] Richard of Hexham, 82–3; John of Hexham, 117.

[50] Richard of Hexham, 84–5.

[51] Richard of Hexham, 100; John of Hexham, 118. The need to re-victual themselves may have been one of the principal reasons for their sally against David's supply train. Certainly, David seems not to have expected such offensive action and was incensed at the attack, which prompted him to renew the siege of Wark (Richard of Hexham, 84).

spread out his main army to ravage the vicinity, William the Lion blockaded Alnwick with his *familia* 'lest perchance a group of knights should break out from it and so disturb the robbers who were pillaging all around them'.[52]

The second explanation lies in the very small size of the northern castles' garrisons. In 1138, the garrison of Norham consisted of only nine knights with an unspecified number of retainers, while that of Wark seems not to have exceeded twenty-four horsemen.[53] In 1174, ten knights and forty sergeants held Wark against sustained assault by William the Lion.[54] In a purely defensive role, such small numbers were considered perfectly adequate. Richard of Hexham records how even though some of Norham's nine knights were wounded, they incurred great ignominy for surrendering to David too easily, since they had plenty of provisions and the ditches and keep were very strong.[55] It is eloquent testimony to the supremacy of the art of defence over that of assault that strongholds such as Wark, Prudhoe or Carlisle could successfully hold off the assaults of entire Scottish armies numbering in thousands.[56] Neither David or William ever attempted to take Bamburgh.[57]

Yet no matter how effective in defence, such limited garrison numbers did not permit the formation of a mobile field force or direct engagement with enemy forces of any size outside the protection of their walls.[58] Without the ability of the

---

[52] Newburgh, 183. Earlier that year William had blockaded Carlisle with part of his army while he led the main force first on a raid through Northumbria then back to Cumbria to assault Appleby, Brough and other fortresses (*Gesta Henrici* I, 65).

[53] Richard of Hexham, 83. Both Richard and John of Hexham note that when Wark finally surrendered to David late in 1138, the starving garrison had eaten all their horses save one still alive and one in salt. As a recognition of their gallant defence, David gave them free egress with their arms and supplied them with twenty-four horses (Richard of Hexham, 100; John of Hexham, 118). This suggests that the garrison comprised this number of horsemen, but whether all were knights or whether some were mounted sergeants is unknown.

[54] *PR 20 Henry II*, 105. This figure provides a useful check on Fantosme, who gives a not unrealistic estimate of the garrison strength of Wark in 1174 as 'more than twenty knights' and 'the best sergeants that ever baron had in his service' (Fantosme ll. 1193–4). Compare this modest garrison to that of thirty knights and sixty archers with armour that defended Mowbray's rebel stronghold of Malzeard in 1174 (Gerald of Wales, *De vita Galfridi archiepiscopi Eboracensis* (hereafter *Vita Galfridi*), *Opera* IV, ed. J. S. Brewer (RS, 1873), 367).

[55] Richard of Hexham, 83.

[56] See, for example, the first siege of Wark in 1138 (Richard of Hexham, 77–8); Carlisle, 1173 (Fantosme ll. 645–68); Wark, 1174 (Fantosme ll. 1185–1269); Prudhoe, 1174 (Fantosme ll. 1643–85).

[57] In 1138, the '*juvenes*' of Bamburgh taunted the Scots as their army passed by the fortress, '*temere praesumentes de munitione valli quod extruerant ante castrum*' (John of Hexham, 118). Some of the enraged Scots stormed this outwork and slew about one hundred people (John of Hexham, 118; Richard of Hexham, 84–5). This was not an attempt to take the castle itself, which the Scots were clearly intending to bypass. Similarly, when in 1136 David succeeded in taking Alnwick, Carlisle, Wark, Newcastle and Norham, he failed to gain Bamburgh, but the circumstances suggest that this was a failure of guile or diplomacy, and that he had not actually invested this impregnable site.

[58] Henry I's campaign of 1124 furnishes a fine example of the effective operation of this process. The army that defeated Amaury de Montfort and Waleran de Meulan at Bourgthéroulde was composed of elements of the *familia regis*, which had been stationed, seemingly in units of one hundred strong, in neighbouring castles then drawn together to form a small but formidable field force of around 300 knights supported by mounted archers (Orderic VI, 348–51; *ASC* 'E' 1124; Robert of Torigni's interpolations in Jumièges, 296). See especially M. Chibnall, 'Mercenaries and the *Familia Regis* under Henry I', *History* lxii, 19–21, where the comparison is rightly stressed between the small sizes of garrisons in English castles revealed by the Pipe Roll of 1131 and those of castles in Normandy. Operations in Normandy were always on a radically different scale to those on the Scottish march. In

garrison to make effective sallies, the castle was thus unable to protect the surrounding countryside from ravaging, the most immediate and fundamental expression of enemy hostilities. With a powerful invading force operating in the vicinity, the castle could only provide a static defence, sheltering the persons, property and livestock of those fortunate enough to have gained the safety of its walls. Castles might hold up an attacking commander if he laid siege to them, or tie down elements of his army in blockade, but such decisions were largely at the discretion of the invader. Here at last, however, we find the essential defensive value of the castle. For the conquest of a disputed region could only be achieved by the occupation or the destruction of its castles. The mechanism of ravaging, though vital for the victualling of an army living off the land and for the provision of booty could not in itself effect long-term strategic gains.[59] It was only in exceptional circumstances arising from Stephen's political and military embarrassments that David's series of forays in 1138 succeeded in gaining the cession of Northumbria the following year, despite his defeat at the Standard.[60] In 1173 by contrast, Henry II's summary rejection of William the Lion's claims left the Scots king in no doubt that he could only gain Northumberland by conquest.[61] The principal objective in war therefore was not simply the despoliation of these disputed areas through ravaging but their physical occupation.

Hence for all their ability to inflict widespread economic damage, the capture of key fortresses lay at the heart of Scottish strategy. David's first act of intervention in 1136 had been the seizure, achieved less by force than by the exploitation of the uncertainties of succession and allegiance following the death of Henry I, of the chief border castles of Carlisle, Wark, Norham and Newcastle.[62] In 1138, he conducted the sieges of Norham and Wark with singular determination, and succeeded in destroying both before finally retreating north.[63] A study of Jordan

---

1216, John drew forces from at least twelve garrisons to form a force under the direction of Fawkes de Bréauté, whose task was to draw Prince Louis' forces away from the sieges of Windsor and Dover (*Rogeri de Wendover flores historiarum*, ed. H. O. Coxe, 5 vols (London, 1841–50), III, 349; *Rotuli litterarum patentium in turri Londinensi asservati*, ed. T. Duffus Hardy, Record Commission, 1835, I, 194b; R. A. Brown, *English Castles*, 199).

[59] On ravaging see M. J. Strickland, *The Conduct and Perception of War under the Anglo-Norman and Angevin Kings, 1075–1217* (unpublished Ph.D. thesis, Cambridge, 1989), 237–79.

[60] Richard of Hexham, 105. In 1139, Stephen ceded Earl Henry the county of Northumberland except the castles of Bamburgh and Newcastle.

[61] Fantosme ll. 271–420.

[62] Richard of Hexham, 71–2. As Matilda's uncle, and having been the first among the magnates to swear homage to her as Henry's successor in 1126, David was in a strong position to attempt to assert Angevin claims in the north. His intervention had been very swift; Henry I had died on December I, 1135, Stephen was crowned on December 22, and David moved into Northumbria in January (R. H. C. Davis, *King Stephen* (London, 1967), 16–18, 21). Huntingdon, 258–9, says David took the border castles by guile, but the ease and speed with which this series of great fortresses surrendered strongly suggests that their garrisons initially accepted David's overlordship on his niece's behalf. Richard of Hexham, 72, says that he took '*fidelitates quoque et obsides de potentioribus et nobilioribus ejusdem regionis, ad conservandam fidem imperatrici nepti suae*'. The arrival of Stephen's army by February forced David to return all these castles save Carlisle, which Stephen granted to Earl Henry along with the honors of Huntingdon and Doncaster, promising also to consider Henry's claim to the county of Northumberland (Richard of Hexham, 72).

[63] Richard of Hexham, 82–3, 84–5, 94–5, 99–100; John of Hexham, 117–8. David was so determined on the destruction of Wark that he specifically exempted its siege from the cessation of hostilities negotiated by the legate Alberic at the end of 1138 (Richard of Hexham, 99).

Fantosme reveals that the capture of the Cumbrian and Northumbrian castles was William the Lion's overriding concern. In 1173, he had approached Wark, Alnwick, Newcastle, Prudhoe and Carlisle, but with a singular lack of success.[64] His campaign the following year, however, brought him initial gains in Cumbria, with his army taking Liddell, Appleby, Brough and Harbottle, and reducing the garrison of Carlisle to desperate straits.[65] Much of the ravaging carried out by the Scots, indeed, must be seen as preparation for investing these border castles.[66] In 1138, for example, David laid waste the crops in the vicinity of Wark before enforcing its blockade, while in a well-known passage in Jordan Fantosme, Philip of Flanders is made to equate ravaging with the necessary prelude to siege: 'Let him not leave them, outside their castles, in wood or meadow, as much as will furnish them a meal on the morrow. Then let him assemble his men and lay siege to their castles. They will not get help or succour within thirteen leagues around them.'[67]

The need to invest castles forced the Scots to abandon a war of movement to which the majority of their troops were best suited and made their armies vulnerable to attack by a relieving army. In 1173, William the Lion narrowly avoided being caught by an English force under Richard de Lucy while besieging Carlisle.[68] His siege of Bowes in 1174 made him the target of an army led by Geoffrey Plantagenet, bishop elect of Lincoln, and later in that same campaign it was while his army lay dispersed before the walls of Alnwick that William was attacked and captured by an English relief force.[69] Such instances, I suggest, provide the key to understanding Anglo-Norman defence strategy and the function of the border fortresses. For castles were never intended to bear the brunt of enemy attack in isolation, but rather to operate in conjunction with the deployment of the Anglo-Norman field armies.

No doubt acutely aware of the inability of the frontier castles to prevent major invasion, Anglo-Norman kings or their commanders instead relied first and foremost on containing Scottish incursions by fielding the feudal host as quickly as possible. Hence Malcolm III's invasion of May 1091 was rapidly halted at Durham by the concentration of an English force just south of the city, while a punitive counter-raid may have been launched shortly afterwards by Nigel d'Aubigny.[70] Rufus himself returned from Normandy in July of that year, and by September was leading a joint land and naval force against Scotland.[71] In early 1136, David I had seized the four great border fortresses of Alnwick, Norham,

---

[64] Fantosme ll. 477–668.

[65] Fantosme ll. 1455–1507; *Gesta Henrici* I, 64–5.

[66] Hence in 1138, David laid waste the crops around Wark before enforcing its blockade. His main army then marched to the Tyne, burning the crops around Bamburgh, Mitford and other sites as they went (Richard of Hexham, 84–5). A raid on Belford and the surrounding area was a prelude to William the Lion's assault on Wark in 1174, while the previous year he had harried the Northumbrian coastal strip as part of his attack on Alnwick, Warkworth and Newcastle (Fantosme ll. 1149–87, 559–60).

[67] Fantosme ll. 445–8.

[68] Fantosme ll. 705–58.

[69] William's siege of Bowes is mentioned only by Gerald of Wales, *Vita Galfridi*, 367, a sobering reminder of the limitations and lack of comprehensiveness inherent in the major chronicle sources. For Alnwick, *Gesta Henrici* I, 65–7; Newburgh, 182–5; Fantosme ll. 1709–1816.

[70] *De miraculis et translationibus sancti Cuthberti*, in Simeon, II, 338–40; *ASC* 'E' 1091; Simeon, II, 221–2; F. Barlow, *William Rufus* (London, 1983), 288–91.

[71] *ASC* 'E' 1091; Worcester, II, 28; Barlow, *William Rufus*, 291–4.

Wark and Carlisle, but further offensive action was curtailed by Stephen's swift arrival at Durham in February.[72] David's invasion of Northumbria at Easter 1137 was speedily barred by 'the greater part of the earls and barons of England' who had assembled at Newcastle, and David was forced to accept a cessation of hostilities till November and the return of King Stephen from Normandy.[73] The campaigns of 1138 began in a very similar manner to those of 1136. David launched a lightning attack in midwinter and besieged Wark, but he had only reached Hexham before Stephen arrived in the north, again by early February.[74] Thus each of David's initial incursions had been repulsed by the deployment of large field armies within a month of the inception of Scottish hostilities. In 1173 and 1174, tactical commitments elsewhere had delayed the English host from marching north immediately, thereby allowing William the Lion considerable freedom of movement.[75] Yet in both these campaigns the eventual arrival of the English army was the decisive strategic factor, forcing the rapid withdrawal of the Scots, and in 1174 effecting the capture of William himself.

It is thus clear that individual castles or those of a vicinity were not intended to operate in a vacuum. Despite their ability to resist direct assault, even the strongest fortress could not withstand prolonged blockade, and it was therefore imperative that the enemy should not be given the opportunity to press a sustained siege. A crucial factor in John's loss of Normandy was his inability to consistently field a powerful relieving army.[76] The prolonged and heroic defence of their castellans should not disguise the fact that defences like Château Gaillard, for all their sophistication, were never intended to be held in isolation for such extensive periods. William the Lion's successful campaign against the castles of Cumbria in 1174 was only made possible by the preoccupation of the royalist forces with increasing rebel activity further south. In this context, it is significant that in both 1138 and 1174 the Scots did not attempt to garrison the castles they took, but demolished them.[77] This was presumably in order to facilitate subsequent incursions, but must also have been motivated by the recognition that they could not supply or relieve garrisons in the face of a substantial English army.

---

[72] Richard of Hexham, 72.

[73] Richard of Hexham, 76–7.

[74] Richard of Hexham, 77–81.

[75] In 1173, de Lucy's forces had been investing Leicester from 3–28 July. The town was taken but the siege of the castle was raised when he moved north against William (Diceto, I, 376; *Gesta Henrici* I, 58). The following year, the royalist forces were confronted by increasing rebel activity in England; the operations of Earl David of Huntingdon, Earl Ferrers and the garrison of Leicester against Northampton and Nottingham (Fantosme ll. 1107–1130; *Gesta Henrici* I, 68); the forays of Mowbray's garrisons of Axholme, Malzeard and Thirsk, finally curtailed by Geoffrey Plantagenet (*Gesta Henrici* I, 68–9; Diceto, I, 379; *Vita Galfridi*, 364–7); and a fresh landing of Flemings in East Anglia, who under the command of Hugh Bigod burned Norwich (*Gesta Henrici* I, 68; Diceto, I, 381).

[76] John's bold but unsuccessful attempt to relieve Château Gaillard in late August 1203, saw the disintegration of the last field force of any adequate size he was able to muster in Normandy. His lack of support and the treason endemic among the Norman baronage caused him to leave Normandy, while his attempts to assemble an army from England in May 1204 to relieve Rouen met with failure. As a result, Philip was left to reduce the fortifications of the duchy at will (K. Norgate, *John Lackland* (London, 1902), 95–102; W. L. Warren, *King John* (London, 1964 reprint), 84–88).

[77] Thus in 1138, David first had Norham destroyed, then Wark (Richard of Hexham, 83, 100). In 1173, William the Lion's Flemings wanted to demolish Prudhoe, although in the event the Scots did not lay siege to the castle until the following year (Fantosme ll. 559–604). If Jordan is to be believed, William garrisoned Appleby when it fell to him, but demolished Brough (Fantosme ll. 1469–74, 1506).

Finally, it was the field armies which proceeded to carry war into Scotland itself in 1072, 1080, 1091, 1138, 1173, 1209 and 1216.[78] And it was from the northern castles that such forays were launched. Hence Wark was the jumping off point for Stephen's raid into Lothian in 1138, while in 1174, the army that seized William the Lion at Alnwick assembled at Newcastle, launched its strike from there and returned to Newcastle the same night.[79] The offensive role of the castle in occupation and conquest has, of course, long been recognised,[80] and nowhere is this more apparent that on the Scottish march. At each stage in a gradual northerly advance, areas of effective Norman control were deliniated by the foundation of key fortresses. The building of Newcastle in 1080 saw the Tyne replace the Humber as the principal boundary of *de facto* rule, while that of Carlisle in 1092 established the Solway as the frontier of the north-western march and consolidated the annexation of Cumbria.[81] By the early twelfth century, Wark and Norham marked the Tweed as the furthest limits of the Anglo-Norman kingdom.[82] Thus rather than seeing castles as being established in some form of defensive network, their location and purpose is better understood if we regard them as being initially conceived as instruments of offence. They subsequently continued to serve this function by operating in conjunction with deployment of the feudal host.

Effective though the deployment of the Anglo-Norman field army was, however, this mechanism of defence was not without serious flaws. If the army was delayed or committed elsewhere, the Scots might make significant gains or inflict widespread damage. Nor could the feudal host stay in the north indefinitely. Logistics and the term of feudal service were crucially limiting factors.[83] There was, moreover, always the eventuality that the Scots might invade more than once in any given year. In February 1138, Stephen's army had repulsed David's initial invasion. Yet by April, David had again crossed the border, and this time no English force barred his way. He invaded a third time in September, to be met at Northallerton by the feudal host supplemented by the shire levies of Yorkshire.[84] Such frequent hostings are suggestive of the extent of military service that the Scottish kings might command, but in contrast, it is doubtful whether the Anglo-Norman feudal levy, designed to combat armies whose timescale of operations

---

[78] *ASC* 'E' 1072, 'D' 1073; Simeon, II, 195–6; Worcester, II, 9; Simeon, II, 211; *Chronicon monasterii de Abingdon*, ed. J. Stevenson, 2 vols, (RS, 1858), II, 9–10; *ASC* 'E' 1091; Worcester, II, 28; Richard of Hexham, 81; John of Hexham, 117; Fantosme ll. 800–4; *Gesta Henrici* I, 61; *Memoriale fratris Walteri de Coventria* (hereafter Walter of Coventry), ed. W. Stubbs, 2 vols (RS, 1872–3), II, 200; *Matthaei Parisiensis, monachi sancti Albani, chronica majora* (hereafter *Chronica majora*), ed. H. R. Luard, 7 vols (RS, 1872–3), II, 525; *Chronica majora* II, 641–2; Walter of Coventry, II, 229.
[79] John of Hexham, 117; Fantosme ll. 1718–22, 1817–25; Newburgh, 183, 185.
[80] See, for example, J. Le Patourel, *The Norman Empire* (Oxford, 1976), 65–7, 72, 303–18, 351–3 .
[81] Simeon, II, 211; Barrow, 'The Scottish Border', 143–7; W. E. Kapelle, *The Norman Conquest of the North. The Region and its Transformation, 1000–1135* (London 1979), 141–2.
[82] Hunter-Blair, 'Early Castles', 155–7; Simeon, I, 140.
[83] In 1091, many of Rufus's invasion army had died of cold and starvation after his supply fleet was wrecked by storms (*ASC* 'E' 1091; Worcester, II, 28), while in 1138, failure of supplies forced Stephen's withdrawal from Lothian following his punitive expedition against David (Richard of Hexham, 81). In 1137, the English army mustered at Newcastle, fixed a truce with the Scots till November of that year, and 'after forty days they retired to their own quarters' (Richard of Hexham, 76–7). The English were fortunate that the Scots honoured this truce and did not invade once the host was disbanded.
[84] Richard of Hexham, 77–88.

was similarly restricted, made allowance for such recurrent military activity.[85] Particularly for operations into Scotland itself, the standard period of service must have been augmented by the retention of knights for wages, although the proportion of stipendiaries in the English armies of 1138, 1173 and 1174 is unknown. A strong force of Flemish and Norman mercenary knights was present at the Standard under the command of Walter de Gant, while a significant element of John's army of 1216 that harried Lothian was composed of *routiers*.[86] Yet whatever the army's composition, there was little that could be done to prevent the Scots harrying across the border again once the main English force had withdrawn.

Such factors made it imperative to strike a decisive blow against the Scots as quickly as possible. Reprisal raids into the Scottish lowlands were undertaken in 1138, 1173 and 1216, but to remove the threat of subsequent raiding, commanders needed to bring the Scots to battle. Conversely, recognition of the impossibility of any prolonged stay north of the Tyne by English field armies and of the far-reaching limitations of their own troops in pitched battle caused Scottish kings to adopt a policy of non-engagement, deliberately denying combat to the English. Hence in 1138, David retreated with his army into an impenetrable swamp to await the imminent retirement of Stephen's forces. Although he avoided the ambush planned for him by David at Roxburgh, Stephen could only ravage Lothian before once more marching south because, according to Richard of Hexham, 'the king of the Scots and his men dared not give battle'.[87] In April of the same year, a mere rumour of an advancing English army caused David, whose own forces had been thrown into confusion by a Galwegian mutiny, to fly in haste back to Norham, abandoning untouched the supplies he had gathered at Durham.[88] Similarly in 1173, William the Lion was forced into a precipitous withdrawal by reports that an army under the justiciar, Richard de Lucy, was nearly upon him. He withdrew to Roxburgh and declined battle till the English were themselves forced to withdraw by news of Robert of Leicester's invasion of East Anglia.[89] In 1174, it was while beating a retreat north that William was attacked and captured at Alnwick.[90] Alexander II likewise withdrew before John's army in 1216, taking refuge beyond the Forth, prompting Matthew Paris to ascribe to King John the remark, 'so shall we hunt the red fox-cub from his lairs'.[91]

Tactical withrawal in the face of an enemy army was, of course, a commonplace of contemporary warfare, as had been recently emphasized by John Gillingham in his study of William I's generalship.[92] Yet in the case of the Scots, avoidance of battle was less a tactical option than a necessity. Perhaps more than any other army of the twelfth century, the strategy, tactics and military effectiveness of the Scottish

[85] For a comprehensive discussion of the feudal host see Hollister, *Military Organization*, 72–135.

[86] *Relatio*, 182, where Ailred also notes that William of Aumâle had knights, presumably stipendiaries, from Ponthieu and the Pas de Calais; *The Chronicle of Melrose* (hereafter *Melrose*), ed. A. O. and M. O. Anderson (London, 1936), 62. Among the other royalist forces at the battle of Fornham in 1173, Humphrey de Bohun led '300 of the king's stipendiary knights' (*Gesta Henrici* I, 61), while Geoffrey Plantagenet, the elect of Lincoln, had many stipendiary knights under his command during his campaign of 1174 against Roger de Mowbray (*Vita Galfridi*, 364).

[87] Richard of Hexham, 81; John of Hexham, 117.

[88] Richard of Hexham, 82.

[89] Fantosme ll. 713–832.

[90] *Gesta Henrici* I, 65–6; Newburgh, 182–3.

[91] *Chronica majora* II, 641–2.

[92] J. Gillingham, 'William the Bastard at War', *Studies ... Presented to R. Allen Brown*, 141–58.

army was profoundly circumscribed by the composition of its forces. In an age when few armies could be said to be truly homogeneous, those of the Scots were markedly hybrid in both racial and military terms. The armies of 1138 and 1173–4 comprised two basic components, an indigenous native levy, itself composed of a multiplicity of tribal elements, and an Anglo-Norman or 'Frankish' element consisting of the royal *familia*, Franco-Norman feudal settlers and other external mercenary units. The composite nature of the Scottish army is clearly revealed by Ailred of Rievaulx's description of their battle formation at the Standard in 1138. In the first rank were the Galwegians. In the second, under David's son Earl Henry, the Cumbrians and the men of Teviotdale along with Henry's knights and archers. The third line was composed of the men of Lothian, the men of the islands, and the men of Aberdeenshire, while the King himself formed the last unit with his *familia*, mercenary knights, the Scots – that is those dwelling north of a line between the Forth and the Tay – and the men of Moray.[93]

. The bulk of the Scottish army was composed of native infantry, but the majority of these troops were very poorly equipped.[94] Defensive armour was denied to most by its prohibitive cost. Ailred mentions hides and shields of calf skin, to which could probably be added wicker or wooden targes of some form, but to observers south of the Tweed, they were effectively 'inermes'.[95] Offensive armament consisted of a long spear supplemented by javelins and long knives.[96] The Scots shared this use of the long spear with the tribesmen of North Wales, but in the twelfth century there is no evidence that the Scots had developed the disciplined formations of pikemen known as schiltrons that were to prove so effective against cavalry in the later wars of Independence.[97] Instead, the Scots and Galwegian tribesmen relied on speed and agility, and the terrifying effect of their wild charges, very similar, one may imagine, to the onrush of the Highland clansmen in the battles of the '15 and '45.[98]

Contemporaries were clearly struck by the disparity in arms and armour between the native Scots and the Anglo-Norman knights. Both Henry of Huntingdon and Ailred dwell on this factor at length in the pre-battle orations which they create for Ralph, bishop of Orkney, and Walter Espec respectively prior to the battle of the

---

[93] *Relatio*, 190–1. No such equivalent detail of the composition of the Scots' army survives for William the Lion's campaigns of 1173–4, but in addition to the Galwegians there were contingents from Ross, Moray, Buchan and Angus, as well as the troops led by Earl Duncan II of Fife and Earl Waltheof of Dunbar (Fantosme ll. 300, 471–6; *Gesta Henrici* I, 66).

[94] For the native levy see G. W. S. Barrow, *Regesta Regum Scottorum, II. The Acts of William the Lion, King of Scots 1165–1214* (Edinburgh, 1971), 56–8.

[95] *Relatio*, 186. John of Hexham, 120, says the Scots infantry were '*nudi ipsi et paene inermes*'. Fantosme noted of the Scots' muster at Cadonlee in 1173 '*tant i out de nue gent*' (l. 475), while to Diceto, the Galwegian tribesmen were '*agilem, nudam*' and distinguished by their shaved heads (Diceto, I, 376).

[96] Diceto, I, 376; *Relatio*, 186.

[97] *Giraldi Cambrensis opera* IV, ed. J. F. Dimock (RS, 1868), 177, 181; W. M. Mackenzie, *The Battle of Bannockburn: A Study in Medieval Warfare* (Glasgow, 1913), 47–8; G. W. S. Barrow, *Robert Bruce and the Community of the Realm of Scotland* (Edinburgh, 3rd edn, 1988), 220–1, 226–9. I have avoided using the term 'pike', since it is unlikely that these spears were as yet the immense 16′ weapons of the 16th-17th centuries. The true pike, which could only be handled by well-drilled men, seems to have been introduced to Scotland just prior to the battle of Flodden (W. Seymour, *Battles in Britain*, 2 vols (London, 1975), I, 196, 205).

[98] Cf. *Relatio*, 189–90.

Standard.[99] Yet that such observations were not simply literary *topoi* or the preserve of hostile Anglo-Norman writers is indicated by the corroboration afforded by Guibert of Nogent in his *Gesta Dei per Francos*. Guibert describes the Scots on crusade as 'fierce in their own country, unwarlike elsewhere, bare-legged, with their shaggy cloaks, a scrip hanging from the haunches, coming from their marshy homeland, and presenting the help of their faith and devotion to us, to whom their numerous arms would be ridiculous'.[100]

If ecclesiastical observers were so conscious of this imbalance, then Anglo-Norman commanders must have been still more so. The formation adopted at the Standard, though drawing directly on the experience of Tinchebrai and Brémule, was particularly effective in neutralizing the superiority in Scottish numbers and in exploiting the lack of armour among the native infantry by the use of massed archery.[101] David himself was equally aware of the shortcomings of the majority of his troops, and in his initial deployment had intended to place his knights and better equipped foot in the first rank, so that, in Ailred's words, 'armed men should attack armed men, and knights engage with knights, and arrows resist arrows'.[102] The lessons afforded by his brother-in-law's victories had not been wholly lost on David either, but the Galwegians objected to this formation, claiming it was their time-honoured prerogative to lead the first attack. To avoid bloodshed between the Galwegians and his Normans, David was forced to concede this demand with disastrous results.[103]

The quarrel between these two elements of David's army highlighted a second major weakness that hampered the military effectiveness of the Scottish forces. Bitter enmity existed between the native Scots and the knightly settlers, who exercised a political and cultural influence over the Scottish kings out of all proportion to their small numbers.[104] During David's march south in April 1138,

---

[99] *Relatio*, 186, 189–90; Huntingdon, 262–3. Huntingdon, 38, had earlier pointed to the superiority of the invading Anglo-Saxons' weapons over those of the Picts and Scots: 'And since they [Picts and Scots] fought with javelins and spears, and they [the Saxons] strove very stubbornly with axes and long swords, the Picts were unable to sustain so heavy an onslaught, but consulted their safety in flight'.
At the Standard, Ralph of Orkney is made to say of the Scots:
> Her people have neither military skill nor order in fighting, nor self command. They do not cover themselves in armour in war; you are in constant practice of arms in the times of peace that you may be at no loss in the chances of the day of battle. Your head is covered by a helmet, your breast with a coat of mail, your legs with mail leggings, and your whole body with a shield. Where can the enemy strike you when he finds you are sheathed in steel? What have we to fear in attacking the naked bodies of men who know not the use of armour? (Huntingdon, 262–3).

For a discussion of these passages within the context of the genre of pre-battle orations see J. R. E. Beliese, 'Aelred of Rievaulx's Rhetoric and Morale at the Battle of the Standard, 1138', *Albion* xx (1988).

[100] Migne, *Patrologia Latina* clvi, 686. The translation is taken from A. A. Duncan, 'The Dress of the Scots', *The Scottish Historical Review*, 29, (1950) 210–12, who suggests that the scrip mentioned refers to the sporran.

[101] Cf. J. Bradbury, 'Battles in England and Normandy, 1066–1154', *ante* vi, 1–12. At the Standard, the best knights were placed in the front rank, interspersed with archers and spearmen (*Relatio*, 191; Richard of Hexham, 91). All the English chroniclers agree on the devastating effect of the bowmen against the Galwegians, who finally broke and fled. Their defeat demoralised the rest of the Scots army, who turned in flight (*Relatio*, 196–7; Huntingdon, 263–4; John of Hexham, 210; Richard of Hexham, 92).

[102] *Relatio*, 189–90.

[103] *Relatio*, 189–90.

[104] By the early thirteenth century the Barnwell annalist could write: 'The modern kings of Scotland count themselves as Frenchmen in race, manners, language and culture; they keep only Frenchmen in

the lives of the king and his *familia* had been put at grave risk by a Galwegian mutiny at Durham, while the quarrel between Alan de Percy and Malisse, earl of Strathearn, immediately prior to the Standard threatened to throw the army into confusion only hours before battle was joined with the English.[105] William the Lion's capture in 1174 was followed by a violent anti-feudal reaction particularly in Galloway, which revealed how hated Norman cultural and institutional innovation might be.[106] To exacerbate matters, there was little love lost between the native elements themselves, and old hatreds and separatist feelings were quick to surface once the king's cohesive authority was weakened. Hence in the chaotic retreat from the Standard in 1138, scattered bands of Scots, Galwegians and 'Angles' – that is the English of Cumbria and Lothian – fell upon each other despite the danger from the English pursuit.[107] Once William the Lion had been captured in 1174, Gilbert son of Fergus made strenuous efforts to assert Galwegian independence, which were prevented only by the intervention of Henry II.[108]

  The third and most critical limitation inherent in the Scottish armies was the lack of a powerful cavalry arm. In an attempt to supplement the native levy, David I and his successors had embarked on a policy of enfeoffment to create a nucleus of heavy cavalry.[109] Yet though the process of feudalisation was well advanced by the third quarter of the century, the number of knights owed per fee was very small in comparison with *servitium debitum* south of the border. Extant royal charters of enfeoffment record only three fees owing more than five knights (two of ten, one of twenty) while the normal service was one knight, or a fraction of one. The tables of extant enfeoffments compiled by Geoffrey Barrow, although not exhaustive, suggests a *servitium debitum* for the late twelfth century of just over 100 knights.[110] To place this figure in context, it need only be noted that the English force which seized William the Lion outside Alnwick, and which was a special task force not the entire strength of the English host, consisted of about 400 horsemen.[111] To augment these feudal quotas, the Scots kings employed

their household and following, and have reduced the Scots to utter servitude' (Walter of Coventry, II, 206). Cf. Fantosme, ll. 383–408, 637–44.

[105] Richard of Hexham, 82; *Relatio*, 190. The unsuccessful attempt by Earl Ferteth and five other native earls to attack Malcolm IV at Perth was attributed by the chronicler of Melrose to their anger that the king had accompanied Henry II on his expedition to Toulouse, an act felt to highlight both unwonted subservience to a foreign monarch and his absorption into an alien political and social world (*Melrose*, 36).

[106] *Gesta Henrici* I, 67–8; Newburgh, 186–7.

[107] Richard of Hexham, 94; John of Hexham, 120. Similarly, following William's capture in 1174, the Scots fell on the 'English' in the army (Newburgh, 186–7).

[108] *Gesta Henrici* I, 79–80. Henry II sent Roger of Howden and Robert de Vaux, the castellan of Carlisle, to gain the submission of Uhtred and Gilbert, joint rulers of Galloway. On their arrival, they found that Uhtred had been murdered by his brother's son, and consequently rejected Gilbert's offer of an annual tribute if Henry would free him from the overlordship of William the Lion.

[109] See G. W. S. Barrow, 'The Beginnings of Military Feudalism', and 'Scotland's Norman Families', both in *The Kingdom of the Scots*, 279–314, 315–336. The Norman settlement of Scotland is the subject of Barrow's subsequent Ford Lectures for 1977 (G. W. S. Barrow, *The Anglo-Norman Era in Scottish History* (Oxford, 1980)).

[110] Barrow, 'The Beginnings of Military Feudalism', 311–14. Barrow notes of this cavalry force: 'It was no doubt useful to deal with rebellion in the remote and ungovernable parts of the kingdom, in the far north and west. But even here, William found it easier on one occasion (1212) to ask for mercenaries from England to supress an insurrection' (Barrow, 'Beginnings of Military Feudalism', 286).

[111] Fantosme ll. 1668–70. Newburgh gives the same figure, but as he drew on Fantosme's poem, it is uncertain whether his estimate is independent (Newburgh, 183).

stipendiary knights.[112] Nevertheless, the Scottish kings could never field sufficient knights to confront the English host on anything approaching equal terms. At the Standard, for example, John of Worcester numbered the knights in the Scottish army at only 200, a figure which must have been greatly exceeded by those of the Anglo-Norman host, judging from the roll call of great lords present at the battle with their retinues.[113] Recognition of this crucial weakness underlay the respective strategies adopted by the Scottish and English armies. As we have seen, the Scots were forced to adopt a policy of non-engagement, while the English sought to exploit this disparity by the deployment of their field armies in a far more confident and aggressive manner than would have been possible in other theatres of war.

Contemporary appreciation of these factors is neatly encapsulated by Jordan Fantosme's description of how William the Lion was taken unawares by the arrival of an English army as he lay before Carlisle in 1173:

> The messenger told them [the Scots] his full story of how he had seen the proud array of knights and men in armour who will launch an attack on them before sunrise. 'The army of de Lucy, that man of wisdom and good sense, will be at grips with your men ere midnight. Look to yourselves by the Divine Majesty, lest you be shamed and dishonoured. ... Take my advice – it is the best that can be given to you – betake yourself to the safety of Roxburgh! If you tarry longer here, a mocking song will be sung of you. Thibault de Balesgué did not trounce the French as badly as you will be trounced by the hardened soldiers from the south, if you and they clash in battle.'[114]

Although William himself wanted to stay and fight, his councillors insisted on the wisdom of withdrawal, so that, as Jordan contemptuously remarks, 'not a single man of his army that had been before Carlisle but scurried in arrant cowardice, without any attack being launched or any hurt inflicted'.[115]

Such a passage, designed as it was for the ears of the Anglo-Norman nobility, conveys the arrogant self-confidence of English arms. Yet that this was no empty rhetoric was fully borne out by the outcome of the engagement at Alnwick in 1174. Despite being largely neglected by military historians, the battle of Alnwick sharply

---

112 At the Standard, David had a bodyguard of English and French knights (*Relatio*, 192). Huntingdon, 264, says that Earl Henry's line was composed of English and Norman knights from his father's *familia*.

113 John of Worcester in Worcester, II, 111–12. Among those Norman lords at the Standard were: William of Aumâle, Walter de Gant, Robert de Brus and his son Adam, Roger de Mowbray, Walter Espec, Ilbert de Lacy, William de Percy, Richard de Courcy, William Fossard, Robert de Stuteville, Bernard de Baliol '*cum multitudine equitum*' sent by King Stephen, William Peverel, Geoffrey de Halselin and Robert de Ferrers, together with the knights of Archbishop Thurstan of York (Richard of Hexham, 86–8; John of Hexham, 119; *Relatio*, 182–3). The *servitium debitum* quotas of these lords' baronies for which information is available, calculated chiefly from I. J. Sanders, *English Baronies. A Study of their Origin and Descent, 1086–1327* (Oxford, 1960), gives an (incomplete) total of over 375 knights. In times of war, it seems unlikely that the muster of the feudal host was based closely on such artificial and exact knight service quotas; particularly in times of invasion, lords must have turned up to the host with whatever forces they had at their disposal. Nevertheless, the quotas do provide a rough minimum estimate of the number of knights that may have been at the Standard, to which should be added a substantial number of stipendiary knights.

114 Fantosme ll. 718–35.

115 Fantosme ll. 755–8.

reveals the high degree of professionalism of the Anglo-Norman forces. While mustering at Newcastle, the forces led by Rannulf de Glanville received detailed intelligence of the Scottish positions. In particular they learnt that the main Scottish army, including some of William's knights, was widely dispersed and occupied in plundering, leaving the king and his small *mesnie* to blockade the castle of Alnwick.[116] Rather than attacking the outlying foraging parties or attempting to force a pitched battle with the main Scottish forces, the English lords decided on a bold tactical stroke. Abandoning the support of infantry for speed of movement, they formed an assault force of approximately 400 horse and rode for Alnwick at full speed.[117] On arrival in the vicinity, they hid in a copse where they rendezvoused with a scout who provided exact information on William's deployment.[118] Their attack caught the Scots king completely unawares, and he and his retinue, which seems not to have much exceeded sixty knights, were quickly overpowered. The English then beat a hasty retreat with their captives to the safety of Newcastle.[119] As Glanville and his commanders had no doubt calculated, the Scots army rapidly broke up in confusion when deprived of its king and fled north in disarray.[120]

There could be no finer example of the quality of contemporary generalship, utilizing speed and surprise to the full. The incautious deployment of the enemy and the Scots' numerical disadvantage in knights were carefully exploited, yet at the same time careful use of regular intelligence ensured that when the English committed themselves to battle it was with the maximum advantage possible.

---

[116] Fantosme ll. 1718–24; Newburgh, 183. The significance of Alnwick as an engagement has been largely obscured by reliance on William of Newburgh. Although he drew on elements of Jordan Fantosme's poem, his later account, written in or shortly before 1196 (A. Gransden, *Historical Writing in England, c.500–1307* (London, 1974), 263), is substantially different, being elaborated and distorted for greater dramatic and didactic effect. According to Newburgh, the English lords who assembled at Newcastle on 12 July were sharply divided concerning their subsequent course of action. Some urged caution; part of their purpose had already been achieved by the Scots' withdrawal northward on hearing of their muster, and it would be rash to expose their scanty forces – 400 horse and no infantry – to the vast barbarian army of 80,000 men, 'to be devoured like a piece of bread'. Others argued that victory would be assured by the justice of their cause, and finally bolder counsel prevailed. Next morning, therefore, they set off with all haste, all the while being covered by a dense fog which obscured their whereabouts. This caused a crisis of confidence, with some urging withdrawal, but after a spirited reply by Bernard de Baliol, they rode on. Suddenly the fog cleared, and to their joy the English beheld Alnwick castle, which they hoped would afford them refuge if pressed by the enemy. Much to their surprise, however, they also caught sight of William the Lion stationed in the fields below the castle with only a small escort, the rest of his army being dispersed in plundering. The Scots king initially mistook the advancing English for a group of his own knights returning from foraging, but on realizing his error, he rushed into the attack. Heavily outnumbered, however, he was quickly overpowered and seized along with the majority of his retinue (Newburgh, 183–5).

Newburgh thus presents the English victory as a wholly fortuitous happening, brought about not by military skill and human daring, but divine providence. In particular, Newburgh was eager to stress the miraculous correlation of William's capture with Henry II's penance at Becket's tomb (Newburgh, 188). When compared to Fantosme's poem, however, the full extent of Newburgh's embellishment is clear. The fog, so vital for the dramatic impact of Newburgh's tale, is wholly absent from Fantosme, who surely would not have failed to mention so graphic a detail had it been a reality. All references to scouts and intelligence reports are omitted, the indecision and disagreement of the army leaders is heightened; the element of finding William by surprise is wholly invented.

[117] Fantosme ll. 1725–45; Newburgh, 183–4.

[118] Fantosme ll. 1758–61.

[119] Fantosme ll. 1762–1909; Newburgh, 184–5.

[120] Newburgh, 186–7.

Conversely, William the Lion was found consistently wanting in the use of intelligence, and he paid a concomitantly heavy price for the neglect of so crucial a branch of the military art.

At Alnwick, William the Lion had not been given a choice about giving or denying battle – he had effectively been ambushed. Yet what of the Standard, the one principal exception to the otherwise consistently implemented Scottish rule of non-engagement? For the decision to join battle at Northallerton in 1138 was unequivocally David's. He had even rejected the offer of the cession of Northumbria to his son, made by the English commanders in return for his withdrawal.[121] Without a better knowledge of David's ultimate strategic goals, we shall never be certain why he joined battle when twice previously that year he had declined any engagement and retired north. Perhaps he believed that the annihilation of the main English force would enable him to effect a permanent occupation of Northumbria, or less likely, to allow him to thrust further south into England. David was an able commander, who had shown himself cautious and pragmatic on several occasions, and we must presume that he felt the odds to be weighted in his favour. He may have felt that he had the advantage of surprise. John of Worcester notes that 'hoping that he should come upon them unawares, he left many vills untouched, and did not allow his men after their wont to burn anything on that day', taking advantage of a dense mist for cover.[122] In the event Thurstan's army was anything but unprepared, and David's decision to press home the attack must have stemmed from confidence in both numbers and in his original plan of deployment.

Yet for all the valuable recent emphasis on the terrors of battle, its great risk, and the infrequency of pitched battle, the vagaries of human nature and in particular the dictates of glory, honour and reputation cannot be overlooked. Jordan Fantosme's poem provides a graphic account of the pressure placed on William the Lion to declare war in 1173 by '*le gent jeufne et salvage*', against the advice of his older, more mature councillors.[123] Duby has shown how important young knights as a collective body, the *juventus*, might be as a catalyst for war,[124] and we need look no further than the revolt of Robert Curthose or that of the Young King to see these forces in action. It would be unwise to assume that these pressures were never extended to the battlefield. Henry of Huntingdon gives the distinct impression that Earl Henry and his retinue were itching for battle. Despite seeing the disintegration of the main Scottish army, he 'paid no heed', in Huntingdon's words, 'to what he saw was being done by his side, but yearned solely after glory and valour'.[125] His charge of the English ranks was magnificent, but like that of the Lord Edward at Lewes, it did little to save the bulk of the army from defeat.[126] Similarly, in 1173 it was only with great difficulty that William the Lion's councillors dissuaded him from joining battle with de Lucy's army that was

---

[121] Richard of Hexham, 88; John of Hexham, 119; *Relatio*, 192–5.

[122] John of Worcester in Worcester, II, 111.

[123] Fantosme ll. 362–408. Cf. ll. 637–44.

[124] G. Duby, 'Youth in Aristocratic Society', *The Chivalrous Society*, trans. C. Postan (London, 1977), 112–22.

[125] Huntingdon, 264. Cf. *Relatio*, 197–8.

[126] Huntingdon, 264, says that although his charge was repulsed, Henry withdrew '*gloriose tamen re gesta*'. For Edward's charge at Lewes, see M. Prestwich, *Edward I* (London, 1988), 45–6; D. A. Carpenter, 'Simon de Montfort and the Mise of Lewes', *BIHR* lviii (1985), 4–5.

coming to the relief of Carlisle.[127] The following year, rather than attempt flight when surprised by the English at Alnwick, William snatched up his arms and was first into the fray.[128] William of Newburgh, moreover, describes how on William's seizure at Alnwick, many Scottish knights 'returned presently at full gallop and threw themselves rather than fell into the hands of their enemies, deeming it honourable to share their lord's peril'.[129]

Military or political pragmatism was thus not always the overriding factor in knights' behaviour in the field. For if Anglo-Scottish warfare in the twelfth century serves to reinforce recognition of the professionalism of the Anglo-Norman armies and their commanders, it also reveals the profound dichotomy which confronted the Scottish kings in war. David I had been born and raised as an Anglo-Norman knight and baron, while his grandson William gloried in the chivalric world of north-western France.[130] In war, both kings as individuals adhered closely to the conventions of knightly conduct in operation south of the Tweed.[131] Yet the nature and composition of the forces available to them severely restricted their military capability, compelling them to adopt an astute but inglorious policy of non-engagement. When it was an option, tactical withdrawal could be readily appreciated as shrewd generalship, when an invariable necessity it gravely compromised the Scottish kings' reputation in war. Even Jordan Fantosme, who clearly recognized and had much sympathy for William the Lion's predicament, was not above equating retreat with cowardice – 'mult grant lascheté'.[132] It is not surprising then if the sense of frustration and anger engendered by this military imbalance occasionally found expression in tactical decisions that both kings lived to regret. It was Allen Brown who stressed the crucial importance of understanding the mentalité of the Anglo-Norman warrior aristocracy, and the great importance of status, symbolism and nobility.[133] He would have been the first to recognize that in studying the actions of the knighthood, we ignore such irrational but highly important dictates as glory, shame and reputation at our peril.

To conclude, let us return to Ailred of Rievaulx and the speech he creates for his friend and patron Walter Espec immediately prior to the Standard. 'Why', he has Espec say, 'should we despair of victory, when victory has been given to our race [the Normans] as if in fee by the most High?'[134] He then goes on to list Norman conquests and victories from England to Apulia, and continues:

> Who then would not laugh, rather than fear, when to fight against such men runs the worthless Scot with half-bare buttocks? They are those, and only those, who of old thought not to oppose us, but to yield when William, conqueror of England, penetrated Lothian and Scotland as far as Abernethy,

---

[127] Fantosme ll. 713–50.

[128] Newburgh, 185.

[129] Newburgh, 185.

[130] Ritchie, *Normans in Scotland*, 125 ff.; Duncan, *Making of a Kingdom*, 197, 227–8, 255. As a youth, William was present at Henry II's siege of Toulouse (Fantosme ll. 1250–3), and took part in the tournament circuit of north-west France (*L'Histoire de Guillaume le Maréchal*, ed. P. Meyer, 3 vols (Société de l'Histoire de France, 1891–1901), ll. 1303–41).

[131] See Strickland, *Conduct and Perception*, 65–9.

[132] Fantosme ll. 755–8.

[133] See, for example, R. A. Brown, 'The Status of the Norman Knight', *War and Government*, 18–32.

[134] *Relatio*, 185; '*Cur enim de victoria desperemus, cum victoria generi nostro quasi in feudum data sit ab Altissimo?*'.

where the warlike Malcolm was made ours by his surrender: they oppose their naked hide to our lances, our swords and our arrows, using calf-skin for shields, inspired by irrational contempt of death rather than by strength.[135]

Ailred here indulges shamelessly in the Norman myth.[136] Yet in a very real sense, as the strategy adopted by the twelfth-century Anglo-Norman armies to secure the northern border showed, Norman military supremacy over the Scots was no mere literary creation, but a stark reality.

---

[135] *Relatio*, 186. The translation is taken from A. O. Anderson, *Scottish Annals from English Chroniclers, A.D. 500–1286* (London, 1908), 197.
[136] On the Norman myth see R. H. C. Davis, *The Normans and Their Myth* (London, 1970).

BENOIT OF ST MAURE
AND WILLIAM THE CONQUEROR'S *AMOR*

H. B. Teunis

In the historical literature about the government of Henry II, Benoit of St Maure is an absentee. Neither Warren nor Clanchy mentions his name.[1] Although Benoit, in his *Chronique des ducs de Normandie*,[2] consecrates 8,000 lines to the government of William the Conqueror, historians have not paid attention to the manner in which Benoit describes William the Conqueror's reign. Perhaps Benoit is regarded as unreliable. But he did have certain views of that reign. And why should we not study this view and try to give it a place in the history of its time?

Which view are we talking about? To start with Benoit of St Maure cannot be called a theorist. He did not try to formulate a doctrine about kingship as for example John of Salisbury did. He did not try either to present as advice to the king a specific view of kingship in the form of a chronicle as, for example, Suger of St Denis did.[3] Benoit was not a royal councillor. But he definitely had an idea about how relations in the realm ought to be ordered, what should be the role of the ruler, what should be the role of the aristocracy and also what the aristocracy should not do.

One can say that these ideas are presented very precisely by Benoit by a few well-chosen words in crucial places before he starts the colourful description of events. The first years of the government of Duke William were, as is well known, characterized by rebellions. Benoit begins the part of his chronicle that treats the government of Duke William by saying that the duke would in the end crush all the rebels. He also emphasizes that Duke William continued the policy of his father:

> Tex oct le pere moct amez
> hauciez, creüz e alevez
> qui puis firent, son lor poeir
> au fiz honte e damage aveir.
> Se li peres les oct cheriz,
> moct s' en aperçut poi le fiz.
> Moct les trova vers sei cruaus
> desleiez e parjurs e faus.[4]

Duke Richard, William's father, had loved the barons. He had enlarged their power and repute. But the barons did not respond positively to this attitude, which the son

---

[1] W. L. Warren, *Henry II*, London 1973; M. T. Clanchy, *England and its rulers*, London 1983.
[2] C. Fahlin ed., *Chronique des ducs de Normandie par Benoit*, Uppsala 1951.
[3] Frits Hugenholtz and Henk Teunis, 'Suger's advice', *Journal of Medieval History* 12, 1986, 191–206.
[4] Benoit, 34047–54.

also possessed. They proved themselves to be 'desleiez, parjurs e faus'. Therefore there can be 'pais ne concorde ne amor' between them: no *amor*, no good understanding, no peace. The rebels are, for that reason, continually named *felon, deslei*. The duke loved William of Arques, he honoured him and made him a great person, but William of Arques could not love the duke and therefore he was 'deslei, enorgoilliz, enfelonniz'.[5] This also holds true for Count Guy of Brionne. William loved him very much, but Guy became disloyal.[6] William did not have a bond of this kind with the French king. In the relationship with the French king, mutual service is mentioned, but there is no bond of love. When there is a war between them, no bond of love is being broken.[7] There is such a bond between the duke and archbishop Mauger, who is deposed,[8] and between the duke and a group of barons who are rebelling c.1060. Then there is

> paiz n'amor ne bienvoillance
> n'acordement ne bienestance[9]

There was also a bond of love according to Benoit between Emma and Edward, and between Harthacnut and Edward.[10] This is a clear indication that in a bond of love, affection is a component part. So William the Conqueror loves Edward's wife, the sister of Harold and he loves his own wife Mathilda very much.[11] They do not only respect one another, each also has really good intentions towards the other. A bond of this kind joined Edward to William. Benoit speaks of *amor, cherement*. Therefore Edward helped William and since Edward did not have a son, William became his successor.[12] It was to him that he preferred to entrust the realm. William forged a bond of love with Harold too.

> od amor e od buenne fei
> li fist teu joie e tel honnor.[13]

But Harold does not keep it, and that is wrong. William does the same thing with Tostig, with William fitz Osbern and with the English barons whom he includes in his following.

> e ja seit ce que grant amor
> lor mostre e fait grant honnor.[14]

That William rewarded his knights after the conquest of England had as a consequence that they loved no man on earth more than him. They showed their gladness and love, and served him readily.[15] When the English appeared to be

---

5 Benoit, 34677–81.
6 Benoit, 34945–56.
7 Benoit, 35381.
8 Benoit, 37313.
9 Benoit, 38257–8.
10 Benoit, 36365 and 36371–3.
11 Benoit, 37375 and 41069.
12 Benoit, 36437–46.
13 Benoit, 38814–15.
14 Benoit, 39056–8, 40211, 40251–2.
15 Benoit, 40264.

rebellious after the Conquest, it was evident that they did not want to preserve the peace, neither for fear nor out of *amor*.[16] This also holds true for the rebellious Eustace of Bologne.[17] William's famous speech before he died is very clear on this point too. It begins in this way:

> moct vos ai, fait il, toz amez
> e chers tenuz e si gardez
> e desfenduz que torz ne laiz
> n'os e esté ne diz ne faiz.[18]

And to his son he says:

> par ceus ou j'ai eü amor
> ou plus connosseie valor
> par ceus ai esté honnorez.[19]

Only after these lines do passages follow about the service of God and the maintenance of justice.

William kept the realm together by creating a bond of love with the most important persons of his *regnum*. Whoever rejected this bond was suppressed strenuously. When the rebels were eliminated, peace governed the country. The story of Benoit is, in fact, the history of this fight. The bond of love which ought to exist according to Benoit, has several elements. It is based on mutual respect. The duke honours the barons and gives them material benefit. The barons recognize him as their lord and serve him. The bond of love has an affective element too. It is used to describe the bond with marriage partners and members of the same family as well as the bond between the duke and his barons. There is benevolence, cordiality for one another; it is well meant. Therefore the rejection of this bond is an evil, and worth being combated. The hierarchy which this bond implies – after all the duke has to be served – evidently does not hamper the reciprocity, nor the affection.

The *amor*, therefore, is a rather complicated notion. In Benoit's chronicle it is the central idea. His story, full of fighting, is the story of the crusade against the violators of the *amor*. This view of the facts is Benoit's own idea. This becomes evident when we compare the chronicle of Benoit with the sources from which Benoit takes his material. In her edition Fahlin regrettably does not mention the sources which Benoit has used, as Holden did in his edition of the *Roman de Rou* of Wace. But it is possible to compare the crucial places where Benoit uses the notion of *amor* with the relevant passages in his sources.

As has already been noticed by Andresen – who is not very useful here – Benoit's most important source is the *Gesta Normannorum Ducum* of William of Jumièges.[20] Benoît used a manuscript with the interpolations of Robert of Torigni and by implication also with those of Orderic Vitalis.[21] This is not his only source

[16] Benoit, 40434.
[17] Benoit, 40451.
[18] Benoit, 41595-8.
[19] Benoit, 41659-61.
[20] H. Andresen, 'Ueber die von Benoît in seiner normannischen Chronik benutzten Quellen, insbesondere über sein Verhältnis zu Dudo, Wilhelm von Jumièges und Wace', *Zeitschrift für Romanische Philologie* 11, 1887, 500.
[21] E. M. C. van Houts, *Gesta Normannorum Ducum*, Groningen 1982, 270-2, 274-5, 279.

however. His story about the first period of William's reign is for a large part founded on the *Roman de Rou* of Wace.[22] For the end of the reign Benoit takes a great deal of material from the *Historia Ecclesiastica* of Orderic Vitalis,[23] and his use of the *Vita Guillelmi* of William of Poitiers is often obvious.[24] It would be possible to identify the sources of Benoit for each episode as Holden did in his edition of the *Roman de Rou*. The passages in which Benoit used the word *amor* and its derivatives can be located in his sources,

In the chronicle of William of Poitiers, the word and the notion of *amor* or *caritas* is not a central idea. Here Duke William is the victor. He subdued the rebellious Norman barons, King Henry I, Count Geoffrey Martel and Harold. According to William of Poitiers, what was the secret of his success? Here William is very clear:

> Ad hoc ipse ut esset decori amicis vel adjumento, tantum satagebat quantum esse valebat; et procurabat semper ut sibi quamplurimum amici deberent. Tunc florescebat in adolescentia principans uni provinciae; nunc regnis dominatur annos natus circiter quadraginta quinque.[25]

The secret of his success was that he always operated in such a way that those who were loyal to him owed more to him than he did to them. In this way he was able to surround himself with friends and to obtain victories thanks to them. With regard to England he acted in the same way. Edward decided to make William his heir remembering the benefits which bound him more to him than bonds of kinship.[26] In order to make Harold a loyal mediator, he showered presents upon him during his visit to Normandy. Here already William of Poitiers indicates what the great misdeed of Harold in the future would be: 'Qua mente post haec Guillelmo haereditatem auferre, bellum inferre, auses es ...?'[27] The oath was a corroboration of the relation William, as usual, created. Harold had let himself be treated honourably, had accepted many presents and by this had entered upon the obligation to serve William. He did not keep this obligation, and that, according to William of Poitiers, was his misdeed and the reason for his downfall.

In like manner, according to William of Poitiers, Duke William held intercourse with his followers. After the landing, he encouraged them by saying that Harold did not have the right to dispense his wealth to his followers since it was his, William's, wealth and he promised to distribute it to them. 'Nos quae dono accepimus beneficiis comparavimus, requirimus.'[28] Here the circle is completed: by protecting Edward as an exile and by helping him, William obtained the crown of England; by his promise to distribute the possessions won, he acquired the fidelity of his followers and, in fact, the opportunity to win the crown. According to William of Poitiers, Duke William acted according to the *do-ut-des* principle. Towards Harold, William repeats this once again by way of a messenger: William is the heir 'ob maximos honores et plurima beneficia que illi atque fratri suo, necnon hominibus eorum, ego et majores mei impendimus (to Edward)'.[29] Before

---

[22] A. J. Holden ed., *Le Roman de Rou de Wace* iii, Paris 1973.
[23] M. Chibnall ed., *The Ecclesiastical History of Orderic Vitalis* ii, Oxford 1969; iv, Oxford 1973.
[24] R. Foreville ed., *Guillaume de Poitiers, Histoire de Guillaume le Conquérant*, Paris 1952.
[25] *Gesta Guillelmi*, 26.
[26] *Gesta Guillelmi*, 30.
[27] *Gesta Guillelmi*, 114.
[28] *Gesta Guillelmi*, 158.
[29] *Gesta Guillelmi*, 174.

the battle begins he says the same thing to his followers: 'Si more virorum pugnent, victoriam, decus, divitias habituros.'[30] Before the coronation the commanders of the Normans assemble. They decide to recognize William as king because he is suitable for that office, and because they may expect still more advantages and honour from his raising to kingship.[31] This last sentence is said by William of Poitiers without any disapproval; it is the legitimate foundation of their support. They may indeed expect advantage and honour in exchange for support. That is the rule which governs their relations.

This is quite a different rule from Benoit's maxim of *amor*. The hierarchy is different: the duke in a sense acquires his position by giving; in Benoit's chronicle the duke's leadership is taken for granted. For William of Poitiers, the point is the bond of loyalty, and here the affective element is not brought to the fore. The point is not benevolence to one another, but the creation of a group of loyal people, who, induced to promise fidelity, have to keep their word. The reciprocity is inherent in the *do-ut-des* concept. There is resemblance between *amor* and *do-ut-des* only in this respect. When we compare Benoit's passages using the notion of *amor* and the same material in the text of William of Poitiers, we do not find a word or notion *amor* in the *Gesta Guilelmi*.[32]

The image of William the Conqueror in the *Gesta Normannorum Ducum* is what the Germans call a *Herrschergestalt*. Everybody is bound to *fidelitas*. Those who rebel in the beginning of the reign are characterized as 'ab eis fidelitate aberrantes'.[33] Trusty followers can be overloaded with honour, but the marks of honour are not the reason for their fidelity. Disloyalty is inexplicable. Toustain is 'zelo succensus infidelitatis'.[34] Mauger had received benefits so that he should stay loyal, not to become loyal.[35] Guy of Brionne had received the castle of Brionne in order to strengthen the bond of fidelity; when he became disloyal he was compared with Absalom.[36] The campaigns against Geoffrey Martel and Henry I were conducted for other reasons than those against the 'optimates qui a duce deviarent fidelitate'.[37] This obligation to be loyal to the ruler is the foundation of the relationship between ruler and subjects. Edward sent Harold to William 'ut ei de sua corona fidelitatem faceret',[38] an oath of fidelity without doubt. After that

---

[30] *Gesta Guillelmi*, 182.
[31] *Gesta Guillelmi*, 218.
[32] Benoit, 40146 – *Gesta Guillelmi*, 230 (the kingdom of Engeland).
Benoit, 40160 – *Gesta Guillelmi*, 237 (Copsi).
Benoit, 40211 – *Gesta Guillelmi*, 240 (William fitz Osbern; diligere: a personal affair).
Benoit, 40351 – *Gesta Guillelmi*, (important English barons).
Benoit, 40264 – *Gesta Guillelmi*, 244 (William's chevaliers, milites).
Benoit, 40288 – *Gesta Guillelmi*, 246 (Normandy).
Benoit, 40434 – *Gesta Guillelmi*, 264 (English people).
Benoit, 40451 – *Gesta Guillelmi*, 264 (Eustace of Bologne).
Benoit, 40797 – *Gesta Guillelmi*, 244 (Edwin, Morcar and Waltheof).
William loves his *patria*, not the barons – *Gesta Guillelmi*, 258.
[33] Jumièges, 115.
[34] Jumièges, 118.
[35] Jumièges, 119.
[36] Jumièges, 122.
[37] Jumièges, 124.
[38] Jumièges, 132.

he obtained rewards, but it became evident that Harold disrupted the bond of fidelity and so he became a perjurer.[39] Those, too, who rebelled in England after the Conquest, sinned against the basic rule of faithfulness: Eustace of Boulogne 'commits perfidy',[40] and there is a conspiracy that betrays loyalty.[41]

In this concept there is very little reciprocity. The hierarchical element is very strong. The foundation of the government of William the Conqueror, according to William of Jumièges, is most surely not *amor*. Where the chronicle of Benoit is an amplification of a story in William of Jumièges, a notion like *amor* does not show up. William of Arques, William of Jumièges says, had received benefits.[42] Benoît translates:

> cist le deüssent aveir cher
> e s'onnor creistre e essaucier,
> mais unc neu sorent jor amer.[43]

Duke William had loved William of Arques and enhanced his honour, but William of Arques could not love the duke. William of Brionne had received rewards in order to strengthen the obligation to fidelity.[44] Benoit says:

> fu norriz cherement
> moct par l'ama, moct le tint cher,[45]

but he is 'orgoilli', 'enfelonni'. To withdraw from the obligation to service, according to Benoit, is not to love him any more.

Benoit did not find his conception of love in William of Jumièges, his main source, nor in William of Poitiers. The notions of *fides* and *amor* do, however, appear in the interpolations of Orderic Vitalis.[46] But I will not try to draw a specific concept out of these interpolations. To do this other works of Orderic Vitalis would have to be brought into the discussion and something has already been said about it.[47] Comparison of the texts of Benoit and Orderic shows that Benoit did not find his idea that there ought to be *amor* between ruler and barons directly in Orderic Vitalis.

He may, however, have found it in Wace. For his story about the beginning of the reign, Benoit takes a lot from Wace. And Wace says:

> cels qui sis pere teneit chiers
> truva mult orgueillus e fiers.[48]

This is the same conception as the one we can see in the chronicle of Benoit. About William of Brionne Wace says: 'William le tint mult chier'.[49] A bond of love

[39] Jumièges, 133.
[40] Jumièges, 138.
[41] Jumièges, 139.
[42] Jumièges, 119.
[43] Benoit, 34679–81.
[44] Jumièges, 122.
[45] Benoit, 34943, 34945, 34955, 34956.
[46] Jumièges, 156, 158, 159 (Perfidus, fidelis, fides); 159, 161 (amor).
[47] M. Chibnall, 'Feudal society in Orderic Vitalis', *ante* i, 1978, 35–48; M. Chibnall, *The World of Orderic Vitalis*, Oxford 1984, 121–8.
[48] Wace, 3245–6.
[49] Wace, 3605.

exists too between William of Arques and Mauger,[50] and between earl Godwin and the Danish people.[51] It is absent, on the other hand, in the relation between the French king and William.[52] According to Wace a bond of love exists also between Edward and William.[53] But, according to Wace, this is not the reason why Edward makes William his heir. The reason for this is that Edward thinks William is the best.[54] William does not forge a bond of love with Harold.[55] Harold does swear an oath, however, and therefore his taking the crown is an injustice.[56] At the beginning of the expedition to England, William asks everybody to love him, including the French king. In chorus everyone shouts to him:

> Ja n'en verreiz un coarder
> nus nen a de morir poor,
> se mestier est (if necessary),
> por vostre amor.[57]

In the *Roman de Rou* the conception of love plays an important role. Barons have it with one another, an earl and a foreign people also have, like William and his barons, a bond of love. The difference between the chronicle of Benoit and the *Roman de Rou* is that for Benoit this bond of love is an exclusive affair between William and his barons and family. At crucial moments the chronicle of Benoit speaks about this bond of love: at the beginning of the reign, at the beginning of the story about the great rebellions of William of Arques and William of Brionne, and to explain the fact that Edward indicates William as his heir, to condemn the attitude of Harold, to characterize the new relationship with the English and to typify the agitation after the Conquest. The theme is resumed in the great speech of William before he died.

According to Benoit, the bond that links William and the barons together is a bond of love. It is their exclusive possession and William is the fountain of love. That is the characteristic of his government. When the barons respect this rule, peace is the consequence; war, when they do not respect it. This view of the government of William the Conqueror is the creation of Benoit.

The notion of *amor* was known to his predecessor, Wace, but it was without doubt also known to his public, or, more precisely, to his intended public. This was not, in the first place, Henry II, as has often been supposed. Although Benoit hoped that his work would please Henry II, a direct link between him and Benoît cannot be proved. A hint from Henry II was not the origin of the conception of Benoît's work.[58] Benoit was acquainted with court life and his intended public is to be

---

[50] Wace, 3402.
[51] Wace, 4676–7.
[52] Wace, 5125–6.
[53] Wace, 4749–52, 5400.
[54] Wace, 5553.
[55] Wace, 5665–724.
[56] Wace, 5900–8.
[57] Wace, 7452–4.
[58] R. H. Bautier, ' "Empire Plantagenêt" ou "espace Plantagenêt". Y eut-il une civilisation du monde Plantagenêt?', *Cahiers de Civilisation médiévale* 29, 1986, 144.

sought in the aristocracy that moved in court.[59] It is clear that we cannot see courtly love in the strict sense of the word in Benoit's conception of love.[60] Benoit was a cleric. Did he use monastic and theological notions of love to shape his vision? Was the love of all, which was the starting-point for William's government, a transplant into the secular realm of the monastic conception of *caritas*, love of all,[61] or of the theological conception of *caritas*, the inborn disposition to love oneself and one's neighbour in the name of the love of God?[62] It would be an interesting investigation to compare the monastic and theological conceptions of love with the secular notions. I think the resemblances would be considerable. But this is *not* to say that the monastic and theological conceptions were Benoit's and Wace's direct source of inspiration. The aristocracy itself was acquainted with the notions of *amor* and *caritas* in the practice of their daily living.

These notions cannot be reduced to clerical conceptions, but they find their origins in the structure of the social intercourse of the aristocracy. In the countless disputes that arose the most preferable way of finding a solution was one that enabled both parties to become friends again.[63] In the *Leges Henrici Primi* this is called 'to proceed by love' (amor). To come to an agreement is the best method of settling disputes. This idea was well known in Western France too, as has lately been brilliantly shown by Stephen White.[64] In the charters made up in the region from which Benoit came, we come across the word *caritas* regularly.[65] Clerical writers used the word *caritas* contrasting it with *iustitia*, instead of the latin word *amor*, which had the connotation, in their language, of love for a specific person or object.[66] What does the word *caritas* mean in the charters made up in the monasteries? I take two examples from the cartulary of St Serge, near Angers.

In the first charter we are told 'that a certain Rainaldus, nicknamed Jeruzalem, after receiving the benefits of the place of the saints Sergius and Bacchus from the monks who lived there, had given a piece of land he had bought himself, sited at Juinniacum, on the condition that if he should not have an heir by his legal wife or if legal heirs that is to say a son or a daughter should be lacking entirely, then the land would be theirs. When in fact the heirs did indeed fail – that is to say there was only one daughter of his and another who was born to her, and was buried by the monks in their cemetery – and when the monks were about to take over the land as their own, Hugo the son of Wismandus and Willelmus de Loarciacum from whom it was held, claimed the land as though Rainaldus had not given it to the monks at all. When the abbot Achardus had started a legal process, it was decided that this gift had to be proved in court. When, however, the time of the plea was near, Hugo and Willelmus, after consultation with their friends, transferred the

[59] W. F. Schirmer, H. Broick, *Studien zum literarischen Patronat im England des 12. Jahrhunderts*, Köln-Opladen 1961, 77–80; D. B. Tyson, 'Patronage of French vernacular history writers in the twelfth and thirteenth centuries', *Romania* 100, 1979, 197–8.

[60] G. Duby, 'A propos de l'amour que l'on dit courtois', *Mâle Moyen Age*, Paris 1988, 74–82.

[61] R. M. Karron, 'Friendship and love in the lives of two twelfth-century English saints', *Journal of Medieval History* 14, 1988, 305.

[62] A. M. Landgraf, *Dogmengeschichte der Frühscholastik* i, 1, Regensburg 1952, 165 and passim.

[63] M. Clanchy, 'Law and love in the Middle Ages', J. Bossy ed., *Disputes and Settlements. Law and human relations in the West*, Cambridge 1983, 47.

[64] S. D. White, *Custom, kinship and gifts to saints. The laudatio parentum in Western France 1050–1150*, Chapell Hill and London 1988, passim.

[65] White, 256 n. 43.

[66] E. James, ' "Beati pacifici": bishops and the law in sixth-century Gaul', Bossy, 44; see note 70.

land to them and agreed that this land in its totality without further difficulties would be theirs except for 3 solidi census. To confirm this agreement Abbot Achardus gave 20 solidi to Willelmus 'in caritate', and to Hugo two arpents of land to build upon on this condition, that he would be his man, and that, if he would die without a legal heir, and if an heir by his legal wife, that is a son or a daughter, should be lacking – excluding the children of other kin – then the land with the buildings on it would belong to saint Sergius'.[67]

Here we have one of the many *convenientiae* which are contained by the cartularies.[68] As is said further on, this document is the written record of a 'convenientia'. Rainaldus and his wife did not have children together, nor other legal heirs, so the gift could be effected. Then the lord claimed the land. This was often the case. A plea was not held. An agreement was reached without any formal procedure. Love prevailed over law, the *Leges Henrici Primi* would say. When this agreement had been reached, Hugo and Willelmus received so-called countergifts. This happened in order to confirm the agreement. It is a part of the agreement in its totality, but the basis of the agreement, the *convenientia*, is mutual consensus about the principal question to whom the land belonged. When this consensus had been reached – the land belonged to the abbey – the abbot gave Hugo and Willelmus countergifts *in caritate*, in love. The bond of love existed from that moment and was founded upon consensus. On this basis, the agreement could be worked out more fully.

Not only abbots tried to bring about a bond of *caritas* and to strengthen it. Another charter says that a certain Radulfus de Barleia, very ill, had been received in the monastery and had become a monk. With the approval of his brother and his lord he had given all his sources of income to the monastery. 'This being done, he died shortly afterwards, was carried to our church and buried there solemnly, and his name was written in the martyrology between the names of the brothers. According to custom, he was succeeded by his brother Rainaldus, who very quickly forgot all this, that is to say the gift and his brother's concession, so that he preferred to attack the gift of his brother rather than to defend it. But the monks confronted him with the confirmation of the witnesses who were present, and

---

[67] Y. Chauvin, Cartulaire de l'abbaye Saint-Serge et Saint-Bach d'Angers ii, Caen 1969, 233–4, no. 206 (1083–1094).

> quod Rainaldus cognomento Jeruzalem accepto sibi beneficio loci sanctorum Sergii et Bachi dedit monachis ibidem Deo famulantibus quandam terram quam sibi emerat prope Juinniacum sitam tali ratione ut si heredem ex legitimo conubio non haberet, aut quandocumque legitimi heredes id est filius vel filia ex eo deficerent, eadem terra eorum esset propria. Cujus heredes cum omnino defecissent id est una filia ipsius propria et alia ex eadem nata que a predictis monachis in cymeterio eorum est sepulta, ac ipsi eandem terram velut propriam accipere voluissent, calumpniati sunt eam Hugo filius Wismandi et Willelmus de Loarciaco de quorum feuo erat ac si eam Rainaldus illis minime dimisisset. Cum quibus domnus abba Achardus inito placito judicatum est ut per quoddam juditium illud donum probaretur. Cum autem perventum esset ad terminum judicii accepto cum amicis consilio Hugo et Willelmus illud dimiserunt atque eandem terram penitus solidam et quietam exceptis tribus solidis de censu concesserunt. Haec autem ut robustior haberetur dedit domnus abbas Achardus Willelmo XX solidos in caritate, Hugoni vero duos arpennos terrae ad edifia facienda tali ratione ut homo ejus fieret, et si sine legitimo herede moreretur vel si aliquando heredes ejus ex legitimo conubio procreati filius scilicet vel filia deficerent excepta prorsus alia progenie nepotum aut aliorum parentum sicut aedificati fuerint Sancto Sergio remanerent.

[68] H. B. Teunis, *Anjou 1050–1125. Heersers en heiligen in de Middeleeuwen*, Amsterdam 1986, 55–70.

proposed to defend according to the law what they received according to the law. When he heard this, and saw that the assertion of the monks was true, and learned about the confirmation of the witnessess he requested from the abbot through a monk that he should give him 'pro federe caritatis' some skins of foxes and then he would agree with all things faithfully and defend them for ever. The monks, who preferred the man to be peaceful rather than angry, peacefully gave him what he demanded and so he came to the chapter with his brother Rotbertus and one of his knights, and transferred all the things his brother had given, without any deceit, to the holy martyrs Sergius and Bacchus and to the abbot Bernardus and the other brothers, and after putting the deed of donation of these things in the abbot's hand, he put it personally on the altar.'[69]

Radulfus de Barleia's brother, Rainaldus, who succeeded him, did not recognize the gift of his brother. The monks threatened him with a legal process, but Rainaldus did not let it take place. For the bond of love he requested some skins of foxes, and only after would he agree with everything and defend the gifts. The monks did not approve of this. They wanted him really to consent and not to buy his agreement. This is an attitude that can be observed repeatedly in the cartularies. In order to achieve an agreement, however, the monks gave way to Rainaldus' demand. It would have been better, they thought, to give something afterwards. After all, it is the consensus that creates the real bond of *caritas*.

The starting point for the agreement is the consensus and the assurance that what binds, the *caritas*, prevails over that which almost caused separation. It is a bond which, as appears from the charters, implies recognition of the position of each party: the gift of the piece of land in the first example was recognized, but the monks honoured the donors with gifts too. It also implies a benevolent attitude towards each other, a declaration of the intention of further co-operation and often a cordial relationship. This does not obstruct the pursuit of one's own interests; on the contrary, the creation of a good relationship prevented a conviction, a defeat, and also prevented more harm being done to one another.

This is not to say that in most cases an agreement based on consensus and *caritas* was brought about. But the realization that it was preferable to maintain a good relationship, as that among friends, was alive in the aristocracy. It was the antidote against unworkable distrust. The high value of this mixture of respect, benevolence

---

[69] Cartulaire Saint-Serge I, 282–4, no. 243 (1094–1103).

his peractis, post paululum defunctus est, et ad ecclesiam nostram delatus, ibique est honorifice sepultus et in martyrologio inter fratrum nomina fideliter est asscriptus. Huic seccessit sicut mos est, frater ejus prefatus Rainaldus, qui tam citissime horum omnium oblitus, fratris scilicet donationis et proprie concessionis, ut potius fratris elemosinam infestaret quam defenderet. Dicebat enim se numquam ita sicut monachi acclamabant concessisse; monachi vero eum per presentium testium aggredientes assertionem, rem tam legaliter adquisitam legaliter defendere volebant; ille vero hoc conspiciens et veram esse monachorum acclamationem, et testium affirmationem cognoscens, requisivit abbatem per monachos quatinus ei pro federe caritatis pelles vulpinas daret, et sic omnia libentissime et fideliter concederet et tueretur perpetualiter. Monachi vero, virum illum magis habere cupientes pacificum quam iratum, quod petebat pacifice contulerunt, et sic veniens in capitulum, adducens secum Rotbertum, fratrem et de militibus suis unum, cuncta, sicut frater dederat, remoto omni ingenio, Deo et Sanctis martyribus Sergio et Bacho, et abbati Bernardo et ceteris fratribus omnino remisit, et donum hujus rei in manu abbatis prius positum ipse presentialiter super altare portavit.

These notices may seem a little early, but I found it – in this particular cartulary – also in a notice dated 1114–1151 (Cartulaire Saint-Serge II, no. 86).

and promotion of one's own interests was familir to the aristocracy for whom Benoit wrote. This value he made the corner-stone of his vision of the government of William the Conqueror. With this he appealed to a deep-seated aristocratic notion.

The relationship between the duke/king and his barons was indeed, Benoit maintains, such a relationship of *caritas*, or speaking in secular terms of *amor*.[70] For William it was always his starting-point; he honoured his barons, he wanted a real understanding, he procured advantages; the barons from their side recognized his position as leader. This vision at the same time was a call for unity. Whoever did not want this bond, acted immorally; he could count upon a merciless treatment. The preferable thing in all respects for all people was, according to Benoit, to comply with the desire of the ruler to have a bond of *caritas* or *amor* with every one.

In my view it is not by accident that Benoit came up with this concept between 1170 and 1180. As Beryl Smalley said: 'It emerged from the muddle of anti-Becket propaganda that Henry II had no coherent theory of royal power to oppose to Becket's defense of the church'.[71] Can Benoit have had the intention to provide for this need? By doing this couldn't he count on attracting the attention of Henry II? Clanchy says about this period: 'The constitutions of Clarendon of 1164 mark the starting point of what a modern lawyer would call "law reform" or "legislation" '.[72] King Henry in fact looked for a solution in legal codification, not in the transformation of an aristocratic value into something like an ideology of kingship. I am not quite sure that Benoit's work would have received the benevolent approval of Henry II. But his idea was not bad in itself. It was, after all, rooted in the hearts of the people.

---

[70] The word 'amor' does show up in the cartularies, in the sense of 'desire', for example 'pro amore celestis patrie dimisit calumpniam', Cartulaire Saint-Serge II, 390 no. 328 (1055–1083).
[71] Cited by Clanchy, 133.
[72] Clanchy, 153.

CONTROVERSIAL SCULPTURES:
THE SOUTHWELL TYMPANUM,
THE GLASTONBURY RESPOND, THE LEIGH CHRIST*

Pamela Tudor-Craig

Of the three pieces here discussed, the Glastonbury Respond has not yet received any treatment in the literature. The Southwell tympanum was catalogued as of c.1120 by Professor Zarnecki in the great Romanesque exhibition,[1] where the full length of its soffit was newly revealed. The Leigh Christ was dated by the VCH[2] to c.1100 and by Nicholas Pevsner[3] to c.1220 – a substantial difference of opinion – but neither view has been challenged during the last twenty years. The time has come perhaps to attempt again to put these three items in context.

As long ago as 1927, Armitage Robinson said of the earlier churches at Glastonbury: 'No interpretation can at the present time be other than provisional. Excavation has as yet gone only so far as to offer a few tantalising details. But it is in the interests of excavation itself that these notes are written; and so long as we keep facts and theories carefully distinct, no harm can come from adventurous suggestions'.[4] In spite, or perhaps because, of the power which Glastonbury holds over the imagination, those words are still partially valid. The plans published by Ralegh Radford of the progress in the development of this sacred site from the eighth to the twelfth centuries are usefully assembled in James Carley's monograph of 1988.[5] A remarkably small proportion of the Radford plans is actually blacked in. His plan for the Abbey of c.1100 must take the record for paucity of evidence. Note also its cautious date. The church built by the first Norman abbot, the Thurstan of Caen who had the monks shot down when they refused to give up their Gregorian chant in favour of the new usage from Fécamp in 1083, was pulled down by the Abbot Herlewin who succeeded him in 1101.[6] Does Radford attribute his

---

* In his last precious year Allen Brown came to the Twelfth-century Harlaxton Conference, which he filled with his vigour and excitement. He gave us a rousing paper on his favourite castles. I was deeply honoured when he asked me to pay a return visit to 'his' Battle Abbey Conference, and dedicate this paper to the memory of a great and courageous man.

[1] *English Romanesque Art 1066–1200*, Arts Council 1984, 123, 165.

[2] VCH *Worcestershire* ii, 194; iv, 106–10, illus. with sketch on p. 107.

[3] N. Pevsner, Buildings of England, *Worcestershire*, 1968, 211–12.

[4] J. Armitage Robinson, 'Historical Evidence as to the Saxon church at Glastonbury', *Proceedings of the Somersetshire Archaeological and Natural History Society* lxxiii, 1927, 40–9.

[5] J. P. Carley, Woodbridge 1988.

[6] The Peterborough version of the Anglo-Saxon Chronicle, under the year 1093, explains that the soldiery shot arrows at the monks from the 'up-floor' (Robinson, 46 n.1) or 'upper story' (Carley, 15, quoting *ASC*, 160). Robinson interprets the description as referring to a gallery above the aisles of the Saxon church. For the musical implications of this account see D. Hiley, 'Thurstan of Caen and Plainchant at Glastonbury: Musicological Reflections on the Norman Conquest', *Procs BA* lxxii, 1987, 57–90.

crumbs of a north transept with apsidal chapel and his return wall (which might be the footings of the pulpitum screen) to Thurstan or Herlewin? We are on much stronger ground when we turn to the records of furnishings. King Edgar, upon acceding to the kingdoms of Mercia and Northumbria in 957, appointed Dunstan immediately to the bishopric of Worcester, then two years later to London, and twelve months after that to Canterbury. Edgar consoled the bereft Glastonbury monks with magnificent gifts: bells, his coronation robe and a cross woven in gold and silver.[7] It may have been that very cross into which the arrows of Thurstan's soldiery stuck during the notorious raid of 1083. The last abbots before the Norman Conquest were scarcely better than Thurstan. Aethelward (c.1024–53) cut up the precious and well preserved body of their benefactor, King Edgar, in order to fit it into the reliquary already designed for it. The corpse bled and Aethelward went mad. Aethelnoth took the gold and silver from the Abbey books and sold them for his own profit – which proves that Glastonbury had splendid holy books before he got at them, if we had ever doubted it.

Dunstan's involvement in the building up of his scriptorium and the production of those beautiful books is well recorded. By the principle of osmosis, scholarship has associated almost every great manuscript lavishly illustrated with line drawings to the Canterbury over which Dunstan presided from 960 until his death in 988. There appear to be only two manuscripts which can be directly linked with tenth century Glastonbury. The first is the sacramentary known as Leofric's Missal[8] which contains a Glastonbury calendar. It has delicate fluttering line drawings and an acanthus border added 969–78, showing that by then the Glastonbury scriptorium was thoroughly conversant with the supreme achievements of the Reims school, with all that this implies. The other manuscript, known as St Dunstan's Classbook,[9] provided the famous drawing, generally accepted as being in Dunstan's own hand, of the Saint at the feet of Christ. The formality and rigidity of this drawing is not necessarily a reflection of Dunstan's artistic status as a gifted amateur: the drawings of the Sherborne Pontifical[10] executed at Canterbury very soon after Dunstan's arrival are more professional in the placing of the figure within the space, but similarly dry in handling.

The Glastonbury museum holds a group of splendid blue lias marble fragments clearly associated with the glorious abbacy of Henry of Blois, which strides across the twelfth century.[11] It contains fragments of thirteenth-century sculpture of very high quality.[12] It contains evidence of early fourteenth-century sculptural embellishment.[13] But what has surfaced from the series of pre-Conquest

[7] Carley, 12.

[8] Oxford Bodleian, MS Bodl. 579, see E. Temple, *Anglo-Saxon Manuscripts 900–1060 (A Survey of Manuscripts Illuminated in the British Isles* 2), London 1976, no. 17 and pls 53–6.

[9] Oxford Bodl. MS Auct. F.4.32; Temple, no. 11, pl. 41, and J. Backhouse, D. H. Turner, L. Webster, eds, *The Golden Age of Anglo-Saxon Art 966–1066*, London, British Museum, 1984, no. 31, p. 51 and pl. 31.

[10] Paris, Bibl. Nat. MS Lat. 943; Temple, no. 35 and pls 134–8; *The Golden Age of Anglo-Saxon Art*, no. 34, pl. 32.

[11] Henry of Blois was abbot from 1126–71, but from 1129 he held the abbacy in conjunction with the bishopric of Winchester. He rebuilt the conventual buildings and gave Glastonbury precious altar furnishings and major relics. See Carley, 20.

[12] J. J. G. Alexander and P. Binski, eds, *The Age of Chivalry*, Royal Academy, London 1987, no. 296, illus.

[13] N. Stratford, 'Glastonbury and two Gothic Ivories in the United States', in F. H. Thompson, ed. *Studies in Medieval Sculpture, Society of Antiquaries Occasional Papers*, NS, iii, 1983, 208–16.

churches? Ralegh Radford has accepted portions of a standing cross as coming from Dunstan's time. I would prefer a much earlier date for these, recalling Bewcastle and Ruthwell.[14] However, there are three items over which we should tarry.

The Glastonbury museum also has a collection of fragments of wall painting, displayed with shells in which pigment was mixed. The larger pieces appear to have been painted in earth pigments with a curtain pattern. Some of the smaller pieces have black lines on a white ground. Lawrence Keen finds instructive comparison for these apparently simple linear designs with patterns used on high relief tiles of the tenth and eleventh centuries.[15] The examples from Winchester are stratified to the Old Minster, reconstructed 980–94. There is a difference of opinion about the date of the Bury St Edmunds tiles. Cathy Haith thinks that they must come from the first stone church on the site, as refounded by Cnut in the eleventh century.[16] Richard Gem and Lawrence Keen kept open the possibility that the Bury tiles were from the timber buildings of 924–39.[17] The rest of the group – tiles from St Albans and from All Saints Pavement at York – all have clear, but unspecified, pre-Conquest dates. Nevertheless, the stratification at Winchester gives colour to the suggestion that the painted fragments at Glastonbury may have come from St Dunstan's time. As Gem and Keen insist, tiles may have been used as a wall dado. The apparent curtain element at Glastonbury suggests the same context. The simple linear patterns at Glastonbury could have been part of a design of simulated tiles.

In the Glastonbury museum there is also a life-size carved head, carved in one piece with its backing stone [Pl. 1]. The facial dimensions are approximately 7½ " (20cm) across and 9 " (22cm) deep. A dowel hole at the top suggests it may have once served as a corbel, and the neck dies away in a way compatible with this interpretation. The proportions of this head are very Roman – summary curls, low brow, relatively shallow and well-spaced eyes, pronounced jaw, nearly open mouth. These proportions are used whenever classical work is being copied. However, the interpretation here is subtly different from late twelfth- or early thirteenth-century work. I find parallels in Carolingian illumination, hinting that this head could belong to the almost lost sculptural world of the Carolingian revival. As illuminators in Reims pored over late classical codices, did not contemporary sculptors study the Roman monuments then standing in some quantity – even now standing in some part – in the same city? There are cogent comparisons for the Glastonbury head on the ivory book cover of the Lorsch Gospels[18] [Pl. 1a] or in such drawn heads as the St Matthew (fol. 21 verso) from the Gospel Book of Hincmar, illuminated in Reims in the first half of the ninth century[19] [Pl. 1b].

---

[14] For which there is a voluminous bibliography.

[15] R. Gem and L. Keen, 'Late Anglo-Saxon finds from the site of St Edmunds' Abbey', *Suffolk Institute of Archaeology and History* xxxv, 1984, 1–30.

[16] *The Golden Age of Anglo-Saxon Art*, nos 142 and 143, pp. 136–7, entry by C. Haith.

[17] Gem and Keen, 30.

[18] For the cover of the Lorsch Gospels in the Vatican museum in Rome see P. Lasko, 'Ars Sacra 800–1200', *Pelican History of Art*, Harmondsworth 1972, 26–7 and pl. 25. As Lasko says, it is generally agreed that the book cover, showing Christ treading on the asp and basilisk, was based on late antique prototypes of the sixth century.

[19] Reims, Bibl. Muncipal, J. Hubert, J. Porcher, W. F. Volbach, *Carolingian Art*, London 1970, pl. 105, p. 118 and p. 349.

From below

Plate 1 *Glastonbury head. Limestone head in the museum at Glastonbury Abbey. Here dated to the mid tenth century. Direct facial view*

Plate 1b *St Matthew from Gospel Book of Hincmar. Reims, Bibl. Mun. First half of ninth century*

Plate 1a *Ivory book cover of Lorsch Gospels (c.830)*

We know that Dunstan's scriptorium at Glastonbury was familiar with the art of the Carolingian revival – that it was probably the first house in England to have the chance to study Carolingian models at first hand. It is logical to assume that the models Dunstan will have provided, and those models were no doubt all on a small portable scale, will have been studied by craftsmen working in all media, and some of those media will have been on a larger scale.

On the other hand, an early twelfth-century date would seem more likely for the well-known wheel-shaped carving of the Agnus Dei with a beaded edge. This piece is fixed to the wall, and it appears to have escaped observation that the back is also carved in high relief. Only a small part of that carving is now visible, though it seems that the central section is heavily damaged. The far end of it is carved with the tail, and the near end has the two paws of what must certainly have been a wolf. Between the two paws, rendered in very high relief and well preserved, is the severed head of St Edmund. High standing crosses with carving on both sides are not unusual, but to find one with some claims to be considered as late as the twelfth century, and bearing so striking a subject as pendant to the Agnus Dei, is occasion for thought – and perhaps for bringing the two-sided sculpture away from the wall. Comparison inevitably springs to mind with the Sigmund relief from Winchester, which featured in both the Anglo-Saxon and Romanesque exhibitions.[20]

Perhaps more interesting than William of Malmesbury's rather ungracious description of Ine's church of the early eighth century as widened with porticus and given a tower by Dunstan[21] is the account, in the Life of the Saint, of his childhood vision at Glastonbury, then very shabby, of the buildings he would erect there 'Sic inquit aedificabitur locus iste ad preparanda corda illorum Domino qui hoc in loco per hunc puerum Domini credituri sunt'. You do not recall with pride in later life that you foresaw the buildings you were going to put up, nor do devoted chroniclers record such ideas, if all you did put up was a couple of lean-tos and a beastly little tower. It is difficult to interpret William of Malmesbury's comments – 'a basilica was produced of great extent in both directions, wherein if aught be lacking of seemliness or beauty, there is at any rate no want of necessary room' in terms of the additive building Radford attributes to Dunstan. It sounds much more like the pillared structure he dates c.1100. How could a large community manage in those sequential spaces till 1101? The 'solaria' between the columns in 1083 sound more like Dunstan than his successors. This however, is matter for the archaeologists to sort out.

Whichever group of buildings Dunstan achieved, it had doorways and openings, and there is a candidate for a respond from such a doorway [Pl. 2]. It is quite small, and altogether odd. The reason why it has lain so long unobserved is that it had been re-carved in the later Middle Ages on the other side. On the reverse it was modified to carry a grotesque figure of which the arms, with buttoned sleeves, survive. They embrace a water spout which was cut through the stone. It was displayed at Glastonbury with the spout side upwards, and only my propensity

[20] *The Golden Age of Anglo-Saxon Art*, 140, pp. 133–5, illus and *English Romanesque Art*, 97, pp. 150–51, illus.
[21] Wm. Stubbs, 'Memorials of St Dunstan', RS 63, 1874, 92 and 271, quoted by Carley, 11 n. 17: 'The result of his labours was that, as far as the design of the ancient structure allowed, a basilica was produced of great extent in both directions; wherein, if aught be lacking of seemliness or beauty, there is at any rate no lack of necessary room'.

*Plate 2 Glastonbury respond. Here dated to the mid tenth century.
From above*

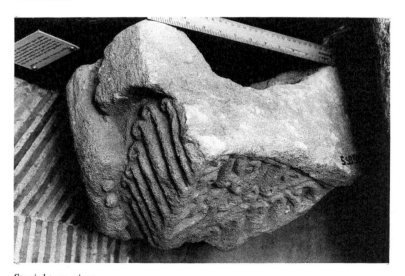

Straight on view

*Plates 2a–d (opposite) (a) Beatus page from psalter from Winchcombe Abbey.
c.1020–30. Cambridge University Library Ff.1.23 f.5
(b) Painted capital in crypt of St Germain at Auxerre. Before 857
(c) Canon Table from Bury Gospels. Christ Church Canterbury, c.1020–30, BL Harley
76 f.10
(d) Three strap ends found at Winchester. Winchester Museums Research Unit BS SF
6624, 6810 and 1396, with head of key, BM MLA Netherton SF 1389. All dated to the
mid tenth century*

a

c

b

d

never to leave a stone unturned, plus the skilled help of Jerry Sampson, brought this richly carved capital to light. Its front surface is concave, and it dies away either side on the diagonal. It is at once more sophisticated and less conventional than any ordinary Corinthian capital. It is a Corinthian capital designed from first principles. Such forays of originality are surely rare in capitals of the post-Conquest period. One could imagine the artist trying to decipher the shorthand for a Corinthian capital on the Lorsch Book cover [Pl.1b]. For comparable bravura compare the Beatus page from the Winchcombe Abbey Psalter of c.1030–50[22] [Pl. 2a]. As Francis Wormald said 'the leaf having the appearance of ostrich feathers was inspired by the Carolingian acanthus scroll of the ninth century and was introduced into England during the last years of the ninth century and the early years of the tenth century'.

A similarly painstaking derivation from capitals of the ninth century like those in the Musée of the Abbaye of St Germain at Auxerre account for the disarming capital at Sompting. Auxerre reminds us that capitals sometimes fell within the province of the painter. In the crypt of St Germain of 865–57 what would read like a plain respond if the painting had gone was in fact ornamented with capital and shaft in trompe-d'oeil [Pl. 2b], as the plain groined vault has ribs and a boss of paint. This is but one step from architecture designed by or reflecting the observation of illuminators. The canon tables of a Canterbury manuscript of the early eleventh-century Bury Gospels,[23] probably one of the first manuscripts acquired from Canterbury by Bury abbey upon its foundation in 1020, comes as almost a shock. Before we are sarcastic about the instability of this interlacing arcade we might ponder whether we know of any actual interlaced arcading to which we can give an earlier date than this [Pl. 2c]. I do not wish to suggest that this illuminator was an architectual innovator of the first order – but that he was surely copying something now lost to us – early eleventh-century architectural ornament that was to have a strong bearing on the full Romanesque style in this country.

For the rest, further comparisons for the pot hooks with which the Glastonbury respond is decorated can be made with the detail of tenth-century strap ends, found in excavations at Winchester, or with the decoration of the head of a key in the British Museum.[24] The other end of the early tenth-century key from York[25] has little holes bored in it very like the Glastonbury drill holes [Pl. 2d].

In short, I deduce that the most likely provenance for the wallpainted fragments, the relief head and the respond at Glastonbury is the abbey of St Dunstan's rebuilding. They are traces of a sub-Carolingian oeuvre in all media from the context that produced for Dunstan's friend and ally the Benedictional of St Aethelwold,[26] the most thorough tribute to the Carolingian School of a century before.

[22] Cambridge University Library, MS Ff. I, 23, fol. 5, Temple cat. 80 pls 249–53.
[23] BL MS Harley 76, Temple 75, pls 221, 230, 231.
[24] Winchester City Museum, Winchester Research Unit, BS.SF 6624, 6810, 1396. The key fragment is British Museum MLA Netherton, SF 1389. All discussed in *The Golden Age of Anglo-Saxon Art* cat. 82. 83, 84, and key fragment cat. 86.
[25] York City Council through Yorkshire Museum, 1979. No. 6833, see *The Golden Age of Anglo-Saxon Art*, no. 20, p. 39, illus. Compare also the motifs on the Disk Brooch of the first half of the tenth-century Stockholm Statens Historika Museum, SHM 9154, *The Golden Age of Anglo-Saxon Art*, no. 17, p. 36 illus.
[26] BL Add. MS 49598, usually dated to Aethelwold's episcopacy, 963–84. See *The Golden Age of Anglo-Saxon Art*, 37, p. 59, where the date is given as c.970–80. However, the rubric says that the

At Glastonbury investigations are hampered by lack of precise archaeological stratification. No such problem awaits the student of the Southwell Tympanum [Pl. 3]. It has long been in the position where it remained until 1983. It had begun to show signs of structural stress, and was taken out in that year for conservation. It was then shown at the Hayward Gallery in the Romanesque exhibition of 1984[27] before going back to the temporary position it now occupies, a pace forward of its previous site. It was described and illustrated in its previous position in the 1801 Dickinson's *History of Southwell*.[28] The tympanum was set into the north corner of the west wall of the north transept to serve as a makeshift tympanum to the doorway leading to the staircase which gives access to the triforium. The researches of Arnold Klukas[29] have sufficiently shown the importance of the upper levels of our Anglo-Saxon and Romanesque major churches to liturgical practice to remind us that this doorway would not have been, in the earlier Middle Ages, the mere workman's access it later became. However no such door in another English great church was so ornamented in the twelfth century. Nor is there any question of this carving being in its original position. It is plain enough that it has been broken off at the left-hand end, losing the head of David. More, a crude piece with a pair of grooves across it was botched into the right-hand end to shape it up for the doorway. The botch provides little evidence, but its tooling is diagonal, consistent with the practical conclusion that it ought to be twelfth-century. The last doubt as to its being a re-used piece was silenced when it was taken out, for the soffit was found to continue under the door jambs, with a Ringerike plant like the termination of the dragon's tail at one end, and a grotesque caryatid figure at the other. These features were in good condition but not so sparkling as to suggest that they had never been outside. Their condition would suggest, in fact, a certain length of years in an exposed position.

Benedictional was written for Aethelwold's personal use by one of his monks called Godeman. Aethelwold made Godeman abbot of Thorney, Lincs, in 972. It ought to follow that Godeman's work on the Benedictional – and the rubric also makes it plain that the elaborate decoration was planned from the first – must antedate his promotion. A date bracket 963–72 for the Benedictional brings it within the period when Dunstan's influence was strong at Glastonbury.

[27] *English Romanesque Art*, 123 catalogue entry by George Zarnecki, p. 165, illus.

[28] William Dickinson, *Antiquities Historical, Architectural, Chorographical and Itinerary in Nottinghamshire and the Adjacent Counties*, Newark 1801, drawing largely upon the author's *History of the Antiquities of Southwell* of 1787. I am indebted to Richard Beaumont for this critical reference. Dickinson's text on the Southwell tympanum (pp. 79–81 of vol. I in the 1801 edition) is of great interest as a model of observation, and in my view of well-founded interpretation: 'The stone, on which there is this curious piece of carving ... forms the head of a doorway leading to the staircase of the large tower [it must be remembered in the first years of the nineteenth century the two western towers were without their spires, so the central tower was unrivalled] ... This is one of the oldest parts of the building, and there can be no doubt but that the sculpture is, at least, coeval with the wall, in which it is inserted, *if not older* [italics mine] ... There has been a great deal of unnecessary carving if this stone was originally designed for the place it now occupies, as the most finished part of it is a border on the underside, which passes a considerable way into the wall at both ends and is not noticed by a cursory observer ... even the front of the stone, on which is the hieroglyphical representation, is not perfect, and does not, on a minute examination appear, from the contiguous stones, to have ever been so since it was placed in its present situation ... I esteem this stone as exhibiting one of the earliest specimens of Saxon sculpture in this Island ... Its design ... satisfactorarily demonstrates that even among the Saxons, rude as they were, efforts were made now and then within the circle of the sciences ...' The tympanum is engraved opp. p. 80, and is inscribed 'Over the Door leading to the Belfry'.

[29] Arnold Klukas, 'The Continuity of Anglo-Saxon Liturgical Tradition in Post-Conquest England as Evident in the Architecture of Winchester, Ely and Canterbury Cathedrals', *Les Mutations Socio-Culturelles au Tournant des XI–XII Siècles (Etudes Anselmiennes (IV Session))*, Paris 1984, 111–23.

The relieving arch behind the 'tympanum' in the thick twelfth-century wall suggests that the structure was designed to accommodate this relatively thin stone from the beginning. It does not appear to have complained at the massive Romanesque weight above it until fairly recently, (though a suspicion that the structural crack was old and a good excuse for removal in 1983 may be entertained).

It is my belief that the Southwell so-called 'tympanum' was placed in its transept position during the early twelfth-century building works. The alternative supposition that between 1120 and 1787 a broken piece of ancient carving – broken no doubt in the first place in extracting it from its original position and further mutilated to fit the new one – was placed over an almost hidden doorway would be difficult to support. These things are usually rediscovered re-used back-to-front in new structural works, from the late fourteenth-century cloisters at Canterbury to post-Reformation close and canonry walls at Winchester.

It follows that a carved stone re-used after breakage in the early twelfth century ought to be earlier than the time of re-use. It further follows from the condition of the newly discovered full length of the soffit carving that it was probably originally in a more exposed position, and from its relative thinness, that it came from a wall thinner than those of the early Norman build.

Southwell Minster was founded in 956.[30] A fourteenth-century copy of the original charter survives. By its terms, Eadwig, king of the English, presented Southwell to Oskytel, archbishop of York. Oskytel survived until 971, but his successor Ethelwold resigned for a quieter life. Southwell in 960 was not Kent, with Dunstan at Canterbury. Until 954, two years before the foundation of Southwell, York had been under the control of the heathen Norwegian, Erik, son of Harold Fairhair, king of Norway. Pagan Norwegians liked dragons, and the kind of dragon they liked best is illustrated by the weathervane from Heggen in the Ringerike style, looking like nothing so much as the dragon on the Southwell carving [Pl. 3a]. Introduce St Michael and Christianity has won. They also liked struggles between men and beasts. Christen the men Samson or David and nothing is lost.[31]

By 1020 Southwell Minster was a pilgrimage site, housing the relics of St Edburga, daughter of a king of the East Angles, of whom we shall hear more. By 1051 there was a house for the archbishop of York also at Southwell. In that year archbishop Aelfric died there. So we know that the church must have been of substance before the Conquest. It follows that it had ornamented doorways, or at least one ornamented entrance. But it is an article of faith[32] that there are no

---

[30] Sir Frank Stenton, 'The Founding of Southwell Minster', *Transactions of the Thoroton Society* lxxi, 1967, pp. 13–17.

[31] Signa Horn Fuglesang, 'The Relationship between Scandinavian and English Art from the late 8th to the mid 12th centuries', *Sources of Anglo-Saxon Culture*, ed. P. E. Szarmach, Kalamazoo 1986, 232.

[32] H. M. Taylor, *Anglo-Saxon Architecture* iii, Cambridge 1978, 1059, is cautious on this subject: 'there are none [tympana] from before the Conquest which can be claimed with certainty as surviving *in situ*'. He goes on to defend the Majesty sculpture now over the south porch doorway at Castor, Cambridgeshire, as a pre-Conquest tympanum, – a view with which I concur, adding that it argues a very narrow door with a stilted arch above it. Taylor then relates the interlaced animal carving on the tympanum at Knook to later tenth-century illumination, and by way of the tympana at Hoveringham and Long Marton reaches Southwell. Hoveringham and Long Marton show conflicts between a dragon and an angel 'with the details which relate them to a lintel at Southwell' . . . Quite. The eleventh-century tympanum set into a frame of 1792 at Castle Farm, Coleshill, Strattenborough is another pre-1066 candidate.

tympana before the Norman Conquest, an article not challenged here. Tympana are the signature of English Romanesque. So for that matter, is their subject matter, derived ultimately from Cluny, of the Christ enthroned in a mandorla: Barfreston, Malmesbury, Ely, Rochester, reiterated in wall painting, Kempley, Canterbury Chapel of St Gabriel, or in manuscript, the Bury Bible. It is all very authoritarian, heiratic, assured, volumes of thought away from St Michael and King David, marginally victorious over lion and a dragon that threatens to metamorphose into chaotic foliage at Southwell. Michael has a hold on his human proportions, but his garments are hatched in the elementary way associated with manuscripts like the Junius Psalter,[33] a Winchester book of 925–50 where the most important initial is David opening the lion's jaw, the 'D' of Dixit Dominus [Pl. 3b] (the Lord said to my Lord . . .), or the famous page of Aethelstan offering a book of St Cuthbert, from Bede's *Lives of St Cuthbert*, another Winchester book of c.937.[34] In other words, the restrained and elementary nature of St Michael's garments suggest the generation just before the influx of Carolingian books associated with St Dunstan.

The subject of St Michael was highly popular in the pre-Conquest period. The cross shaft at Shelford by Trent has the Virgin and Child on one face, and the Archangel on the other. As Fuglesang has observed, the tympanum at Hoveringham in Nottinghamshire and the stones at St Nicholas Ipswich [Pl. 3c] have St Michael with dragons like Southwell.[35] Ipswich also is a heavily Viking influenced area. But are these carvings tympana? Masons resorted to various subterfuges in late eleventh-century or early twelfth-century buildings. At Bredwardine (Herefordshire) it is patent that they re-used the lintel from an earlier doorway and ran their blind tympanum – perhaps originally painted – above it. At Barton Seagrave they made up a tympanum with the help of a lintel and some single stones cut down to match. Hoveringham, already mentioned, has a lintel with Michael and two dragons, made up with some oddments of St Peter and two ecclesiastics. At Leckhampton in Buckinghamshire and at Moreton Valence a so-called tympanum with two dragons, a hand of God and two extras are reset in a bigger space created in the late eleventh century. The examples at Uppington (Shropshire) and Byton (Herefordshire) are more interesting still, and so are amazingly undistinguished tympana at Little Tey and Little Braxted in Essex. The special features these objects share is that the carved block is not a straight lintel but a gabled lintel. At Little Tey and Little Braxted they filled in the spaces under their early twelfth-century arch with almost anything – no doubt it was painted over. At Uppington and at Byton they just cut them about and set them in the wall. At its lowest, a large block that will span a door opening is too good to throw away. The Byton Agnus Dei panel has been severly cut down and set askew, but the peak of the gable survives. At Uppington the block has been broken and lengthened – as has happened at Southwell. If these carvings had not survived in an early Norman context would anyone have suggested a post-1066 date for them? The fact that they were re-used front outwards, and not reversed and carved again on the fresh side, tells volumes about the available standards of sculpture in post-Conquest parish churches. Even the cathedral sculpture, like the Chichester Raising of

[33] Oxford Bodl. MS Junius 27 (Sc.5139); see Temple, no. 7, p. 38, pl. 26.
[34] Cambridge Corpus Christi College MS 183, Temple, no. 6, pl. 29. The same simple drapery occurs on the Cuthbert Stole of before 916.
[35] Fuglesang, *Sources of Anglo-Saxon Culture*, 232. Taylor (see n. 32) adds Long Marton to this list.

Plate 3 Southwell Tympanum. Here dated to pre-Conquest Minster

From below showing soffit

Plate 3a Weathervane from Heggen. Late tenth century. Universitet Oldsaksamling, Oslo

Plate 3c Relief from St Nicholas, Ipswich, of St Michael and the dragon. Here considered to be pre-Conquest

Plate 3b Junius Psalter. Dixit Dominus opening. Second quarter of the tenth century. Oxford Bodl. MS Junius 27 f.118

Plate 3d Relief from St Paul's. Before 1035, Museum of London

Lazarus, may not have been as good as work of before the Conquest, and in the villages it was zigzag and beakheads all the way. Look at Tickencote.

I am claiming therefore, that this bunch of ornamented features with thematic material either darkly mysterious or associated with dragons, conquered and otherwise, is not a sequence of proto Norman tympana but of earlier lintels and elementary pediments, re-used in early Norman buildings. The penchant for such gabled lintels or pedimented lintels can again be demonstrated by reference to Carolingian manuscripts like the Gospel Book of Ebbo.[36]

Plain though it is now, such a pedimented lintel crowned the door of Charlemagne's Palatine chapel at Aachen. In the Romanesque exhibition the Southwell tympanum was associated with its closest relatives – the boar tympanum and the Michael and the dragon slab from St Nicholas Ipswich and the gabled lintel of St Michael and the dragon from St Bees Priory, Cumbria.[37] From their appearance these pieces need not have been carved after the Conquest. Professor Zarnecki gave the inevitable comparison with the Ringerike relief from St Paul's,[38] associated with the reign of King Canute [Pl. 3d]. At c.1030 I would suggest the St Paul's relief as the latest of a series of potential comparisons for Southwell, of which the Castor dragon and the Mustair dragon were venerable ancestors. You have only to compare the Southwell tangles with the plain reptilian tail of St Michael's domestic dragon at the end of the Anglo-Saxon tradition in the great Psalter Cotton Tiberius C VI[39] to realise where Southwell's sympathies lie.

The soffit of the Southwell gabled lintel bears a repertory of motifs of ultimately classical origin, as well as others of Viking source whose affiliations lie more readily with the detail of the tympanum, if it is a tympanum, from All Saints Lathbury, another piece which might be claimed for a pre-Conquest origin.[40]

In short, I would like to attribute the Southwell gabled lintel (which we will continue to call a tympanum) for the church built there by archbishop Oskytel soon after 956, or at the latest for the early eleventh century when the relics of St Edburga had brought increased prosperity to the house.

Edburga was held in special esteem in the church which holds the last subject of this enquiry: the blessing Christ at Leigh in Worcestershire [Pl. 4]. The church at Leigh is dedicated to St Edburga which is not surprising since relics of Edburga had been given to Pershore by Earl Odda who died in 1056, and Leigh had belonged to Pershore before the Conquest.[41] At Domesday Leigh included an occasional residence of the abbots of Pershore, and there were four mills in the parish. It follows that there must have been a church. The VCH plan[42] shows the bones of the standing church which were assumed by the authors to be of c.1100. Pevsner said 'Norman'[43] presumably on the evidence of the stepped buttresses and

---

36 Epernay Bibl. Mun. MS 1; *Carolingian Art*, pls 94–7 and p. 349.

37 *English Romanesque Art*, no. 124, p. 166, illus. St Bees is the acid test. The Benedictine nunnery of St Mary and St Bege was founded c.650, destroyed by the Danes and refounded by William de Meschines in c.1120. Do we have to assume a total vacuum between 650 and 1120?

38 *English Romanesque Art*, no. 95, p. 149, illus.

39 BL MS Cotton Tiberius C VI, c.1050. See Temple, no. 98, pl. 310.

40 *English Romanesque Art*, no. 104, pl. p. 63.

41 Efforts to find the earliest date at which St Edburga was associated with Leigh have so far proved fruitless. The VCH records have been destroyed.

42 VCH *Worcestershire* iv, 106–10.

43 N. Pevsner, *Buildings of England, Worcestershire*, Harmondsworth 1968, 21 and pl. 19.

of features, block capitals to the chancel arch and the blind niche which used to house our figure outside the north door, which could be secondary. The long narrow nave and chancel suggests a classic pre-Conquest plan, of which the chancel arch was subsequently enlarged. Heavy repointing and a certain amount of sandstone replacement make the diagnosis of the critical north nave and chancel and south chancel walls at Leigh difficult. The walls at approximately 3' (31–34") are not thin. Taylor found many Anglo-Saxon walls of that thickness and a few thicker.[44] The stepped buttresses are almost certainly additions. They interspersed at irregular intervals a series of flat buttressess of little projection, entirely composed of the paler sandstone, which recall the building practice of many later eleventh-century buildings, like the transepts of St Albans Abbey. A peculiar feature of the interior of Leigh church has gone unexplained, and largely ignored. Riding high above the chancel arch on its western face, in the angles of the walls, are two groups of clustered shafts. Their bases are of simple form, and no further detailing is visible from the ground. They would appear to have served some secondary structural feature, such as a gallery *carried across the chancel arch wall* (italics mine). The Taylors described structural evidence for upper chambers on all *four* sides of the church at Norton.[45] It is a feature more easy to accommodate in our knowledge of eleventh- than twelfth-century buildings. In the absence of clearer documentation a date after the middle of the eleventh century, when Pershore's prosperity was improved by Edburga's relics, would seem appropriate for the building or rebuilding of a church dedicated to her in one of Pershore's dependant villages.

The VCH dated the Leigh blessing Christ c.1100.[46] Nicholas Pevsner disagreed, and chose an early thirteenth century date. He was reminded, no doubt, of the great trumeau figures of Chartres, Reims and Amiens, but his context does not convince. However he assumed that the statue had been a recumbent figure from a coffin-lid, with the wrong head and arms added. This interpretation was probably partly provoked by the condition and inaccessibility of the Leigh figure in Pevsner's day. It has now been cleaned at the Victoria and Albert Museum and brought indoors. The head has been refixed, but there is no reason to think it is not the original. The only part of the figure which is clearly an addition is the head of the cross held in Christ's left hand. This lacks the limewash evident in the hollows of the other re-set pieces, as it is on the figure as a whole. There are considerable traces of presumably medieval paint, in particular areas of red down the outer fold of Christ's garment, especially on his left-hand side. As a blessing Christ, it can hardly come from a coffin lid.

The Leigh Christ has one feature that at first sight suggests a date bracket way beyond the latest period that could be offered on other grounds: the tunic of Christ is parted over the heart as traditionally placed on the right side of his chest. English scholars immediately think of the imagery associated by Dr Marian Roberts with

---

[44] Taylor, *Anglo-Saxon Architecture* iii, 959–60. Taylor did not discuss Leigh.
[45] H. M. Taylor and Joan Taylor, *Anglo-Saxon Architecture* i, Cambridge 1965, 465–9; Taylor, iii, 758, 800, 835.
[46] The height of the figure is 4' 10" (165cm). At its widest it measures 27" (68cm) and at narrowest 14" (35cm).

Plate 4 Figure of the blessing Christ at Leigh, Worcestershire. Here dated to the second half of the eleventh century

c

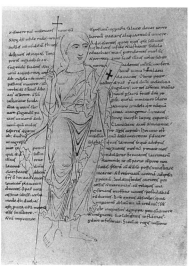

d

*Plates 4a–d (a) Gospel Book from the Meuse region. Paris, Bibl. Nat. Lat. 9453 f.125.
Second half of the tenth century*
*(b) Drawing from Gregory the Great, Pastoral Care. Mid to third quarter of the tenth
century. Oxford, St John's College MS 28 f.2r*
(c) Anglo-Saxon Homilies, c.1020–30. Trinity College Cambridge MS B 15 34 (369) f.1
(d) The Harrowing of Hell. Mid eleventh century. BL Cotton Tiberius C VI, f.14

the presentation of the Relic of the Holy Blood to Westminster Abbey in 1247.[47] However, as Roberts herself suggested, the iconography of Christ showing the wound is much older, going back to tenth-century sources. She quotes the critical folio in BL MS Cotton Galba AXVIII, fol. 21.[48] This illumination shows Christ seated, enthroned, in a mandorla. His right hand is blessing and left carrying a cross – as at Leigh. He is surrounded by martyrs, confessors and virgins with angels in the outer spandrels. This manuscript is particularly relevant because Francis Wormald associated it so tellingly with the fragment of a wall-painting discovered at Winchester and stratified to the pre-903 building.[49] He was able, therefore, to make the convincing suggestion that the wall-painting at Winchester was once part of a Civitas Dei. It follows that the other known pre-Conquest representations of Christ exposing the wound in his side, in Ottonian wall-paintings, are not so remote from the English manuscript nor from the Leigh sculpture.[50] The common factor could have been a major wall-painting in the New Minster at Winchester. Personal devotion to the pierced heart of Christ, so well illustrated in The Meuse Gospel Book (Paris Bibl. Nat. MS Lat. 9453, fol.125) [Pl. 4a] of the second half of the tenth century has been convincingly related by Roberts to the gift to Aethelstan from Hugh Duke of the Franks of Longinus' Spear. There was no decline in this devotion in the eleventh century, as is well attested by the prayers of St Anselm, written 1070–80 before he became archbishop of Canterbury.[51] His phrase 'Why, O my soul, were you not there to be pierced by a sword of bitter sorrow when you could not bear the piercing of the side of your Saviour with a lance? . . .' could not be more heart-rending had it come from the pen of a late fourteenth-century mystic.

If Pevsner's date is unconvincing, it is hard to find a place for the Leigh Christ in the sequence of column figures that lie behind great French trumeau figures of c.1220. It does not go alongside the Bourges St Stephen of c.1200, or the Chartres column figures of c.1140 – or their prototype, the column figure of Agnes, Imperatrix Augusta, wife of the emperor Henry III, the eleventh-century figure in the Regensburg museum. The Leigh figure fits nowhere along the graph of gradually thawing damp fold drapery that this sequence suggests. It belongs to the freer interpretation of Classicism that we associate with the English line drawing style from the time of Dunstan. One notable Leigh feature, the tendency for the drapery to sink between the legs, which may have led Pevsner to believe that the figure was originally recumbent, can be seen in a drawing from St Augustine's Canterbury of the mid tenth century[52] [Pl. 4b]. Compare also the hem of the blessing Christ in this manuscript with that of the Leigh Christ. The Leigh tunic

---

[47] M. E. Roberts, 'The Relic of the Holy Blood and the Iconography of the thirteenth-century North Transept Portal of Westminster Abbey', *England in the Thirteenth Century: Proceedings of the 1984 Harlaxton Symposium*, Harlaxton 1985, 129–42.

[48] Temple, 36, fig. 33, here dated to before 939.

[49] Francis Wormald, Anniversary Address to the Society of Antiquaries 1967, *Antiqs Journ.* xlvii, 1967, pl. II, pp. 159–65, illus pls XXIII, XXIVb, XXV. For Ottonian wall paintings of this subject see B. Brenk, *Tradition und Neuerung in der christlichen Kunst des ersten Jahrtausends*, Studien zur Geschichte des Weltgerichtsbildes, Wiener Byzantinishtische Studien, iii, Vienna 1966, 238–42, quoted by Roberts, footnote 31.

[50] Hubert et al., *Carolingian Art*, pl. 144, pp. 157, 351.

[51] *The Prayers and Meditations of St Anselm*, translated with Introduction by Sister Benedicta Ward SLG, Penguin Books 1979, especially Prayer to Christ, p. 95.

[52] Gregory the Great's *Pastoral Care*, Oxford, St John's College MS 28; Temple, cat. 13 and pl. 42.

hem shows the urge to flutter that is the hall-mark of Anglo-Saxon drawings, and appears in surviving sculpture like the mourning angels at Bradford on Avon. At Leigh the most significant feature is the hem above Christ's right foot. It does not only flutter: it is deliberately turned back and lifted in a little bunch. The figure of Philosophy from another manuscript of c.970 at St Augustine's Canterbury has the same flick of the hem rationalised into a ruched band.[53] If it were not for her unfortunate squint (which I am sure was intended to suggest her inward looking cast of mind rather than the need for optical correction), this monumental figure could be readily imaged as a majestic sculpture. All pre-Conquest figures have that freedom of draughtsmanship, that ever-present catching of an up-draught of wind, that distinguishes them from the formal confinement that characterises post-Conquest work in all media, for example, the mid-Romanesque jamb of the chancel arch at Kilpeck. The problem of the missing range of late Anglo-Saxon figure sculpture can be addressed, as it were diagonally, by comparing small ivories with manuscripts, and both with the traces of large sculptures. Comparison between, say, the Winchester ivory of two angels and the Winterborne Steepleton relief from a crucifixion has its validity. So does comparison between the famous crucifixion page in BL MS Harley 2904 and the Headbourne Worthy shadow. After all, Headbourne Worthy is just outside Winchester. But the fragment of an arm at Bitton in Somerset from a life-size rood also makes sense by reference to MS Harley 2904, and we have the testimony of Bradford on Avon, Breamore, Romsey and Langford for the existence of mighty roods, which are reflected in the ivory in the Victoria and Albert Museum.[54] A similar parallel can be drawn between the ivory Christ enthroned in the Metropolitan Museum, New York, and the Christ in Majesty from the Anglo-Saxon Homilies of c.1020 in Trinity College, Cambridge[55] [Pl. 4c]. The practice, observed here, of actually writing on the knees of Christ 'Rex Regum' might be the explanation for the recessed and flattened panels on the knees of the large relief of Christ Enthroned at Barnack. These two works of art are not only instructive in their relationship to one another, but in their relationship with Leigh, in particular with the narrow head type which is so striking at Leigh. It is very much a feature of the eleventh century – compare a wall painting fragment at Beauvais or MS Cotton Tiberius C VI, the Harrowing of Hell, [Pl. 4d] – and as such enters the Cluniac stream at Cluny itself. It is found therefore, at Vézelay and at Autun but in every other way those great tympana speak a totally different formal language from Leigh.

The subject of the triumphant blessing Christ was greatly favoured in the eleventh century. Jonathan Alexander has published a sequence of the Christ trampling the asp and basilisk from manuscripts of the late eleventh century at Mont-St-Michel.[56] The standing Christ, with the emperor Henry II and the empress

---

[53] Cambridge Trinity College MS O.3.7, Boethius' *De Consolatione Philosophiae*; Temple, cat. 20, pl. 44.

[54] P. Williamson, *The Medieval Treasury*, Victoria & Albert Museum, 1986, 96 illus; *The Golden Age of Anglo-Saxon Art*, cat. 118, pp. 117–18, col. pl. XXVI. My comment only applies to the ivory Christus, generally accepted as English work.

[55] The ivory (?) pectoral Cross, Metropolitan Museum, New York (17.190.217), *Golden Age of Anglo-Saxon Art*, no. 124, pp. 121–2, illus. The drawing of Christ in Majesty is on fol. 65 of Aelfric's Homilies, Cambridge Trinity College MS B.15.34, *The Golden Age of Anglo-Saxon Art*, cat. 63, p. 78, illus.

[56] J. J. G. Alexander, *Norman Illumination at Mont-St-Michel 966–1100*, 1970.

Kunigunde crouching at his feet, flanked by the three archangels and St Benedict, form the gold-plated antependium from the Benedictine monastery at Reichenau, founded by Henry in 1015.[57] The standing Christ remained a popular topic on the Continent – witness the sequence of trumeau figures – but in Romanesque England it appears to have been ousted by the seated Christ in Majesty. We have no evidence of standing figures of Christ from the twelfth or early thirteenth century in this country, though I believe the iconography was brought back to England from France in the trumeau figure of the north door at Westminster Abbey, and thence reflected in the Westminster retable of 1268. Quite apart from stylistic difficulties, an iconographic context for the Leigh Christ after the Conquest would be difficult to assemble. If the ivory diptych of the eleventh century in the Bargello, Florence, showing Christ on the asp and basilisk paired with St Michael defeating the Devil is English work, we have another relevant example, for we have already stressed the popularity of St Michael – one borne out by many church dedications – in the English pre-Norman Conquest period. This diptych, and the Leigh Christ, are very much in the triumphalist tradition.

So where would the Leigh Christ have been placed? Both the VCH and Pevsner thought his position in any early Norman niche over the north door was secondary. The example of Bitton reminds us that fine late Saxon sculpture could be set very high. If I am right in interpreting the long narrow nave at Leigh as a structure to be associated with a building dedicated to St Edburga and put up soon after her relics reached the abbey at Pershore in the mid eleventh century, then the Christ could have stood within the gable, either outside the west door or above the chancel arch, possibly in association with an eastern gallery. Alterations to the chancel arch at Leigh were among the first things to be done after 1100, and the Christ could have been displaced as soon as that to the position it so long occupied over the north door.

In any event, the Leigh Christ deserves a niche in the canon of eleventh century English sculpture, alongside the much more famous Bristol Harrowing of Hell.[58] They spring from the tradition of Christ as Hero, to which the Southwell gabled lintel also belongs, the tradition that knew enemies not only as plunderers, exploiters and foreigners, but as pagans. That option, still expressed in the St Paul's fighting beasts of c.1030, was not again a real possibility after 1066.

In a recent volume of the Battle Abbey proceedings[59] Eric Fernie has suggested an Anglo-Saxon basis for some of the regional variations, especially in decorative matters, of Anglo-Norman architecture. In the exploration of the justice of this perceptive thesis it is helpful to identify surviving evidence of pre-Conquest decorative features. The corpus of surviving pre-Conquest architectural sculpture is necessarily small. The best was no doubt in the greatest buildings, and these, as Fernie pointed out, were all destroyed: 'No English cathedral retains any standing masonry of undisputed Anglo-Saxon date'.[60] Glastonbury however must have

---

[57] In the Cluny Museum in Paris, *Carolingian Art*, 170–1.

[58] *Romanesque Art*, cat. 96. I find the suggestion that this piece was originally a coffin lid as puzzling as the same suggestion made by Pevsner in the case of Leigh. Certainly the Bristol Harrowing of Hell tapers, but surely in the wrong direction.

[59] Eric Fernie, 'The Effect of the Conquest on Norman Architectural Practice', *ante* ix, 1986, 71–85, especially 71–7.

[60] Fernie, 71.

been, *pace* William of Malmesbury, one of the most influential centres for all the arts. Southwell was a minster, and both there and at Pershore, and at its dependency Leigh, there was a cult of the royal saint Edburga.

Anglo-Saxon illumination is peerless. We should keep a weather-eye for the slightest evidence of the sculpture that accompanied it. Since it was imitated in the twelfth century, some earlier pieces may still be accredited to later hands. No-one upholds an Anglo-Saxon provenance for the York Virgin any longer, but other more movementé, eccentric pieces may still carry Romanesque labels. A few of them have been discussed in this paper.

HISTORIOGRAPHY AND HAGIOGRAPHY AT SAINT-WANDRILLE: THE 'INVENTIO ET MIRACULA SANCTI VULFRANNI'

Elisabeth M. C. van Houts

The monastery of Fontenelle, later known as Saint-Wandrille, was founded by Wandrille and his nephew Godo in the years 645 to 649/50. During the first two centuries of its existence it acquired extensive property scattered over a large area which stretched from the Pas-de-Calais in the north to Provence in the south.[1] Economic prosperity enabled the monastery to become an important centre of Carolingian learning and culture. It had an impressive library, an active scriptorium and a school which attracted people from as far away as Frisia and Italy.[2] Hagiography and historiography flourished. The earliest product was the *Life of Saint Wandrille* written in the seventh century and revised probably about a hundred years later.[3] Other lives were written about the abbots Lambert (d. 688) and Ansbert later archbishop of Rouen (d. after 690), and about the monks Condedus, Erembert later bishop of Toulouse (d. after 687/8) and Vulfran; Vulfran had been bishop of Sens and missionary in Frisia before he retired to Saint Wandrille where he died before 696/7.[4] The *Gesta abbatum Fontanellensium*, which was the first *gesta abbatum* modelled on the *Liber Pontificalis* to be written, was composed here probably during the abbacy of Ansegisus (823–833) and a short series of Annals exists of slightly later date.[5] The three most important saints of the monastery were Saint Wandrille, Saint Ansbert and Saint Vulfran, who rested side by side, Saint Wandrille in the middle, in the crypt of the abbey church.[6] The

---

[1] F. Lot, *Etudes critiques sur l'abbaye de Saint-Wandrille*, Paris 1913; Dom J. Laporte, 'Fontenelle ou S. Wandrille', *Dictionnaire d'Histoire et de Géographie ecclésiastiques* xvii, 1971, cols 915–53.

[2] J. Fontaine, 'La culture carolingienne dans les abbayes normandes: l'exemple de Saint-Wandrille', *Aspects du monachisme en Normandie (ive–xviiie siècles)*, ed. L. Musset, Paris 1982, 31–54; R. McKitterick, *The Carolingians and the written word*, Cambridge 1989, 173–5.

[3] *Vita Wandregisili*, ed. B. Krusch, *MGH rer. Merov.* v, 1910, 4–24. *Bibliotheca Hagiographica Latina (BHL)*, Subsidia Hagiographica, nos 6, 11, 70, Brussels 1900–1986, nos 8804–5.

[4] Ed. W. Levison, *MGH rer. Merov.* v, 1910, 606–12 (Lambert) *BHL* no. 4675; 613–41 (Ansbert) *BHL* no. 520–520b, 644–51 (Condedus) *BHL* no. 1907, 652–6 (Erembert) *BHL* 2587, 657–73 (Vulfran) *BHL* no. 8738. The dates of the texts are discussed by A. Legris in *Analecta Bollandiana* xxvii, 1898, 265–306; W. Levison in *Neues Archiv* xxv, 1900, 593–607 and Laporte, 'Fontenelle', cols 930–31.

[5] *Gesta sanctorum patrum Fontanellensis coenobii (Gesta abbatum Fontanellensium)*, ed. Dom F. Lohier and R. P. J. Laporte, Rouen-Paris 1936. For discussions of the date, see W. Levison in *Revue Bénédictine* 46, 1934, 241–64; P. Grierson in *EHR* lv, 1940, 275–84 and M. Sot, *Gesta episcoporum, gesta abbatum*, Turnhout 1981, Typologie des sources du Moyen Age occidental, vol. 37, 34–5. *The Annales Fontanellenses priores (Chronicon Fontanellense)*, ed. Dom J. Laporte, Rouen-Paris 1951, Mélanges publiés par la Société de l'Histoire de Normandie, 15e serie, 63–91.

[6] *Gesta abbatum Fontanellensium*, 20.

last authentic reference to all three saints dates from 853 or 854, when they are mentioned in a charter of King Charles the Bald.[7]

In 858 the pressure of the vikings proved to be too much and the monks were forced to flee.[8] They left Saint-Wandrille taking with them manuscripts, charters and the relics of their saints. During the years of exile the monks recorded their wanderings in the *Miracula Sancti Wandregisili*, our main source for the reconstruction of their journey.[9] They spent about ten years in their own lands in the north of France. From 868 to 885 they found refuge with the nuns of Blangy as is testified by the *Miracula Sanctae Bertae*.[10] Probably forced once more to flee from the vikings, they went south-east to Chartres where they stayed only a few months. Then, in 885 or 886, they returned to the north. There is no information about their whereabouts until 944, when at the orders of Count Arnulf I of Flanders the relics of their saints, which were then at Boulogne, were transferred to the monastery of Saint-Pierre at Ghent, an event which is described in the *Sermo de Aduentu sanctorum Wandregisili, Ansberti et Vulframni in Blandinium*.[11] From that day onwards the Flemish community claimed to be in the possession of the relics not only of Saint Wandrille and Saint Ansbert, but also of Saint Vulfran. And it is precisely this claim which a century later led to the writing of the *Inuentio et Miracula Sancti Vulfranni*, which relates the discovery of the relics of Saint Vulfran at Saint-Wandrille.[12] But before we can discuss this text we must first briefly sketch the history of the refoundation and the intellectual life of the monastery.

Twice before in the tenth century people had tried in vain to rebuild the monastery.[13] Both attempts had originated in the monastery of Saint-Peter at Ghent; the first by Abbot Gerard of Brogne (941–53) came to nothing, and the second, about two decades later by the monk Mainard, collapsed after only a few years (c.960–66). Finally, in 1008, the third attempt was successful. This time the initiative came from Abbot Gerard of Crépy-en-Valois, who had the support of Duke Richard II. It was shortly after his arrival at Fontenelle that the body of Saint Vulfran was allegedly discovered. Abbot Gerard was murdered on 29 November 1031 and his former pupil Gradulph, then monk at Sainte-Trinité at Rouen, succeeded him. He continued the work of his predecessor; the new abbey church was dedicated in September 1033. Some years later he sent his monks to the new foundation of Saint-Peter at Préaux, and he was about to be appointed as *uicarius* of the archbishop of Rouen when he died on 6 March 1047. Gradulph was succeeded by his brother Robert, who remained at Saint-Wandrille till 1062 when he was transferred to Saint-Germain-des-Prés near Paris.

[7] Lot, xxxv and 33; *Recueil des actes de Charles II le Chauve roi de France*, ed. G. Tessier, i, Paris 1943, 424 (no. 160): . . . *ubi preciosi confessores Christi Wandregisillus, Ansbertus atque Vulfrannus corpore requiescunt.* . . .

[8] Lot, xxx–xlvi; Laporte, 'Fontenelle', col. 919; H. van Werveke, 'Saint-Wandrille et Saint-Pierre de Gand (ixe et xe siècles), *Miscellanea Mediaevalia in memoriam Jan Frederik Niermeyer*, Groningen 1967, 79–92, esp. 80–1.

[9] *AA.SS Martii* iii, 281–301; excerpts in *MGH SS* xv, 406–9; *BHL* nos 8807–9.

[10] *AA.SS Iulii* ii, 54–60; excerpts in *MGH SS* xv, 564–6; *BHL* nos 1267–70.

[11] *Une translation de reliques à Gand en 944. Le Sermo de Aduentu Sanctorum Wandregisili, Ansberti et Vulframni in Blandinium (Sermo)*, ed. N. N. Huyghebaert, Brussels 1978; *BHL* no. 8810.

[12] *Inuentio et miracula sancti Vulfranni*, ed. Dom J. Laporte, Rouen-Paris 1938, Mélanges publiés par la Société de l'Histoire de Normandie, 14e serie; *BHL* no. 8740.

[13] Lot, xli–xlvi; Laporte, 'Fontenelle', cols 919–20 and L. Musset, 'Monachisme d'époque ducale en Normandie: le problème de la continuité', *Aspects du monachisme en Normandie*, 56–8.

The main task of the three abbots was to rebuild the patrimony of the abbey, either by the recovery of lost Carolingian lands or by acquisition of new property. In their quest for land the monks made active use of the saints' lives and of the *Gesta abbatum Fontanellensium* to trace former possessions. In 1024 Count Dreux of the Vexin handed back Chaussy-en-Vexin, which according to his *Vita* had at one time belonged to Saint Ansbert, who had given it to the monks.[14] And during the abbacy of Gradulph (1031–47) the *Vita sancti Condedi* was used as evidence to persuade Count William of Arques to restore *Belcinnaca*, an island in the Seine where Saint Condedus had lived as a hermit and which he had given to Fontenelle. Using information from the *Vita* the monks forged a diploma of King Theodoric III dated 673 and they drew up a genuine one for Count William.[15] But despite their efforts only a small fraction of the original patrimony was recovered.

This use of Carolingian material for the production of charters leads us to the intellectual life at Saint-Wandrille after the restoration. Hardly any manuscripts of the pre-viking period have survived and only a handful of the eleventh century.[16] The oldest preserved manuscript, which may have been written at Fontenelle, is the early eighth-century copy of the first *Life of Saint Wandrille*, now Paris BN MS Lat. 18315.[17] Another one written by the scribe Harduinus about a century later is Rouen BM MS 524 (I. 49) which contains Bede's *De ratione temporum*. There is hardly any doubt that he is the same as the learned computist and scribe Harduin, master at Saint-Wandrille, who died in 811.[18] Four eleventh-century manuscripts have thus far been traced. The *Collationes* of Cassianus, now Paris BN MS Lat. 2136, were copied by a scribe called Algrimus at the orders of Abbot Gerard.[19] From the middle of the century dates Rouen BM 322 which contains the *Concordances of the Gospels*.[20] Between 1033 and 1053 the monk William was responsible for the beautifully written *Sacramentarium*, now Rouen BM MS 272 (Y 196).[21] The same William was almost certainly the scribe of the bulk of the most important of all these manuscripts, Le Havre BM MS 332. Ff 8–110v contain a collection of hagiographical texts (lives, miracles and hymns) concerning the saints of the monastery: Saint Wandrille, Saint Ansbert, Saint Vulfran, Saint Condedus, Saint Erembert and Saint Lambert, as well as the oldest surviving copy of its house chronicle, the *Gesta abbatum Fontanellensium*.[22] During the period

---

[14] Lot, 37–8 (no. 7) and *Vita Ansberti*, ed. Levison, 619.

[15] Lot, lxix, 23–4 (no. 1), 56–7 (no. 15); *Vita Condedi*, ed. Levison, 647–8 and 648 note 1; M. Chibnall, 'Charter and chronicle: the use of archive sources by Norman historians', *Church and Government in the Middle Ages*, ed. C. N. L. Brooke, a.o., Cambridge 1976, 1–17, esp. 2–3.

[16] *Catalogue des manuscrits en écriture latine portant des indications de date, de lieu ou de copiste, vol. vii: Ouest de la France et Pays de Loire*, ed. M. C. Garand, a.o., Paris 1984, xix–xx; G. Nortier, *Les bibliothèques médiévales des abbayes bénédictines de Normandie*, Paris 1971, 72–7.

[17] *Vita Wandregisili*, ed. Krusch, 4–5; the possibility that the manuscript was copied at Saint-Wandrille is discussed by Fontaine, 'La culture', 37 note 1.

[18] *Catalogue* vii, 518; Nortier, 6–7.

[19] *Catalogue* ii, 473; Ph. Lauer, *Bibliothèque Nationale. Catalogue général des manuscrits en écriture latine* ii, Paris 1940, 335; *Trésors des abbayes normandes. Catalogue de l'exposition organisée en l'honneur de l'année des abbayes normandes*, Rouen-Caen 1979, 139–140 (no. 166).

[20] *Catalogue* vii, xx and *Catalogue général des manuscrits des bibliothèques publiques de France* ii (Rouen), ed. H. Omont, Paris 1888, 329–30.

[21] Dom F. Lohier, 'Notes sur un ancien sacramentaire de l'abbaye de Saint-Wandrille', *Mélanges d'Histoire offerts à Charles Moeller* i, Louvain-Paris 1914, 407–19; *Catalogue* vii, 277.

[22] *Catalogue* vii, 157; *Catalogue général*, ed. Omont, ii, 332–5. The identification of the scribe is Garand's (*Catalogue* vii, xx).

1033 to 1053 therefore the scribe William copied virtually all that was known about the early history of Saint-Wandrille into one book. The manuscript tradition of the saints' lives and the *Gesta* suggest that William's exemplar was not the original but a copy.[23] The exemplar was probably destroyed after Le Havre BM MS 332 had been finished. The manuscript is illuminated and contains several large miniatures representing the saints of Saint-Wandrille.[24] This is, however, not the only evidence for the production of pictures or paintings made in the scriptorium. For according to the *Miracula sancti Vulfranni*, a second collection of miracles written before 1066,[25] one of the monks had given some parchment with a picture of Christ to the daughter of the nun Eulalia who both lived at Saint-Wandrille.[26] And finally the *Inuentio et Miracula Sancti Vulfranni* itself is our only source for the important evidence that the monks were acquainted with saints' lives written not only in Latin but in the vernacular as well. According to the *Inuentio* Theobald of Vernon, canon at Rouen, knew Abbot Robert, for he told him how Saint Vulfran had cured him of eye problems. This Theobald, so the story ends, translated many saints' lives including that of Saint Wandrille into the vernacular and he used them for the composition of songs.[27] Unfortunately none of Theobald's work has survived. As far as the writing of annals is concerned it seems very likely that a beginning was made during these years, despite the fact that the *Annals* in their present form in The Hague KB MS 128 E 14 ff 1–11 were composed during the first decade of the twelfth century.[28] This is the evidence we have of the intellectual background against which we can place the *Inuentio et Miracula Sancti Vulfranni*.

[23] Both the *Gesta abbatum Fontanellensium* and the saints' *Lives* know a 'Flemish' and a 'Norman' branch in the transmission of the texts. In all cases the Flemish version is the original, see *Gesta*, ed. Lohier-Laporte, xix and Lot, cxxviii–xxxiv and saints' *Lives*, ed. W. Levison, 616–17, 645, 653 and 659–61.

[24] *Trésors*, 140 (photograph of f. 62r showing Saint Vulfran).

[25] *BHL* no. 8741. Edition in *AA.SS, Martii* iii, 150–161. A list of selected miracles, though not in the correct order, is given as an appendix to the *Inuentio*, ed. Laporte, 79–81. There Laporte suggests as a date the last quarter of the eleventh century, in 'Fontenelle', col. 931, however, he dates the *Miracles* a little later than the *Inuentio*. The terminus post quem is Easter 1057 (*AA.SS, Martii* iii, 150 (§ 1) and *Inuentio*, 79).

[26] *AA.SS, Martii* iii, 158 (§ 26): *Sanctimonialis, nomine Eulalia, Fontanelle degebat; huic erat filia, quae a quodam monacho pictacium accepit, in quo uidebatur imago Salvatoris, quasi pendentis in cruce, honeste expressa, et nomina ipsius descripta. Haec itaque domum rediens secum detulit matrique custodiendum ob reverentiam videlicet Dominici characteris commisit* ... Later on in the story the *pictacium* is said to be made of *percamenum*.

[27] *Inuentio*, 68–70 (165): *Illud preterea nequeo preterire silentio quod Tetbaldus sanctae Ratumagensis aecclesiae canonicus abbati Rotberto retulit* ... [erasure in manuscript] *de seipso.* ... *Hic quippe est ille Tetbaldus Uernonensis qui multorum gesta sanctorum sed et sancti Uuandregisili a sua latinitate transtulit atque in communis linguae usu satis facunde refudit, ac sic ad quandam tinnuli rithmi similitudinem urbanas ex illis cantilenas edidit.* This passage is one of the earliest references to vernacular songs based on saints' lives. G. Paris suggested that Tetbaldus may have been the author of the Old French *Vie de Saint Alexis*, which is commonly dated to the mid-eleventh century (*Bulletin de la Société des Antiquaires de Normandie* xx, 1898, 365–6). This is rejected by *La Vie de Saint Alexis*, ed. C. Storey, Génève 1968, 22–4 and *The Life of St Alexius* in the Old French version of the Hildesheim manuscript, ed. C. J. Odenkirche, Brookline-Leyde 1978, 55 note 32. The use of saints' lives for the composition of vernacular songs is discussed by J. Stevens, *Words and Music in the Middle Ages: song, narrative, dance and drama 1050–1350*, Cambridge 1986, 235–65, esp. 263–5.

[28] J. P. Gumbert, 'Un manuscrit d'Annales de Saint-Wandrille retrouvé', *Bibliothèque de l'Ecole des Chartes* cxxxvi, 1978, 74–5; G. I. Lieftinck, J. P. Gumbert, *Manuscrits datés conservés dans les Pays-Bas* ii, Leiden 1988, 250 no. 922. The Annals have never been edited, except for a fragment (1060–1110) which was published in the *Recueil des Historiens de France*, nouvelle édition, xii, 1877, 771.

The same Le Havre manuscript on ff. 110v–135bis, contains the oldest and only complete copy of the *Inuentio et Miracula Sancti Vulfranni*. It is written in a different, slightly later, hand and the text contains many erasures and revisions. Since, as I shall discuss below, the bulk of the text was composed at Saint-Wandrille between the summers of 1053 and 1054, it seems highly probable that Le Havre BM M 332 is the autograph. It is clear that the scribe and author meant the text to be a natural continuation of the preceding part.[29]

The author cannot be identified. All we know is that he was a monk of Saint-Wandrille and that before he entered monastic life, that is well before 1053, he was a *clericus* at Asnebecq (Orne).[30] This is how he describes himself in one of the miracle stories at the end of the *Inuentio*. He tells how a little girl, the daughter of a *uir nobilis*, at the castle of Asnebecq suddenly fell ill while playing outside with other children. Her mother called for help and it was her *clericus*, the author of the *Inuentio*, who not having any medical knowledge suggested that lighting a candle for Saint Vulfran might cure the girl. Through the saintly intervention the girl recovered.[31] The *uir nobilis*, it has been suggested, may have been Roger de Beaumont, who presumably was the lord of the castle, for in 1086 he gave the church of Saint-George at Asnebecq to Saint-Wandrille and in 1136 his grandson Robert de Neubourg held the castle.[32] The author knew the Beaumonts well, for he refers by name to Humphrey, Roger's father, as the founder of Saint-Peter at Préaux, and his son Robert was a substantial benefactor of the monastery.[33] A connection between the *clericus* of Asnebecq and the Beaumonts would also explain his choice to enter the monastery of Saint-Wandrille; though if this hypothesis is correct it seems strange that Roger is not identified but referred to only as *uir nobilis*. Once at Saint-Wandrille, where he probably arrived either during the abbacy of Abbot Gradulph or else of Abbot Robert, the anonymous monk became interested in the history of his monastery and in its saints. He was one of the fifteen monks who in May 1053 carried the relics of Saint Vulfran to Rouen and was therefore an eyewitness to the event which he shortly afterwards descibed in the *Inuentio*.[34] He may also have written *Miracula Sancti Vulfranni*, which I have mentioned earlier on. That work shows clearly that it was the author's responsibility to collect and verify the stories recorded, and, where possible, to

---

[29] I have been unable to consult either the manuscript or its microfilm. The authors of the *Catalogue* vii suggest that this part of the manuscript contains a 'mise au net du texte', but they refrain from identifying it as an autograph. I rely entirely on the italics in Laporte's edition for my observations that some passages are written on erasure (*Inuentio*, p. 13). A second manuscript of the *Inuentio* is Rouen BM MS 1211 (Y 237) pp. 69–90, which dates from the thirteenth century and contains only a fragment, see *Catalogue général*, ed. Omont, i, 303.

[30] According to Laporte he was a clericus after he became monk (*Inuentio*, 5).

[31] *Inuentio*, 70–2 (§ 67): *Cuiusdam uiri in regione illa nobilis filia pro etate paruula, ut etatis illius mos est, in platea castelli quod Asnebec dicitur simpliciter ludebat . . . Unde graui percussa merore ad me clericum suum direxit (sc. mater) quatinus si quid nossem remedii transmitterem aut dicarem agendum egrotanti.*

[32] *Inuentio*, 71 note 116; for the grant of the church, see Lot, 96–7 and for Robert de Neubourg, see Orderic, vi, 466.

[33] *Inuentio*, 45–6 (§ 33) and Lot, 62–4, 65–6 (nos 19, 21; Fauroux, nos 128–9).

[34] *Inuentio*, 50–1 (§ 39): *. . . preciosum sancti Uulfranni corpus electi quindecim fratres . . . dispositum iter tandem arripuimus . . .*

gather tangible evidence of Saint Vulfran's intercession which was then handed over to the sacristan.[35]

The date of the *Inuentio* can be established with more precision than the limits of 1053, the year of the procession to Rouen, and 1062, the last year of Robert's abbacy, as suggested recently.[36] The author wrote the text shortly after the temporary transfer of relics to Rouen, which can be dated to 25–31 May 1053, the return on 31 May coinciding with the vigil of the *Translatio* of 1 June. The fact that there is no mention of the rebellion of Count William of Arques, who is referred to as still holding Arques, in the autumn of 1053 or the battle of Mortemer in February 1054 supports such an early date for the bulk of the text.[37] The author, however, extended and revised his text. Towards the end of the *Inuentio* he announces that he will add two miracles which happened on the anniversary of the *Translatio* to Rouen, that is presumably on 1 June 1054.[38] And the reference that Archbishop Malger held his office only a few years (*paucis annis*) can only have been written after his deposition during the council of Lisieux in August or September 1055.[39] Since Hugh, archdeacon of Rouen, who died on 16 September 1057, is mentioned as being still alive, we can conclude that the author ceased revising well before that date, possibly because by then he had started already the composition of the second collection of *Miracula sancti Vulfranni*.[40]

The story of the *Inuentio* develops along two lines. The main theme is the discovery of the body of Saint Vulfran by Abbot Gerard shortly after the refoundation, the transfer of his relics to the abbey church on 1 June 1027 and the

---

[35] A clear example can be found in *AA.SS, Martii*, iii, 154–5 (§§ 13–14) where the author says that he went to Rouen to talk to the parents of a small boy who by accident had almost swallowed the clasp of his cloak but who had been been saved by Saint Vulfran; the parents gave him the clasp which he in turn handed over to the sacristan.

[36] Thus far the text has been dated as follows: Lot, xlii note 3 suggested 'composé en 1053 ou peu après'. Laporte first suggested 1073x87 (*Inuentio*, 5–6) but later rectified this to 'avant 1066' ('Fontenelle', col. 932). Dom Huyghebaert proposed 'vers 1060 ou peu après' (*Sermo* ci) and *Catalogue* vii, 157 suggested 1053x63.

[37] The date of the *Translatio* to Rouen is given by the *Inuentio* (50, § 39), and accepted by Lohier 'Notes', 415, as *viii kal. Iunii* (25 May, Tuesday). The journey to Rouen took two days. The return journey started on the following Sunday, which I understand to have been 30 May (*iii Kal. Iunii*), which in 1057 was Whitsun Day. Since their outward journey took two days it is logical to assume that the return journey took equally long, which means that the monks arrived back at Saint-Wandrille on Monday 31 May, the vigil of 1 June (*Kal. Iunii*). Dom Lohier suggests, without giving any reasons, that they returned on the Sunday following 30 May. Dom Laporte has a completely different interpretation. He emended the text to *viii kal. Iulii* (24 June, Thursday) so that the day of return, being the following Sunday, would become 27 June (*v kal. Iulii*). For this date is given in the fourteenth-century copy of Usuardus *Martyrologium* from Saint-Wandrille (Rouen BM MS 1212, see *Catalogue* vii, 528): *Ipso die relatio corporis beati Wlfranni ab urbe rothomagensi quem deus ad laudem sui nominis claris assidue glorificat miraculis* (Dom Lambert, 'Un calendrier de l'Abbaye de Fontenelle (xiiie–xive s.), *Revue Mabillon* i, 1905–6, 321–40, esp. 335). For William count of Arques, see *Inuentio*, 39 (§ 28): *Vuillelmus uidelicet qui postea Arcas castrum in pago Tellau primus statuit*. The siege of Arques had certainly begun in October 1053. The Battle of Mortemer took place in February 1054. For a reconstruction of events, see D. Bates, *William the Conqueror*, London 1989, 36–7. See also below note 105.

[38] *Inuentio*, 74 (§ 72): *duo adhuc tantum narrationi ceptae miracula, in die deuectionis annuae peracta, addere proposuimus*. They are told in §§ 73–4. § 75 contains the epilogue which ends with a doxology.

[39] *Inuentio*, 39: *Malgerus qui postmodum in urbe Rotomagensi paucis annis archiepiscopatum tenuit*.

[40] For Hugh the archdeacon (*Inuentio*, §§ 39–40, 51–3), see D. Spear, 'Les archidiacres de Rouen au cours de la période ducale', *Annales de Normandie* xxxiv, 1984, 17–18 and *Trésors*, 95 (no. 105).

procession to Rouen in June 1053 followed by the miracles. Parallel to these chapters runs the history of the monastery and of Normandy from the viking invasions to the early 1050s. The *Inuentio* is therefore a mixture of hagiography and historiography. To say this is of course anachronistic because in the Middle Ages there was no sharp distinction between the two forms of writing. For the monk of Saint-Wandrille, the history of the relics of Saint Vulfran and the history of his monastery could not be separated. The present discussion of the *Inuentio*, however, will be facilitated if we first look at it as an example of hagiography and return later to its historiographical aspects.

The narrative belongs to an established hagiographical genre in which the *Inuentio*, or discovery, of the relics of a saint is described and often also their *translatio*, or transfer, to a new tomb or shrine.[41] The best known examples are the *Inuentio sanctae Crucis*, the discovery of the Holy Cross, by Empress Helena and the *Translatio sancti Benedicti et sanctae Scholasticae*, which describes the transfer of the bodies of Saint Benedict and his sister Scholastica from Rome to Fleury. The *Translatio* was written by Adrevald of Fleury and widely copied all over Europe. As a result of its popularity it exercised a great influence on the development of the genre. The author of the *Inuentio* almost certainly knew it, although it is not possible to show any direct borrowings. No manuscript from Saint-Wandrille has survived but the text was available in other Norman libraries.[42] The account of the discovery in the *Inuentio* follows a common pattern. Usually one person, through visions or otherwise, is inspired to find the relics of a saint (Abbot Gerard of Crépy), the body is intact (*integerimum sanctum corpus*), there is corroborating evidence to authenticate the find (the tomb of Saint Vulfran was located on the right hand side of Saint Wandrille's and the saint's body was wrapped in *sacerdotali veste* as described in his *Vita*) and the relics are buried in the church (*translatio* on 1 June 1027). The second half of the narrative is a proper *translatio*, for the detailed description of the journey from Saint-Wandrille to Rouen and back again in May 1053 and the accompanying miracles belong to that genre. But the story in itself presents many problems.

First of all the author does not date the actual discovery of Saint Vulfran, an event which he places at the beginning of Abbot Gerard's tenure, nor does he say whether any miracles at that time took place.[43] Secondly, the allegedly authentic evidence found in his grave consists only of refences based on the *Vita sancti Vulfranni*.[44] Even the information that the names on two empty tombs were those of Saint Wandrille and Saint Ansbert and the name on the unopened tomb was that of Saint Vulfran can be deduced from the *Vita*, and can therefore hardly count as

---

[41] M. Heinzelmann, *Translationsberichte und andere Quellen des Reliquienkultes*, Turnhout 1979, Typologie des sources du Moyen Age occidental, vol. 33, 77–99; R. Aigrain, *L'Hagiographie. Ses sources, ses méthodes, son histoire*, Paris 1953, 186–92.

[42] *Les miracles de Saint Benoît, écrits par Adrevald, Aimoin, André, Raoul Tortaire et Hughes de Sainte-Marie, moines de Fleury*, ed. E. de Certain, Paris 1858, 1–14. For the transmission of the text and its manuscripts, see A. Vidier, *L'Historiographie à Saint-Benoît-sur-Loire et les Miracles de Saint Benoît*, Paris 1965, 141–9.

[43] *Inuentio*, 32–3 (120) the discovery is described as having taken place before the start of the building of the abbey church (36, 124) and which can be dated to 1011 (twenty years before the death of Abbot Gerard).

[44] For corresponding passages, see *Vita Vulfranni*, ed. Levison, 672–3.

corroboratory evidence.[45] And although the author added two chapters with historical arguments, which I shall discuss below, this part of his claim is unconvincing.[46] Thirdly, he can only produce a date, 1 June 1027, for the transfer of the relics together with those of two other Merovingian saints, Erembert and Condedus (found at the same time?) and of the recent acquisitions Maximus and Venerandus, which, he says, from then onwards was celebrated annually.[47] But, again, no miracles. As a matter of fact there is no contemporary evidence for the find at all, nor for the prominent role assigned to Saint Vulfran in the cult of saints at Saint-Wandrille before 1053. There was no special feast for him apart from the usual celebration on 20 March and none of the charters mentions his name. After 1053, however, new feasts for him and other saints, who thus far had not been celebrated individually, and for the *Translatio* of 1 June were added to the liturgical calendar, and his name begins to appear in charters.[48] If the *Translatio* of 1027 had been celebrated annually one would have expected it to be listed in the liturgical calendar, like the feast of the dedication of the abbey church on 12 September 1033, which, according to the *Inuentio*, became an annual feast. This discrepancy was noted by Dom Lohier, but he concluded that the *Translatio* of 1027 was probably an unofficial celebration which did not become a liturgical feast until 1053.[49]

A closer inspection of the dating clause, however, which correctly refers to Richard III as ruler in Normandy but incorrectly to King Henry as holding the *regnum Francorum* against the wish of his mother, reveals that it is probably a fabrication made with the help of two undated charters of Saint-Wandrille.[50] King Henry's troubles with his mother Constance and his exile to Normandy date from 1033. During this visit he attested charters as a witness, like the one confirming the grant of the churches of Arques to Saint-Wandrille which can be dated to Easter 1033, but he also authenticated earlier documents, one of which is the confirmation by Richard II and Richard III of the grant by Imma de Pontechardon to the same monastery in 1025x6.[51] This grant is mentioned in the *Inuentio* in the chapter preceding the one which discusses the *Translatio* of 1027 and there other gifts of Imma, including the silver shrine for Saint-Vulfran, are listed.[52] The importance

---

[45] L. Musset, however, accepts the references to inscriptions as genuine ('Le problème de la continuité monastique entre l'époque franque et l'époque ducale: les apports de l'épigraphie', *Histoire réligieuse de la Normandie*, ed. A. Chaline, Chambray 1981, 57–69, esp. 59).

[46] See p. 242.

[47] *Inuentio*, 38–9 (§ 27), 39: ... *et idcirco dies illa ... per annos singulos ibidem recolitur.*

[48] Lohier, 'Notes', 412–14. The only pre-1053 charter to include a reference to Saint Vulfran is known exclusively from a twelfth-century note in Le Havre BM Ms 332 and may well have been interpolated (Lot, 70 (no. 25)). The post-1053 charters are Fauroux, nos 154, dated 1047x63 by Fauroux but probably belongs to the later half of Abbot Robert's tenure; 207 (Lot, no. 35) dated c.1055x66 and 234 (Lot, no. 40) dated 1082x7.

[49] Lohier, 'Notes', 415.

[50] *Inuentio*, 39 (§ 27): *Facta est autem haec translatio anno dominicae incarnationis millesimo uigesimo septimo, Kalendis Iunii, Henrico rege Francorum regnum preter matris suae uoluntate inuasum tenente, principatum uero Nortmannie tertio Richardo legali modestia* (MS: *modesta*) *disponente nam is defuncto patri Richardo secundo, de quo supra meminimus, in regno successerat.*

[51] Fauroux, no. 69 (Lot, no. 13) 13 April 1033: *signum Henrici regis qui temporibus profugus habebatur in hac terra.* Fauroux, no. 55 (Lot, no. 12) 1025x26: *signum Henrici regis.* J. Dhondt, 'Une crise du pouvoir capétain 1032–4', *Miscellanea Mediaevalia in memoriam Jan Frederik Niermeyer*, Groningen 1967, 137–48.

[52] *Inuentio*, 37–8 (§ 26).

of the sequence of the chapters in the *Inuentio* is the fact that according to the author of the *Inuentio* Imma's benefactions predated the *Translatio* and that the *Translatio* took place at the time of King Henry. If the reference to King Henry is a simple chronological error, in which case it would be the only one in the *Inuentio*, we can overlook it and still accept the story of the *Translatio*. If, as I tend to believe, it is not an error, then we must suspect the author of having fabricated a date, which he inserted into the history of his monastery, as 'evidence' that the *Translatio* of 1 June had been celebrated since 1027. For in 1053 during their campaign to launch Saint Vulfran's cult, the monks had need of such proof. For them the date of 1 June was important because it was on the vigil of 1 June, as I have shown, that his relics, and those of the other saints, returned from Rouen to Saint-Wandrille.[53]

But finally the most damning weakness of the story of the discovery of Saint Vulfran at Fontenelle was the existence of a rival claim by the monks at Saint-Peter at Ghent. Ever since the *Translatio* of the relics of the saints of Saint-Wandrille from Boulogne to Ghent at the orders of Count Arnulf I of Flanders in 944 the Flemish community had claimed the possession of the bodies of Saint Wandrille, Saint Ansbert and Saint Vulfran. The earliest authentic testimony of their claim is the original charter of King Otto II dated to 977, which refers to the presence of all three saints at Ghent.[54] A possible earlier source is the *Sermo de aduentu sanctorum Wandregisili, Ansberti et Vulframni in Blandinium*. The original version of this text, which has not survived, was written in or shortly after 944. Today the *Sermo* only exists in a later revision of c.1118, which definitely contains the name of Saint Vulfran. Its most recent editor, Dom Huyghebaert, who stripped off the later layers in order to lay bare the original account, concluded that the original never mentioned the third saint, but that at a very early stage, certainly before 977, the name of Saint Vulfran had been interpolated and that the interpolated text in turn became the backbone of the Flemish claim.[55] His conclusions are very difficult to follow mainly because he wants us to believe in a versatile interpolator whose activity can only be characterised as extremely erratic. However, we owe to Dom Huyghebaert the important suggestion that it must have been the *Sermo* which aroused strong feelings at Saint-Wandrille and which led to the composition of the *Inuentio*.[56] For the author of the *Inuentio*, in his discussion of the discovery of the body of Saint Vulfran, reproaches the authors of a *libellus de translatione et miraculis sanctorum*, which he does not identify but which can only be the

---

[53] For the launch of the cult of Saint Vulfran, see *Inuentio*, 49 (§ 37): *Nam gloriosa sanctissimi patris Uulfranni merita tali dignatus est occasione mortalibus declarare et ad patrocinium fidelium cunctis reuelare, quae paucis eatenus ad notitiam noscuntur peruenisse, adeo ut crebra miracula quae apud eius sacratissima ossa fieri uidebantur ne illi quidem imputarentur.* The ceremony of the *Translatio* as described in *Inuentio* § 27 may well have been part of the dedication ceremony of the new abbey church six years later on 12 September 1033. Similarly the silver shrine and pallium, gifts of Imma and Archbishop Robert, said to have been for Saint Vulfran, may have been gifts in general for the relics of the saints of Saint-Wandrille.

[54] *MGH Diplomata Ottonis II*, 167–8 (no. 149). For a discussion of the earliest Flemish sources, see Van Werveke, 'Saint-Wandrille', 88.

[55] *Sermo*, ed. Huyghebaert, cvi–xii (date of original text), cxxiii–v (date of Saint-Vulfran interpolations), lxxviii–xcviii (date of early twelfth-century revision). For the interpolation of the name of Saint-Vulfran, see text, 3, 5, 24, 30–1, 52, 58; the interpolator 'forgot' to add the name in the text of 48. See also, N. Huyghebaert, 'L'énigme des reliques de Saint Vulfram, archévêque de Sens', *Revue Bénédictine* lxxxvii, 1977, 181–94.

[56] *Sermo*, ed. Huyghebaert, ci–iii.

Sermo, for having falsified the text by interpolating the name of Saint Vulfran.[57] Since the monk of Saint-Wandrille was trying to prove that Saint Vulfran had never left Fontenelle he could only assume that the presence of the saint's name in a Flemish text was due to an interpolation.

It is clear that the presence or absence of the name of Saint Vulfran in the earliest written sources forms the main argument in favour or against the opinion that the saint had been transferred from Normandy to Flanders, not only in the modern controversy on this point but also in the Middle Ages. The debate as an intellectual discussion comparing the available source material, was initiated by the author of the *Inuentio* himself. In two chapters, following the account of the discovery of Saint Vulfran's relics, he points out that neither the *Miracula sancti Wandregisili* nor the *Miracula sanctae Bertae*, which were both written during the monks' exile, mention Saint Vulfran. They only mention the saints Wandrille, Ansbert and Berta and their miracles. The reason for the absence of a reference to Saint Vulfran in the *Miracles* was, the author claims, that the saint was still reposing in his tomb at Fontenelle.[58] There is no doubt that the author of the *Inuentio* is correct in his observations, but ingenious though his deduction is it is not necessarily valid. Does it really make sense, as Professor van Caeneghem has pointed out, to think that the monks of Saint-Wandrille would have taken with them only two of their three patron saints?[59] If they had time to dig up two bodies they could surely have dug up the third as well. As a middle way out of this tricky problem Van Caenegem suggested that the monks of Saint-Wandrille may have travelled in at least two groups, one carrying the bodies of Saint Wandrille and Saint Ansbert, and the other one Saint Vulfran's. The groups and relics met again in Boulogne, from where all three saints were transferred to Ghent. The fact that the *Miracles* refer to only two out of three saints would be a reflection of the separate travel arrangements. His suggestion, like the argument of the monk of Saint-Wandrille, is ingenious.

There is only one more question which remains to be considered. Why did the monks of Saint-Wandrille become so suddenly, it seems, interested in Saint Vulfran in 1053? According to Dom Huyghebaert it was the *Sermo* which triggered off the dispute. If he is right it would mean that the monks probably got hold of a copy in the early 1050s, presumably directly from Ghent. There is no information of any contacts between the two monasteries at precisely this period. But the marriage of Duke William and Matilda of Flanders, which took place probably in 1050 or 1051, generated closer links between Normandy and Flanders in general and it seems very likely that the two monasteries benefitted from intellectual exchanges, if only to revive their rival claims. Moreover the monks had become more interested in the history of their monastery, as is clear from the copying of Le Havre BM MS 332. One of them, while reading the saints' lives and miracles carefully, may have

[57] *Inuentio*, 35 (§ 22): *Sed quia quorundam temeritas eo uanitatis processit ut libellum de translatione et miraculis sanctorum infalsare presumpserunt, non mirum uero tale quid hos perpetrasse, cum diuinae auctoritatis libros corrupisse quosdam nouerimus.*

[58] *Inuentio*, 33–5 (§§ 21–2), 35: *Nam et in illa hystoria antiquorum diligentia litteris procurata, in qua sanctorum nomina et miracula, scilicet Uuandregisili et Ansberti continentur scripta, huius sancti nomen uel mentio nusquam reperitur uel semel inserta ... legant qui uelint gloriosum illud miraculum quo in libello de uirtutibus sanctae Bertae continetur ... ubi profecto de hoc sancto et glorioso praesule Uulfranno omnimodis reticetur, utpote qui in illa translatione, paganorum metu perpetrata, illic, non interfuit, neque enim a loco suo quo sepultus fuerat cum ceteris translatus erat alibi ...*

[59] R. C. van Caenegem, 'The sources of Flemish history in the Liber Floridus', *Liber Floridus Colloquium*, ed. A. Derolez, Ghent 1973, 71–83, esp. 78–80.

spotted the absence of the name of Saint Vulfran and put it together with the knowledge that, during the building work for the new abbey church at the time of Abbot Gerard, tombs and relics had been found. Such a connection could easily have led to the story of the discovery of the actual body of Saint Vulfran, and the launch of his cult, as is testified by the procession and the feast of the *Translatio* of 1 June.

Yet, the refoundation of the monastery of Saint-Wandrille had only become possible thanks to the persistance of the monks of Saint-Peter at Ghent. Therefore, despite the profound disagreement as to which of the two communities possessed the body of Saint Vulfran, the author of the *Inuentio* as a chronicler had to acknowledge his own monastery's debt towards the Flemish abbey. We shall therefore now discuss the *Inuentio* as a source for the refoundation at Fontenelle. Whereas skillfully avoiding any reference to Ghent as the actual place of rest of the relics of Saint Wandrille, the author could not avoid mentioning the place as the home of Abbot Gerard of Brogne (941–53) and the monk Mainer.[60] For those two initiated the revival of monastic life at Fontenelle. Although the *Inuentio* is our only source for their story, much of the information which it provides is corroborated by other documents. Thus, according to the anonymous monk, Abbot Gerard of Brogne, in the possession of the relics of Saint-Wandrille, recovered Rivecourt-sur-Oise, an ancient property of Fontenelle, which had been usurped by a man called Thierry, and this man has been identified as Thierry II, count of Beaumont-sur-Oise from 936 onwards.[61] Stimulated by this success the abbot came to Richard I at Rouen, where he negotiated the return of the relics of Saint Wandrille in exchange for the site of Fontanelle. He showed the charters but failed to persuade Richard and his advisers and was forced to return home.[62] Charters from Saint-Peter at Ghent show that from 944 onwards there existed at Saint-Peter a separate 'congregatio sancti Wandregisili' with its own abbot as part of the Flemish community. Professor van Werveke has shown that the same monks formed the two communities and that the division was a pure administrative device to keep the memory of Fontenelle alive and to conduct what was strictly speaking Fontenelle business at Ghent.[63] In this way they recovered, as we have seen,

---

[60] *Inuentio*, 22 (§ 9): *Gandensis coenobii abbas Girardus nomine*. He ends § 11 (*Inuentio*, 24) as follows: ... *atque sanctum Vuandregisilum consumpto nequiquam tanto labore ad locum unde eum extulerat festinus reuexit* (sc. *Abbas Gerardus*), *ubi apud Deum et homines in magna gloria et honore nunc usque requiescit*. Compare the last phrase with the rubric of the *Inuentio*, 14: *Incipit prologus in miraculis sancti Uulfranni pontificis, cuius corpus sacratissimum in magna gloria apud Deum et homines Fontinellae requiescit*.

[61] *Inuentio*, 22–3 (§§ 9–10). The identification of Thierry is due to J. Depoin, *Les comtes de Beaumont-sur-Oise et le prieuré de Sainte-Honorine*, Pontoise 1915, 237 note 2. For Abbot Gerard de Brogne, see Dom J. Laporte, 'Gerard de Brogne à Saint-Wandrille et à Saint-Riquier', *Revue Bénédictine* lxx, 1960, 142–66.

[62] *Inuentio*, 23–4 (§ 11): ... *seque in promptu sancti Vuandregisili corpus habere retulit* (sc. *Abbas Gerardus*), *quod suo restitueret loco, si terrae sibi redderentur quas cartarum posset approbare priuilegiis. At ille suorum usus consilio principum cartas exhiberi praecepit et coram omnibus recitatas exponi. Quo facto murmur et contradictio fieri cepit ab omnibus qui se dicebant nequaquam posse carere propriis honoribus quod sibi armis et sanguine predecessorum suorum pepererat bellicosa uirtus siue quos sibi ipsi diuturno adquisierant seruitio multisque sudoribus*. Emily Zack Tabuteau's scepticism as to the validity of this reference for the use of Carolingian charters in tenth-century Normandy is unjustified (*Transfers of property in eleventh-century Norman law*, Chapel Hill-London 1988, 213–14).

[63] *Liber Traditionum sancti Petri Blandiniensis*, ed. A. Fayen, Ghent 1906, 87–8: *In nomine regis aeterni, Womarus abbas ex constitutione domni abbatis Gerardi, congregationis sancti Wandregisili confessoris Christi, sociorumque ejus*. Van Werveke, 'Saint-Wandrille', 82–7.

Rivecourt-sur-Oise, Pecq near Paris, and also Bloville (Pas-de-Calais). That the close association between the two communities could lead to (possibly involuntary) usurpation of Saint-Wandrille land is shown by the case of Bloville, which later appeared as part of the patrimony of Saint-Peter. All three properties recovered during the exile of the monks of Saint-Wandrille were situated outside the area governed by the *comes* of Rouen. The main reason for Abbot Gerard's failure to regain Fontenelle was probably that his visit was ill-timed, coming as it did only a few years after the murder of Richard I's father, William Longsword, at the instigation of Arnulf I, count of Flanders, the very man who was Abbot Gerard's lay-supporter.[64] It would not have been surprising if Richard I and his advisers were suspicious at that time and in consequence negative in their response to a possible grant of land on the banks of the Seine in the heart of their country to what must have been in their eyes a group of Flemish monks backed by Count Arnulf I.

The second attempt a few decades later, in 960, by Mainer monk of Saint-Peter, was more successful. At that time, according to the *Inuentio*, Richard I gave his consent to the restoration of Fontanelle by a certain Turstingus to Mainer. Charter evidence shows that this Turstingus, who was probably a direct descendant of the viking companion of Rollo who had been given the land, was a benefactor of Saint-Ouen at Rouen.[65] A grant from Richard I concerning different lands in the vicinity of Fontenelle which is only known from a charter of his son Richard II probably dates from this period as well.[66] As soon as Abbot Mainer had established himself, so the story goes, his abbot (at Ghent), sent him books, charters, ornaments and saints' relics.[67] Apart from the charters, which were probably the original Carolingian ones, it was material of rather secondary quality: the monks of Ghent kept the original manuscripts of the saints' lives and the *Gesta abbatum Fontanellensium* and parted with copies, but more importantly they kept the bodies of the saints of Fontenelle.[68] The last memorable deed of Abbot Mainer, according to the *Inuentio*, was the acquisition of two new saints, Maximus and Venerandus, not from Ghent but found near the eastern borders of Normandy.[69] His brief abbacy at Saint-Wandrille came to an end when Richard I asked him to reinstall monks at Mont Saint-Michel. Abbot Mainer left in 966 and died in 991.[70] The author of the *Inuentio* describes the period which followed as one of lamentable decline and irreparable damage, which lasted until the arrival of Abbot Gerard of Crépy-en-Valois in 1008. He can only recall the fact that after Mainer there were three abbots about whom he decides to remain silent. This passage is unfortunately

---

[64] William Longsword was murdered in December 942. Norman sources blame Count Arnulf I. For a discussion, see Ph. Lauer, *Le règne de Louis IV d'Outremer*, Paris 1900, 276–83. For the close relationship between Count Arnulf I and Abbot Gerard de Brogne, see E. Sabbe, 'Etude critique sur la biographie et la réforme de Gerard de Brogne', *Mélanges Félix Rousseau*, Bruxelles 1958, 497–524, esp. 515–23.

[65] *Inuentio*, 24–6 (§§ 12–13). For Turstingus, see Fauroux, nos 42 and 53. the identification is due to J. Adigard des Gautries, *Les noms de personnes Scandinaves en Normandie de 911 à 1066*, Lund 1954, 326–7 (no. 1).

[66] Fauroux, no. 52.

[67] *Inuentio*, 26–7 (§ 14): ... *libros quoque et cartas et quaedam ornamenta sed et filacteria cum preciosis sanctorum pigneribus ab abbate suo et fratribus sibi indulta illuc conuexit.* The abbot then was Womar (953–81), who at first had acted as abbot of the congregation of Saint-Wandrille (above note 63).

[68] See above note 23.

[69] *Inuentio*, 27–8 (§ 15).

[70] For Abbot Mainer at Mont Saint-Michel, see Dom J. Laporte, 'L'Abbaye du Mont Saint-Michel aux xe et xie siècles', *Millénaire monastique du Mont Saint-Michel* i, 1966, 53–80, esp. 57–63.

written on an erasure and it is possible that at one stage it contained their names.[71] An epitaph from Jumièges identifies one of them as Enfulbertus who died in 993.[72] After his death the abbey may have been ruled jointly with Jumièges, a situation which is suggested by a charter of Count Walter II of the Vexin addressed to the monks of both institutions.[73] But at least one ducal charter shows that grants were still being made to Saint-Wandrille without any reference to Jumièges.[74]

It is difficult to establish the sources for the early history of the monastery available to the author of the *Inuentio*. He gives a hint of having received oral information from old men which he wrote down for posterity.[75] Very probably he had access to stories circulating at the Mont-Saint-Michel where Mainer spent the last twenty-five years of his life. And it is of course equally possible that he received information directly from Ghent, if there were contacts between the two monasteries, as I have discussed above.[76]

The author of the *Inuentio* may have exaggerated the decline at Saint-Wandrille before the arrival of Abbot Gerard of Crépy, his hero, if only to make a more impressive case for his achievements. He tells how Abbot Gerard of Crépy had accepted an invitation from Duke Richard II, conveyed to him by the duke's chamberlain Roscelin, to become abbot of Saint-Wandrille.[77] Roscelin, the chamberlain, is known from four ducal charters which all date from after 1017, but if the *Inuentio* is correct his office must date from before 1008, unless of course the use of his title is anachronistic.[78] The greatest achievement of Abbot Gerard was his discovery of the relics of Saint Vulfran. But equally impressive was the abbot's power to arrange for so many benefactors to finance his enterprises. The most important are listed as Archbishop Robert, his wife Herleva, Imma de Pontechardon and the monks Ansfridus and Osbernus, brothers-in-law of Duke Richard II.[79] Only the gifts of Imma and the two brothers have survived in charters.[80] There is thus no room for doubt that the *Inuentio*'s praise for Abbot Gerard as being very skilled in temporal affairs is fully justified.[81] From the time of his abbacy onwards the history of Saint-Wandrille can be followed in the charters

---

[71] *Inuentio*, 28–9 (§ 16): *Uerum hic illius honor et amplitudinis incrementum, lamentabilis fuit Fontinellae deiectio et inreparabile detrimentum. Nam post eius recessum sub tribus rectoribus de quibus silere decreuimus per aliquot annos nullo rerum genere creuit, quinpocius in multis detrimenta sua indoluit.* The words *sub tribus . . . decreuimus* are written on an erasure.

[72] His epitaph says that he had been decanus at Jumièges and abbot at Saint-Wandrille, that he died in 993 and was buried at Jumièges (*Gallia Christiana* xi, cols 176–7.

[73] In April 1006x7 Walter II count of Amiens (998–1017x24) granted exemption of toll to the monks of Jumièges and Saint-Wandrille (J. J. Vernier, *Chartes de l'abbaye de Jumièges*, Rouen 1916, 16 (no. vi); D. Bates, 'Lord Sudeley's ancestors: the family of the counts of Amiens . . . during the 11th century', *The Sudeleys – lords of Toddington*, The Manorial Record Society of Great Britain, 1987, 34–48, esp. 35–6.

[74] Fauroux, no. 7 (29 or 30 May, 996x1006).

[75] *Inuentio*, 25 (112): *Quod quia ueterum relatione nobis est compertum, ad posterorum notitiam litteris censuimus transmittendum.*

[76] See above p. 242.

[77] *Inuentio*, 31–2 (119): *Unde admodum gauisus princeps inclitus ilico uirum strenuum ex officio cubiculariorum nomine Roscelinum destinauit ut Fontinellae monasterium illius dederet potestati.*

[78] Fauroux, nos 44–5, 49?, 55 (for Saint-Wandrille).

[79] *Inuentio*, 37 (§ 25 Herleua), 37–8 (§ 26 Imma), 38–9 (§ 27 Archbishop Robert), 39–40 (§ 28 Ansfridus and Osbernus).

[80] Fauroux, nos 46 and 46bis (Lot, no. 9) and 55 (Lot, no. 12).

[81] *Inuentio*, 32 (§ 19): *. . . sagacitate in rerum temporalium procuratione prouidentissima.*

as well as in the *Inuentio*, which on the whole confirms the picture as given by the documents. There is no need therefore to dwell on the later history of the monastery, except for one passage in the *Inuentio* which concerns Abbot Gerard's successor Gradulph. It deserves special attention for the light it throws on the role of the abbot in the ecclesiastical affairs of Normandy.

According to the *Inuentio* the abbot was contemplating whether or not to accept the appointment, at the suggestion of Duke William, as *uicarius* of Archbishop Malger, when he suddenly died on 6 March 1047.[82] The date of the abbot's death shows that the negotiations leading up to the appointment took place in the early months of the year 1047 and probably coincided with the aftermath of the battle of Val-ès-Dunes. Although the defeat of the Norman rebels in the Cotentin cannot be dated precisely it is commonly assumed that the battle took place late in the winter of 1047. The ducal victory led to the proclamation of the Truce of God in October of the same year. Professor De Bouard has convincingly argued that Duke William together with his uncle Archbishop Malger and his cousin Abbot Nicholas initiated the peace movement in Normandy.[83] It seems very likely that the preparation of these measures occupied so much of the archbishop's time that he needed a deputy to help him with his episcopal duties in the diocese. That the choice fell on Abbot Gradulph is not surprising. Apart from handling the business of his own monastery he had been the co-founder of the abbey of Saint Peter at Préaux and was involved in the refoundation of the nunnery at Montivilliers. Although in an earlier chapter the author revised a reference to Archbishop Malger after his deposition he did not alter the present one.[84]

By now we have moved on to the discussion of the *Inuentio* as a source for the history of Normandy and it is time to look at the passages concerning the dukes. As far as the viking invasions are concerned the picture painted by author of the *Inuentio* is similar to that of Dudo of Saint-Quentin and William of Jumièges, though on a much smaller scale.[85] Rollo is called *quidem Nortmannorum dux*, a leader stronger than other warriors, who settled on the banks of the Seine, distributed lands amongst his comrades and fighters and instituted laws. In this way he created one people out of many different tribes or nations.[86] After Rollo was christened he died and left his realm to his son William. The monk of Saint-

---

[82] *Inuentio*, 46–7 (134): *Sed cum Fontinelle locus diatim sub tanto rectore proficeret atque illius fama bonitatis multis spectabilis foret, episcopalis autem honor sanctae sedis Rotomagensis paululum multis ex causis declinaret, uisum est pontifici Malgerio prefatae metropolis quod et omni clero plebique non mediocriter placuit ut eundem Gradulfum abbatem sibi substitueret et uicarium sub se benedictione episcopali insigniret, ut res quibus se minus sufficere perpendebat ille sua uice suppleret.* For the different meanings of *uicarius*, see J. F. Niermeyer, *Mediae Latinitatis lexicon minus*, ed. C. van der Kieft, Leiden 1976, 1089–91.

[83] I owe the suggestion that the appointment of a *uicarius* was connected with the aftermath of the battle of Val-ès-Dunes to Dr Marjorie Chibnall, for whose advice I am very grateful. For the truce of God, see M. de Bouard, 'Sur les origines de la Trève de Dieu en Normandie', *Annales de Normandie* ix, 1959, 169–89.

[84] For Abbot Gradulph's involvement at Préaux, see *Inuentio*, 45–6 (§ 33) and *Gallia Christiana* xi, Instr. 202a (qui partim fundator illius loci extiterat), and at Montivilliers, see Faroux, no. 90 (hujus operis maxime procuratoris). For the revision, see above note 39.

[85] *Inuentio*, 20 (§ 6). I have been unable to trace any direct borrowings from either Dudo's *De Moribus* or William' *Gesta*.

[86] *Inuentio*, 20–21 (§ 7).

Wandrille does not have much to say about William Longsword for he refers only to the refoundation of the abbey of Jumièges and the death of William caused by the betrayal of Herluin (of Montreuil). It is interesting, though, that he does not blame Count Arnulf of Flanders as other Norman sources do.[87] He is more exuberant about William's son Richard who is described as having managed, after a difficult start, to maintain the rule of his father over a realm which his grandfather had acquired with force of arms and courage and which in glory and wealth almost equalled the Roman empire.[88] Coming nearer to his own time, the author of the *Inuentio* devotes two chapters to Richard II. First he pictures him as a benefactor of the church: bishops, clerks, abbots and monks came flocking towards him and enjoyed his generosity. Not only Greeks and Armenians but even messengers from Mount Sinai came to Normandy to benefit from Richard's gifts of gold and silver.[89] This passage is a reference to the story of Simon, formerly monk of Mount Sinai who had come to France where amongst other places he visited Rouen, before he finished his life as a recluse in Trier. His story was well known in Normandy, especially at Sainte-Trinité at Rouen, where Abbot Gradulph had been monk before he came to Saint-Wandrille. He therefore may have been the source of this information.[90] The second chapter on Richard II is one of the most important of the *Inuentio*. It deals with the relations between Normandy and England in the first half of the eleventh century and having been written shortly after 1053 the chapter contains the earliest Norman account of these events.[91]

The author starts his account with the marriage of Emma sister of Richard II and Aethelred king of the English. Two sons are mentioned, Edward, who was the eldest, and Alfred. Then follows a remarkable statement, namely that Edward while still a little boy, at the orders of his father and with the consent of the people, had been anointed and consecrated king. The writer goes on to give a misleading chronology of the death of King Aethelred, the invasion of King Canute son of King Svein, the exile of the aethelings to their maternal uncle in Normandy, who educated them as if they were his own sons, and Emma's marriage to King Canute, and to convey genealogical information about Emma's children by her second marriage. But what is surprising is the remark that Edward the Confessor while still very young had been crowned king. This statement is false. There is no contemporary evidence from Anglo-Saxon sources to confirm it. Edward was born between 1002 and 1005, the year when he first appears as a witness in charters.[92] For the first fifteen years of his life he could not have been regarded as his father's successor, simply because he had half brothers olders than himself, sons of

---

[87] *Inuentio*, 21–2 (§ 8).

[88] *Inuentio*, 22: ... *diuitiis et gloria Romano quondam imperio pene exaequauit* (sc. *Richardus*).

[89] *Inuentio*, 29 (§ 17): *Quamobrem factum est ut ad eum undique cateruatim confluerent pontifices et clerici, abbates et monachi, quos mira semper liberalitate studebat munerari. Huius rei testes idonei Greci sunt atque Armenii quos eo tempore fama tanti uiri suis a sedibus eduxit, quosque solo illius liberalitas relicti suis Greciis ad intuendum patriam Nortmannorum inuitauit. Nam et a monte Syna legatos frequenter habuit per quos sanctis caelestem illic degentibus uitam, plurima in auro et argento munera direxit.*

[90] A. Poncelet, 'Sanctae Catherinae uirginis et martyris translatio et miracula Rotomagensis saec. xi', *Analecta Bollandiana* xxii, 1903, 423–38; R. Fawtier, 'Les reliques Rouennaises de sainte Catherine d'Alexandrie', *Analecta Bollandiana* xli, 1923, 357–68.

[91] *Inuentio*, 29–31 (§ 18). For the full text, based on Laporte's edition, see Appendix.

[92] F. Barlow, *Edward the Confessor*, London 1970, 29.

Aethelred from a previous marriage. How then should we explain this passage in the *Inuentio* written at Saint-Wandrille at a time that King Edward was still alive and reigning in England? The author of the *Inuentio* was not alone in attributing to Edward some notion of kingship early in his life. For in the anonymous Life of King Edward written in 1066–7 a similar though less explicit passage can be found. There it is said:

> When the royal wife of old king Ethelred [Emma] was pregnant in her womb, all the men of the country took an oath that if a man child should come forth as the fruit of her labour, they should await in him their lord and king who would rule over the whole race of the English. . . . Accordingly the boy then born was declared beforehand by the oath of the people to be worthy to be raised at some time to the throne of his ancestral kingdom. . . .[93]

On the strength of this passage Frank Barlow in his biography of the Confessor has suggested that it is quite possible that an oath of allegiance of some sort was sworn as part of the terms of Emma's marriage contract.[94] And yet, during his long exile on the Continent Edward remained an active contender for the English throne supported by his Norman cousins. Perhaps he himself or his supporters invented the story of the oath at the time of Emma's marriage with Aethelred. Or if such an event had really taken place they may have exaggerated its importance so that it gradually became a story of a coronation. There are other pieces of evidence which support the suggestion that Edward himself used the title of king well before he was actually crowned. Two ducal charters for Fécamp and Mont Saint-Michel bear his name and royal title among the witnesses.[95] Moreover, William of Jumièges refers to Edward as King Edward even for the period before his accession to the throne. Since William wrote most of his work including the chapters on English history before 1060 he too may have had in mind a story that Edward considered himself to be king.[96] It is therefore possible that when the author of the *Inuentio* wrote that Edward had been crowned king as a little boy, he did so in good faith.[97]

The rest of chapter 18 is important as evidence that some of the arguments, used by the Normans to defend their case in 1066 were already circulating in Normandy about a decade before that date. For the author of the *Inuentio* stresses the blood relationship between Edward and Richard II by calling Edward a nephew (nepos) of Richard. He says, in an earlier part of the chapter, that Duke Richard II educated the aethelings as if they were his sons.[98] He points out that Edward returned to

---

[93] *Vita Eadwardi*, 7–8: *Antiqui regis Aethelredi regia coniuge utero grauida, in eius partus sobole si masculus prodiret omnis coniurat patria, in eo se dominum expectare et regem, qui regeret uniuersam Anglorum gentem. . . . Natus ergo puer dignus premonstratur patrie sacramento, qui quandoque paterni regni sullimaretur solio . . .*

[94] Barlow, 31–2.

[95] Fauroux, nos 76 (Mont Saint-Michel), 85 (Fécamp).

[96] Jumièges, 109–110 (VI, c. 9) and 120–1 (VII, c. 5). For the date, see the introduction of my forthcoming edition (*The Gesta Normannorum Ducum of William of Jumièges, Orderic Vitalis and Robert of Torigni, vol. i (Introduction and Books I–IV)* (Oxford Medieval Texts)).

[97] One charter for Saint-Wandrille, which can be dated to 13 April 1033, bears the signatures of Edward (without title) and Alfred (Fauroux, no. 69).

[98] Compare Jumièges, 109 (VI, c. 9): *tanquam fratres sibi eos adoptauerit (sc. Dux Rotbertus).* For the possibility of a blood-brotherhood relationship between the Aethelings and their Norman cousins,

England with the support of the Normans, a statement which implies that Edward was indebted to his cousins in Normandy. He tells the story of the murder of Alfred, Edward's younger brother, by Earl Godwin, brother-in-law of Edward. And finally he describes the generosity of King Edward in conferring honours and gifts of gold and silver on those Normans, both laymen and ecclesiastics, who had accompanied him to England. There can be no doubt that the author was influenced by the recent developments in Anglo-Norman relations of the years 1050–1. King Edward's designation of Duke William as his heir was still relatively recent news in 1053–4, when the *Inuentio* was first written, and Robert Champart, former archbishop of Canterbury who had been directly involved in the decision making, was still living close by at Jumièges.[99] He was the outstanding authority on Anglo-Norman relations and no doubt a well-informed, though biased, source of information for these events. The fact that the monk of Saint-Wandrille does not actually refer to these events should not surprise us. He is extremely cautious in his description of contemporary political circumstances.

Duke Richard III is only mentioned briefly in the dating clause of the *Translatio* of 1 June 1027, which I have already discussed, which is followed by the statement that he was the eldest of four brothers, himself, Count William of Arques, Archbishop Malger and Duke Robert.[100] As far as Duke Robert is concerned the author of the *Inuentio* gives an account of his reign, which, though much shorter, is similar as the one by William of Jumièges. He says that as a result of bad advice Robert weakened the flourishing *regnum* he had received from his brother, but that later on he made amends.[101] The largest of these was his pilgrimage to Jerusalem. His death by poison on the way back at Nicaea is mentioned and the *Inuentio* is our only source for the information that permission was given for the duke, unlike other mortals, to be buried in the church of that city.[102] This story may well be true, for one of the duke's companions was Gerard Fleitel, who at the end of his life retired as a monk to Saint-Wandrille and who no doubt was responsible for the circulation of stories concerning the pilgrimage.[103] The first years of the reign of Duke Robert's young son William were catastrophic for Normandy. The author of the *Inuentio* does not explicitly refer to any of the struggles between the magnates who were competing for power. Like William of Jumièges he blames the *discordia*

---

see E. M. C van Houts, 'The political relations between Normandy and England according to the Gesta Normannorum ducum', *Les mutations socio-culturelles au tournant des xie–xiie siècles. Etudes Anselmiennes (ive session)*, Paris 1984, 85–99, esp. 91–2.

99 Robert Champart died in exile at Jumièges in 1055 (*Annales de l'abbaye Saint-Pierre de Jumièges*, ed. Dom J. Laporte, Rouen 1954, 57). For the events of 1050–1, see Barlow, 103–9; S. Körner, *The battle of Hastings, England and Europe 1035–1066*, Lund 1964, 158–63, 181–9; D. Douglas in *EHR* lxviii, 1953 and E. John in *EHR* xciv, 1979, 241–67.

100 *Inuentio*, 39.

101 *Inuentio*, 41 (§ 28): *Hic autem Rotbertus acer animo et prudens priores suos uirtute quidem et potentia exequauit, sed prauorum consultui, utpote in primeuo iuuentutis flore constitutus, aequo amplius attendens, regnum quod florens susceperat in multis debilitauit.*

102 *Inuentio*, 41–2 (§ 28): . . . *profectus Ierosolymam, profunde penituit. Sed in redeundo malignorum perpessus insidias, qui eius aequum. quod iam experti erant, uerebantur imperium, ueneficio, ut didicimus, apud urbem Niceam occubuit, ibique intra sanctam ciuitatis illius basilicam, quod nulli alii mortalium concessum est, honorifica donari sepultura promeruit.*

103 Fauroux, no. 108 (Lot, no. 22). For a fifteenth-century note concerning a relic of Saint Stephen brought back from the Holy Land by Gerard Fleitel, see *Inuentio*, 40.

principum for internal unrest in Normandy.[104] But, so he ends the first part of his narrative before he sets out to describe the procession of May 1053, finally with God's help the adult prince was allowed a brief period of peace.[105] This paragraph refers to the Truce of God in October 1047 and the months leading up to the rebellion of Count William of Arques and the battle of Mortemer.[106] As the political situation in Normandy was still explosive in 1053–4 and it was still uncertain whether Duke William would be able to maintain his authority, there was no reason for the monk of Saint-Wandrille to praise Duke William excessively.

My conclusions can be summarised in three points. The *Inuentio* was the product of a long tradition of the writing of history and hagiography at Fontenelle which had started with the composition of the *Life* of its founder in the seventh century. The story of the *inuentio* or discovery of the body of Saint Vulfran, written down between the summers of 1053 and 1054, is a fabrication which was part of a campaign to launch the cult of Saint Vulfran. If it was not invented in the early 1050s, as I think is likely, it certainly cannot go back earlier than the abbacy of Gerard de Crépy (1008–31), which is still considerably later than the rival claim put forward by the monks of Saint-Peter at Ghent from 944 onwards. Secondly, as a chronicle of the refoundation of the abbey at Fontenelle after the viking invasions and its history up to the summer of 1053 the *Inuentio* is a valuable and trustworthy source for the history of the monastic revival in Normandy. And finally, the chapters concerning the Norman dukes, especially Richard II, Robert I and William, are important as a contemporary record for the history of Normandy and in particular the Anglo-Norman relations before 1066.

---

[104] *Inuentio*, 47 (135): *Huic* (Abbot Gradulph) *successit frater illius pro carnis origine nomine Rotbertus anno ferme xii principatus Uuillelmi comitis quem genuerat Rotbertus comes inclitus … Hic autem a patre ualde tener ac paruulus in regno relictus multa incommoda et aduersa pertulit, sed iuuante se gratia diuina, cum ipsa pueritia omnia discrimina quibus opprimebatur exuit, suorumque ultor acerrimus inimicorum, qui sibi fideliter obsecuti fuerant honoribus extulit, potentia sublimauit; finesque sui regni crebris munitionibus aduersus finitimas gentes, ne earum paterent incursibus, uehementer firmatas cinxit, atque nunc usque sub celestis regis imperio monarchiam regni pro arbitrio potenter disponit, cunctis per circulum regnis et nationibus aut federatis sibi oportunus aut infensis formidolosus. Inuentio*, 48 (136): *… Preterea discordia principum inter se conflictantium propter predicti principis pueritiam Nortmannorum patriam uehementer atterebat, ferro rapinis et flammis urentibus cuncta longe lateque incursabat, et in ultimam uastitatem obtima quaeque et electa uberrimi et speciosi quondam regni loca redigebat.*

[105] *Inuentio*, 49 (137): *… Pacis aliquantulum requiem iam adulto principe seque sibi in libertatem uendicante miseratus concessit, seditiones incendia et rapinas domesticas inhibuit; non tamen manum uendicem usquequaque sustinuit sed reliquias scelerum populi sui clementius paterno flagello corrigere non destitit.*

[106] For the Truce of God, see De Bouard, 'Sur les origines', 169–89. Note the similarity between the wording of the *Inuentio* (above note 105) and William of Poitiers, who writes: *imprimis prohibere caedes, incendia, rapinas* (*Gesta Guillelmi*, 14).

APPENDIX

Inuentio et Miracula sancti Vulfranni, § 18 (ed. Laporte, pp. 29–30)

Huius (sc. Richardi II) sororem Immam nomine Anglorum rex Adhelret in coniugio sortitus duos genuit filios quos patria lingua Eguuarth et Alureth placuit noncupari. Quorum Eguuardus, qui prior natu erat, tener admodum et in puerilibus adhuc annis constitutus, rex, iubente patre et fauente populo terrae, unctus est et consecratus. Nec multo post, prefato genitore suo a presentibus exempto, Canutus Danorum rex, filius uidelicet Sueni regis, Anglorum regnum nauali exercitu fretus uiolenter inuasit, et quoad uixit potenti uirtute pro arbitrio suo disposuit. Vnde factum est ut prefati infantuli transito mare ad patrum confugerent Richardum. A quo gratissime excepti et liberaliter acsi filii educati sunt, et dum uixit in terra Nortmannorum cum maximo honore retenti. Interea Canutus rex acer ingenio et armis strenuus in regno quod arripuerat confortatus, reginam Immam predicti regis Adelredi relictam, fratre Richardo consulto fauente, legaliter in uxorem accepit, ex qua filium Hardecanutum, filiam quoque Grumith nomine genuit, quae postea . . . quam ad nubiles annos peruenit Romanorum atque Saxonum imperatori Henrico nobiliter, ut sobolem regiam decuit, et in magna saeculi gloria nupsit; cui filia solummodo, quia in breui defuncta est, adidit; quae ut adoleuit carnale commercium sponsi caelestis amore respuit, sumptoque sacro uelamine uirginitatem suam regi omnium Deo dicauit. Exacto uero non modico tempore sub tribus regibus, Canuto uidelicet de quo supra retulimus, et Haroldo filio eius quem de concubina Alueuia genuit, sed et Hardecanuto naturali eius filio, Eguuardus gloriosi principis Richardi nepos in regnum paternum, adnitentibus sibi Normannis rediit, et in solio regie dignitatis post multa quae inserere longum est, demum resedit. Vxorem quoque filiam Gotuuini magni terrae illius principis qui fratrem suum Alureth iam pridem cum multis crudeliter atque in dolo peremerat accepit, eosque quos secum de Nortmannis duxerat utriusque ordinis amplis honoribus extulit, auro et argento ditauit. Sed de his omissis ad rem redeamus.